IN THE

NAME

OF

GOD

IN THE

NAME

OF

GOD

IN THE

NAME

OF

GOD

The True Story of
the Fight to Save Children from
Faith-Healing Homicide

CAMERON STAUTH

Thomas Dunne Books
St. Martin's Press ≋ New York

THOMAS DUNNE BOOKS.
An imprint of St. Martin's Press.

IN THE NAME OF GOD. Copyright © 2013 by Cameron Stauth.
All rights reserved. Printed in the United States of America.
For information, address St. Martin's Press,
175 Fifth Avenue, New York, N.Y. 10010.

www.thomasdunnebooks.com
www.stmartins.com

ISBN 978-1-250-00579-3 (hardcover)
ISBN 978-1-250-03760-2 (e-book)

St. Martin's Press books may be purchased for educational, business,
or promotional use. For Information on bulk purchases, please contact
Macmillan Corporate and Premium Sales Department at 1-800-221-7945,
extension 5442, or write specialmarkets@macmillan.com.

First Edition: October 2013

10 9 8 7 6 5 4 3 2 1

For Richard Pine and Arthur Pine

With special contributions by Gabriel Stauth

AUTHOR'S NOTE

Because it is a violation of the laws of the state of Oregon to reveal the identity of any person who reports child abuse, a very limited number of names and identifying characteristics in this book have been altered to protect privacy.

CONTENTS

Acknowledgments   *xiii*

Prologue: Genesis   *1*

Part One: The Book of Matthew

1. The Serpent   7

2. God's Perfect World   26

3. Death and Dismemberment   38

4. The Exorcist   58

5. The Crime Family   86

Part Two: The Book of Judas

6. Betrayed with a Kiss   111

7. The Getaway   126

8. The Snitch   141

9. Crime Scene Investigators   153

10. Guilt and Innocence 177

11. The Wages of Sin 201

12. The Love of Judas 215

Part Three: The Book of Revelation

13. The First Great Awakening 239

14. Sacrificed on the Altar 266

15. Angel Baby 295

16. Police Work 316

17. Clackatraz 337

18. Tender Mercies 367

19. Healing the Blind 389

20. The Father, The Son 413

21. It Is Finished 432

Epilogue: Exodus 445

Index 451

ACKNOWLEDGMENTS

The author wishes to gratefully acknowledge the generous help of the many people interviewed for this book, particularly those whose courageous cooperation caused personal risk and pain.

Editor Peter Joseph worked tirelessly on this long project, and his unmatched expertise and talent guided it from beginning to end.

The book could not have been written without the research, interviewing, organization, writing, editing, and computer-technology assistance of Gabriel Stauth, and working with him was one of the joys of my life.

Adrienne Stauth was pivotally important in structuring the story that is told here, and her gift for narrative is evident throughout.

Mark Christensen was the first to critique the manuscript, and his advice was essential.

Two books were vital to this book's research: *The Last Strawberry*, by Rita Swan, and *God's Perfect World*, by Caroline Fraser.

Meg Brookman, Brenda Hollister and Cindey McGuire adroitly

transcribed thousands of pages of material, in a process that at times seemed endless.

Lori Brockman contributed to the book in limitless ways.

Richard Pine of InkWell Management made the book possible.

Thank you all.

GENESIS

Oregon City, Oregon
January 27, 2010

"Why do you want to talk to me?" I asked the man in mirrored sunglasses. He was trying not to be noticed, but the glasses weren't helping with that on a day that was several gradations of gray outside and much darker in the bar. Even the rain was opaque, drifting down like falling ash. The place was called The Verdict and was across the street from the Clackamas County Courthouse, where the life of one of his best friends was being destroyed, mostly because of him.

"I don't want to talk to you," he said. "This will be the end of me."

"The end, how?"

"I'll lose everything. My wife. My family. My job. My friends. I may even go to hell."

"Then why are you?"

"Because it will be the beginning, too. The omega and alpha."

"So, some good will come from it?"

"Depends on what you call good."

"But . . ."

"You're trying to make sense of this. If you really want to understand it, don't," he said, softly and sadly.

I'd been around inscrutable oxymoronics ever since I'd moved to Oregon, without much to show for it, and this was beginning to feel too familiar. For the last nine months, I'd been trying to find a source within the ultra-secretive, radical-fundamentalist Followers of Christ Church, and I thought I'd finally found one. A highly placed official had told me that this man, an informant, was the most pivotal person in the recent series of arrests for child homicide within the church. But I didn't know what to make of him. For all I knew, he was just another broken soul from that strange church who was trying to get even with people who'd hurt him.

Then he took off his sunglasses, and I could see that his eyes held much more than mere sadness. There was something in them that very few people have: open, unconditional love—for me, for the bartender, our rude waitress, and everybody else in his field of vision. His aquamarine eyes were disillusioned but gentle—uncommonly clear, almost translucent—glistening with forgiveness even for sins not yet committed against him, but someday almost sure to be, as punishment for his rebellion.

This was not shaping up as the usual version of: "I'll give you inside information for your book." In the standard scenario, the people who offer to crack open a story invariably portray themselves as the heroes. He said he was the villain. And the heroes always have documentation that's intended to prove exactly how heroic they are. But he'd refused to put anything in writing. I didn't even know his last name. To me, he was just Patrick.

He looked anxiously out the window at the TV remote-broadcast vans, and hid behind his glasses again. It was his friend that he was afraid of. We were in the Verdict because his buddy, Jeff Beagley, whom he would be driving home, would never go into a bar. Jeff, on trial with his wife for the death of their child, might need one of his much-loved Cokes at the end of the day, but if he did, he'd go to the adjacent coffee shop, The Alibi.

We watched cops, lawyers, criminals, and conspirators file into the old limestone courthouse, which was once white but had faded to the color of flesh. Patrick knew almost all of them, and sorted out the good guys from the bad—based on their character, not their professions: the kind cops and the callous ones, the decent Followers and the venal.

"Things are out of control," he said. "Before this is over, one of those people over there is going to kill somebody."

"You mean, let another kid die?"

"Yes. But not just that," he said. "This, too." He pantomimed a gun with his hand, cocked it, and shot.

I dismissed that. Too melodramatic. I didn't know, at that time, that he hated melodrama, but had been dragged against his will into a life of confounding complexity that was headed inexorably toward peril.

Nor did I know that he would soon tell me the most fascinating and disturbing story I have ever heard. It was an insider's account of the sacrifice of innocent people, mostly children, upon the altar of Christian fundamentalist faith—and about his mission to end this evil, even if it destroyed him.

"The media's jumping on this story like it just happened," Patrick said, "but the Followers have been up to this crap forever. I'll tell you how it started, and you can put it in your own words."

"I'll be honest," I said, "I'll probably make you guys sound pretty weird."

"You can't possibly make us sound any weirder than we are." Patrick's mouth struggled into the most sorrowful smile I've seen. "Don't start with Jesus, though," he said.

"Why not?"

He looked at me kindly, with the patience usually reserved for small children. "Because this isn't about religion. I wish it was that simple."

"What is it about?"

Patrick spit out his answer as if it were poison. "People."

PART ONE

The Book of Matthew

And whoever shall receive one such little child in my name re-
ceiveth me. But whoever shall offend one of these little ones . . . it
were better for him that a millstone were hanged about his neck,
and that he drowned in the depths of the sea.

—Jesus of Nazareth,
The Book of Matthew, 18:5–6

I

THE SERPENT

They shall take up serpents; and if they drink any deadly thing,
it shall not hurt them. They shall lay hands on the sick,
and the sick shall recover.

—The Book of Mark 16:18

London, England
1705

The Dark Ages were over and revolution smoldered, soon to flame.
Kings and priests were hated. The common man was on the rise,
ready to seize the power of not only governments, but God himself. It
was the Age of Enlightenment.

An English writer named Charles Gildon, struggling to make
sense of the cataclysm, wrote a book called *The Deist's Manual* that
described the forty great religions of Europe, including a newly
founded, wildly rebellious church known as the Followers of Christ.

The Followers had originated in London in the late 1600s, identified by neither a founder nor a place of worship, which kept them
safer from the torturous wrath of the Church of England. Prudently,
when they met secretly in each other's homes, they didn't even pray
out loud.

At the dawn of the 1700s, they rose slowly to prominence in a mi-
lieu of clean and sober Christianity that was not far removed from the

sexless, humble piety of the Pilgrims. The Followers, though, thought that the Pilgrim's life of obedience and restraint was hardly worth living. They believed in a joyously mystical, almost orgasmic universe of miracles and wonder: a kingdom of heaven on earth that they alone ruled as supreme beings, operating without restraints.

The religious movement they helped create was called the Great Awakening.

Gildon, an atheist turned Anglican fundamentalist, wrote:

> The Followers of Christ are the heirs of Salvation. They are above ordinances.
>
> They walk Here as if they were Above. They meet at the houses of their members for a silent contemplation of the Angels in Heaven.
>
> They hold themselves nearer to those that are of Their opinion than those with whom they have any tie of Birth.
>
> Some call them Visionaries. Some call them Revelation Men.
>
> Their divinity is concerned with the Most Mysterious Things in the nature of God.

Not everyone agreed. Gildon had sulfurous detractors, including mainstream Presbyterian Daniel Defoe, author of *Robinson Crusoe*, who once insulted Gildon by saying, "Charles Gildon is a man with six well-fed whores and a starving wife."

It was an era of bitter religious contention, believed to be temporary, as the Age of Enlightenment began to unfold its wings, in yet one more attempt to finally make the world rational.

Bow, New Hampshire
1829

"Mary is dying!" Mark Baker screamed. His eight-year-old daughter was writhing on the floor, gnashing her teeth. She suddenly became lifeless, her eyes open but empty. Her mother crouched over her as her father raced for the doctor, lashing his horses as he stood rigidly in his wagon.

By the time he returned, Mary had recovered. But her fits began to recur.

One night Mary was lying in bed and heard a voice cry her name three times. She later recalled that when she replied, her body began to rise. It rose one foot off the bed and remained there. Then she was lowered gently back down. She levitated again, and was lowered. Then again. She knew it could *not* have happened—but that it had— and she believed forever-after that she was possessed by a strange and wondrous power.

Mary continued to suffer horrible fevers, seizures, ulcers, pain, and paralysis, and her suffering did not cease when she tried homeopathy, hydrotherapy, and various healing diets, including grain-based vege- tarian regimens created by Seventh-day Adventist John H. Kellogg, and by the Reverend Sylvester Graham, who claimed his new flour could cure almost anything.

Physicians couldn't help Mary. The only two choices she had were those who had begun to use ether and operated aggressively, or the traditionally passive doctors—the two options categorized at that time as those who killed you, or those who let you die.

Finally she turned to a protégé of the famous Dr. Franz Mesmer, and found relief.

Dr. Mesmer, of Vienna, had initially employed magnets to heal, believing that a universal force of animal magnetism existed in all people. Benjamin Franklin had tried to bottle this magnetic power in 1784 as a "powder of sympathy," but when he failed, the biomedi- cal version of the cure was abandoned and Mesmer began to simply place his hands soothingly on a patient's midsection—just above the navel, in the hypochondrium region—sometimes for hours at a time. It seemed to work.

With this treatment, Mary Baker experienced a rebirth of her health.

Mary considered Mesmerism to be not only scientific, but a logical extension of the biblical practice of laying on of hands. It cast out not only fevers, but demons: two for the price of one. She refined the theatrical practice, dressed it with theology, and began to sell it herself.

Mary's therapy and the exotic belief system she built around it gained acclaim and gave a nice jolt to the tepid religious rut that had overtaken America. Her growing group of acolytes became part of the Second Great Awakening, along with other radical, all-in churches that made big promises of worldly glory and heavenly ascendance.

The one with the flashiest backstory was the new Mormon Church, founded in 1830, which offered its adherents wealth and membership in a pre-doomsday super-race—as well as the right to have a *lot* of wives, all submissive. The Mormons believed that two warring tribes of Israelites had been the original settlers of America—the bad Red Israelites, and the good White Israelites. Jesus, they said, had materialized on the East Coast shortly after his resurrection to try to stop a genocidal race war that the Red Israelites eventually won, as evidenced by the fact that when Columbus came to America he met no surviving Caucasians.

The Mormons even had a living witness to their story: Joseph Smith, who swore he'd heard the whole thing in New York from a warrior-angel who gave him golden tablets and magic reading glasses. The tablets and glasses soon disappeared, but Joseph Smith had enough material to write *The Book of Mormon,* and attract a following of thousands of modern, or latter-day, saints. They alone were God's chosen people, Smith said, destined for an End Times heaven that far surpassed the standard Christian utopia.

The seductive Mormon inducements trumped those of another group founded a few years later, the Seventh-day Adventists—who also promised eternal ecstasy, but demanded a monastic lifestyle of no dancing, card playing, music, self-adornment, reading, or meat-eating. Not even celebrations on Christmas or birthdays.

The most popular of the rebellious charismatic churches was that of the backwoods-based, snake-handling, poison-drinking Pentecostalists, who guaranteed a fabulous hillbilly heaven, but only for the *ultra*-trusting. They arose in the late 1880s as part of an offbeat segment of Radical Reformation evangelicals that included The Foot Washers, The Plain People, The Dunkers, and the Peculiar People, named after an alternate translation of Deuteronomy's "The Chosen People."

A group offering not just similar perfection, but "higher perfection," was the even wilder Followers of Christ, who had migrated from England to Canada for religious freedom and were trickling down to America with an exciting, exclusive offer of daily face-time with God himself, *plus* submissive wives, perfect health, and superiority over everyone on earth—except for one minor sacrifice: Nobody could ever go to a doctor. They thought healing was God's job, not that of crude physicians, who at the time also served as barbers. The Followers—convinced, like the others, that they alone were God's chosen people—even claimed that one of their first American settlers, James McDonald, had baptized Joseph Smith in the 1820s, shortly before Smith had begun to take dictation from angels and write his own bible.

The basic concept of these New England churches was simple: You can be perfect (*if* you're one of us) because we are not of this poor material world, but God's perfect world.

In this manner, among these people, modern faith healing in America was born.

Among all the mystics, Mary Baker came closest to perfecting the art of ethereal branding and franchising. She became the print media's preeminent drama queen, enmeshed in poisonous feuds and outrageous claims during the creation of her faith-healing empire. Mary grew rich and famous teaching others how to make money by treating illness with no overhead.

After the early loss of her first two husbands, one to yellow fever and one to desertion, she made headlines in the highly publicized Salem Witchcraft Trial of 1878 by instigating a lawsuit against her ex-boyfriend for casting a spell on her with a form of witchcraft that she called malicious animal magnetism. She lost the case, but stayed in the news cycle when her third husband—Gilbert Eddy, who'd sealed their marriage deal by agreeing to a no-sex clause—was arrested for killing her ex-boyfriend. Eddy soon died of heart disease, despite Mary's fervent attempts to convince him that clogged arteries were impossible in a perfect world.

Mary blamed Eddy's demise on "mental murder," committed by one of her students. But she was unable to produce the neural murder weapon and the case was dismissed.

Nonetheless, Mary Baker Eddy became the only woman in world history to found a major religion, the Christian Science Church. It became one of the most powerful churches in American history, and one of the most hated. For the next century, as its influence and wealth grew, it helped protect a constellation of radical faith-healing churches, including the Followers of Christ, as children, elders, and other vulnerable people began to die by the thousands at the hands of faith healers—with no consequences whatsoever—across a growing country founded by the Pilgrims on one primary principle: freedom of religion.

ONEIDA, NEW YORK
1840

Follower James McDonald had a son shortly after he'd baptized Joseph Smith and moved in the 1830s to the emerging utopian colony of Oneida, where he claimed that his son not only had the gift of divine healing, but could even raise the dead. The claim shocked the people of Oneida, which wasn't easy, because the town was the home of the anything-goes, proto-swinger Perfectionist religion, which coined the phrase "free love."

More shockingly, McDonald's son, Jacob, openly kissed other men on the mouth. That same act had previously resulted in the arrest of the Followers minister, Jacob Cochrane, on a charge of adultery and promiscuous behavior. Cochrane's legal defense: The Holy Greeting was a centuries-old custom, based on the biblical assertion that Jesus had kissed his disciples on the mouth. Therefore, Cochrane said, because the Followers were, unlike the era's *pretender* churches, directly linked to Jesus, the kiss was not sodomistic at all, but holy: hence, the name, Holy Greeting.

The claim didn't help Cochrane with his Oneida jury, even though the Perfectionists did believe that mankind had begun to live in a "new age" that allowed "complex" marriages. Cochrane went to jail.

Jacob McDonald wisely hit the road, and soon enlisted in the Union Army. The Followers were pacifists, but were also idealistic, and willing to kill for the abolition of slavery. Abolition was an obsession among them, along with temperance, courtesy, medical self-care, good hygiene, thrift, and raising the dead.

As a young soldier, McDonald, according to Followers' lore, was sitting alone on the tongue of a wagon one evening, reading Scripture, when a Divine Apparition floated out of the trees. The Holy Ghost commanded Brother McDonald to defy convention, heal the sick, redeem the wicked, and let Him worry about the lawyers.

With this calling, Brother Jacob McDonald drifted west and began to baptize sinners in a chain of saved souls that eventually reached Brother John Evans, one of the many Followers who was part of the Oklahoma Land Rush of 1893—"a glorious period in our time," according to the Followers' genealogy. Brother Evans, a cowpoke who could speak in tongues, was ordered by his pastor to, "Teach the Brethren, here and elsewhere, up and down this unfriendly World. And those that hear thee shall wear a starry crown."

Evans and a small band of Followers families—the Caldwells, Cunninghams, Youngs, Morrises, Eellses, and Smiths—joined a wagon train in 1898 for their exodus from Oklahoma. They headed for the lush gardens and rich gold mines of Idaho, which had just been made a state, following its abolition of polygamy.

The West, they believed, would be their American Eden.

CALDWELL, IDAHO
1939

The snake in the garden wasn't doing its job. The fat blacksnake was supposed to be eating the garden's grasshoppers and spiders, but little Eleanor Evans could clearly see the insects climbing all over their vegetables. Snakes that big didn't usually eat bugs, but the pond the snake lived in was just about empty of the bullfrogs and bluegills it liked, and in the Dust Bowl year of '39, as Eleanor later recalled, just about anything would eat just about anything. Some people were even eating their blacksnakes, which wasn't too smart, because the blacksnakes ate the rattlers.

Around this time of day, with the sun straight up, the rattlers would sometimes slide into the dusty garden, but not if they smelled the blacksnake, which could handle a rattlesnake bite. Blacksnakes were like the Followers that way. Eleanor had seen her dad snatch up great big rattlesnakes by their tails and proclaim, "In Jesus' name, Devil be gone," then cast them down, and watch the snakes crawl away to die. Snake handling was kind of a contest among the men, to see who *really* had faith. It didn't always turn out so well for those with lack of faith, but whose fault was that?

Once a rattler had bitten her great-uncle Wilbur, but he just prayed it out and was fine. People respected Wilbur, because he was one of the Oklahoma pioneers, but he'd made everybody mad by fighting in the Great War, which was probably why the snake bit him. He had a sore arm after the bite but he lived almost forever until he got sugar diabetes, and he almost prayed his way out of that. Now he was in the Peaceful Valley Cemetery, just up the road, buried in a long row of Evanses, next to the sections of Cunninghams, Morrises, Smiths, and Beagleys. He'd been laid to rest next to his daughter, who'd started to have a baby, but couldn't. Her baby wouldn't come all the way out, they said—just the poor thing's little blue head—and she and the baby had gotten sick and died.

It was a beautiful cemetery, though—especially the places where they buried all the kids, because folks always did something special with their kid's graves, like putting cribs or bed frames around them, so it would look like their children were just sleeping. The Followers were crazy about their kids.

Eleanor was just six in '39 but she already had a couple of friends in the cemetery. It didn't spook her, though, because she'd already been dead herself, and knew it didn't amount to much. It happened when she had pneumonia as a little kid. That was back in Hailey, next to the rich town of Sun Valley, before they were forced out of there when the powerful folks got mean. Eleanor remembered that when she got sick her grandma had held her by the cook-stove to keep her warm, while her dad and the elders prayed over her. But then she got real sleepy and died.

They said her arms flopped down and she was limp as a dishrag. She wasn't breathing, of course, and everybody said her body turned the color of an eggplant. That's when Grandma handed her to Mom—who'd been dead herself, as a baby—and they laid hands on her. It didn't work the first time, according to Mom, and she just got more purple. She was dead quite a while, Mom said, so they had to keep her close to the stove so she wouldn't be cold when she came back to life. They praised the Lord and anointed her. They raised a ruckus, because everybody loved her to death. She was good with her little brother, Donny, and was a big help around the house.

Eleanor didn't remember coming back. But everybody else sure did. They talked about it all the time. It was a regular family story.

Out in the garden, while Eleanor was picking beans by the lazy old blacksnake, which was like a pet, her grandma came out with a big wicker basket and they started gathering tomatoes. The tomatoes weren't much at all that year—they were as bad as the dried-out snap-beans, and even worse than the apples and pears, which were just runty little things you couldn't even make a cobbler out of.

Grandma Evans always told Eleanor to be real careful of the

spiders. You had to be, she said, even if you were born holy. When Grandma would come across one, she'd flick it with her finger, and knock its web apart. Eleanor had promised to keep her eyes open for spiders, but she really didn't, because the spiders didn't look very scary—not like the rattlers did—and she was trying to learn to think for herself.

But when Eleanor was reaching for a tomato, a spider got her. That's what happened, she thought, when you didn't listen to your elders. Grandma got worried, because it looked to be a black widow.

Grandma found the two bite marks and put an Epsom salt poultice over them, but Eleanor's arm still swelled up, and there was yellow pus all up and down it. Her skin got so thin that it split in places. After the men got home, they all circled around Eleanor, prayed silently, according to the ancient custom, and anointed her forehead. Her dad sent word for everybody to remember Eleanor in their prayers, so pretty soon it didn't hurt so much.

That night her arm got so fat she thought it would burst, so they called for her second cousin, Vernon Thaine, to come over, because he had special powers. Vernon got real sad-looking and prayed for hours while Eleanor watched the fireplace and tried to keep her arm from aching. Vernon was the sweetest person she knew. Everybody loved him. While he was humming a hymn to her she fell asleep thinking that Vern might be a Prophet someday, like Vic Baldwin, their minister. Vern wasn't as handsome as Vic, but he was a better healer. He did it at tent revival meetings in what some of the preachers were calling the Third Great Awakening, which included Prohibition. In Caldwell, thank the Lord, they still had temperance, so the worldly people in the Valley had to go all the way to Boise for their whiskey.

In the morning, when her arm didn't hurt so much, Eleanor's dad told her that the whole thing was lucky, because it showed her what God could do. It was like when Dale Cunningham got his foot mangled in a thresher but came out fine. He had a little limp, but that was good, because it reminded him that he was born holy. If he hadn't been born holy—like all the heathen Mormons in the valley—he'd have lost that foot. Sometimes the Mormons and the other worldly farmers lost their fingers and even whole hands from nothing more than a bite from a widow or a tiny little rattler.

By nightfall, though, everybody forgot about her arm because Grandma was in a dither. She'd found a note from Pastor Vic Baldwin to Eleanor's cousin Ophelia. It was all about him wanting to meet Ophelia at the motel down by the Simplot potato plant. Ophelia was just fifteen, and that was why Grandma was so mad. Grandma talked about calling the sheriff but Grandpa put a stop to it, saying that the Followers took care of their own.

The next day Grandma and Grandpa barged in on Vic and Ophelia at the motel. Grandpa had his hunting rifle and Grandma had a big six-shooter. When they got home, Grandma told Eleanor that she'd yelled, "You better leave her alone, or I'll *get* you," and that old Vic had just about wet himself.

The church went crazy after that. Some people were up in arms about Pastor Vic doing something like that to a little girl, but most of them said that Ophelia wasn't really all that young, and that Vic had a right, because he was a Prophet. Prophets were right up there with Jesus, almost like his Disciples. It started to look like nothing was going to happen. That's when Walter White stepped in.

Everybody knew that Walter White was heavenly-holy—in the Word, as they said—and that he had a lot of flash, but nobody knew how serious he was until then. He only preached once in a while, and the only reason he did it at all was because a couple of years ago he was on a train trip and glanced down at his hands, which looked like they were covered with maggots, eating away—so of course he talked to God, and God said he had to start preaching. On that day, Walter White became the Prophet, though he kept it to himself at first.

Walter got up at the service on Thursday night and said that God had decreed that the Caldwell church had to break up. He told them God had commanded him to take his people from this place of fornication forever.

But nobody really wanted to leave. There was no good place to go where the worldly people would leave them alone. That's when Walter starting talking about this little town outside of Portland called Oregon City. He made it sound like paradise. Things grew there without watering, he said, because God kept it wet almost all year 'round, and there were sky-high Christmas trees you could build a whole house out of, giant fish called sturgeon that looked like sea monsters and lived to be a hundred years old, elk ten feet tall, and strawberries as big as your fist.

Oregon City was their future, Walter said. There were hardly any Mormons there, not too many sheriffs, and no rattlesnakes at all. He said they'd be safe there until the end of time.

Pretty soon, just about everybody followed Walter to Oregon City, except for a few families with old folks who weren't up to it.

They traveled the old Oregon Trail, which was now a paved road, and entered the little riverside town with a thrill of hope. Oregon City was as beautiful and bountiful as Pastor Walter had claimed. It was heaven.

Oregon City, Oregon
Thanksgiving, 1963

When Walter went off on his harangue about End Times, which he said was set for 1969, it made Eleanor think about the new Skeeter Davis song "The End of the World." Eleanor couldn't get the tune out of her head, even while Walter was yelling about the Beast, the Jews, 666, The Rapture, Armageddon, false prophets, and the rest of it. She lost track, and that made her think she had a devil, because she knew she should be scared to death. They only had six more years before Jesus would return to take the Followers to heaven and send all the people from the world to hell, and here she was, wasting time on a silly song.

Everybody else was hanging on Walter's words, except Eleanor's brother Donny. He was kind of young in the mind, she thought, and ate like a pig, and now he was chewing gum in church, which wasn't smart. "That was enough," Eleanor later said, "to get Walter all teed off. It didn't take much by that point."

Walter had changed, she thought, after they arrived in Oregon City. He got very bossy, and chastised people from the pulpit, especially after he'd had some wine for his digestion. He'd had a few glasses at their big Thanksgiving dinner, and was giving Donny the evil eye.

Eleanor thought that Walter had gotten mean because things were actually *too* good in Oregon City. There was lots of work at the sawmill down by the waterfall, they all helped each other build fine new houses, and growing a garden was like falling off a log. The deer ate the gardens, but all you had to do was to build two fences five feet apart, because a deer could jump the first one, but couldn't get a run at the second, so—bang!—venison. It wasn't legal, but so what? As far as the law was concerned, it was also illegal to shoot geese out of season, but there were about two thousand Followers and only six police, and one of them was drunk every time you saw him.

The luxury that had made a lot of people soft, though, had made Walter hard. All of a sudden, Walter, glaring down at Donny from the pulpit, yelled, "Whatta you eatin', Donny? Wanna stand up and tell ever-body?"

Donny hung his head but Walter got louder. "Can you hear me, Donny? Can you *hear* me?"

Eleanor kept her face from showing anything, but Cousin Vernon Thaine, God bless him, leaned forward and gave Walter a *look*, right in front of everybody. Vernon could get away with that because he was an elder, and the most loved man in the church. He'd been very kind to the Hickmans after their little girl passed from polio, and he was a big help to the Beagleys, who'd just lost a child. He was every bit as sweet as he'd been when he prayed the poison out of Eleanor's arm.

"Brother Walter," Vernon said softly.

Walter, with his big, boxy face and strong hands, squared up his shoulders and looked like he'd been slapped. He stared Vernon down and said, "Why, you don't know enough to tan your own hide."

Vernon took it in. He even gave Walter a kindly look, like Jesus had bestowed upon his tormentors.

"Even a *possum* knows how to tan its own hide!" Walter yelled.

Vernon breathed out hard. He'd left family back in Idaho to go with Walter, and so had the Beagleys, Smiths, Cunninghams, Crones, and Hickmans.

Nobody else said anything, including Eleanor.

But she never forgot it.

For Eleanor Evans, that was the beginning of the end. Before the year was over, Eleanor—twenty-nine, unmarried, and unemployed—left the church. Because she was the first person ever to leave the Oregon City Followers of Christ Church—and many years later, become one of the first to join Patrick in his historic rebellion against the church—she eventually came to consider her act of individuality to be the beginning of the beginning.

When 1969 came, the world did not end. But the life of Walter White did. There was never another preacher in the church able to place the primacy of ideas over that of personalities and never a new doctrine to help congregants discern right from wrong.

But many in the church were happy with the lack of authority, and the Followers of Christ became the largest and most powerful church—and voting bloc—in town.

THE FOLLOWERS OF CHRIST CEMETERY
OREGON CITY, OREGON
DECEMBER 23, 1974

"Hairy Christmas," fifty-nine-year-old Vernon Thaine said to eight-year-old Patrick Robbins, as the boy stood over his father's new grave. Patrick looked up at Vernon with tight, dry eyes and forced a smile.

"Only the good die young," Vernon said softly, looking into the grave. Vernon put his arm around Patrick and rocked him from side to side, until Patrick could finally cry.

Patrick thought that Vernon was as good as they get, and totally free of fear. The old man would even say something funny at your dad's funeral if that's what it took to coax a smile out of you. Vernon was also Patrick's doctor. He'd been a medic in World War II—one of the Followers' many Conscientious Objectors—and could cure just about anything. He knew everything that doctors knew, and he was the one doctor who didn't think he was God, which gave him a big advantage. Vernon was the closest thing they'd had to a preacher since Uncle Walter, though Walter, everybody said, had really been more like Jesus than just a pastor.

The service was held up while Patrick had his cry, and when he finished, his pal Timmy Wyland came over with some of Patrick's other young friends and gave him a hug. Patrick had been the only boy in the house since his brother died of the flu, but he still felt like he had the best brothers ever. Then the teenagers and grown-ups started to line up for him, and it was pretty cool to have the holiest people on earth promise to take care of him forever. When sixteen-year old Jeff Beagley came along, he gave Patrick the Holy Greeting, on the lips, and it made him feel grown-up, but even sadder, because it meant that he was old enough now to take care of his mom. She was standing off to one side, looking as white as death and as lost as ever. But after the folks got done with Patrick, they went to his mom and gave her envelopes with something to help out, and that put some life back into her ghost-face. Some of the envelopes were pretty thick, and she got more than she could hold, so she gave a big handful to Patrick.

Then something really crappy happened, as if Patrick didn't already have enough to forget.

His big sister Ella, who everybody was shunning because she killed her unborn baby, pulled up in an old beater. Ella was with that woman people called the Widow, not because she'd lost a couple of husbands, which happened to a lot of wives in the church, but because poison from a black widow spider had gotten into her brain a long time ago and made her crazy. The Widow stayed in the car, which was smart, because the Followers hated her for helping Ella kill her own baby, just like the worldly did. But Ella started marching across the wet cemetery in high heels. When she got close, three of her home-school girlfriends broke ranks and ran over to her, which wasn't very nice to Patrick and his mom. The girls set up sort of a flying wedge, like in touch-football, and they headed for the grave. Sis looked like she was crying. She looked a lot older, too.

Ella, all sobby, came up to Patrick's mother and held her hands out. Mom wouldn't even look at her. It was embarrassing, and just made his sister cry harder.

Then, in a moment Patrick would remember forever, Ella knelt down to his face. "I'm still . . . ," she said, but had to stop. "Your. Family. . . . You know that, Patrick."

Patrick got very calm, at least for an eight-year-old at his dad's funeral. "No you're not." He looked around him. "This is my family."

Later on, he heard that everybody thought he was a hero, and maybe even a future Prophet, but that sure wasn't how it felt at the time.

Ella lost it, and nobody had a clue what to do until Vernon put his arm around her and led her back to the road. That was a relief. The Widow met them by the car, and for some ungodly reason Vernon shook her hand. But at least they left.

After that the Followers all went back to the church to decorate their giant Doug-fir Christmas tree, wrap presents, play volleyball and board games, and eat a lot. The moms made really good things on days like this. Extra-crispy chicken. Beef Stroganoff made with country-fresh cream and homemade egg noodles. Chocolate cake filled with vanilla pudding. Strawberry parfait pie with ice cream right inside it. Fudge with the Beagleys' huge hazelnuts. And always pure-white divinity fudge—that was a tradition, and kind of a joke, since of course they were the only divine people on earth. Even after Patrick was stuffed, the women kept giving him their best desserts and lots of big hugs. All the guys clowned around to make him feel better, and toward the end of it they gathered around him and his mom and said a healing prayer. It wasn't even silent, which made it very special. Timmy Wyland's dad led it. He was almost as nice as Vernon—the kind of man who seemed like everybody's dad.

Then the Morris Brothers Band started playing happy music, like "Jingle Bell Rock" and the Elvis version of "Here Comes Santa Claus." Jeff Beagley and the other teenagers started dancing—fast— but still touching each other, which was the only proper way. Jeff danced with a girl named Marci, who was barely a teenager. Jeff's dad yelled out that Jeff was robbing the cradle, and Marci laughed. After that, Les Morris sang "Have Yourself a Merry Little Christmas," and all the grown-ups danced.

By the time they left, Patrick felt surprisingly okay. His mom said that they wouldn't need to worry about money for a year or two, be- cause God and Walter had been watching over them that day. By then, Patrick figured, she'd be with somebody else—maybe her sec- ond cousin Darryl Eells, since his wife had just died of something or other. Mom was brave about the whole deal, but she was still a mess.

In bed, Patrick made himself tired by repeating the Now-I-Lay- Me-Down-to-Sleep a whole bunch of times. He tried pretending his dad was praying with him by the side of his bed, like always, but it didn't help. Then he thought about how his dad had told him, after Dad got real sick, that no matter what happened, he'd always have The Family. That did help.

As he drifted toward the relief of sleep, Patrick thought about how bad it would be if Darryl was his new dad. But he pushed the thought away. It was easy. He was getting really good at not thinking about things.

GROSSE POINTE, MICHIGAN
JULY 1975

It was a perfectly ordinary heavenly summer day, full of miracles and wonder, as devout Christian Scientist Rita Swan drove to her ultrasound appointment—to see if her unborn baby might die—completely free of the devilish force of fear.

Rita already knew what the doctor would say: The ovarian cyst that had been threatening the life of her son was gone.

A few days before, God had guided Rita to Jeanne Laitner, a gifted fellow follower of Christ the Scientist. Laitner, the most revered practitioner in Detroit's Christian Science Church, had in a matter of moments obliterated the cyst with the power of prayer. One moment the ugly growth had been lodged in Rita's left ovary, bleeding and burning like a knife wound, and the next—*Gone!*—blasted away by a laser of divine love.

So the ultrasound—which Rita was doing partly just to pacify her poor, befuddled obstetrician—was not exactly boring, but very anticlimactic. The only interesting part was the macabre experience of being in a hospital, with its dehumanizing machines, the presence of death, and the cheap-motel smell of Lysol that covered the stench of germs, human waste, and fear.

Rita's doctor, who'd felt the frightening lump during a prior pelvic exam, said he had great news: It had disappeared! This was the kind of day he *lived* for! A polycystic growth would have drastically increased her chance of a miscarriage, and even its removal would have been dangerous.

Rita, who'd been raised with Midwestern good manners, reacted appropriately. She knew that there were more things in heaven and earth than could be dreamed of in her doctor's philosophy, but this was no time to rub it in. He was mortal, so she couldn't expect him to be perfect.

Rita drove home to her husband, Doug, to share the sweet irony of the doctor's supposed success. Rita and Doug were intellectuals—he had a PhD in mathematics and she had a PhD in literature, from Vanderbilt—and were intelligent enough to recognize a multiverse that existed far beyond the limited human intellect, in the glimmering realm of the spirit. In that world, the impossible happened every day to those lucky few who had discovered that only the goodness of God was real, and that all suffering was illusion.

For the rest of her pregnancy, Rita was, as she later put it, "on cloud nine."

Little Matthew Swan was born on March 3, 1976, with Rita's obstetrician present. The First Church of Christ, Scientist—the official name of the Christian Science Church—had begun to recommend a doctor's attendance at birth, as well as prenatal care, and Doug and Rita bowed to that wisdom. The Church was quite rational, and so were they. After all, Jesus himself had possessed such a gift for logic that his teachings had long captivated many of the most brilliant minds on earth.

Jesus of Nazareth was, according to Christian Science doctrine, not just the son of God, but the finest scientist of his day.

Absolutely nothing, Dr. Rita Swan was convinced, could possibly go wrong, from that day forward until the end of time.

2

GOD'S PERFECT WORLD

There is nothing either good or bad, but thinking makes it so.
—*HAMLET*, BY WILLIAM SHAKESPEARE, QUOTED ON PAGE
ONE OF *SCIENCE AND HEALTH*, BY MARY BAKER EDDY

FATHER'S DAY
GROSSE POINTE, MICHIGAN
JUNE 19, 1977

"Good morning, Christian soldier," Doug chirped to his son when Rita brought Matthew to their bedroom.

Doug's voice was music to Rita—lyrical, melodic, and rich with comfort—and he loved to talk to her. Their marriage was perfect. It was born of a bond forged ethereally in heavenly splendor and nurtured materially by the paradise of wealthy Grosse Pointe, just inland from the waterfront palaces of the Ford and Dodge auto heirs on windswept Lake St. Clair. Doug, thirty-seven, was teaching at the Detroit Institute of Technology, while Rita, thirty-three, was breast-feeding Matthew and spoon-feeding her Wayne State students pearls of wisdom from her academic focus, Percy Bysshe Shelley, not the least of which was one that beautifully espoused a central Christian Science belief: "Death is the veil which those who live call life; They sleep, and it is lifted."

On this special father-child day, it was clear to Doug that God was in his heaven. Sunlight streamed in on his seven-year-old daughter, Catherine, and his beloved little boy, cradled in the arms of his Midwest Madonna, who was slender and sweet, with inviting eyes and a pretty face, but without a hint of pretension. All was right with the world.

At least, almost all. A couple of months ago there had been a reappearance of Rita's cyst, which had apparently been obscured by her pregnancy, rather than healed by Jeanne Laitner. It had become twisted and began to putrefy. Rita tried Christian Science healing, but the cyst caused unbearable pain and nausea so severe that she could no longer breast-feed. She asked her doctor for a religiously condoned injection for the pain, "a hypodermic," as Mary Baker Eddy had called it. But the doctor refused to just mask the pain of a potentially lethal condition.

Doug didn't know what to recommend. He'd been traumatized by caring for his mother while she'd died of untreated colon cancer, but he and Rita both thought the most dangerous thing they could do was to show lack of faith in God by relying on medical treatment. People *died* from lack of faith, not because God was punishing them—as unstudied fundamentalists might presume—but because they'd turned away from the most potent power imaginable. Faith had cured people since antiquity. There were countless well-documented accounts of it. They had seen it happen themselves: sudden reversals, spontaneous remissions, miracles—and so had their friends.

When Rita had been a child on the plains of Kansas, she'd even prayed her cat back to health after it was bitten by a prairie rattlesnake. The cat's head had swelled to practically the size of a lion's, but she'd held it with a child's undiluted love, ignored her fear, and welcomed it back to life.

Rita thought it was no coincidence that her first medical crisis had been caused by a serpent. By the time the cyst occurred, she was certain that illness was the product of a spiritually troubled state of mind. More than a hundred years earlier, in a foreshadowing of what was emerging in the mid-1970s as mind/body medicine, Mary Baker Eddy had shown that belief could not only create illness, but also quell it.

Rita had been intellectually convinced, ever since she and Doug had attended and then taught at the Christian Science Church's Principia College, that disease was a figment of the imagination, made real only by the *belief* that it was real. She thought it was illogical for a Christian to believe that death was an illusion—due to the existence of heaven—but could *not* see that disease was illusory, too. Disease was just a melodrama of the mortal mind, like paranoia, greed, and jealousy—a soap opera that the enlightened need not suffer. The only *real* reality was the Divine Mind that ruled God's perfect world.

But even Jesus had used his own saliva to cure blindness, so Rita soon went to the doctor, had the cyst removed—just as it was about to burst and kill her—and that was that. Almost. She was suspended from teaching her Sunday-school class, because the Church was less forgiving than God, but who wasn't? That was Christianity's whole point, wasn't it?

Even during Rita's suspension, God revealed his grace again. Matthew came down with a fever, but Jeanne Laitner came over, reminded Rita that fever was just fear, and summoned the Holy Spirit. It blew into the room like a blast of fresh air and washed away Rita's fear, and with it, Matthew's fever. Piece of cake. Jeanne collected her payment and left.

The same thing had happened to Matthew again about a month before Father's Day. Same treatment, same result. Rita and Doug, thrilled, testified in church. In the Christian Science Church's unstructured, preacher-free service, their story was hardly the most dramatic, but was one of the most heartfelt.

On this morning of glorifying fatherhood, though, it looked like the baby's fever was back. Even though the fever was undoubtedly just a fear-based triviality in God's perfect world, it was still scary. Rita and Doug knew that worry caused an endless cycle of suffering, but they were parents, and it was their *job* to worry. Sitting on the bed,

Doug looked into Matthew's eyes and couldn't find their familiar sparkle. The baby was lost in a fog. Doug was sure, though, that Jeanne Laitner could rescue this memorable family holiday.

Jeanne said she couldn't come over, but did promise to apply distant healing—praying for Matthew in her own home—which was standard operating procedure. It was more convenient—and after all, the prayers were meant to summon the will of God, not that of the patient. Jeanne told them that her focus wasn't on somebody's silly symptoms, but The Almighty: So get over your self-fulfilling fear, she seemed to say, write me a check, and have a good day.

That admonition hit Doug hard, because on this warm summer morning his hands and feet were cold with the fear that he was the cause of this. He thought it was no coincidence that this was happening on Father's Day, because he had one dark secret he'd never told Rita or anyone else, and now it looked as if God was shoving it in his face. During his mother's illness, he'd promised himself that if he ever had children who were seriously ill that he'd take them to a doctor. He hadn't told Rita because he was afraid his lack of faith might poison her thinking, and weaken their family's immunity to evil.

But Rita also had a secret. She, too, thought it was no coincidence that this was happening on Father's Day, because she was furious with her father. Her mother, long disabled by feelings of helplessness and hopelessness, had recently seemed to go nuts—she'd stripped naked and rolled in the snow, crawled under beds, and shaved her head—and Rita had gone home to help. Her father, however, had been so defensive and insulting that she'd abruptly left. Her mother's Christian Science practitioner told Rita that the whole problem was the false belief in menopause, but that perspective hadn't solved anything. Since then, Rita had done endless metaphysical work, praying for her mother's relief, and for peace with her father, but she still felt like her family was surrounded by a cloud of evil thoughts: what Mary Baker Eddy had called malicious animal magnetism.

And what if *most* of the malicious animal magnetism was coming straight from *her*? With *Matthew* paying the price?

Jeanne Laitner logged her start-time, and got all prayered-up, as Christian Scientists put it. By the end of it, she was sure she'd achieved relief for Matthew.

But Rita soon called back. Jeanne, still patient, told Rita that Matthew might be cutting a tooth. Or maybe even *two* teeth, given how hard she'd just prayed.

That evening, Rita called again. Matthew was soaking his crib with sweat and couldn't move. She was terrified.

Late at night, unable to escape the fear that seemed to be stealing Matthew's life, Rita and Doug, with both their secrets still unspoken, decided to take their little boy to the emergency room. By the time they reached their decision, though, it was too late.

It was after twelve. Emergency rooms, they believed, closed at midnight.

GROSSE POINTE, MICHIGAN
TUESDAY, JUNE 21, 1977

When Jeanne Laitner returned to the Swans' home it was obvious that Matthew wasn't just teething. His body was rigid, and his handsome little face—once so animated, with oversized, old-soul eyes—now looked like a death mask. Rita's cheeks were wet with tears and sweat.

Even so, it was an honor that Jeanne had come personally.

It was a greater honor when Jeanne began to pray out loud, in front of Rita, because it showed her faith in Rita's piety. Jesus had warned his disciples in the Sermon on the Mount that praying aloud with other people present risked contamination of a privileged communication with God. "Do not give dogs what is sacred," Jesus had said. "Do not cast your pearls before swine." Instead, Jesus said, "When thou prayest, enter into thy closet, and when thou hast shut thy door, pray to thy Father in secret." So that's what Jeanne always did, except around the most faithful. Or in an emergency.

Mary Baker Eddy had been an advocate of silent prayer, and called

it praying in the closet. She thought it produced better medical outcomes. And for her own purposes, in an era of litigious religious wars, it limited her liability, and was more judicious from a legal point of view.

"Matthew," Jeanne intoned, "you *cannot* be sick. You live in the kingdom of God."

When Jeanne finished, she triumphantly told Rita that nothing in material-world medicine—she called it "materia medica"—could equal what she'd just done: unless, of course, her work had been contaminated by the poison of "false parental thoughts." In short: Calm down, and leave the praying to the professionals.

Rita bowed her head and agreed to keep the celestial wavelengths open for Jeanne. It was humiliating, but humiliation was the best path to humility.

Jeanne came back that evening to find Matthew asleep—finally healing, it seemed—and she talked warmly with Rita and Doug in the living room, confiding trade secrets. "I've learned a *lot* about disease," she said. "You naturally would, in this business. And I know that Christian Scientists are nearly always wrong. They always imagine the worst. It's a fascination with fear." She made them feel safe.

And sure enough, when the morning star arose, Matthew emerged from his daze. Rita held him on the porch in God's glorious sunlight. A truck went by, and Matthew, fifteen-months old, said his baby-talk word for truck, "Guck."

Rita called Jeanne with the wonderful news. "I need that, Rita!" Jeanne snapped. "I worked extremely hard."

Rita asked for a follow-up appointment, but Jeanne refused. "Now that Matthew has turned this corner," she said, "his progress in Christian Science will be steady and sure."

The miracle of Matthew's recovery glimmered before the Swans' eyes, and a life of devotion beckoned. Rita offered God her gratitude.

Prayer, for Christian Scientists, doesn't include deal-making, no matter how dire the circumstances. Christian Scientists and the other

denominations that practice faith healing—the Pentecostalists, Jehovah's Witnesses, Seventh-day Adventists, Mormons, the Church of
the First Born, the Followers of Christ, and the myriad smaller
sects—don't promise God that they'll give up bad habits or contribute
more money in exchange for deliverance. They don't say please, just
thank-you.

But if, in so doing, God rewards their reverence, they are not
averse to showing ever-greater gratitude.

They spread the word, sacrifice their savings, support the politics of their faith, and do whatever else it takes to save the world
from sin.

They consider this reaction to be a natural, sensible law of the universe. They call it "giving back," even though to others that may sound
a lot like fulfilling a contract.

But who's to blame them for that? Don't most of us do whatever it
takes to make sense of this often senseless life?

Wednesday, June 22, 1977

Rita and Doug had five minutes to make a life-changing choice. It
was already 7:25 in the morning, and Doug needed to leave no later
than 7:30 for his first class at the Detroit Institute of Technology.
Matthew was failing. The choice was: trust Matthew's life to Jeanne
Laitner, or turn their backs on a belief in God's personal protection
that they'd both held since childhood.

"I'm afraid of what medical science will do to him," Doug said.
He'd heard hundreds of horror stories from Church members.

But Rita was afraid it was already too late, no matter what they
did. Matthew's resurgence had faded into utter detachment. He
wouldn't eat, wouldn't smile, and his once-wise baby eyes were as
hard and lifeless as marbles.

At the last minute, Rita and Doug came up with a compromise:
They'd use a different Christian Science practitioner. They called a

woman from their congregation who had healed Matthew of a fever two months earlier, and invited her to their home.

The practitioner, June Ahearn, didn't seem to be as ego-driven as Jeanne Laitner, but one of the first things she said was, "I am getting a strong message of temptation towards materia medica. I want to ask you, quite frankly, if there has been any history in your family of resorting to medicine?" Rita told her about having the cyst removed, but didn't mention that it had saved her life.

"Materia medica can do *nothing* for you," June said. She thought the only hope was to, as Christian Scientists often say, let-go-and-let-God. She cited a Christian Science parable of a man hanging from a branch over the edge of a cliff. The solution—of course—was to let go, and trust Providence. Rita didn't respond immediately and June eyed her condescendingly, as if to say: What part of letting yourself fall off a cliff don't you *get*? June said that no matter *how* tempted they were, Rita and Doug could *not* play God, as Adam and Eve had, when they'd eaten from the tree of knowledge of good and evil. Knowledge was God's domain. They were in over their heads.

June also probed Rita about other sins that might be separating the Swans from God's healing power, and Rita confessed the fight with her father. June, excited, insisted that Rita write her father and beg forgiveness. The goal was atonement—not as groveling repentance, as some crude sects might believe—but to restore personal power by regaining, as Mrs. Eddy had put it, at-one-ment with God.

Rita also mentioned her friction with Jeanne Laitner. June, shocked, feared she might be getting in the middle of a fight fueled by malicious animal magnetism.

Rita ignored June's histrionics and stayed civil. But Matthew's life was *leaving* while June spouted what was starting to sound to Rita like religio-babble about how dangerous it would be to take Matthew to a doctor.

Rita, disheartened, called Jeanne Laitner back. She admitted to Jeanne that she'd seen June, and Jeanne didn't take it well. To pacify Jeanne, Rita told her that Matthew was making progress.

"My, my, I should say so," Jeanne said in a high, supercilious tone. "I'm *always* willing to give the other person credit, but in this case, where I worked so *very* hard, it wouldn't be right for another practitioner to come on the case and just . . . heal . . . it."

Rita was appalled by what seemed to be unadulterated egotism. Back to June.

June, still fixated on Rita's spat with her dad, shared the case history of a patient she'd healed of gallstones by coaxing him to admit a grudge against a relative. As soon as the patient achieved at-one-ment, the so-called "gallstones" were gone. It was a miracle!

The next day Matthew began gnashing his teeth. Every time his spine moved he recoiled in soundless agony. Rita lifted him onto a pillow and sang Mrs. Eddy's "Mother's Evening Prayer."

> *Oh, make me glad for every scalding tear,*
> *For hope deferred, ingratitude, disdain!*
> *Wait, and love more for every hate, and fear no ill,*
> *Since God is good, and loss is gain.*

Then Rita began to pray fervently and read Mrs. Eddy's book until she was prayered-up enough to write her father. June Ahearn, however, never mentioned the letter again, and Rita's father never answered it.

June came over that night, but again accused Rita of sabotaging her work with fear. "You don't have to stand over Matthew like a hawk," June said. "I have been very successful in my work."

The next day, Rita skipped church. She lay on the floor weeping as she cried, again and again, "He's just a baby!"

When June came by after church, Rita pulled herself together and asked June to pray alone with Matthew in his room. After some time, Rita heard a happy cry. Hoping against hope, she bounded up the stairs.

Rita burst into the room and saw Matthew grabbing both of June's thumbs. "It's so cute!" June crowed. She had been making Matthew's stuffed clown dance for him, and then . . . miraculously . . . he'd reached out to her. He was holding on to "Aunt June" with all his might. "Look at him!" said June. "Like a little rose lying there!" This was the kind of day that practitioners *lived* for!

Rita's heart shattered. No longer could she see the world through the eyes of those she had once trusted most. All she saw was her baby reaching out in pain.

Even so, she called June later that day and apologized for how distraught she'd been. "Really?" June said coldly. "I didn't catch any hint of that."

Rita told her about Jeanne Laitner's jealousy, but June proclaimed that she enjoyed fending off "mental malpractice," and said there were a lot of "kooks and cliques" in wealthy Grosse Pointe's swanky branch of the Christian Science Church. She didn't ask about Matthew.

At midnight, Matthew began screaming. Rita called June, who said she was certain that mental malpractice had destroyed her perfect healing. Rita told her that they couldn't continue with Christian Science healing, because it just wasn't working.

"It's you and Doug, with your fear, that are holding this thing up," June said. But she agreed to send over a nurse.

The Church of Christ, Scientist, appoints its own nurses, who work at in-patient Christian Science hospitals and perform outpatient care. They're trained only in metaphysics, not medicine, and don't consult with doctors.

Although patients often die, the hospitals are largely immune from legal consequences, because of mandates that were created in 1974 by Richard Nixon, whose aides Robert Haldeman, John Ehrlichman and Egil Krogh—most famous as Watergate felons—were Christian Scientists. The mandates prohibited prosecution of failed faith healings. Nixon also engineered passage of state and federal religious-shield laws that gave faith healing the same essential legal status as medical treatment. Christian Science hospitals were allowed to bill Medicare at the same rate as medical hospitals.

Nixon's Realpolitik motivation for advocating religious freedom was probably to bring the powerful fundamentalist Southern churches into the Republican fold, as part of his no-redneck-left-behind Southern Strategy that made religious conservatism an integral part of Republican politics, even after the Old South became the far-more-sophisticated Sunbelt. The Democrats had controlled the South ever since Republican Abraham Lincoln had attacked it, but Nixon's courtship of Neck of Color Americans changed Southern politics permanently.

Even so, Nixon's mandates were endorsed by Ted Kennedy, chairman of the Senate Subcommittee on Health, who needed the money and votes of the Christian Scientist Church members in his home state of Massachusetts, where Mrs. Eddy had founded and headquartered the church. Later, Massachusetts senator and presidential candidate John Kerry also embraced most Christian Science positions.

Only one state resisted the mandates: Nebraska, where state senator Ernie Chambers, known as the Maverick of Omaha, led the opposition, keeping Nebraska free from unfettered faith-healing abuse.

Chambers, a black civil rights activist and eventually the longest-serving senator in state history, later gained national prominence for filing a lawsuit against God, seeking to block God from "causing grave harm to innumerable persons." The suit was dismissed by a judge who ruled, "Thou shalt not sue God."

When the nurse arrived, Rita was on the floor with Matthew, trying to feed him homemade cream pudding as her tears dropped onto the carpet. Rita had managed to feed Matthew a strawberry, his favorite food, but it had taken almost four hours.

The nurse—trained only in religion—parroted the wisdom that fever was just fear. She did nothing except talk to Rita, didn't stay long, and was afterward hard to reach.

A day later, as Matthew slid into what seemed to be seizures, June Ahearn returned and enthused, "Look how active he is! Everything looks lovely now."

"Is there any intelligence directing that movement?" Rita asked flatly.

"Yes! If there's movement, Divine Mind is directing it."

Rita and Doug leaped at an escape strategy: the contrived claim of a broken bone, which the Church allowed to be treated by a doctor. June agreed to it, but warned them not to mention the fever.

At the hospital, six nurses gathered around the baby within ten minutes. A young doctor named Sharon Knefler quietly asked questions, but Rita could not answer. Everything suddenly seemed so . . . sane. Finally Rita was able to speak and soon learned that Matthew had spinal meningitis, with a brain abscess, extreme cranial pressure, and hemorrhaging in his eyes. Doctors tested him to see if he had bacterial meningitis, which was often deadly—but was treatable with antibiotics—or viral meningitis, which was generally far less lethal, but not if it had advanced to this stage.

Rita called June for support, but June refused to set foot in a hospital. No other practitioner would come.

A doctor said that a Catholic priest would speak with Rita and Doug, and they gratefully agreed. The kindness of the priest reawakened their hope, and they mustered the courage to hear the results of the testing.

Matthew had bacterial meningitis. It was treatable. Doctors began immediate intravenous antibiotics. If Matthew recovered, it would happen fast.

Rita and Doug went home and took turns praying. Their prayers seemed to connect them with a power that was far more benevolent than the God of June Ahearn and Jeanne Laitner.

They wondered if this was the ultimate test. If Matthew survived, did it mean that they should dedicate their lives to helping Christian Scientists combine prayer *with* medicine? It would be a painful mission. They would lose their friends and be scorned by most Christian Scientists. It would be almost impossible to make a living with that mission. But . . . for Matthew, they would do anything.

Shortly before midnight, they got a call.

3

DEATH AND DISMEMBERMENT

None of us—no, not one—is perfect. And if we were to love none who had imperfection, this world would be a desert for our love.

—Thomas Jefferson

Grosse Pointe, Michigan
June 29, 1977

Rita prayed that Matthew's doctors were calling to say that he had responded to the medication. She knew virtually nothing about medicine, but suddenly that seemed like the most reasonable thing to pray for.

It was June Ahearn. She said she was now doing "treatment for the family." That meant she was praying for Rita and Doug to straighten up and stop killing their son. Doug told June to forget it. He and Rita didn't need treatment, Matthew did.

June still refused to treat Matthew, though. She said she could face Church sanctions for praying for someone in a hospital.

Rita called a Christian Science colleague at Wayne State and begged him to pray for Matthew. He was a passive man who seemed as if he'd be easy to persuade, but when he heard that Matthew was on what he referred to as "medication and machinery," he declined.

Then they called one of the highest-ranking church members in the state, Dean Joki—who had lost his own son during Christian Science treatment—thinking that he might understand. Joki demanded repentance, though, and Doug said, "I am very repentant—that I let that poor baby suffer on under Christian Science as long as I did."

"Oh come now!" said Joki. "That kind of resentment isn't going to heal anything."

Joki did inform the Swans that they would probably not be prosecuted if Matthew died. Michigan had passed a religious-shield law, because former President Nixon had threatened to cut off federal funds for child-abuse prevention to any state that didn't.

Reports of Rita using materia medica to heal her cyst swept through her church, and some congregants blamed this act of treachery for causing Matthew's illness. People also said that the incredible Jeanne Laitner, who'd been dismissed by the Swans, had just healed another little boy with the exact same disease.

Matthew underwent a successful operation to relieve the pressure on his brain. But antibiotics—which would have cured him in the early stages of the disease—couldn't control his infection. His brain activity ceased.

As her little boy lay dying—finally looking angelic again, now that his pain had passed—Rita went to the office of her Wayne State colleague to plead with him to pray for the soul of her son. He agreed to "err on the side of mercy." But first, he said, they had to take Matthew out of the hospital.

Rita was disgusted. "Would you," she demanded, "get all prayered-up, march into the hospital, and insist on taking the baby out?"

"Oh," he said casually, "I can't tell you what to do."

He didn't even seem to know that it was illegal to remove a gravely ill child from a hospital.

Matthew Swan, age sixteen months, died at 1:00 a.m. on July 7, 1977.

Rita asked Jeanne Laitner to scatter her son's ashes into the windy waters of Lake St. Claire, and Jeanne did so.

Shortly after that, Rita found out that the other boy with spinal meningitis that Jeanne Laitner had claimed to heal had the less virulent, viral form of the disease. Rita never spoke to Laitner again.

Rita and Doug resigned from the Church. A woman from Detroit's United Church of Christ reached out to them and they attended a service. They stood before the members, and asked the congregation of strangers to pray for their son.

Later, Doug Swan noted, "I always blamed myself and the failure of Christian Science for Matthew's death. Never Rita. And I am sure she blamed Christian Science and herself. Not me."

Rita and Doug wanted to wage war on faith-healing abuse, and told a number of people what had happened to them. Some were sympathetic, some were critical, and some were afraid of the Church. Most just weren't interested.

Rita wrote an eloquent reminiscence of Matthew's life and death, "The Last Strawberry," and submitted it to several magazines and newspapers. They all rejected it, letting Rita know that criticizing Christian Science was simply not acceptable.

Rita and Doug Swan remained married, and remained alive, at least partially. Their life had become wreckage, and its continuation seemed to offer nothing but pain. Doug's grief, as time passed, seemed to grow even darker, and Rita suffered an almost sadder fate, losing interest in life as depression overwhelmed her.

She couldn't understand it when people said things like, "Time heals all wounds," and "Life goes on." When a wound is deep enough, time stands still. And sooner or later life doesn't go on, and the best that people can hope for is that when their life stops, their heart will stop beating first.

The first chapter in the war against faith-healing abuse in America had ended—almost before it had begun.

OREGON CITY, OREGON
JULY 1997

Dr. Larry Lewman, chief medical examiner of Clackamas County, poised over the chest of a deceased little boy, then lowered the whining blade of his Stryker saw onto the child's breastbone. Blood, tissue, and white shards of bone splattered against his thick green apron.

The medical examiner—more commonly called a coroner—then cut the boy's ribs apart with medical-grade, stainless-steel pruning shears. He removed the child's chest wall, and severed the boy's descending colon from his rectum with a huge knife. He removed all the organ attachments up to the boy's tongue, and ended the evisceration by lifting the boy's block of abdominal organs out of his body, grasping the tongue at the top, and the colon at the bottom.

"God. All. Mighty. Not again," Lewman muttered. It looked almost immediately as if the boy had died needlessly. How could this *possibly* be happening in the late twentieth century?

Two days earlier, six-year-old Holland Cunningham had awakened his father, Carter, complaining of a terrible stomach ache. Carter and his wife, alarmed, immediately began to provide health care for Holland. They prayed for him and anointed him with oil. Then they called two family members and asked them to remember Holland in their prayers. Everyone knew what that meant. Those two called others, who forwarded the message, as the alarm spread throughout the congregation.

By the end of the day, most of the church members were focusing their love on Holland, and the next day, more than a hundred people were in the Cunninghams' small home, praying, anointing Holland with cooking oil, laying hands on him, and eating. Lots of food was required at church-wide healings, and there were no better cooks in Oregon than the wives of the Followers of Christ. They usually made everything from scratch, because they felt their husbands and children deserved no less.

It was obvious to Dr. Lewman that Holland Cunningham had

suffered terrible pain, because about two-thirds of Holland's bowel was black and rotten and smelled terrible.

Lewman, a tall and muscular man of fifty-six, could see that Holland had been born with an internal hernia in his bowel that could have easily been repaired. Lewman wasn't surprised to find a birth defect, because they were relatively common among the Followers, due to genetic abnormalities that stemmed from frequent intermarriages among a small group. In the vernacular, they had too many kissin' cousins.

Holland's hernia had eventually twisted off the blood supply to most of his bowel. Even as Holland lay dying, the diseased parts of his bowel could still have been surgically removed to save his life. But Holland's father hadn't considered surgery, and didn't allow his wife to have a voice in the decision, because that would violate the Church's biblical adherence to male domination.

Lewman closed Holland up and went to his office to write his report. He couldn't remember how many Followers kids he'd autopsied, because there had been too many, but he could remember the first, almost ten years ago, back in 1989. At that time, four-year-old Alex Morris had come down with a cold that had slowly turned into a lung infection. Inflammation had burned the boy's lungs until his chest hurt from just breathing, as his immune system pumped white blood cells into his lungs that coagulated into pus. Alex coughed and cried for about a month and a half. He was treated with prayer, anointment with oil, and the laying on of hands, but died.

Lewman later recalled that he'd begun Alex's autopsy by checking for encephalitis, because that was a common cause of sudden death among kids. He sliced the back of Alex's head from ear to ear, creating two flaps, then pulled the front flap over Alex's face, so that he could later put the boy's face back into place without causing severe disfigurement. Then he tugged the rear flap down the back of the neck, all the way to the top of Alex's spinal column. With the boy's scalp out of the way, Lewman cut a circle into the top of Alex's skull with his Stryker saw, then lifted off the skull's cap, or calvarium. Then he snipped the cranial nerves that connected Alex's brain to his spinal cord, and lifted the brain out. It looked okay. That meant something in Alex's lower body had killed him, which probably meant that his parents had a significant window of warning. Lewman pulled Alex's face back over his nose, cheeks, and forehead, and stitched the flaps.

The next step was examination of the internal organs. That was generally a relatively clean procedure. But when Lewman cracked Alex's chest with his saw, almost a gallon of pus burst from it. It splashed onto Lewman, the floor, and everywhere else.

At that time in Lewman's career, he had done about 2,000 autopsies, and by 1997 he had done about 5,000. He would do at least 5,000 more by the twilight of his career, in 2013. But years later, Lewman still vividly remembered Alex's autopsy, partly because the boy had died what seemed to be an unnecessary death, and partly because Alex had been an exceptionally adorable little kid, with child-actor features and a face that was beautiful even in death.

At least, it had been beautiful before the procedure began. Even after it, though, Alex still looked fairly presentable. When Lewman performed scalp incisions at the back of someone's head, a mortician could hide the ear-to-ear mutilation by cutting a hole in the coffin's pillow, to obscure the incisions. That created an extra step for the mortician, but the Followers always used the same funeral home, which offered what it called "affordable, simple options," and the undertakers there were happy to provide a few little extras from time to time. Once, when a Follower died with a huge tumor on her side, they cut a hole in the casket to accommodate it.

Another Follower's autopsy that Lewman had tried to forget but couldn't had been that of a newborn whose arm had been pulled almost all the way off during birth. The maiming had occurred because the baby wasn't coming out properly, and the midwives conducting the birth had tried to reinsert some of the baby's body parts. It was a bizarre thing to try, but all of the midwives that the Followers used were Followers themselves, and none had any medical training. That wasn't required by Oregon law, which tends to venerate personal choice.

By 1997, Lewman and his associate George Coleman had compiled evidence of eighteen Followers children dying of curable diseases over just the last ten years, in a congregation of about 1,200 people. Ten had died just after childbirth, from infection, untreated head injuries, and other preventable causes of death. Others died of diabetes and meningitis. Lewman and Coleman calculated the odds of this degree of infant mortality among a group this size, and it was approximately 26 times higher than normal. Lewman was certain that even more infant deaths had been covered up by church members who falsely claimed that children had been stillborn, a situation that did not require the reporting of the death. "The definition of being born is to take one breath," Lewman later said.

Followers' wives were also dying during birth at an excessive rate. Four had died in the last ten years, all from preventable causes, and one from a type of infection that hadn't killed anyone else in America since 1910. The death rate among Followers women giving birth was approximately nine hundred times the norm.

Dr. Lewman was repelled by this needless tragedy, but others in the office didn't seem to be. The deputy medical examiner at that time, Dr. John Schilke, later said that he could not remember a Follower's case that he could, as he put it, "get excited about." The county's district attorney, James O'Leary, did not consider any of the deaths to be crimes.

O'Leary reportedly told George Coleman that the Followers' acts were protected by the Constitution, but Coleman continued to protest. "I almost became a bore," Coleman later said.

Most of the approximately half-dozen medical examiners in the Clackamas office wrote no more than a couple of sentences in their reports about the deaths of the Followers' women and children. Their reports of the deaths were generally based upon the accounts that were provided by the elders of the church, who always offered benign versions.

Most of the medical examiners did think that the Followers were oddballs—rugged, outdoorsy men who kissed each other on the mouth—but they believed that people who based their lives around religion probably wouldn't lie, so they classified all the fatalities as natural deaths.

Lewman became disgusted with the local government. He expected more from it. He'd come to the eccentric but progressive state of Oregon because it was one of only six that had replaced the old system of electing medical examiners instead of appointing them. In most states, coroners didn't even need to be doctors. The only requirement, Lewman later said, was "that you live in the community, know how to breathe, and get fifty percent of the votes, plus one." Because of that, coroners were often incompetent and corrupt.

Of course, everyone in the Clackamas County government told Lewman that they *hated* to see the death of a baby or a young mother. But they also hated religious intolerance.

Lewman's boss, Dr. Schilke, believed—quite correctly, based on Oregon's religious-shield law—that parents had the *right* to withhold medical care. Oregon—a live-free-or-die haven—had one of the country's strongest laws protecting faith healers.

Before Lewman had moved to Oregon in the mid-1980s, the state did have a law that gave children the right to medical care. It had been passed after two Followers children had died of meningitis, with others coming to school with badly-set broken bones. But the law had been gutted during the Nixon administration.

The legal situation was almost as bad in neighboring Idaho. At least twelve Followers children in Caldwell, Idaho, had died unnecessary deaths over the past several years. Buried in the Peaceful Valley Cemetery, the kids were descendants of the group of Followers who'd stayed there after Walter White led the others to Oregon. Nobody there had ever been prosecuted. Nor had there ever been any arrests at the Followers' two other branches near Caldwell, or in the branches in Oklahoma, and Grants Pass, Oregon.

Less than six months after Holland Cunningham died, Lewman found himself working on another Followers case, that of five-month-old Valerie Shaw, who died on New Year's Day. Her parents said she'd never been strong, but that her death was still a shock. They had taken her to the traditional Followers' New Year's Eve party—one of their much-loved dances, with an All-Followers band—and right after that she passed. The parents thought it was tragic. But death happened. If anyone knew that, the Followers did.

However, when Valerie's great-uncle Darrell heard about her death—from a police officer, since he was no longer in the Church—he was suspicious. Darrell Shaw had left the Church twelve years earlier, and had been shunned ever since. "They didn't even call me," he later said, "when my parents passed away." Shaw was able to endure the isolation of shunning, and rebuild his life, but others could not.

A friend of Shaw's, who dropped out at approximately the same time, never did fully recover. When he left the Church, disgusted by all the needless deaths, he was shunned by his wife, who soon divorced him, and by his children, parents, friends, and brother. He also lost his job, because most Followers worked in affiliated businesses centered around the construction industry. Broke and homeless, he went door-to-door in the Followers' neighborhoods, asking for understanding, but no one would even let him in. Finally, with nowhere to live, he was taken in by someone from a church in nearby Gladstone. Every day of his life, since that time, he had thought about those he loved most, and wondered why they could not find love for him.

By the late '90s, about twenty people had left the Church, and dropouts often went off the deep end into permanent homelessness and self-destruction, mostly because of the shunning.

Sometimes people were shunned for just a few weeks if they did something minor, like using profanity in front of women and children. A worse transgression, like a man cheating on his wife, might result in nobody talking to him for up to a year, though he'd still be allowed to go to church. To be accepted again, he would need to make humiliating acts of contrition, like public confessions, major donations, and repeated pledges to sin no more.

If a wife was caught cheating, though, she would almost certainly suffer from the Followers' sexist double-standards and be divorced by her husband. Men were allowed to divorce, but women weren't. A cheating, divorced woman would be shunned forever—just like the dropouts. Decades could pass without her receiving phone calls or letters, even during family illnesses and deaths. If a friend, or even one of her children, saw a shunned woman in public, they would look away.

That happened even to the highly esteemed Ernest Nichols, Walter White's former right-hand man, who dropped out in 1964 because of Walter's authoritarianism. When Nichols left the church, five of his children never spoke to him again, even when he was dying. Nichols became an itinerant for some time and never preached another sermon, but somehow found peace, and was said to harbor no bitterness.

Often, though, the loneliness, loss of self-esteem, and sense of betrayal caused by shunning drove people to alcoholism, drug addiction, and other avenues of numbness, and occasionally it pushed them into an anger and confusion that bordered on madness. In ways, shunning was a more painful punishment than the placing of a prisoner in solitary confinement, because the isolation of shunning was inflicted by those who had once been the victim's most loved, trusted, and needed intimates.

One dropout in the 1990s got hooked on meth and mixed up with a group of meth-cooking backwoods Wiccans with rotten teeth and leprous skin. They lived in tepees and crude cabins in the dank, mossy outback of Clackamas County, outside a little town called Sandy, which was the quintessential encapsulation of eccentric Oregon: a wholesome ski town, but home to the state's only Bed & Bondage establishment.

The Wiccans committed the unthinkable crime of raping girls just past puberty, while they were still very dependent and impressionable, to produce infants to sacrifice. That had happened at least twice in the 1990s, with no arrests ever made. The Wiccans eventually faded from sight, and the former Follower overcame his addictions and got a job.

Even when the ex-Follower was out of his mind on meth, though, and capable of almost anything, the Wiccan life still seemed like a horror movie to him—but strangely familiar. The Wiccans were more deliberate in their human sacrifices than the Followers, but *far* fewer Wiccan kids had died. And many of the Followers' kids died slowly and painfully, while the Wiccan deaths were quick. Besides, the Followers let adults die, too, even when they were begging to go to the hospital.

Although shunning was a horrible fate, even a life of loneliness and rejection was better than that of those who stayed in the church and ended up disabled, chronically ill, in constant pain—or dead, like little Valerie Shaw.

When Dr. Lewman began to eviscerate Valerie Shaw, he was appalled. In the midst of her ravaged urinary tract, which was yellow with infection, he found a garden-variety blockage of one of her urinary tubes. It could have been surgically repaired in about an hour, and its symptoms would have been clearly noticeable: things you couldn't miss, such as difficulty urinating. Nausea. Fever. Vomiting. Pain.

She'd *never been strong*? That was one way of putting it. The Followers were pleasant people, Lewman thought, but most of them seemed to be brainwashed. They'd forgotten one fundamental fact: Freedom of religion must include freedom within a religion—freedom of thought, freedom of speech, and the freedom to follow your conscience—or it's not a religion at all.

Larry Lewman, once again, tried to interest the legal authorities in the deaths of the Followers' children. He was optimistic. The former DA, who had felt the Followers could not be prosecuted, had been replaced by a friend of Lewman's, a tough legal veteran named Terry Gustafson, who'd prosecuted seventeen homicides, hated to grant plea-deals, and loved a good fight. She specialized in protecting children, having joined the DA's office at a time when female prosecutors handled most kids' cases, because they were considered more sensitive. While Terry Gustafson had been an assistant DA, she'd repeatedly nagged her boss to go after the Followers, and now that he was gone it looked like she had her chance.

But when Lewman told Gustafson that he had solid forensic evidence of a crime, she looked sad. She said the whole thing made her sick, and that she wanted to help. But she wasn't sure she could.

The state legislature had just beefed up Oregon's already-powerful religious-shield law once more, and Gustafson feared the new law. It had been passed when the Oregon District Attorneys Association sponsored a bill to increase the punishment for murder by abuse, to help stop child and spousal abuse. The Christian Science Church had used the opportunity to push for an amendment to the bill that added a religious shield against manslaughter.

Gustafson had argued against it, but the legislators told her that they respected the Christian Scientists, and weren't terribly concerned about the Followers. "Nobody in the state government, at that time, was even thinking about the Followers," Gustafson later said, "except me."

When the bill went to Governor John Kitzhaber—who was a physician, and supposedly astute about medical issues—Gustafson vehemently exhorted him in the media and in the statehouse to veto it. Her unremitting campaign against the amendment embarrassed him, she thought, by violating Oregon's gentle ethic of play-nice politics.

The governor signed the bill. It became the last law ever passed in America to grant a religious shield for felony child abuse. The law officially made Oregon the weakest state in the country when it came to protecting kids from radical faith healing. But it pleased most of the state's DAs, who also seemed largely indifferent to the Followers, and it heightened their allegiance to the governor.

"Kitzhaber was in like Flynn with the prosecutors," Gustafson later said, "and he knew exactly what he was doing when he signed that bill, but to advance his interests he chose to do it." By that time, she considered the governor an enemy, and assumed the feeling was mutual.

The new law, she thought, made the Oregon religious shield impenetrable. She believed that it not only crippled her chances of getting felony convictions, but created so much ambiguity about the relative wrongdoing of faith healing that even minor infractions would be much harder to prosecute.

Bottom line: no prosecution.

Meanwhile, Terry Gustafson was still getting calls from neighbors of Followers who reported hearing children screaming and crying. She hated it.

For Dr. Larry Lewman: Plan B.

THE WINTER OF 1997–1998

When Larry Lewman was invited by television reporter Mark Hass to be on the panel of ABC affiliate KATU's popular weekly talk show, *Town Hall*, he quickly accepted. It would give him plenty of face-time with Hass.

After the show, Lewman buttonholed Hass and spoke the language of the media: "I've got a sensational, exclusive story."

Lewman told Hass that there had been a recent cluster of deaths among children in a local church called the Followers of Christ, that avoidable death had been going on for years, that the kids' parents were responsible, that other members covered for them, and that they were getting away with virtual murder because of laws that Nixon had pushed through.

Mark Hass liked and respected Larry Lewman, always had. Lewman—who was articulate, honest, and outspoken—had been the state's chief medical examiner for twelve years and had a national reputation. But the doc's story seemed too weird. A conspiracy? To kill children? Among members of a folksy church? Their own kids? The Nixon angle? This has been going on for *how* long? How come nobody else had the story?

There was no evidence. No criminal complaints. No other accusers. No police investigations. And obviously the Clackamas County DA didn't buy it.

Lewman was considered by some to be a bit of an oddball. It seemed to be a trait that was common to the profession, possibly because MEs went decades without seeing a live patient—or maybe because they'd *have* to be strange to want that grisly job, instead of one in which they saved lives and made big money. But this claim was just outrageous.

Even so, Hass was a pro, and did some research on the relatively new, ponderously slow Internet. He couldn't find anything at all about the Followers of Christ. But lo and behold, Nixon *had* passed a federal statute requiring religious-shield laws. And the Oval Office *had* been chock-full of Christian Scientists. In fact, Chief of Staff Bob Haldeman had apparently gotten sick recently and died, while refusing to let his family take him to a doctor.

But was there any *news* here? As in, something you could prove? And would attacking freedom of religion be healthy for the station? Not only that, Hass was a devout Presbyterian himself, who also hoped to run for public office, and he had to be sensitive about church/state issues.

Nonetheless, on Sunday he drove out to the Followers' church, which sat at the very end of the old Oregon Trail among a series of strip malls. The church was nondescript—no steeple, no stained glass—identified only by a hand-lettered sign. Hass entered the old building and sat down amid a throng of worshippers. Those who acknowledged his existence were only frigidly polite, and he could feel stares from every direction. It wasn't quite like the nightmare of being naked in church, but was close enough.

The service was . . . not a service. No sermon. No preacher. No one leading prayers. No Communion or baptisms. Just hymns. A man in front would rise and intone in a stentorian voice something like, as Hass later recalled, "Page three-oh-three, 'My Lord Ye Thee,'" and then they'd sing a ten-minute hymn with at least five verses and about four different notes. Then another. Ten in all. It made Hass' Spartan Presbyterian services seem like Mardi Gras.

At the end of it, the men gathered in the parking lot out front, and the women, girls, and children stayed inside. The teenage boys went out back and somehow got away with openly smoking cigarettes.

Hass tried to ask the guys in the parking lot softball questions like, "How long has your church been here?" And, "Do you have other branches?" Nothing about dead kids. Just icebreakers. But the men gave him hollow, drop-dead smiles. The weirdest thing, though, was that they called each other Brother, yet every time Hass said something, they'd eyeball each other, as if their greatest fear was of one another.

That barrage of stilted, superior silence was more or less all Hass would ever get out of them, and that would remain true over the years to come. They were incredibly quiet and cohesive. Especially after they became notorious.

No other reporter ever got behind the scenes, either, and almost all of the church dropouts stayed quiet. The secrecy of the Followers of Christ endured.

As Hass was winding up his exercise in futility, he did wrench a non-statement from one of the guys. It wasn't much more than a screw-you, but was one of a scant few on-the-record comments ever made by a member of the Followers of Christ. It was something to the effect of: "We believe what we believe because that's what God *wants* us to believe. Obviously." Even then, the guy who made the statement got some dirty looks that made him grin defensively, then shudder.

As Sunday dinner beckoned, they broke into sub-clans and the men kissed each other good-bye. Nobody offered Hass a kiss.

The whole thing felt like a big dead end—just another embarrassment in the name of journalism. But Mark Hass had one more stop.

Larry Lewman had told Hass he should go to the Followers' cemetery. So Hass got in his car and followed Lewman's directions. The cemetery wasn't far. But in Oregon, once you're more than about ten miles outside of any town, especially in the vast rolling incline of the Cascade Mountain foothills, you enter a disorienting labyrinth of variegated green, with views obscured by hanging sheets of moss, and hairpin curves. It's a landscape of prehistoric trees, sawtooth ferns taller than cars, look-alike pastures, unmarked roads, and animal sounds that seem to come from nowhere. It's easy to get lost.

At a largely invisible hard-left, Hass almost crashed into the cemetery.

Birds cried as Hass entered, then suddenly went silent. The squishy grass among the graves was pocked with moss and toadstools, and the grounds were canopied by hulking trees and Pacific Northwest perma-clouds that made the place moldy and putrescent. Slugs and beetles sat on flat gravestones and sow bugs crawled over soggy brown leaves. The place teemed with life, but it was the kind of life that came with decay.

Hass wandered down the rows of about three hundred gravesites, many of them with crumbling pioneer tombstones, and headed toward a newer, hard-marble section. He noticed the grave of what was obviously a child: OUR BABY GIRL, CHERI D. LARKIN, MARCH 22, 1967. And another: BABY BOY WHITE, DEC., 1994. BABY GIRL MORRIS, AUGUST 1990-something—the date was covered with mud. BABY CRONE, JAN. 21, 1965. DWAYNE D. HICKMAN, AUGUST 19, 1966. A mold-covered slab: BABY KING, FEB. 11, 1970. Several were engraved with babies sleeping in cribs, and others had teddy bears, baby shoes, and lambs. Hass saw the freshly sodded grave of the little girl Larry Lewman had just autopsied: OUR LITTLE ANGEL, VALERIE LYNN SHAW, JULY 17, 1997–JAN. 1, 1998. Hass wasn't sure why so many kids had no first name. It seemed dismissive.

He started to count the children's graves.

In Hass' career in if-it-bleeds-it-leads TV journalism, he had been at almost as many death scenes as some policemen. Once he'd gone live-on-air standing among red and white brain matter, and hadn't missed a beat. But he was starting to get a queasy, creepy feeling that seemed to go with the fetid odor of the toadstools.

He was standing among the graves of seventy-eight children.

Hass went straight to the TV station. The next day, KATU began America's first major series of reports on faith-healing abuse. At first, the story sounded bizarre to the other KATU broadcasters. Young reporter Dan Tilkin, who in future years would take over coverage of the Followers, later said, "I was in *disbelief* that people could do that in modern times."

But Hass proved conclusively that there was a faith healing scandal in Oregon. He interviewed Dr. Lewman, Terry Gustafson, some national experts, and a few church drop-outs, and showed that this abomination had been occurring in Oregon City for decades. Hass kept at it for months, until the *Portland Oregonian* picked up the story, as did, eventually, the national media.

Clackamas County was soon under intense outside pressure to crack down on the Followers, coming mostly from the intelligentsia of Portland. But Clackamas County—Clackalackie, to the locals—didn't give a damn about the views of Portland or anyplace else. It was a world unto itself, small in population and huge in area, run by insular Oregon City, the oldest incorporated town west of the Rockies.

The state of Oregon—and particularly Portland, which boasts the motto "Keep Portland Weird"—promotes itself as a Pacific Rim beacon of globalism, inclusiveness, and new-millennium enlightenment. All of that is true, in bits and pieces, here and there—particularly on the campuses of the state's many colleges and white-collar corporations—but it no more represents the greater truth about Oregon than a single home movie reflects a family's everyday life. The larger reality of Oregon is one of quirky, almost otherworldly provincialism, caught up in occasionally brilliant but often solipsistic self-absorption. Oregon City, defiantly self-defined, with a fetish for self-determinism, is very much a part of the real Oregon. In most of the ways that really count, it *is* Oregon.

Mark Hass, later recalling the early days of the war against faith-healing abuse in America—which has been centered around Oregon City for the past fifteen years—referenced the famous line from *Chinatown*, when Jack Nicholson's character realizes he's in a veritable Wonderland: "Forget it, Jake—it's Chinatown." Hass said, "Don't try to understand those people. They just do what they *do* down there. *It's Oregon City.*"

Meaning: The isolated little town of Oregon City is often paradoxical, imponderable, and almost impenetrable—unless you're part of it. Then it all starts to make perfect sense. But after that, the rest of the world no longer does.

Partly because of this aggressively localized outlook, the members of the Oregon City Followers of Christ, despite the notoriety that suddenly hit them in 1998, have remained consistently unrepentant, and almost celebratory, in an angry way. Martyrdom, safe to say, had piqued their narcissistic and rebellious ways.

In 1998, Larry Lewman was certain that the new scrutiny of the Followers had not changed their conduct. His attitude was shared by one of his early confidants, a detective named Jeff Green. When Green was asked that year by a reporter if he thought there would be more deaths among the Followers' children, he said, "I don't think there will be more deaths. I *know* there will be."

Lewman and Green remained somewhat hopeful that new district attorney Terry Gustafson would crack down on the Followers, even after her first negative response. But by the beginning of 1998, even with the glare of media lighting the way toward effective prosecution, Gustafson appeared to feel, in law enforcement parlance, hinky about it.

She thought that arrests would result in such weak cases that defeat would be certain and just invite more abuse. She had a point. There were no good witnesses and almost no circumstantial evidence. Most of the down-home jury pool in Clackalackie—a sobriquet imported by immigrants from rural North Carolina's "Cackalacky"—loved religious freedom and hated big government. Not only that, some people feared the Followers. The Kissers, as they were often called, were obviously off on their own planet, and some of the guys looked tough and acted tougher.

Plus, Oregon had the worst religious-exemption law in America, and in the county seat of Clackalackie they were *proud* of it: *It's Oregon City*. The law, Gustafson later said, "was like a Get Out of Jail Free card."

On top of all that, and worst of all, Gustafson had political problems. She had recently offended a powerful defense attorney by pressuring him to testify as a witness in a case—an unusual request. He'd filed a complaint against her, also accusing her of leaking records to the media as part of her pressure. Suddenly, it seemed to her, the whole state government was against her. "I thought Governor Kitzhaber was behind it," she later said, "because I had been vocal about him not vetoing the religious shield to manslaughter." The full frontal assault on the governor, she said, "was just not how you were supposed to play politics in Oregon."

The state bar, an organ of the state Supreme Court, wanted to yank Gustafson's license, but she fought back, staved off disbarment, and topped it off by winning the election for DA.

But the whole ugly affair still festered under the surface. She never knew when people would start playing politics again.

Terry Gustafson had been elected on a reputation for being tough, especially on the county's burgeoning meth trade. But with dead kids right under her nose, and smug parents acting as if they were above the law, she felt completely helpless.

SAN DIEGO, CALIFORNIA
JANUARY 1998

Terry Gustafson was enjoying the summer-like winter of Southern California, and a brief respite from the political pressures of Oregon City, as she attended a conference on child abuse. For Tough Terry, the grim subject was strangely soothing, because she was passionate about helping kids.

A lecture entitled "Religion-Based Medical Neglect" caught her attention. It was on the relatively unknown topic of children being victimized by faith healing. To Gustafson's astonishment, she learned it was happening all over the country. Year after year, hundreds of people—possibly even thousands—were killed, maimed, disabled, and disfigured. Most of the victims were among America's most vulnerable: children, women in childbirth, and the elderly. But it was extremely well hidden.

The solution, according to the speaker, was politics: boring, messy, humiliating hardball. Nothing else would work, because most religions were preternaturally averse to even minor change. After centuries of holy wars, hate among various religions was as common as love, and lives were destroyed by religion as often as they were saved. In vast, scattered pockets throughout the world, including America, the Dark Ages were alive and well, with people being sacrificed every week in the name of God.

The speaker was riveting: passionate, aggressive, strong, and smart, and had recently given similar presentations in Chicago, Minnesota, Ohio, and Washington, DC. Gustafson had heard innumerable presentations, but never anything quite this uplifting. Finally, she was hearing a *plan,* a way to solve the problem that was eating at her guts: strategies, practicalities, a way to win.

When it was over, she rushed up to the speaker.

"I'm Terry Gustafson. I'm the district attorney of Clackamas County, Oregon. We have a *terrible* problem, and I *really* need to talk to you."

"I'm glad to meet you, Terry. I'm Rita Swan."

4

THE EXORCIST

In our sleep, pain which cannot forget
Falls drop by drop upon the heart,
Until, in our own despair,
Against our will,
Comes wisdom, through the awful Grace of God.
—Aeschylus

San Diego, California
January 1998

On closer analysis, Clackalackie DA Terry Gustafson didn't know quite *what* to make of Rita Swan.

On one hand, Rita was—as Doug had seen her so long ago—the pure essence of Midwest Madonna: plainspoken, pretty, humble, positive, and brimming with love.

In midlife, Rita was more beautiful to Doug than she'd been twenty years earlier. She glowed with an inner peace and confidence that had supplanted her spark of youth, and was imbued with a palpable sense of purpose—driven by the darkness of loss—that made her mysterious.

To Gustafson, Rita's open brown eyes seemed somehow capable of seeing into a person's soul, measuring people not by their ability to help her, or by anything external at all, but by their goodness alone: a frightening proposition for many, but a gift to the good. Mrs. Swan, Terry Gustafson thought, actually seemed to be on a mission from— could it be, in this day and age?—*God*.

But Rita's eyes could also hold a look that was simultaneously focused and detached, a flinty thousand-yard stare that was familiar but hard to place. When you saw it, it was impossible not to think that if you got between Rita Swan and what she needed, you'd be, in the enduringly earthy vocabulary of law enforcement, majorly fucked. Not that Rita would ever indulge in that phrase, or even in the concept of retribution. It wasn't because she was a lady, or still a devout Christian, but because she just didn't need that. Too strong. Too focused on the future. Besides, the sponsor of her mission took care of that kind of thing.

"We've just had two kids die who *shouldn't* have," Terry told Rita. "Both in the Followers of Christ."

Rita exhaled a breath that seemed never to end, as she looked into Terry's face, measuring her up.

"I'm so sorry, Terry." Rita said it with compassion, but in the way a commanding officer might commiserate about troop loss.

"I *know* they're still up to something," Gustafson said. "We've gotten reports from children's services about two kids who may be sick. But they keep moving them from house to house. First to grandma's, then to a sister, then someplace else. We keep trying to get an informant in the church, but they're all too afraid."

"That's the hardest part. In all my years, I've never found a reliable informant who's still in a church." Rita smiled gently. "Are you going to prosecute?"

"I want to. But our laws . . ."

Rita's gaze grew veiled.

Rita Swan knew every religious-shield law in the country. And she knew Oregon's was the worst. "Those laws can *change*," Rita said, with absolute authority. She gave Gustafson that look again. "And maybe you *can* prosecute." The look.

This time Terry placed it. She'd seen it on the faces of parolees, and the victims of violent crime. It was the look of somebody who'd been to hell and back, and wasn't about to go there again.

GROSSE POINTE, MICHIGAN
JULY 1977

Rita Swan left life and went to hell the day she met Matthew's mortician. He said, "You're Christian Scientists? Then you won't want a notice to come out in the newspapers." He was trying to be kind. And the truth was, Rita didn't want people speculating about their tragedy—especially Christian Scientists, who often blamed the victims themselves.

But God in heaven! That meant that this had happened before, often enough to have its own policy, even in this one Detroit suburb.

Drained by the lethargy of loss, Rita went home, went to bed, could not sleep, got up to eat, and could not eat.

People from the church called. One woman tormented Rita with the assertion that she would see Matthew again if she would just "awaken to the truth that he never died." June Ahearn called to remind Rita that when *she'd* been "working" on Matthew, "the pain left his spine." The board chairman of Rita's church warned her that she had no *idea* what it was like to be an ordinary mortal, instead of an eternally saved Christian Scientist, and that if Rita left the protection of the Church, "You'll be at the doctor's office every day."

Several well-wishers also mentioned, with their agendas hardly hidden, that poor Jeanne Laitner was comforted by having saved at least one child with meningitis. Rita didn't bother to tell them about the two forms of the disease. They probably didn't even know the difference between a bacteria and a virus.

Feverish images of Matthew tortured her: him writhing in pain, screaming, reaching for his last strawberry, and looking up at her in agony, yet with complete trust.

Rita could no longer work, and quit her teaching job at Wayne State. Anxious to escape the memories that Michigan held, she and Doug moved to harshly exotic Jamestown, North Dakota, where Doug took a tenured mathematics professorship at Jamestown College.

"We tried to start a new life," Rita later said. She briefly taught literature at Jamestown, but her heart wasn't in it. They had another baby, Marsha, but Matthew's death haunted the whole family. Doug and Marsha's older sister, Catherine, seemed to be suffering even more than Rita was, and their sadness added yet another layer to her loss.

Rita and Doug burned all of their Christian Science literature, except for a set of blue leather books that had belonged to Doug's deceased mother, and they cut off all contact with their Christian Science friends.

Rita also grew estranged from her mother and father. Her parents still embraced Christian Science, despite Rita's tragedy, as well as her mother's ongoing failure to overcome lingering maladies, even though she paid her practitioner $620 every month. Rita didn't speak to them for the next ten years. She didn't know, during that time, that her mother blamed herself for her own illnesses, and that her father blamed his hostility toward Rita for Matthew's death.

Even without that contact with her mom and dad, though, her mother's perennial mien of helplessness and hopelessness permeated Rita, like a congenital illness now exacerbated by her own experiences.

Rita felt singularly alone, partly because she was the only Christian Science mother who had ever spoken publicly about the needless loss of her child. "So many people in faith-healing sects," Rita later said, "dig in deeper after a tragedy, because they can't bear to accept the horror of betraying the trust of a helpless child."

As months that felt like years crawled by, Rita grew wan with grief, and could easily have welcomed death as a friend, if not for the needs of her husband and daughters.

Then, on the first day of 1979, which dawned gray and cold, Rita—devoid of hope, and bereft of any resolutions for a better new year—noticed in her numbness that the United Nations had declared

1979 to be the International Year of the Child. Minors throughout the world, the UN said, were suffering indescribably, with virtually no legal recourse. Children almost everywhere, UN director Kurt Waldheim declared, were chattel: property, with few more civil rights than slaves, even in most democracies.

Suddenly Rita's suffering felt connected to a grief that engulfed the world. On that day, she later said, "I vowed to myself that I would do something each and every day, for the rest of my life, to bring the issues posed by Matthew's death to public attention." But was that remotely possible? The only logical outcome, at that time, seemed to be meaningless martyrdom. She had already tried to bring the pointless cruelty of her loss to light, and had been summarily rejected. The world, she feared, wasn't ready for what she felt compelled to do.

And was she? Her heart had been broken, and with it, her will, the last vestige of which longed only for escape. She would need to create meaning and energy from the empty pit of her own despair, and to do that she would have to heal.

The healing process that she faced seemed like the most dreadful effort imaginable. She would not only have to find forgiveness for others, which seemed difficult but possible, but also forgiveness for herself, which would be far harder.

If she were to heal, the scar that healing would leave would be unholy.

Even so, against the remnants of a will that longed only to let go, her human spirit, along with what felt like an indefinable celestial force, kept her heart beating with hope: not for the betterment of her own life, which was just a burden, but on behalf of Matthew, and the other children she might be able to save from his fate.

She founded The Matthew Project. To do nothing would be to commit the same sin that had been committed against her son: a sin of omission. No one, after all, had killed Matthew. They'd just let him die. That was a sin she would never commit again. Her self-esteem crept back in.

A new spirit entered her.

The first feeling that came back after deadness was fury. No obituary! No remembrance! *She* remembered.

THE UNITED STATES
1977–1990

Rita's heart slowly changed. But to fully recover she also needed to change her mind. "Although we never went back to Christian Science," Rita later said, "ungluing ourselves from its magical thinking did not occur so quickly."

Achieving that meant conceiving of a God powerful enough to create the universe, but unable or unwilling to heal a simple illness. It wasn't a logical proposition. Forget about God working in mysterious ways, or God never giving people burdens greater than they could carry, or any of that ecclesiastic mumbo-jumbo. That weak, mainstream-church crap just didn't cut it, while certain aspects of Christian Science still did make sense. It was even hard to dispute the very first page of Mrs. Eddy's book, with the Shakespeare quote: "There is nothing either good or bad, but thinking makes it so."

That bit of wisdom not only encompassed the whole of Christian Science perception, but was consistent with the compelling, late-seventies concept of create-your-own-reality. The flashy "new" philosophy, initially described by Socrates and Plato, resonated with Rita's long-held Christian Science belief that ideas are the highest reality.

In America, the platonic ideal—the notion that the material world is just a dim reflection of reality—had first been packaged for mass consumption in the Second Great Awakening, by big-thinker William James, whose Godfather, Ralph Waldo Emerson, was an admirer of Mrs. Eddy's. Much more recently, in what the media were calling the Fourth Great Awakening, it was popularized by Rita's fellow Wayne Stater, Wayne Dyer, and would later be repackaged by Dr. Deepak Chopra and a host of mini-gurus, most recently as the Law of Attraction, and as Rhonda Byrne's *The Secret*.

In many ways, the affirmation philosophy of perceptual reality was almost inarguable—although a lot of people thought, as Rita was beginning to, that it was ridiculous. If you believed it, then it was quite conceivable that, as Mrs. Eddy had said, "Evil has no reality. It is neither person, place, nor thing, but is simply a belief, an illusion of material sense."

But Rita had seen the very face of evil—not a demonic red visage with pointy horns, but that of hard-eyed Christian Scientists who indulged every day in recklessness, vanity, and casual disregard for the realities of others' lives. She'd gotten a close look at the banality of evil, and a sight like that engraved itself on your soul.

Rita kept remembering how her own thought processes had shifted so suddenly in the presence of the doctor who'd first examined Matthew, Sharon Knefler, MD. The doctor's intensely practical rationality had felt far more like compassion than the ethereal solicitations of the Church people, who were too hard-hearted to rise above their rigidity and give Matthew the practical help he needed.

But it was hard to let go of the thrilling concept that the power of belief by itself could heal, and that ideas were more real than matter. "There are so *many* deeply entrenched thought patterns that the ex–Christian Scientist has to unlearn," Rita later recalled.

For 150 years, those patterns had been programmed into the brains of Christian Scientists, with virtually no allowance for freedom of thought. Mary Baker Eddy had refused to allow preaching or teaching by anyone but herself, insisting that her adherents read forty-five minutes of specific passages from her book and the Bible each day, with a repetition of the same material by Readers at church every Sunday. These recitations always included a passage written by Eddy called "The Scientific Statement of Being," which begins, "There is no life, truth, intelligence, or substance in matter," and ends with: "Therefore, man is not material. He is spiritual."

To deprogram themselves, every day Rita and Doug would, as she later put it, "*un*-say the 'Statement,' repeating, 'There *is* life, truth, intelligence and substance in matter.'"

Rita's thoughts, fogged so long by unsettled torment, began to clear.

In anger as much as love, bearing a new form of idealism, Rita Swan rose from the dead.

She self-published a limited edition of *The Last Strawberry*, her memoir of Matthew, and was cleansed and illumined by the pain of that process.

Every day she worked on The Matthew Project, researching other faith-healing deaths. However, information about them was scarce, because no faith-healing crimes had been prosecuted in the past ten years. She hammered at the media to hear her story, despite the pain that caused her, but achieved virtually no success. The project's paperwork began to fill their home, to the distress of her youngest daughter, Marsha, who said, "Matthew is dying all over this house."

The trauma of reopening her wound was often agonizing, and the only other person who was convinced it was worth doing was Doug. He was the sole financial supporter of her foundation, and her only professional associate. "Then and now," Rita later said, "we regarded it as *our* work, not mine."

They hit the phones hard, systematically calling the primary people in media, law, and medicine who had the power to stop faith-healing abuse. No one was interested. Everyone with significant clout shared the attitude of a doctor at Children's Hospital, Detroit, who was sympathetic to Rita, but said, "I don't know *anybody* around here that wants to take on the Christian Scientists." The *Detroit Free Press* wouldn't touch the issue.

Rita and Doug soldiered on, and just before the end of their first year of work, they landed an hour-long spot on the biggest talk show of the time, *Donahue*. Their appearance marked the first national unveiling of the issue and resulted in by far the most attention it had ever received, generating six hundred letters. The *Detroit Free Press* called Rita back and said, "If *Donahue* does it, then it's a story." She was also scheduled for *Larry King* three times, as well as *Good Morning America*, but was disinvited each time when the Church refused to send someone to counter her claims.

In 1980, she and Doug filed the first wrongful-death suit ever against the Church of Christ, Scientist. The suit went to trial in 1983, after thousands of hours of pro-bono work by the Detroit law firm of Charfoos & Christensen. The courtroom was packed with national media, all hungry for a sensational, two-to-three-week story about religious abuse in America.

The first day, the Church filed for dismissal, and a new judge, who was suddenly substituting on the case, threw out every complaint but one. "It was very humiliating and painful," Rita later said.

On the second day, according to Rita, "the judge gave a long speech about the power and dignity of the First Amendment," focusing, of course, on freedom of religion. Then he dismissed the rest of the case. Trial over.

The media dutifully flipped their perspective and spread the word that religious freedom was alive in America.

Rita and Doug appealed, but in 1986 the Michigan Supreme Court refused to overturn the dismissal, again citing the First Amendment. It sickened Rita. "People think there's a religious exemption for faith-healing crimes in the Constitution," she said later. "Even judges. I still don't know why." She tried to interest the press in the Fourteenth Amendment, which guaranteed equal rights to children, but she found that the amendment wasn't simple and sexy enough to take traction with the media.

Rita's national attack, which had taken seven years, had failed, but she fought on, state by state. Rita gradually gained the support of a few lawyers, physicians, and other people who were appalled by faith-healing abuse. She transformed The Matthew Project into a foundation called Children's Healthcare Is a Legal Duty, or CHILD, challenging state religious shield laws one at a time, and uncovering abuse case by case.

Year after year she struggled, working mostly alone as Doug refocused on his career, with no government grant, charitable funding, or a single penny from any church in America. CHILD survived solely through the financial sacrifices of Rita and Doug, and captured the attention of a growing group of pediatricians, child-abuse researchers, family-law attorneys, professors, elected officials, and other children's advocates. Although CHILD's annual budget was typically meager, with Rita receiving no salary for twenty years, she began to publish an esteemed quarterly newsletter—enhanced considerably by her talent and training as a writer—that became the country's primary resource for information about faith-healing abuse.

She also began publishing articles in newspapers, law journals, and medical journals, including *The Los Angeles Times*, the *Quinnipiac Law Journal, Advances in Pediatrics, American Atheist*, and the *Brown University Child and Adolescent Behavior Letter*. She also made about fifteen major presentations at conferences on child abuse in Philadelphia, Los Angeles, San Diego, Iowa, and elsewhere.

Mother Church, as the Christian Scientists often referred to it, had a vast treasury, and used it to fight Rita at every step from its lavish Boston headquarters. Her army-of-one was up against not only the church's internationally respected newspaper, *The Christian Science Monitor*, and its television and radio networks, but also a panoply of rich and famous Christian Scientists, some former and some current, whose ranks have included, over the years, Treasury Secretary and Goldman Sachs CEO Henry Paulson, Marilyn Monroe, Elizabeth Taylor, Robert Duvall, Ellen DeGeneres, Val Kilmer, Spalding Gray, Henry Fonda, Lionel Hampton, Bruce Hornsby, Doris Day, Mickey Rooney, Audrey Hepburn, Ginger Rogers, Milton Berle, Carol Channing, Lady Astor, Joan Crawford, director Frank Capra, writers J. D. Salinger, Theodore Dreiser, Dalton Trumbo, and Danielle Steele, astronaut Alan Shepard, Muppeteer Jim Henson, millionaire George Getty, the family of *TV Guide* media magnate Walter Annenberg, two CIA directors, one FBI director, four governors, and one Monkee, Mike Nesmith. Rita was battling socially and financially powerful people—

the proverbial one-percenters who own or control most of the country's assets. She was also tangling with the Church's high-pedigree legal team, which included former secretary of state Warren Christopher, and preacher's son Ken Starr, who later pushed along the impeachment of President Clinton.

During this time, Christian Science spokesperson Stephen Gottschalk characterized Rita as "too dark, too bitter." He said, "Her arguments and statistics are often very twisted. She doesn't want to admit that healing actually works. She's a sad woman."

Despite this opposition, Rita began to document suspicious deaths of Christian Science children from meningitis, diabetes, diphtheria, measles, kidney infection, septicemia, cancer, and appendicitis. She also discovered uncontrolled outbreaks of polio at Christian Science schools and camps, including one that paralyzed eleven children in Connecticut, and epidemics of measles, such as one at the Christian Science Principia College, her alma mater, that infected over 200 people.

She traveled extensively, exposing deaths that would have otherwise gone unnoticed. One of the first was the death of four-year old Shauntay Walker, who died of meningitis. Shauntay's Christian Scientist mother kept her home from preschool for seventeen days, as the little girl suffered in much the same way that Matthew had. When the girl's aunt threatened to call the police, Shauntay's mother sent her daughter to another Christian Scientist's home, where she died. Shauntay's mother, Laurie Walker, was convicted of involuntary manslaughter and sentenced to six hundred hours of community service, but the conviction was overturned with the help of attorney Warren Christopher.

Next came the case of seven-year old Amy Hermanson of Sarasota, Florida, a musical prodigy who began to lose weight and become lethargic over a four-week period. Amy was too sick for her music lessons, but her teacher didn't intervene, because she knew Amy's parents were Christian Scientists. Shortly before Amy's death, her mother took her to visit a neighbor, and the neighbor urged Amy's mom to take her daughter to a doctor. The mother refused, and moments later Amy crawled into the room on her hands and knees, begging her mother to take her home. Days later, Amy died at home of untreated diabetes, incoherent and unable to focus her eyes. Her parents were convicted, but the conviction was overturned due to the state's religious-shield law.

After several years of hit-and-miss media coverage of faith-healing deaths, and sometimes almost no coverage at all, Rita was finally able, in 1988, to achieve widespread media focus on a needless death. A two-year-old boy, Robyn Twitchell of Boston, died at home of a severe abdominal infection, triggered by an easily removable intestinal blockage. He died in a comfortable neighborhood that sat "in the very shadow of the Mother Church," according, to *The New York Times*. For a month, the little boy had been listless and moaning in pain. He eventually began vomiting excrement and even pieces of his own bowel. His scrotum turned black from tissue death. Robyn died in his father's lap, as his mother and a practitioner prayed.

The Twitchells were indicted. Robyn's dad, who admitted in court that he'd had recent root-canal surgery, with Novocain, cried throughout his five days on the stand. The practitioner testified that just before Robyn died, he'd had a "super-good day." But prosecutors proved that the toddler could have been saved even in the latest stages of his decline, and Robyn's parents were convicted of manslaughter.

The conviction was soon overturned because of Massachusetts' religious-shield law. The Church tried to save face by running exculpatory full-page ads in *The Boston Globe*, a strategy that Rita's critic Stephen Gottschalk admitted was ineffective. "Toes haven't uncurled since," Gottschalk said.

The same year, Rita helped Massachusetts legislators repeal parts of the state's shield law. It was her first major victory against Christian Science, after eight years of work.

"To actually get that done in the home state of the Christian Science Church was quite a feat," Rita later said, "but it probably wouldn't have happened without the ghastly death of Robyn Twitchell."

But then, more failures. In Arizona, twelve-year-old Ashley King stopped coming to school when she could no longer walk, because of advanced bone cancer. Police went to Ashley's home, but her Christian Science mother wouldn't let them in. They forced entry and found Ashley, who tried to please her mother by hiding her leg, which bore a tumor that was 41-inches in circumference. Her buttocks and genitals were covered with bedsores. In the hospital, alone with her nurses, Ashley said, "I'm in so much pain. You don't know how I have suffered." She died, but her parents were sentenced only to probation on one misdemeanor charge.

Then a thirteen-year-old Christian Science boy in St. Louis died from untreated diabetes, and shortly after that twelve-year-old Andrew Wantland died of the same disease in Orange County, California. Andrew, like other young, untreated victims of diabetes, started to lose weight and complain of fatigue. He developed an almost-constant cough and missed about a week of school, which his family blamed on the flu. Andrew fell into a coma as his mother, father, grandmother, and a practitioner prayed for him. At the end, he was emaciated and almost devoid of bodily fluids.

Soon yet another boy, eleven-year-old Ian Lundman of Minneapolis, died from diabetes after losing more than one-third of his weight. As he lay dying, he was prayed over by his mother, stepfather, and a Christian Science practitioner, who was being paid by the stepfather's health insurance, provided by his employer.

Ian's mother and stepfather, Kathleen and William McKown, were charged with second-degree criminally negligent manslaughter, but the case was dismissed because of the state's shield law.

Nonetheless, Rita helped Ian's father, Doug Lundman, win an award of $5 million, plus punitive damages against Mother Church of $9 million. It was described as a "staggering blow to the Church—the most damaging it has ever suffered," by Caroline Fraser, in her book *God's Perfect Child*. But the punitive damages were rescinded by a higher court in Minnesota, because they violated "the forbidden field of religious freedom."

Rita launched a campaign to change Minnesota's law. She testified in hearings before the state Senate and House, and so did Doug Lundman. Rita also helped arrange for the testimony of a woman named Sue McLaughlin, who as an infant had been denied care for a metabolic disorder that caused her to be developmentally disabled, and only four-feet, two-inches tall. They lost. The legislators refused to repeal the shield. Certain small improvements were made, though, reflecting a pattern that would persist throughout Rita's lifelong campaign to repeal shield laws, state by state: Even when she lost, she usually achieved minor, piecemeal changes. Across the country, often almost imperceptibly, her one-woman crusade was gradually succeeding. Prosecutors in a number of states, hungry for her expertise on faith-healing abuse and her insight into the minds of its perpetrators, invited her to assess their cases.

As the myriad minor changes in state laws slowly took root, the Christian Science Church began to subtly modify its practices, and more fully include medical attention when faith healing failed. The Church even stopped using the term faith healing, for the most part, and used milder euphemisms, such as saying a patient "gained relief" from prayer. Due in part to the negative publicity engineered by Rita, membership declined drastically. But kids were still dying.

And then, as the cusp of the new century approached, Rita discovered something even more horrific. There were isolated, independent faith-healing churches all over America that nobody had ever heard of, whose members committed crimes that Rita later called "gruesome and heinous." The little churches didn't have the numbers or notoriety of the Christian Science Church, although Mother Church offered them financial aid for legal problems, and helped them to stay largely under the radar of local authorities. Each church was a fiefdom of its own, operating without restraint among neighbors who generally considered them little more than quaint.

The deadliest was in Oregon City, Oregon.

OREGON CITY
NEW YEAR'S EVE, 1990

Patrick Robbins turned red when the high school kids at the church's New Year's Eve party started talking about condoms. They'd just seen a presentation about safe sex at Oregon City High School, where girls onstage had put big plastic bags that were supposed to look like condoms over the entire bodies of some boys, to demonstrate in a funny way how to use birth control.

With *that* kind of talk, as far as Patrick was concerned, this party was getting out of control. The scary thing was, if these kids kept talking about sex, pretty soon they were going to try it.

He glanced at his date, the girl he was in love with, and who he prayed would marry him. Theresa, thankfully, was blushing, too, and looking at the floor.

Patrick's buddy Tim Wyland—who had been in his grade-school class, and was later home-schooled at the same time as Patrick—also seemed to feel pretty squeamish about the direction of the conversation. Tim steered his young wife, Monique, toward the punch bowl. Patrick touched Theresa's arm, made eye contact with her, and they followed.

"Not fittin'," Tim said, shaking his head. Always a gentleman, Tim ladled Monique's goblet full of a delicious icy slush of sparkling grape cider, fresh-squeezed pomegranate juice, crushed huckleberries, and scoops of homemade strawberry sherbet, with frozen strawberries as ice cubes. He filled her plate with fresh-baked cookies and blackberry tarts.

"If I'd have talked like that," Patrick said, "my mom would have washed my mouth out." Actually, she would have beaten him with her stick, as she'd done the time he brought a worldly boy home from school, but that was nobody's business.

The two couples listened to the Thaine Brothers Band, but they could still overhear one of the high school kids—a *girl*—say that before she'd seen the assembly, she'd thought that condoms were called rubbers because they kept you from having a baby if you rubbed yourself with one. The kids laughed, but Patrick couldn't see the humor.

"I worry about the kids holding fast to tradition," Patrick said. He'd heard that the girl who was talking openly about sex—in *church*, not incidentally—was thinking about going to college, something no Follower girl had ever done.

He feared that her attitude might be contagious, and eventually infect Theresa. Theresa always paid him the respect of not acting intelligent around him, but she obviously was, and if she went to college he'd have to break up with her. It wouldn't be very hard for him to find another girl, because even as a young man, he later recalled, he had a certain resemblance to fair-featured Liam Neeson, with piercing blue-green eyes and sandy, reddish hair. But Theresa was special, and impossible to replace.

He had big plans for Theresa, and knew she was interested in him because he'd heard she'd had the Followers' traditional talk with her mother about sex. Before long, he thought, they'd get sealed in the church and reap the rewards of those who stayed pure: a large cash endowment from the church fund, a job that paid enough to support both of them, enough furniture and furnishings to fill their entire house, a lavish honeymoon, a whole new wardrobe for Theresa, and a beautiful wedding with a live band and all the extras. Then, when they started having babies, their family and friends would become permanent babysitters, and help raise the kids. Helping each other out made it easier for everybody, and kept the families close.

It was a good life they'd created for themselves, Patrick thought. It was the way all family life in America should be. It seemed like the worldly, though, were happy to throw it all away as they chased money and meaningless sex.

Of course, not every Follower walked the righteous path. Patrick knew a girl who'd gotten pregnant before marriage. She had gone off to have the baby by herself, in a motel room, and had ended up covered with blood and shame, wishing she was dead. Of course, his own sister, whom the family had been shunning for years, had done almost the same thing, in a hospital room that probably had even more germs than a motel.

Jeff and Marci Beagley wandered over, looking typically tired from the rigors of raising their two daughters, Raylene and Nicole, who were just starting grade school. Patrick thought they were amazing parents, the kind he would like to be. They weren't much older than Patrick—Jeff was 32 and Marci was 28—but were really in a different generation. Generations shifted quickly among the Followers.

Jeff's brother Steve and his sister-in-law Jacqueline joined them. Jacqueline was seven months pregnant, and starting to curtail her physical activities, but she'd still been dancing, and there was a gloss of perspiration on her face that went well with the glow of impending motherhood. Patrick saw Theresa give Jacqueline a private smile as she looked at Jackie's tummy. Theresa had told him she'd give anything to be Jackie—just because Jackie was such a cool girl, is what Theresa said—but he knew what she really meant. It was one reason he loved her. Your kids kept the family alive forever.

When Patrick went to get Theresa's sweater, he heard the high school kids talking about the band AC/DC. Somebody said it stood for After-Christ/Devil Comes. Apparently, one of the kids had been listening to it in bed with his eyes closed, until he sensed something in the room with him, opened his eyes, and saw demons climbing onto his bed. Somebody asked if he'd had the presence of mind to shout, "In Jesus' name, Devil be gone!" He had. So he survived, and smashed the record into a hundred pieces. But the radio still played AC/DC, he said, so you had to be careful.

"Walter called the radio the Devil's Toolbox," one of the girls said.

"I thought that was TV," said her boyfriend, Jerry Lloyd, who was pushing her to get married.

"Both, probably," she said, and everyone nodded.

"Did anybody do that homework on the circulatory system?" the girl asked.

"I didn't," said Jerry. "It doesn't apply to us. That's just for the worldly. They've got that kind of body, I guess."

It was good to hear the kids quoting Walter. And Patrick was glad that they realized their bodies were as unique as their spirits. Holding fast.

As midnight neared, Patrick started to think about his dad, and the funeral party they'd had here, and how Vernon Thaine had helped him cry off some of his loss. Vernon had died this year. Patrick raised his glass of punch and said, "I'd like to propose a toast to Vernon. Rest his soul." Vernon had been almost as revered as Walter White, and had wielded great power, unlike the newer generation of elders who had come along after Walter's death.

"To the eternal Vernon," said Tim gravely. Patrick thought Tim was such a good guy. Very traditional. "One of our last elders," Tim said. "One of the best." They raised their glasses. "Eternal rest."

"And to the little ones we lost this year," Marci said softly. "Cowan Mouser, and Alex Morris, and Mikas Rippey." The young parents of those children looked touched, solemn, and proud. Their sacrifices had been noted not only by God, but by those they loved most.

"Eternal rest," they said in unison.

Spontaneously, Patrick recited "The Family Prayer": "May the love of our families, made eternal by each new generation, rise above discord, difficulty, and even death, as it heads toward the horizon of time."

"Amen," they said.

That was the last time, Patrick later recalled, that the Thaine Brothers Band played. With Vernon no longer around to help his family hold fast to tradition, one of the Thaine brothers soon dropped out, was shunned, and killed himself within about a year—an execrable act, in the eyes of the Followers, that helped justify his shunning. It was also the last time Patrick saw Jerry Lloyd, who also committed suicide, apparently because his marriage proposal was declined. His rejection was humiliating for someone born holy, one that rarely seemed to occur among the Followers, since the girls were just as anxious as the boys to become adults.

And Patrick never again saw Jacqueline Beagley. She was only 25, but eleven weeks later she died after three days of hard labor, with her dead baby still inside her. Before long, Tim's wife, Monique, would also be with the Lord—but Tim, ever strong in his faith, would marry again, and become a father to a daughter he adored.

When the hour of the new year arrived, an elder tolled a bell twelve times, and the Thaine Brothers Band played "Auld Lang Syne." Patrick took Theresa's hand as they sang, and at the end of it he kissed her. She held the kiss long enough to embarrass him, but he felt happy. He looked around the darkened room of friends and family—seeing those he loved holding one another, many with their babies between them, almost all in circles created by interlocked arms, in groups that ranged from infancy to old age. He felt certain that their perfect, linked lives, as the new year dawned, would somehow, miraculously, travel as one to the kingdom of heaven, where they would be together always.

How could it not happen, to those blessed few who were born holy?

AMERICA
THE 1990s

As the 1990s unfolded, Rita Swan uncovered the grotesque underbelly of American faith healing—a collection of splintered, anonymous sects that had no money, no political influence, and no sophistication: in short, nothing to lose. These small, fundamentalist churches thrived mostly in the lawless recesses of rural America and in its largely ungoverned ghettos. The deaths in their congregations were far less obvious than those that occurred in the white-collar Christian Science churches.

The little churches were mostly the black-sheep offspring of the fire-and-brimstone Pentecostal Church, which was strange enough in and of itself. Some members of its offshoots handled snakes, spoke in tongues, and sexually abused girls and boys. Their congregants were often mesmerized by charismatics who predicted the end of the world, though with differing dates. A great many of the members of these churches were happy to sacrifice their own children on the altar of faith—as long as the cops didn't bother them. They all hated cops.

They hated the devil, too. Unlike the Christian Scientists, who had esoteric beliefs about disease being caused by spiritual alienation, the members of these churches thought illness was the result of possession by Satan, pure and simple. So how do you cure illness? You cast Satan *out*.

Their exorcisms were generally nonviolent—just praying, anointing with oil, and the laying on of hands. Of course, the patient was often writhing in agony, but that was a sign the exorcism was working.

On occasion, one of the cracker-barrel exorcisms got out of hand, and backwoods elders would physically attack the devil, which meant attacking the person who was possessed. Then the religious ritual would turn into what cops would call a crime scene, with blood, bruises, broken bones, and sometimes dead children. But the church leaders seemed to think that the only way to beat the devil was to play by his rules.

Rita thought she had seen it all, but these cases were even more gory than most of the homicides that were due to medical neglect. They made her sick. One of the first that she came across was that of a girl in Indiana's Tippecanoe Township, just off East Backwater Road, a poor but beautiful, hickory-shaded hillbilly heaven, where the primary retail core was a Dollar Store. Four-year-old Natali Joy Mudd was found dead by detectives in her own home, with a tumor in her eye that was almost as big as the rest of her head. At the horrific scene, a police sergeant found horizontal trails of blood along the walls of the house. The trails matched the height of the girl's head. Natali had apparently been leaning against the wall as she dragged herself from room to room, blinded, trying to find a way to freedom, before the tumor killed her.

Natali's parents were mild-mannered, church-going folks who

belonged to the preeminent congregation in the area, the 2,000-member Faith Assembly Church. Faith Assembly was a Pentecostal offshoot with branches everywhere from Pasco, Washington, to Queens, New York, a borough with dozens of ultra-fundamentalist churches.

Natali's parents were not charged, because the local prosecutor, in his words, was only "ambivalent" about the Faith Assembly Church, and didn't want to waste money on an unpopular case. The main reason he ignored the case, though, was because of Indiana's strict shield laws.

Rita tried to generate legislation in the Indiana statehouse to change that, but didn't succeed.

Two and a half years later, Natali's five-year-old sister, Leah, died from a tumor in her stomach that was approximately the size of a basketball.

Shortly after Leah's death, the Faith Assembly's meeting hall, known as the Glory Barn, was burned to the ground by arsonists— never indicted—indicating a certain degree of grassroots weariness with the Dark Ages.

Unfortunately, Faith Assembly—which some academic researchers blamed for as many as 100 childhood deaths, with a mortality rate among mothers giving birth that was approximately 870 percent higher than normal—had dozens of splinter groups that were even more out of control than the main congregation. In one just outside Lansing, Michigan, a baby that was born at home without medical care lived only twelve days, yellow from jaundice and racked with seizures, before choking to death with pneumonia. The baby's father, who was mildly reprimanded by authorities, told police, "If my *God* can't help her, no *man* can."

Only nine days later, while the father's case was still open, his fifteen-month-old son died from a large tumor in his abdomen. There were no charges in that case, either.

As Rita continued to investigate the sects, she found that the single most common cause of death among them was infant mortality due to lack of medical care during home births, a problem that had mostly been eliminated among Christian Scientists, who now opposed home births without doctors.

In one of these cases, near the end of the '80s, a Sioux Falls, South Dakota, mom named Joni Clark had given birth to her daughter, Libby, at the perilous birth weight of three pounds twelve ounces. Mrs. Clark, who'd already lost a two-day-old daughter, pleaded with her husband to take Libby to the hospital. But he wouldn't allow it, and a husband's word was law in almost all of these churches.

Joni became frantic when Libby's breathing grew sluggish and intermittent, but the Clarks' pastor, End Times Ministries leader Charles Meade, reminded her that babies sometimes forget to breathe, because they are—as Joni should have known—very *young*. Pastor Meade, along with Joni's husband, warned her that her lack of faith was a deadly threat to her daughter.

Libby soon began to vomit blood, and then died.

Meade quickly relocated End Times Ministries to a luxurious compound in Florida, where he grew wealthy from Internet fundraising. He and his flock later had problems involving lewd and lascivious acts with little girls, but he remained unindicted, with thousands of faithful adherents, until he died in 2010. That was after his predicted End of Times, but he'd already, by necessity, pushed the date back.

With Rita's emotional support, Joni Clark fought off her sorrow, went to law school, and filed a suit against South Dakota's shield law. Rita testified at the hearings, and in late 1990 she and Clark won repeal of the shield law. It was the first repeal in the country. Joni Clark Cutler later attended Harvard's Kennedy School of Government, became a college dean, and was elected to the South Dakota Senate, where she was vice chair of the Judiciary Committee.

After that success, Rita testified in the legislatures of thirteen other states, gradually making progress. Throughout the country she lobbied legislators, mobilized press coverage, and made innumerable presentations at conferences on child abuse and children's rights. From her new headquarters in Sioux City, Iowa, she helped draft legislation, contributed data to studies that appeared in such prestigious publications as the *Journal of the American Medical Association,* and raised funds for CHILD, which still operated on a Spartan budget.

Several of the state law reforms that Rita was involved with were initially successful, but were overturned by higher courts, almost always on the grounds of freedom of religion. She appealed some of the rulings to the US Supreme Court, but none were accepted for review.

Rita also lobbied on the federal level and testified before the US Senate—urging lawmakers to solve the problem in a single action with national legislation. But Congress, apparently afraid to be seen as limiting religious freedom, did nothing to stop faith-healing abuse.

The Christian Science Church opposed Rita in virtually every state, on every issue. The Church often prevailed, with one major exception. In Minnesota, CHILD filed a federal suit arguing that taxpayers should not be required to subsidize Medicare and Medicaid funds that paid for Christian Science nursing, an expense of approximately $8 million per year nationally. The Church fought back, but the US district court agreed with Rita and repealed the law.

It was an enormous victory. Even so, the ruling did not stop the faith-healing abuses of either the relatively mainstream Christian Science Church nor the isolated splinter sects that operated under almost no public scrutiny.

In one case that first came to light in a local newspaper and was then reported in *The Seattle Times,* a faith-healing death occurred in the flatlands north of Spokane, Washington—a close-to-Canada haven for Neo-Nazis, survivalists, and religious fanatics. The case began when a ten-year-old boy named Aaron Norman wet the bed one night. Aaron's mother and father, Judith and Bob Norman, suspected that the boy had actually masturbated instead of urinated, despite the physical evidence, so they demanded a confession. Their actions were guided by two members of The No Name Fellowship, Jeffrey Siegel, and church founder Doug Kleber, a former National Football League linebacker, who encouraged Aaron's father to beat him with a wooden paddle. Aaron would not confess, and died. Aaron's parents were originally charged with murder, but due to complications caused by the state's religious-shield law, the only convictions were of Bob Norman, for manslaughter, and Siegel and Kleber, for criminal mistreatment.

A similarly disappointing legal outcome occurred in Melbourne, Florida, where the parents of two-year-old Harrison Johnson escaped conviction in their son's death because they belonged to the Bible Believers Fellowship, a tiny sect that has since thrived. Little Harrison died after he was attacked by a massive cloud of yellow jackets. They stung him 432 times, according to the coroner's report. His parents, Kelly and Wylie Johnson—who told investigators that they believed that doctors are sorcerers—began to pray immediately after the attack, but didn't call 911 until eight hours after the toddler lost consciousness. When the police investigated, Harrison's father told them, "When people went to Jesus Christ, *he* always healed them. He never *sent* them to anyone, let alone a doctor." The Johnsons were charged, but acquitted, since their decision was faith-based.

Shortly after that, in Wisconsin, a two-year-old boy with autism, Terrance Cottrell, was wrapped in sheets and smothered by his own mother and the minister of her storefront church during an exorcism that was intended to cure his condition. The minister, Ray Hemphill, was convicted only of a lesser charge of recklessly causing bodily harm to a child, and got a light sentence. The mother was never charged, because the state had a strong shield law. Critics also blamed the local DA for not intervening because of his own strong church ties.

One of the most prominent churches Rita fought was the Faith Tabernacle Church. It had about 18,000 members and a number of branches in America, primarily in Pennsylvania and New Jersey, and also in many foreign countries, where faith-healing crimes were often even more common. In Ghana, a Faith Tabernacle pastor who was given five young sisters to cure of "evil spirits" raped all five, but his fine was only the confiscation of one sheep and two bottles of schnapps. In a case in Haiti, more than forty people were tortured to death by a mob for suspicion of practicing voodoo. In Egypt, 47 people were beaten to death in a mass exorcism, and 98 more were injured, including eleven people whose blindness was presumed to be a punishment by God for their sins.

Deadly exorcisms didn't happen only in poor countries, though. In Japan, six people were tortured to death during a group exorcism. In an exorcism in Canada, two-year-old Kira Canhoto's parents restrained her and poured so much water down her throat that she died. In England, 36-year old Anne Orieso strangled to death her five-year-old son, Sylvester, to death, believing that she was killing the devil in him, then waited several days for her son to return—intact and holy.

At a Faith Tabernacle church in Philadelphia, one-year-old Patrick Foster grew lethargic and gaunt over several months while his parents tried to drive the devil from his body with prayer. When his parents, Daniel and Anne Marie Foster, saw that Patrick had a growth bulging from his left side, they prayed even harder. The growth became so big that it wrapped around his liver and heart, and became visible to a neighbor, who called authorities. A social worker found the boy with one eye swollen shut and lips cracked from dehydration. His parents refused to take him to a hospital, but police forced them. Patrick, who weighed eighteen pounds, had a six-pound malignant tumor.

Patrick managed to survive the tumor's removal—a remarkable medical outcome that his parents credited to their prayer. He spent six months in a hospital, was adopted by his aunt and uncle, who were not Church members, and survived.

It was a huge triumph—one of the few with a survivor—even though his parents were never punished.

Another couple in the same church, Dawn and Roger Winterborne, had already lost six children to illness, all younger than age two. At one point, 491 people in the church contracted measles, and six children died. In another Pennsylvania branch of the church, a brother and sister had died, one from diabetes, and the other from an untreated ear infection.

Two parents from the Altoona, Pennsylvania, branch of the Faith

Tabernacle Church, Dennis and Lorie Nixon, had received only two years' probation when they let their sixteen-year-old daughter, Shannon, die from diabetes. Their sentence included community service at a hospital, to learn the necessity of medical care, but Rita thought it was a naïve sentence that did not recognize the intransigence of most faith-healing abusers. Besides, Rita later said, "The hospital didn't want them." Who knew what they might do?

The awful cases went on and on. But no one other than Rita Swan, who was still working mostly by herself, seemed able to see the big picture of faith-healing abuse in America. It was a terribly lonely position, and it was often frightening to be out on the road alone. At this time, she got her first death threats, which scared Doug even more than her, though he never dreamed of asking her to come home.

In a democracy, though, sometimes all it takes is one dedicated, persistent person to change everything, if they know exactly what to do. At least that was the theory. Rita prayed it was true.

SAN DIEGO, CALIFORNIA
JANUARY 1998

When Rita Swan met Terry Gustafson in San Diego, it was no longer quite so easy for faith-healing abusers to stay secret, but it was still almost impossible to convict them.

A few months earlier, though, Rita had finished a groundbreaking study with one of her closest associates, Rhode Island pediatrician Seth Asser, MD, which would soon appear in the journal *Pediatrics*. It documented 172 faith-healing deaths of children in America between 1975 and 1995. "These included babies who in some cases were literally tortured to death," Asser later said.

The deaths were associated with 23 different sects in 34 states. The study was designed conservatively to ensure its credibility, and Rita was sure that it represented only the tip of the iceberg. "Most of the deaths," she later said, "are swept under the carpet."

At age fifty-four, Rita Swan had almost completely abandoned teaching, having spent her career trying to stop legalized religious crime, and to bring full civil rights to children. But her work was marked mostly by moral victories and piecemeal improvements. She had proven there *was* a problem, but couldn't solve it.

But she knew exactly what solving it would require. This was the equation:

First, she needed to find a state with a weak shield law—or to successfully weaken one herself.

Second, she needed a district attorney in that state who was willing to aggressively prosecute a prominent church, such as the Faith Tabernacle or the Followers of Christ.

Third, that prosecutor needed to have a police force that had developed an inside source within the church: somebody who was trusted by the churchgoers, and willing to betray that trust.

The three-part equation was simple, but the problems seemed insurmountable.

First problem: Every state, at this time, had at least some form of a shield law, and achieving even a partial improvement in a state's law could easily take more than a year.

Second problem: Prosecutors hated these cases. They all wanted to get reelected, and the cases were unpopular, weakly supported by witnesses, and hampered by shield laws.

Third problem: No police department had ever been able to infiltrate a church. Nobody would turn Judas. Even the people who no longer approved of their own churches were too frightened to do it.

If those three problems could be solved, though, it would be the key to multiple prosecutions within a single jurisdiction. And multiple prosecutions would be the linchpin to completely dismantling that state's shield law and changing the perceptions of its local jury pools. That would lead to multiple convictions. And the more convictions, the greater likelihood of longer sentences.

Getting multiple, major convictions with long sentences in one jurisdiction would be the key to prolonged local publicity. It would also light up the new set of Internet connections that people were calling the blogosphere, on the sites that exposed religious abuse, including Rita's own CHILD site, the Cult News Network, and the Ross Institute, founded by Rick Ross after his previous employer, the Cult Awareness Network, was bought in bankruptcy court by the Christian Science Church, seemingly as a defensive strategy.

The Net interest would trigger national newspaper, magazine, and television coverage.

As all this media and social networking rolled out, the politicians would come around, and kill shield laws right and left. That would put even more pressure on the higher courts to revisit the issue. Only this time Rita would win.

And then, America would accept it as a fact that faith-healing abuse is a crime.

If all that could happen, it would change American culture. And American history.

But that's what it would take.

So as Rita Swan sized up Tough Terry Gustafson, in a comfortable convention hall in San Diego, she wondered if Gustafson—who was in a position to go after the Followers of Christ—was tough enough to do it.

Hard to tell. But it wouldn't take long to find out.

5

THE CRIME FAMILY

Deliver me, I pray thee, from the hand of my brother . . . for I fear
him, lest he come and slay us all, the mothers with the children.

—The Book of Genesis 32:11

Oregon City
February 23, 1998

Clackamas County detective Jeff Green careened around corners to get to the death site as fast as possible. He wanted to arrive before the Followers of Christ had time to get their stories straight. It wasn't easy. Traffic. Probably too late already.

Green had known about the Followers for years, and had heard Larry Lewman's horror stories about the autopsies of the Church kids. He was primed for the call-out because he'd already cased the Followers' neighborhood and knew the best routes. The Kissers were mostly clustered around their church on Molalla, in places like the Beagleys' split-level house on Canyon Ridge Drive—within walking distance of the church—and Grandma Mitchell's little, green ranch house on Auburn Drive, which had a jacked-up red pickup in front of it at the moment.

You had to know where the grandmas lived, because sick kids often got sent there to stay under the radar, and because it was a tradition to have the babies born at grandma's.

The last two deaths were still raw in Green's mind: little Holland Cunningham, dead from a rotten intestine, and that baby they took to the New Year's Eve party, Valerie Shaw. Who on earth would take a deathly ill newborn to a *party*? From the parents' perspective, though—give them the benefit of the doubt—how could they know the baby was really that sick? Probably only a doctor would know—and *no* doctor was going to see *that* kid.

Dispatch said that this dead kid was Bo Phillips, age eleven. Green knew exactly who they were talking about because an officer from another department had been to the boy's house two days earlier, acting on a tip from a neighbor. The neighbor said the parents claimed Bo was only slightly ill, and the officer talked to Bo himself, who said he was okay. Tough little kid, apparently.

Green mentally cataloged the facts. According to Dispatch, cause of death: undetermined. Time of death: earlier this evening. Several witnesses. Mother and father present. No other units had been notified at this time.

When Green got there, two hundred Followers were jammed into the home of Bo Phillips' grandparents. The Followers looked unremarkable to Green—some of the men were dressed sharp and some were sloppy. Some of the women were frumpy and vacant-eyed, and some looked attractive and smart. But as Green walked in, all of them seemed distant and looked right through him.

The men were grouped in the front yard and garage, many of them smoking. The women were gathered in the kitchen and bedrooms, speaking the shorthand of deep familiarity. As Green waded through, they parted like the Red Sea.

There was definitely an air of sadness in the home, but not shock. Not even overt grief. And yet, a *dead boy* was here. So were his parents, grandparents, aunts and uncles, and their closest friends. The lack of emotion was creepy. "I'll remember that scene for the rest of my life," Green later said.

Green hurried to the bedroom where Bo Phillips lay, and saw what to his investigator's eye was a boy who had suffered a slow and awful death. Bo's dark T-shirt was soaked with an acrid sweat, and his body showed the classic signs of extreme dehydration: a face that was gaunt and tight, and dried-out flesh as thin as butcher paper. He was yellowish. Kidney failure? Liver? The adult diaper they had on him indicated that he'd lost control of his bowels or bladder, due to either the loss of nerve function, or the stress of imminent death, or both. Bo's mouth was still pulled tight and his eyes were blackened and sunken, sometimes a sign of significant pain at the moment of death.

Green had seen lots of dead people, many soaking in blood, sometimes dismembered. Some had been children—victims of accidents, and even kids killed by their own parents. But seeing Bo was different. Here was a child whose parents had almost certainly loved him, and yet they'd done nothing but pray while he died. It was incomprehensible. "I'll never forget his eyes," Green later recalled. "They were haunting."

The detective took Bo's temperature immediately, before it could fall any further. Bo had been dead for about three hours, according to the witnesses in the home. But he still had a temperature of 104 degrees. That was evidence that he'd had a scorching fever, which implied neglect. Even with rigor mortis stiffening Bo's jaundiced torso, his body was still hot to the touch.

Green isolated the main players, starting with mom and dad, kept his voice cordial, and started hitting them with questions. They told him that Bo had been sick for at least two weeks—which contradicted their charade two days ago about his good health. But they probably knew that school officials could confirm the length of his illness, so it wouldn't be wise for them to lie about it at this point. They were smart enough to realize that. Bo, they said, had been complaining of aching muscles and feeling "tired." He had managed to stay in school for a week, but then stayed home. Three days earlier, they said, Bo had vomited several times, and "his forehead got hot." They didn't own a thermometer.

Several days before, prior to the visit from authorities, Bo's dad had called his wife home from an out-of-state trip, and had told people in the church to remember Bo in their prayers. That was a code phrase, Green knew, that meant somebody was desperately ill.

Mr. Phillips said he had begun to realize that Bo was very ill, but thought that praying was the best course of action.

Earlier that day, the parents said, Bo had been in pain and struggled to breathe. Then he lapsed into unconsciousness. It sounded to Green like a diabetic coma. Bo had temporarily regained consciousness, but collapsed and stopped breathing.

No one called 911 or did CPR, but nobody that Green talked to seemed regretful about that.

Green stood close to Bo's father, who was crestfallen but calm. "Why did you let your son *die*?" Green said. "You had all these options available to you."

"Well," said Mr. Phillips, "it was my choice."

Green could barely process it. He had seen so many kinds of crime, and they hardly ever made sense. "But I couldn't believe it," he later said. "This family *let* their son die? Because they made it their *choice* not to take him to get medical treatment?"

The next day, Dr. Larry Lewman, in his thick green apron, cut a Y-incision into the abdomen of Bo Phillips, to determine the cause of death. It was, as expected, secondary infection due to diabetes, coupled with dehydration. Lewman surmised that "the last twelve hours or so were a real horror story. The abdominal pain had to be excruciating."

KATU-TV journalist Mark Hass interviewed Lewman about Bo's death, which came shortly after the deaths of Holland Cunningham and Valerie Shaw. "In some cases," said the doctor, who was as inured to gore as any person can reasonably be, "these were lingering, horrible deaths." He paused for a breath. "*Pain* . . . suffering . . ."

Hass waited patiently.

"*Torture* is a good word," said Larry Lewman, though he could not discuss the disposition of the case on-air.

When they got off, Hass asked, "What now?"

"What now?" said Lewman. "We call Terry."

OREGON CITY
FEBRUARY 24, 1998

The day after Bo's death was perfectly ordinary in Oregon City, or O.C.,
to the locals. The morning's unusually fat drops of rain delighted the ski-
ers headed for Mt. Hood, visible on the eastern horizon, but contributed
to the local epidemic of Seasonal Affective Disorder. Christian Scientist
Robert Duvall's paean to faith healing, *The Apostle,* was playing on Beavercreek Road, just down from the church, and was a big hit with the
Followers, but signaled a menacing cultural shift to the atheists and an-
archists who grew medical marijuana in Old Town bungalows down by
the river. That segment of Oregon City was pure Portlandia, and a part
of Clackalackie's mix, at least equal to the conservatives in the hill country, just outside town, that some called Clackatucky.

Downtown, the Globetrotters were doing their wholesome show
at the Rose Garden, a few miles away from Strip Club Row, just up
from Oregon City in the eastern part of "Pornland," as CBS's Dan
Rather once referred to Portland, because it had more gentlemen's
clubs per capita than anyplace else in America, and a huge problem
with child sex trafficking.

And according to the news, it looked as if Terry Gustafson was
getting ready to launch an assault on the Followers of Christ, a welcome proposition to most, but anathema to a significant minority.

It was a typical day, then, by O.C. standards, with its rich stew of
controversy and cohesion bubbling away. As the locals would say: It's
Oregon City.

Gustafson went public about Bo Phillips' death, and it began to
percolate through the local press. She started attacking the Followers
on some of their most vulnerable issues, including their hypocritical
use of eye doctors and dentists. That tradition had started when

founder Walter White developed some visual and dental problems and was visited by the Lord, who told him that seeing ophthalmologists, dentists, and orthodontists did not show lack of faith or invite eternal damnation. Gustafson called it "an inconsistency that amounts to fraud."

Another soft spot she poked at was the freedom of adults to clandestinely seek medical care, while kids had to follow the rules. Gustafson had learned, for example, that Marci Beagley, matriarch of one of the church's three inner-circle families—the Hickmans, Beagleys, and Worthingtons—had snuck off to have ingrown toenails treated, without suffering repercussions within the church. "Kids," Gustafson reminded the public, "don't have the ability to walk into a medical clinic on their own."

She added, "We can change things here. And I'm quite confident we will."

Larry Lewman urged Gustafson to stay in the forefront of the attack, while he supported her from behind. He had become convinced that at least 25 Oregon City kids had died needlessly over the last ten years, not counting the "stillbirths" that seemed to be suspiciously common among the Followers.

At the same time, in Washington County, adjacent to Clackamas, the faith-healing Church of the First Born was also suspected by local authorities of killing and maiming people through medical neglect. although there wasn't enough evidence to make charges. Even so, that congregation looked like college-town Episcopalians compared to the Followers.

Rita Swan, still in touch with Gustafson, heard about Bo Phillips' death from the DA the day after it happened, then got in touch with Detective Green. The more Rita had researched the Followers, the more she realized that death and disability from faith healing were more concentrated in Clackamas County than any other place in America.

It was becoming clear to Rita: Oregon City was the epicenter of the epidemic. If she could win there, she could win anywhere.

OREGON CITY
MARCH 1998

Rita was confident that Terry Gustafson and her Clackamas colleagues had the guts to go for it, partly because she'd discovered that a few years earlier they'd prosecuted a ten-year-old boy for murder after he shot his younger brother and sister. Putting away a ten-year-old for Juvenile-Hall-Plus-Life showed that Oregon City was a bad place to break the law.

The Clackamas prosecutors had also gained recent national attention for bringing down a bizarre sect called Ecclesia, out in Sandy, the ski town with the Bed & Bondage place. Ecclesia had routinely tortured its children, and Leader Eldridge Broussard had let elders beat his own eight-year-old daughter to death with one hundred blows from a pipe, a hose, and an electrical cord, while other children, including Broussard's son, were forced to watch. Because Broussard was too arrogant to invoke the Oregon religious-shield law, he'd been convicted of first-degree manslaughter, but before he could get shipped to prison, he died of untreated diabetes. His son later started a civil-liberties foundation that opposed, among other things, religious-shield laws.

Defendants who did use the shield law, of course, had a tremendous advantage. While Gustafson was mulling indictment in the Phillips case, a DA in nearby Wasco County who'd just convicted another dad of torturing his child to death said, "I shudder to think what the result might have been if he'd said he'd been praying while he did it."

"I want desperately to prosecute this case," Gustafson told *The Oregonian.* She was seemingly in a strong position to do it, with a budget of about $6 million and a staff of 82, including 26 lawyers—robust resources for a medium-size county. But the accusation of leaking files to pressure the powerful defense attorney still hung over her head, and rumors also ricocheted around the courthouse that she'd shaded the truth during her testimony about the case.

None of the courthouse insiders were particularly scandalized, though, because they knew that perjury was a way of life in virtually every American courtroom. Prosecutors and defense attorneys across the country realize that a witness stand is often the *last* place somebody tells the truth, but it's hard to prove. The officers of the court rarely admit this, though, because doing so would just encourage it.

Probable perjury by the Followers, however, was one of Gustafson's biggest worries. She knew they'd have no problem lying in the service of the Lord.

But even more threatening than fibbing-Followers or the accusation of unethical conduct was the state's shield law. The sad fact was that the Oregon shield law was extremely broad—it offered protection for almost any offense—and most of the locals liked it that way. Gustafson needed help. She turned to Rita Swan.

At Gustafson's urging, Rita relocated to Oregon to help persuade state officials, as well as the media, that Oregon should prosecute the parents of Bo Phillips.

Rita, as the world's leading crusader against faith-healing abuse, quickly made headlines in Oregon, partly by baring her soul, as she had done so often, about how she had lost her own little boy. It was the hardest part of her job.

Rita didn't like the odds in this case any more than Gustafson did. Of the forty states that still had extensive shield laws, covering a multitude of offenses, Oregon was one of only six—to Rita's dismay—that allowed a religious shield against homicide. Oregon's law, the bottom-of-the-barrel worst in the country, now protected parents who committed faith-healing crimes even from many relatively minor charges, such as child neglect.

Rita huddled with Gustafson, Detective Jeff Green, and Larry Lewman, and soaked up Oregon's sensibilities. "Oregon is certainly a secular state," she said many years later, "and is by no means part of the Bible Belt. Along with the state of Washington, it has the highest percentage of nonreligious people. But it's *so* liberal, and *so* tolerant, that sometimes it doesn't see danger. It still has the most religious exemptions for preventive and diagnostic care for newborns, and is the only state with a religious exemption for placing vitamin-K drops in babies' eyes, to prevent blindness and internal bleeding. It even has a religious exemption for wearing a *bike helmet*. Now, to me, that's just hard to explain."

The most rational explanation is that there is no rational explanation. The corollary to It's Oregon City is: It's Oregon. Rita had discovered that reality three years before, in 1995, when she had tried—unsuccessfully—to keep Christian Science lobbyists from adding the ridiculous manslaughter shield. The Church had lobbied vigorously—and convinced the legislators, against all reasonable evidence—that Christian Science represented the entire Christian community. That was maddening to Rita, because membership in Mother Church had dropped drastically over the years, from a peak of about 300,000 in the early 1900s to as few as 20,000 by the 1990s.

In the '95 scrap, the Church had even gotten the unlikely support of the state's District Attorneys Association. When Rita had called the head of the association, she later recalled, "He was very defensive about it. His attitude was, 'we still have a good manslaughter clause, so what are you complaining about?'"

But that same year, Mother Church orchestrated the complete elimination of the manslaughter option, over Gustafson's outspoken opposition, and by this time, the only charge that was still not shielded was a lesser one of criminally negligent homicide. Gustafson, though, feared that even that charge was legally compromised, because it was worded almost identically to the law on manslaughter—which was supposedly *not a crime*. "It was like calling the same crime two different things," Gustafson later said. She thought it created a huge loophole. Defendants could claim that the contradictions between the two laws violated their right to due process of law. If the judge agreed, the case would be thrown out. That exact thing had already happened in Minnesota and Florida, because the shield laws there were equally muddled.

Gustafson was almost certain that if she charged Bo's parents, the judge would dismiss the case before it even came to trial. If that happened, she thought it would harden the Followers' belief that they were above the law, and would ignite a new wave of abuse.

So Gustafson started to back away from the Bo Phillips case. Rita Swan, accustomed to the glacial pace of societal change—and afraid of doing more harm than good—thought Terry was doing the right thing.

But the state's DA's association pressed Terry to go full-bore into court. So did the Oregon attorney general, Hardy Myers, a close ally of her enemy, Governor John Kitzhaber. Gustafson thought she was being set up to fail, as part of a personal vendetta.

Gustafson wrote a letter to Myers about her misgivings. But instead of mailing the letter, and taking the risk of it getting "misplaced," she drove to the capital and read it aloud to Myers. She told him that if he was so gung-ho about prosecuting Bo's parents, he should send a prosecutor from his own office to do it.

Myers refused. "He said he was getting pressure from the governor's office," she later said. Gustafson felt her fears were being confirmed.

After Myers refused to take the case, Gustafson tried to get the feds to try it as a civil rights issue, invoking the argument that children have a civil right to medical care. But the Justice Department wouldn't touch it—because they agreed with Gustafson that the confusion in the Oregon shield law had made a mess of the case. The local US Attorney said, "It's a more appropriate matter for state prosecution."

Gustafson's hesitancy to prosecute was attacked by *The Oregonian*, the Northwest's largest paper. The city's hip weekly, *Willamette Week*, tarred Gustafson as its Rogue of the Week. Then—not quite out of nowhere, it seemed to Gustafson—the accusations about her pressuring the defense attorney, leaking files, and lying in court arose with a vengeance. She was suddenly being investigated not just for professional malfeasance, but for the crime of perjury.

Rita remained aligned with Gustafson. Terry had tried hard to help, and Rita would later present Gustafson with an award for her attempt. But the situation was getting out of control. Spring turned to summer and summer to fall, while the Phillips case remained unresolved.

THE CLACKAMAS COUNTY COURTHOUSE
OREGON CITY
OCTOBER 7, 1998

Terry Gustafson called her entire staff into a large conference room and told them that she was being indicted on criminal charges of perjury, and of intentionally releasing court records. She also announced her retirement.

"She was in incredible control," a deputy prosecutor recalled. "With my whole world crashing down on me, I'm not sure I could have pulled it off." Gustafson left the courthouse in a van full of prisoners. It took her to county jail, where she was fingerprinted and photoed.

She posted bail immediately. The Clackamas County Jail, called Clackatraz by its inmates, was no place to spend the night. The processing room for new prisoners was kept frosty by an industrial-strength air conditioner that often made the Fresh Meat turn blue and tremble. It helped sober up drunks, and let everybody know that this was no place to return to.

Clackatraz was a much harsher jail than Portland's county jail, where inmates were assigned to sterile but comfortable pods, were granted special dietary privileges based upon religion, and even had access to a vending machine. In Clackatraz, nobody ate from late afternoon until breakfast, other than the corrections officers, who usually made microwave popcorn around midnight, and allowed its hot-buttered fragrance to waft through the holding tank.

When Gustafson left office, Attorney General Hardy Myers briefly took personal charge of the Clackamas courts, pending a new election. But he never prosecuted the Bo Phillips case.

It was over. The Followers won. Terry Gustafson lost. Rita Swan lost.

The year came to a quiet end, punctuated only by the usual New Year's Eve parties, including the celebratory soft-rock extravaganza at the Followers of Christ Church, where most of the congregation imbibed delicious homemade punch, while the men of the inner circle enjoyed red wine in a back room, as Walter once had, purportedly for digestive purposes.

With Walter gone, admission to the inner circle—based loosely around the Hickmans, Beagleys, and Worthingtons, and often the White and Wyland clans—was based less on spiritual ascendance than on practical, more prosaic measures of status: money, skills, personality, popularity, and even looks. All of those inner circle families had also lost members at some point, including children, without breaking faith and going to doctors. That was the Followers' most bittersweet proof of piety.

The seeming quiet, though, was deceptive. As the Followers basked in the recently reinforced sanctuary of the Oregon shield law, Rita Swan, a master politician by this time in her life, went back to the Midwest to plan her next movement against the Followers. But she had a great deal of other work to do, and this would have to be her last big effort in Oregon. If she got shot down, Oregon would remain the worst state in the country at protecting kids from religious abuse, and Rita would have to focus on more reasonable states. The Followers, unfortunately, would basically be able to do whatever they wanted.

SALEM, OREGON
JANUARY 1999

Before all the college bowl games were even over, Rita again left her home and her husband, who was still teaching, to launch her final Oregon effort: a major rewrite of the state's shield law. It was the highest possible hurdle, but the only option that remained.

It started with a media campaign that she orchestrated like a maestro, having done it so often before in other states. She got *The Oregonian*'s top investigative reporter, Mark Larabee, to begin a series of articles on the Followers. It became the most exhaustive investigation on faith-healing abuse ever to appear in American print media, and not only triggered other articles and broadcasts throughout the country, but made the issue of critical importance in Oregon. Rita opened doors for Larabee all around the country, and he was the first reporter to glimpse the terrible scope of the national scandal.

In broadcast media, Rita gave extra help to Mark Hass of KATU, whom she considered "a hero" for breaking the story in 1998. He did several more installments on the Followers that further propelled them to national ignominy.

Rita built a national campaign that included coverage in *Time* magazine and on ABC's *20/20*. *Time* wrote about the cemetery and the Bo Phillips case and included tough quotes from Larry Lewman, Detective Jeff Green, and Terry Gustafson, who was still involved, but was preoccupied with her own legal problems. Lewman and Green also appeared on *20/20*, and the issue got far more attention than ever before.

Still, it all came down to politics. Rita teamed up with conservative evangelical-Christian legislator Bruce Starr, a Republican from the prosperous Silicon Forest section of West Portland, and with Democrat Kate Brown, a hyper-ambitious leftist who represented the eastern, Portlandia part of town. They introduced a bill that would de-claw the Oregon shield law, removing key religious exemptions for numerous crimes: murder by abuse or neglect; first and, second-degree manslaughter; first and second-degree criminal mistreatment; child abuse; and failure to provide physical care. Rita was optimistic. Jeff Green came to the state capitol in Salem and told his horror story, and so did Dr. Larry Lewman.

Also testifying was a Follower that Rita had coaxed into going public: Russ Briggs, a heartbroken father of two babies who were buried in the Followers cemetery. He told the legislators that in 1970, when he was twenty, his first son was born more than a month pre-mature, in a traditional Followers' home birth, and for four days the untrained midwives fed the baby out of an eyedropper and prayed, as the baby slowly died. "I stood there," Briggs said, "a twenty-year-old child, sobbing and hurting, and trying to figure out why my child died. If there had been an incubator there," he said, "or modern medicine, I know he would have made it."

A year later, Briggs said, he and his wife, Lorraine, lost their sec-ond son twelve hours after his home birth. When Lorraine got preg-nant again, they left the Church. A few weeks after they left, Briggs' father became gravely ill, but Briggs' mother would not let him enter the house. He never saw his father again. His family would not allow him to attend the funeral, and he began to drink heavily and consider suicide, but ended up joining the Army, and had two daughters.

When his mother became ill in 1976, he rejoined the Church, to be able to see her. But he and his family were still ostracized, and his daughters' friends refused to sit with them in church. In 1981 he was seriously injured and chose to have an operation, against the will of Church members. "The Church expects you to lie on the couch," he said. The hostility increased, and he left the Church forever. His brothers had not spoken to him for twenty years, and a letter he sent to his sister was returned unopened.

In response to this rare public attack by a former Follower, one of the Church's more prominent members at the time, Dale Morris, gave an unprecedented interview to KATU, calling Briggs "a liar and a whoremonger." When asked about the children's deaths, Morris said, "God's will be done. I don't expect you to understand."

Fifteen other people testified in favor of the measure, including district attorneys, nurses, social workers, doctors, law school profes-sors, and child-safety advocates.

Only three testified against it. One was Seventh-day Adventist minister Dan McCullough, who claimed that doctors are never penal-ized for making mistakes. It made no sense, of course, because doctors are often punished for malpractice. Somehow, though, the argument remained a staple that would be cited by various defendants of faith-healing abuse for many years.

Mother Church sent Christian Science practitioner and PR man Bruce Fitzwater, who managed to entertain the conflicting notions that the existing laws were terribly intrusive, but didn't need changing one way or the other.

The third antagonist was from the Church of Scientology, which could generally be counted on to make an appearance in battles against offbeat churches.

There were also the usual attacks on Rita. She was portrayed as a bereaved mom who'd become a radical anti-Church zealot because of a tragedy of her own making. Matthew's death, Fitzwater said, was due to "bad parenting."

In another attempt to turn the hearings into a trial of Rita, Scientology Celebrity Centre spokesperson Gwen Barnard testified that Rita Swan "has an ax to grind, as she, herself, allowed her son to die due to lack of medical treatment. . . . It does not appear to me that she is as interested in saving children as she is on acting out her vengeance on her Church."

Rita let the insults slide, although she privately considered Fitzwater to be not only "sleazy and slick," but a clown. She formed this opinion when a senator on the Judiciary Committee asked him, "If you knew a child under your care was dying and you knew medical help was available, would you not advise them to get medical treatment?"

Fitzwater replied that he wouldn't tell them directly, but would "ummmm . . . give some hand signals" to that effect. Even years later, Rita couldn't talk about the remark without laughing.

To win, Rita stuck hard to the facts. She arranged for Larry Lewman to testify, and he began his testimony with plenty of medical jargon—"craniocerebral trauma," "puerperal sepsis," "anoxia," etc.—and then moved to earthier phrases, such as "horror stories involving prolonged and extreme suffering." He said in plain English that "craniocerebral trauma" occurs when you crush a newborn's head during delivery.

Detective Jeff Green told the legislators what it was like to take the temperature of a dead boy, and to attempt to determine the approximate degree of his suffering by the amount of it still frozen on his face.

The Followers showed up en masse, in what to Rita seemed an obvious attempt at intimidation, but they refused to testify, a blunder in her opinion. Only days into the campaign, Rita thought the whole thing was wrapped up: a victory that would open the door to aggressive prosecution of the Followers of Christ, and lead to the control of other faith-healing lunatics throughout America.

Then she got blindsided by political grandstanding. A liberal from The People's Republic of Eugene, Floyd Prozanski, rewrote the bill to include the dismantling of an existing system of mandatory minimum sentences. His constituents from Bluejean hated that system—probably rightfully so, since it was extremely rigid—but Rita thought that risking her attempt to save kids in order to win this other battle was "a reckless strategy."

Prozanski was inexplicably joined by the godfather of the mandatory minimums, Kevin Mannix, who typically tilted slightly to the right of Caligula, and it turned into a bitterly contentious summer. Rita didn't know what had accounted for this sudden left/right fellowship, and no one she knew could explain it, either.

Rita kept from burning bridges, and weaved her way through the egos, personal agendas, and vendettas. As Terry Gustafson had learned when she'd met Rita in San Diego, Rita could see into people's souls and size them up for exactly who they were. It was one of the few perks of having been to hell and back. She went from office to office in the art deco capitol building, making friends, picking brains, and usually finding out that Bruce Fitzwater had been there first. His main tactic seemed to be creating confusion. He'd tell one lawmaker one thing and another something else until nobody knew what was what, other than that faith healing was in the Constitution. Sort of.

As the legislative session neared its conclusion, approximately 75 various permutations of the bill were proposed, and serially discarded. The final bill was weaker than Rita's initial bill, but still called for the elimination of five key shields: protection from prosecution for murder by abuse, murder by neglect, first-degree manslaughter, second-degree manslaughter, and even criminal mistreatment, a lesser neglect charge that would be easier to enforce.

All of the neglect charges were important, though, because according to Rita's close associate Seth Asser, MD, "Child neglect is the most commonly fatal form of child abuse."

But the final bill also said that if children were older than fifteen, they would have the right to demand medical care. That sounded good to most of the lawmakers, but not to Rita. She thought it might imply that fifteen-year-olds also had the right to *refuse* medical care—possibly while being persuaded or even bullied by their parents.

Even so, she accepted it as a necessary compromise.

Other compromises were a religious shield against giving kids immunizations, one against a blood test for newborns that could detect serious disorders, one against giving newborns vitamin-K eyedrops to help prevent blindness and hemorrhaging, and one that would allow kids to ride bikes without helmets—if that was, somehow, against their parents' religion.

Even passage of that bill looked precarious, though, because of what was perceived as public sentiment against it. One legislator told Rita, "We cannot legislate good parenting."

Just before time ran out in the seven-month struggle to pass a bill, Rita found consensus by adding a critically important bipartisan amendment. It protected cats and dogs from being skinned by fur traders. Not that there was any evidence of that having ever happened, though, particularly in pet-sensitive Portlandia, where a blind dog named Diego had his own Seeing Eye dog. Nonetheless, the larger Oregon existed in a delicate realm of homeostasis between urban and rural, with a lot of mink ranchers in the boonies balanced by PETA people from Portland who set the minks free, and nobody wanted that equilibrium to be upset by the specter of people wearing coats made from Feline Americans. It's Oregon.

The Kitty Coalition prevailed and a bill was sent to Governor John Kitzhaber. Unfortunately, as an MD who was so veto-friendly that his nickname was Dr. No, Kitzhaber had 99 bills targeted for veto on what he called his Hit List, so nothing was certain—especially since he had already *strengthened* the religious-shield laws twice.

At the time, though, Kitzhaber had delicate image issues of his own. He'd been a longtime bachelor—very longtime: he was 48 when he married an equally longtime bachelorette, Sharon LaCroix, who was initially great window-dressing because she was a vivacious blonde and seemed quite bright. But the press and public quickly found her icy, particularly when she adopted chastity as her pet cause. The capital was buzzing with rumors of a split, which did eventually occur, and would soon lead to Kitzhaber's temporary retreat from public life. At the same time, he was trying to socialize medicine within the compulsively self-reliant state. This session, therefore, was not the best time for him to declare war on God.

Seventy-five minutes before Kitzhaber's scheduled yea-or-nay, he closeted with Fitzwater. Then he called a key legislator and told her he wanted to postpone the signing indefinitely.

It looked like the bill was dead. But at the last minute, for reasons never fully presented, Kitzhaber signed the bill.

Before she left Oregon, Rita Swan went to the Followers' cemetery. She saw the headstone of the baby who'd died just after the New Year's Eve party, Valerie Shaw, which bore an engraving of a baby in a cradle. There was a sooty, age-blackened marker for Baby Girl Cunningham, a predecessor of little Holland Cunningham. Baby Girl had probably died shortly after birth, although there was no way to know, because there were no dates on her marker. There were no dates on a number of the children's graves. And nearby there was Bo Phillips' grave, new enough to be free from moss.

Rita went home to Doug, Catherine, and Marsha in Sioux City, where they lived high on a hill outside town, with an expansive view, and horses in their pasture. This was the greatest victory in her long mission. "Oregon's new law," she later noted, "put the children in faith-healing sects light-years ahead of where they were before."

Oregon's new law had real teeth. The most potent aspect of it was the ability to arrest parents on charges of second-degree manslaughter. The penalty for that was six-plus years in prison. It was a much harsher penalty than had ever before existed in Oregon.

The new law appeared to frighten the Followers. No reports of abuse were heard for many years. Other states took notice of Oregon's success, and Rita's work became easier and more fruitful. In the next installment of her career, she was welcomed warmly by the state legislatures of Colorado, Maryland, Massachusetts, and Rhode Island, winning repeal of some or all of their shield laws.

Her media appearances increased in number and magnitude, and the amplified exposure and Rita's tireless lobbying soon led to major modifications in the shield laws of Hawaii, Arizona, Delaware, Minnesota, and North Carolina.

The nation began to change. To Rita Swan, life, at last, seemed to make sense, and her family, finally, had found some peace.

OREGON CITY
OCTOBER 2000–APRIL 7, 2007

The first Halloween of the New Millennium was coming—a kid-focused holiday the Followers loved, even though some of the old people said it was Pagan—but Patrick Robbins and his wife, Theresa, weren't acknowledging it. No decorations, no pumpkin, no parties, no candy to hand out to the kids. When Halloween night came, they would almost certainly go to a movie, as they had the last three years. Their seclusion was because of their bitter punishment by God with barrenness: After eight years of trying, Theresa could not conceive a baby.

Patrick, 34 now, couldn't understand the curse, no matter how much he studied the Bible. He had been God's steadfast servant, and prayed each day for the miracle of new life. He was more in the Word than most of the Followers his age, and was proud when his friends called him a Bible-thumper. He went to church every Thursday and Sunday, like he was supposed to, and had never had even a thought about any woman but Theresa. He still remembered the night he'd kissed her on New Year's Eve, ten years ago, as if it were a scene from a love story.

But after being childless so long, he and Theresa were starting to stand out in the church, and not in a good way. Kids seemed to come so easily to the Followers. His friend Phil Hickman already had five sons.

Sometimes Patrick thought that maybe he was being chastised for his sister Ella's abortion—since mortal sins within a family were often visited upon the innocent—even though he'd refused to respond to any of the three letters Ella had sent him since the last time he saw her, at their father's funeral, twenty-six years earlier. A shunning of that length should have released him from blame, but to be safe, he planned to continue it forever.

One of the women in the church heard that Ella had become a nurse—which made no sense for somebody who would kill her own baby—and supposedly she was even a Marine. That didn't make any sense, either, since she was a woman. If it was true, the Marines must have changed. These were strange times. Hard times. But at least time was passing quickly for Patrick, practically in fast-forward, propelled by the predictability of his schedule of work, church, Theresa, and more work. Months, even years, were flying by on the wings of routine.

To help numb the pain of infertility, Theresa had gone to work. Because she'd been to college, she didn't just clean houses, like the other Followers' wives who worked outside the home, but had a career in Internet technology. She even out-earned Patrick, who was an apprentice carpenter at the Hickmans' construction company. They kept her salary a secret, though, to hide the humiliation. Patrick had done a lot of praying before allowing her to have a career, because it wasn't holding fast to tradition, but he loved Theresa too much to deny her a refuge from grief. Her job, thank God, hadn't changed her willingness to defer to his authority.

Just before Halloween, Theresa went to the home birth of one of the Pedracinis. She was thinking about becoming a midwife, so she could at least help her friends have babies. That wouldn't interfere with her job, because midwifery was just a part-time thing for Followers women, requiring no training.

But Theresa came home from the birth that night in tears. The baby had died, even though they'd laid hands on him, and prayed with fierce conviction. Follower babies had died before, but never in the presence of Patrick or Theresa, and the immediacy of the experience was shattering for both of them. It became even worse when the police investigated the death, and spoke to Theresa. No charges were ever made, but it was humiliating and frightening.

The death had obviously happened for a reason, Patrick thought, but he could not divine it. The Pedracini baby was born holy, surrounded by God's only chosen people. How could this special baby, of all the babies born that day, have died?

The week of the baby's death, Patrick recalled many years later, was when he began to change. The transition started as mere questioning, an act he had engaged in countless times before, but this time, in the empty vacuum of his own childlessness, his questions led not to further certainty, but to a void he had never before visited, where the prayers of even those born holy were not answered.

Even so, Patrick later came to believe, his doubts—about the Church, but not God—would have waned if the next few years had not been so dark and disturbing. Only a few months after the death of the Pedracini baby, another infant died, Michael Conley.

Three months later, Patrick's friend Brent Worthington lost a baby. Brent's wife, Raylene, delivered the child three months early, and it did not survive. They placed it in a grave in the cemetery, with a headstone marked BABY BOY WORTHINGTON. The Oregon City Police Department investigated that birth, but could find no fault with Brent and Raylene.

A couple of years later, in January of 2003, Tyler Duane Shaw, the younger brother of deceased infant Valerie Shaw, died shortly before his second birthday. The Clackamas County Sheriff's Department investigated, but no charges were filed. Eight months after that, another baby died during childbirth, Baby Girl Hansen.

Then, at last, two years passed with no deaths of children in the church. But on February 16, 2006, Julia Lynn Hickman died shortly after birth. The Clackamas County Sheriff's Department and the Oregon City Police Department both investigated that death, and practically everybody in the church was shocked at what they thought was blatant persecution. No charges were filed.

KATU investigator Dan Tilkin, who'd taken over the Followers beat in 2000 when Mark Hass was elected to the Oregon House of Representatives, called the medical examiner and the DA every few months to see if there were any suspicious deaths. "But the answer was always no," Tilkin later said. It looked like the Followers were finally doing the right thing.

But Patrick was beginning to wonder. After all these deaths, he struggled to keep doubt out of his mind. He lived among the most blessed of all the people on earth. And yet death and suffering surrounded them.

He conducted himself piously, without reproach, and prayed for a child of his own. But month after month Theresa did not get pregnant.

It didn't make sense.

He couldn't help it: He felt betrayed.

PART TWO

The Book of Judas

Jesus asked Judas what the priests of the church were like, and Judas said, "Some sacrifice their children, and others their wives, in praise and humility with each other."

—THE GNOSTIC GOSPEL OF JUDAS

6

BETRAYED WITH A KISS

And Jesus said to Judas, "Come, that I may teach you about secrets that no person has ever seen. . . . The star that leads the way is your star."

—The gnostic Gospel of Judas

Easter Sunday
The Followers of Christ Church
April 8, 2007

When the pianist said the final hymn would be "Saved by Grace," Patrick Robbins couldn't help but shudder. He saw that a lot of other people felt awkward, too. The song had a reference to baptism! Nobody here needed *baptism*. They were all *born* holy. Not only that, everybody knew that God didn't just *grant* grace. He made you claw for it every day, by holding fast to tradition and taking care of the others born holy.

But Patrick and everybody started singing anyway, because this was the only pianist they had left, with the former one, David Nichols, from one of the great families, on "sabbatical."

Poor David. He'd been persecuted by the police. Not that he was a complete innocent. Not even close. But consider, as the Followers' lawyer liked to say, the facts of the case. Fact number one: David, who was one of their few college grads, was very strong in the Word.

That's all he ever talked about, though it was partly because he wasn't outdoorsy and didn't have a family. But people respected him for being himself, and for following the example of Saint Paul and staying single. Plus, he could really rock some of the hymns, which didn't make the old people very happy, but Patrick thought the church had to change with the times—at least a little bit. Fact number two: David's father was on the verge of being reborn into the kingdom of heaven, because he had cancer, which almost always seemed to be incurable. The Lord had given David's dad some pretty good-size tumors, and he wasn't far away from ascending—though you never knew, with a Follower. Fact number three: There was a *cop* in the poor sick guy's face, as if he didn't have enough on his mind, trying to make him give up his son for some sort of crime. It was an Oregon City Police Department detective named James Band, who seemed to think he was like Bond, James Bond.

The problem was, there'd been a flood at David's store, Melody Maker's Music, and an insurance guy went in and asked, What's behind that door? Turned out, David had this whole spy thing set up, where he could peek at the teenage boys who lived in his apartments upstairs. David had let kids from the Russian Orthodox community south of town stay there in exchange for helping him restore pianos. He had a good business going. He was never the richest person in the church, not by a long shot, but in addition to giving piano lessons to kids, he bought nice pianos—especially from people who didn't know *how* nice they were—and fixed them up. Then he sold them all across the country for $20,000 or $30,000 each, making a huge profit. He delivered them himself and always had one of the boys go with him.

But the insurance guy saw this video system, and also some child porn, and called the police. What David did was bad, of course, but was it really enough reason to ruin the life of someone born holy? The cop came out and saw that David was taping the boys while they were in the shower. There were hours and hours of tapes. Plus there were tapes of David getting into bed with the boys while they were out on the road, and touching them while they were asleep. It looked like there might have been marijuana involved, too, but nobody seemed interested in that.

So the cop wanted to interrogate David, but David was somewhere in Nebraska with a boy, so Band started making threats. He told David's dad that David's black Hummer and white trailer were going to stick out like a sore thumb on the Nebraska freeways, and the Eye in the Sky would nail him. But Band said that if David's dad could get David to put the kid on an airplane, right away, and then drive home himself, they wouldn't arrest him when he got back. Band, James Band, *promised* this.

David's dad complied. Then a few months later there was a grand jury and David did get arrested. Which was completely not the deal. David went to jail. Worse than that, he got shunned. If his sin hadn't been so shocking, the shunning might have lasted less than a year. But it involved a form of homosexuality, which was practically unforgivable.

So for a while David's dad tried to freak Band out by following him around, and doing things like standing outside Starbucks, in the rain, soaking wet, with the big tumors in his belly hurting like heck, watching Band drink his coffee, just to let the cop know what he'd done.

Then David's father died. It seemed like part of the reason he died was because of the harassment. Even so, everybody in the church thought he had a nice funeral. David's aunt made her famous date pudding.

All that persecution was completely unnecessary, though, because the church would have straightened David out on its own, just like they did with the kids who took stuff from the W. B. Market, which Walter White had owned.

And it wasn't like David had been mixed up with prostitutes and strip clubs, or robbing gas stations, like some people Patrick knew.

But the more Patrick thought about David the less sympathy he had for him. Little *foreign* boys, who couldn't protect themselves? David was from such a good family—born holy—but he went out and behaved like a *worldly* person. Even worse: like a worldly *pervert*.

The songs went on and on and everybody sang along. Patrick liked
to sing—people said he should start a choir—but he wished they had
a preacher, somebody who'd talk about right and wrong, like Walter
had before he'd ascended in 1969. Walter had prophesied '69 was going to be the end of the world, and even though it turned out to be
just the end of him, he obviously did know that something was up.

In the middle of the next-to-last song, Patrick happened to notice
that Bill's wife, Liz, just to his left, had what looked like a tiny, dew-
drop tear sliding slowly down her cheek. She caught him looking and
tried to smile, but couldn't pull it off.

After the service, all the women stayed inside with the kids and
gossiped, as usual, while the teenage boys made themselves scarce as
fast as possible and smoked their Camels out back, where the Prophet
had. Patrick didn't approve of smoking, but at least the boys were
holding fast to tradition. The men went out to the parking lot in front
to smoke, and talked mostly about the spring Chinook-salmon season. Everybody said it was strong that year. A school of about 50,000
of them had returned, mostly from the ocean, swimming upstream
until they hit the dead-end of Willamette Falls—right downtown,
by the courthouse, where you could fish off the sidewalk, over the
fence—and about 5,000 more of the silver monsters were working
their way up the Clackamas River, which was running high from the
spring melt but was still so clear you could see the fish.

The men, as usual, were all happy-go-lucky on the surface, but
some of them acted stressed out. Patrick's one worldly friend at work
said that everybody knew that the Followers had all gone nuts from
not enough sex, drugs, and rock 'n' roll. Sometimes he called it the
Hawaiian Disease: Lackanookie. It was a dirty joke, but Patrick
didn't judge the guy, even though he was from the world. He was a
character, but he actually knew the Bible. Better than some of these
guys.

When the guys started talking about going to their salmon hole in
the Clackamas if the rain held off, Patrick took Bill aside.

"Liz okay?" he asked.

Liz, Bill said, was absolutely not okay. For months, he told Patrick, she'd been absolutely out of her mind with depression, and three days ago when Bill had been driving down Molalla Avenue she'd grabbed the steering wheel and had smashed them into a tree, totaling the car. The only thing she said she was sorry about was that she hadn't aimed for traffic on her side, to kill herself and spare him.

"Dude," Patrick said, "she needs counseling. And medication."

Bill looked shocked.

"My mom had depression," Patrick said softly. He remembered the years of nightly weeping and extra beatings. She finally did break down and get antidepressants, which she said weren't really medicine because all they did was improve your mood. Then she mellowed out a lot, especially in the last couple of years before she died.

Patrick told Bill that antidepressants really helped and were more like vitamins than medicine. Bill said he'd think about it, and sounded serious. When the guys started breaking into family groups for Easter brunch, Patrick kissed Bill good-bye, but he got a funny feeling when he did it. They just weren't connecting. He couldn't tell if it was him, or Bill, or both of them. Bill left with a couple of the Smith families, the ones who loved to talk smack about everybody.

Patrick went inside and found Theresa. Even though they'd been married for almost sixteen years, he was still excited to see her. She was so sweet and prettier than ever. There were a lot of good-looking people in the church, partly due to clean living, but Patrick and Theresa were still considered one of the church's most attractive couples, both just past forty but looking thirty, and both tall and thin. His strong, rugged features had matured, and his eyes, even in blurry family photos, were already beginning to look soulful and troubled, as if they held too many secrets. Patrick and Theresa *still* hadn't been able to have kids, which was frustrating, but it did give them a lot of time together and he never got tired of it. He called her from work a lot, and was even secretly proud that she'd gotten her high-tech job.

As he and Theresa pulled out of the parking lot onto Molalla, they saw Chuck, one of their friends from the church, chugging down the street on a bicycle. Chuck, in his 60s, had a little diabetes, like so many of the old people in the church who loved that good Followers' home cooking. Patrick and Theresa waved, but he didn't see them. His face was red and still too fat, even after months of working out, and his eyes were fixed.

"Looks like he's riding for his *life*," Patrick said.

"Good for him," Theresa said.

"I guess." Theresa still didn't get how messed up it was to face death without a whole lot of options, like his mom and dad had. When his dad died, Patrick was too young to do much more than feel hurt, but when his mom died just after he graduated from high school, he changed a little. Seeing her suffer made him wonder why holy people couldn't at least use painkillers, especially since it was okay to use antidepressants, at least in his family, and to go to the dentist and eye doctor. Maybe her cancer could even have been cured with that operation where they just take out a little lump—a lumpectomy, they called it—which was almost like no operation at all.

Within days, word of Patrick's advice to Bill got out—which was odd, since the only person he'd talked to was Bill himself. Liz had a big mouth, though, and was obviously unglued. It was probably her who'd turned Judas on him. Bill was more trustworthy, partly because he was a man. That might sound sexist to some people, but the Bible said it was true.

Suddenly Patrick was getting the cold shoulder from a lot of people, and Theresa wasn't invited to a couple of things. One little teenage hothead, one of the half-bright Hickman boys, got right in his face and blamed *him* for Liz's depression, because of his lack of faith. The kid was cruel, though—he liked to kill geese just to watch them die, and had gotten in trouble for that with the police.

To cool things off, Patrick had to go to Brent Worthington—the future Prophet, many people said. By this time, though, 28 years after Walter White's death, nobody really knew what a Prophet *did*, or what kind of special link to God he had. It was mostly a matter of opinion. Often as not these days, people generally thought that the

future Prophet—if there ever was one—would just be somebody with a lot of popularity and power, like someone from the inner circle. Those in-crowd people didn't hold any special spiritual position, but they made good money and lived lives that revolved around the church. The Prophet would be their preacher, but almost certainly wouldn't have the same status as Walter, who was considered by some to be a god.

Brent was just a painter, but people listened to him because he was strict, nice, and totally dedicated to the church. He had a rugged, chiseled face with dark eyes, and was quietly charismatic. And Brent also had lost a child, which added immensely to his stature.

Brent's first name was Carl, but everybody called him by his middle name because his first name was the same as his father's—a Follower tradition, just like The Church of the First Born. In Brent's case, the custom had at least spared him from having the unfortunate name of Carl Jr.—hardly ideal for a Prophet—but generally it just caused confusion, because there were too many people with the same names. When the girls married their second or third cousins and had the same last name as their maiden name, it got even harder to keep things straight.

But the birthright of a name—the direct link to one's holy ancestors—was sacred. It was the only reason there were so many kids in the cemetery whose first name was just Baby. It didn't make sense to use up a firstborn-name on a child who was already dead. That's why Brent's son in the cemetery was Baby Boy Worthington. Patrick figured that would probably sound cold to worldly people, but you couldn't expect them to understand the power of tradition and *true* family.

Brent spread the word that Patrick had meant no harm, and smoothed things over. Patrick was relieved, but it meant he owed Brent one, and Brent was a bad person to owe. He took his role as a leader of the church seriously, and wouldn't hesitate to make demands on someone who owed him a favor.

Liz, of course, did not go to a doctor. Before there was even a chance of that, some of the inner-circle guys packed up Bill's belongings and took him and his two kids to a new house, where they'd be safe. They put Liz under constant guard—sort of a citizen's house arrest—so she could cast out her demon.

They held Liz for months, sometimes driving her by her kids' playground at recess, so that she'd see what she could have when she got rid of her devil. That didn't motivate her, though, and she stopped eating. They had to lay her on the floor a couple of times every day and have two men sit on her while another forced food into her mouth. It was harsh, but the guys meant well, and weren't remotely open to the idea of antidepressants. They also did an exorcism, holding Liz down and praying fervently for God to remove Satan from her heart. They were trying to copy Jesus' first miracle, when he'd driven a demon out of a madman, although they were a little more aggressive, and bruised her up some. But Liz, like a modern-day witch, seemed to like her devil, and sabotaged the healing with lack of faith.

One day they left her alone for a minute and she ran. They said she was almost to the street when one of the biggest men got her from behind, clamped his hand over her mouth to keep her from making a scene, and dragged her back inside. Patrick told Theresa about it, but she didn't believe the guys would really do that. So Theresa went to Liz's house, and Liz said it was true. Liz told Theresa that the hand in her face was so big that it looked like the hand of God, and Theresa said that in a way, it was. Liz said she was trying hard to believe that.

About a month later, the same thing happened again: the run, the pursuit, and the hand over her mouth. Patrick thought it was gross. He knew that once in a while that kind of rough-stuff happened to people who had a devil, but it shouldn't happen to a woman. He went to see Bill, but Bill pooh-poohed the whole thing.

Patrick wanted to believe it was for the best, but it bothered him. He knew Liz couldn't heal by turning her back on God, but hadn't God created antidepressants?

Thoughts like that made Patrick worry that he had a devil himself. If he'd kept his mouth shut, none of this would have happened.

He thought about reporting Liz's house arrest. It was illegal, even if it was for her own good. But that just made him feel like a Judas. There was a funny thing about Judas, though. Patrick had read the Gospel of Judas, a book from the nontraditional Gnostic branch of the early Church, which said Jesus had become divine not through birth but by his own mastery of the mysteries of the universe. The book said that Jesus had *asked* Judas to betray him, to make sure the crucifixion happened. Only his execution, Jesus told Judas, would show his absolute commitment to goodness, and capture the imagination of mankind.

Obviously, the Gospel of Judas hadn't gotten into the King James Version of the Bible that the Followers read. But the book made sense on one level. How could one of Jesus' best friends betray him, if there wasn't a greater goal behind it?

Stranger things had happened.

CLACKAMAS COUNTY JAIL
OREGON CITY, OREGON
JULY 1, 2007

As soon as Detective James Band stepped inside the secured area of County, his ears were assaulted by the usual Clackatraz ruckus. One belligerent drunk was acting like Charles Manson in the holding tank, mixing New Age threats with old-con epithets in a largely indecipherable word-salad.

At one point, he became coherent: "I want a blank-et!" the guy screamed.

"What's up with him?" Band asked.

"He wants his blanky," said the booking officer.

"And his bottle," another jailer said.

Band felt for the corrections officers. He was hardwired for empathy, and had a special affinity for these cops. Corrections was the low-rent neighborhood of law enforcement, and offered none of the adrenal rush that made the job fun. The big problem with the crime-and-punishment equation, many cops thought, was that punishment often created more problems than it solved, which was very demoralizing. If somebody could ever find a way to make punishment a dependable deterrent, even for one subset of lawbreakers, it would be a happy day for criminal justice.

"I think we should comply with the blanket request," said one of the COs, sick of the racket. In the old days, they might have just hosed the man down, but County had gentrified. It was still The Traz, though: joyless, cold, and claustrophobic.

Band began to remove the handcuffs from the perpetrator he'd brought in. He didn't work patrol now that he was a sergeant, but he'd helped a uniformed officer with a messy call-out.

His cell phone vibrated. He said, "This is Band, hold please."

Band finished uncuffing his white-whiskered perp, who smelled like whiskey, sweat, and cat pee. He'd just busted the guy in a Domestic for throwing hot coffee on his girlfriend's twelve-year-old daughter, who was freaked but seemed okay.

Band was a team leader in the Clackamas County Major Crimes Unit, an interdepartmental agency that focused on violent crime. It sounded glamorous to civilians, but 80 percent of his caseload was child abuse and domestic violence. For a lot of people in paradoxical O.C., the most dangerous place to be was home. Clackalackie wasn't Portlandia. There were just too many angry, hungry, broken families who lived too close to the town's few rich people, and it made for an edgy atmosphere. It was especially hard on the kids, who saw one kind of life but lived another.

The domestic work was a good fit for Band's skill set, though, because he had a bachelor's degree in childhood development, and was regarded by his bosses as the best in the OCPD at getting abused kids to talk, and juvenile offenders to listen. He was innately pleasant, and into touchy-feely community policing, but he could be all-cop in a hurry. Tall, taut with muscle, and steel-tough, with hair cropped close to his skull, he looked like Mr. Clean, always smiling, but without the earring.

Band was naturally adept at bridging polar opposites, having grown up as a clean-cut neo-hipster on a sleepy Montana cattle ranch in the wild 1970s, just outside Missoula, which was half-college-town and half-cow-town. He'd gotten equal parts of hard labor and pure family love during the vast extremes of snowstorms and scalding sun, as he'd lived the cowboy life and dreamed of becoming a cop. That dream became real when he graduated from Warner Pacific College in Portland, and became a policeman in nearby Mt. Angel, in quiet tulip-farm country, where riotous colors stretched to the horizons every spring. His next professional stop was Oregon City, where he started as a patrolman and advanced quickly.

Band signed the paperwork and said, "My arrestee has been nothing but a gentleman to me"—not exactly true—"so please take good care of him." He gave the jailers a friendly smile and left.

Outside, he punched his hold-button and said, "This is Jim Band. Still there? Sorry. Thanks for holding."

Words rushed out. "I need to report a crime, but I can't tell you my name. This is really important. They put me through to you, but . . ." The caller was breathing hard.

"Slow down. You're doing fine."

To the man on the other end of the line, it seemed as if Band were smiling. He took a breath.

"This guy just got his finger bit off."

"Where? Is he getting medical attention?"

"Medical attention? I doubt that. Very much. I'm not sure where it happened. Wherever it was, he'll be gone now."

"If you don't know where, how do you know this happened?"

"I got a phone call. A lot of people know it happened."

"So it's been reported?"

"No. Just by me. Now."

"Does *anyone* know where the victim is?"

"He's not the victim. The lady who bit off his finger is the victim."

"*Who* is?"

"This lady. She has depression. She needs help. But they won't let her out. They've been holding her."

Band, by this time back in his squad car, sighed. He loved O.C., but it was such a strange jurisdiction. On one hand, it was the epitome of the ugly, unemployed American West, and on the other, it was paradise. The rivers and creeks that ran through it on their way to the Willamette sparkled like melted jewels, rippling with rainbow trout, and the woodlands no more than five miles outside of town were full of bull elk, wild turkeys, and ten-point black-tail bucks.

"We need to meet," Band said. He looked at his watch. His shift had theoretically ended an hour ago, at 5:00 p.m. "Where are you now?"

"Someone's coming."

The line went dead.

OREGON CITY POLICE DEPARTMENT
320 WARNER-MILNE ROAD
JULY 2, 2007

The next morning, Band was still struggling to make sense of the call. His gut said it wasn't a prank, despite all the melodrama. He redialed the number but no one answered and there was no voicemail. He checked the local hospital and clinics, but no patient fit the description. Then, as he re-created the call in his mind, he remembered that the informant had said something like: "Medical treatment? I don't think so. No way."

"Oh my God," he said out loud. "The *church*."

Over the past month, he'd gotten a couple of vague, anonymous reports that two Followers kids needed medical care. He'd handed the tips over to children's services, and that was the last he'd heard. Which was good. It probably meant the kids were okay. But this was different.

Using his skills as the region's up-and-coming major-crimes investigator, Band searched some law-enforcement and government sites that even most cops didn't know about, and called a couple of contacts that *nobody* knew about. By late morning he found the woman with depression—who *was* a church member—living in the home of a friend, in the company of two men that she described as family. Neither of them had a wounded finger.

At first she seemed terrified and wouldn't even talk, other than to deny that she'd bitten someone's finger. Neither of the men would talk, either. But he got rid of the guys and gradually put her at ease. He told her that she sounded very depressed, as if it were somehow obvious.

"Would you be interested in getting evaluated at a hospital?" he asked. "You could talk to somebody. Might help. Couldn't hurt."

She was quiet for over a minute, as Band resisted the urge to fill the awkward silence.

"Can you take me? Right now? Without my husband's permission?"

"You don't need anybody's permission," he said gently.

Band helped her get admitted to Portland's Adventist Hospital, under a condition called Police Officer Hold, which meant that she could decline family visitation, on the grounds that she was a threat to herself and others.

Then Band drove back to O.C. to huddle with the new chief deputy district attorney, Greg Horner. Horner was perfect for this kind of problem, because he was tough, super-smart, and had worked every kind of crime at his prior job in downtown Portland: murder, rape, theft, property, drug, white-collar—whatever the cops hauled in. He was left-brained, to say the least, and made Tough Terry Gustafson look about as scary as The Little Mermaid. Horner had dedicated his life to putting away bad guys, and had never gone over to "the dark side," which was what the DAs called defense attorneys.

Horner knew the Followers chapter-and-verse, and hated the idea of tangling with them. They were tighter than the local Russian Mafia that sold stolen goods online, and even less friendly.

Horner was second-in-command to Clackamas County DA John Foote, who had also been Horner's boss in Portland's Multnomah County, where Horner ran the Unit D violent crimes section, dreaded by perpetrators not only because of Horner's mesmeric power over jurors, but also his penchant for pursuing every lesser crime that was attached to a major felony—an unusual approach among DAs, who usually overlooked secondary crimes, such as theft, if they occurred during a murder. If a murderer that Horner was prosecuting had jay-walked away from the murder scene, though, Horner might nail him for that, too, on the apparent principle that a sentence of life-plus-a-week was better than just plain life.

Foote had brought Horner over when he was elected district at-torney in 2001, and now Horner helped run an office of about thirty DAs. Horner and Foote had met with five church delegates in 2004 to discuss, among other things, the importance of not tampering with evidence at a crime scene, and calling the medical examiner every time a child died. The meeting, Horner later said, had been "very amicable, and they were cooperative."

Hopefully, the Followers would still cooperate. Horner and Band sent investigators out that same day to see if Liz's presumed abuse, which she refused to talk about, was part of a pattern.

Nobody had any luck. The church was incredibly well insulated from any outsiders. Fortunately, though, there didn't seem to be any sick children. The ones they saw looked even healthier and happier than most kids. But Band had learned long ago not to take things at face value. He genuinely liked people, but didn't trust them. Horner never even considered the idea.

The Fourth of July was coming up, and Band and Horner wanted to spend it with their kids. Band had two that he was crazy about, and Horner was a devout Soccer Dad, a role in which he adopted a com-pletely different identity: relaxed, nurturing, charming, and witty. In fact, when two of Horner's friends—one from soccer and one from work—once discovered that they both knew him, it took almost ten minutes for them to decide that they were both talking about the same Greg Horner.

Despite Horner's ability to compartmentalize, though, he, like Band, never completely erased work from his mind. All weekend, as the DA and the cop played the role of family-guy, their kids kept reminding them of the Followers' kids.

They kept thinking, Who *are* these people? Why would they kidnap a mentally ill woman? Have kids died that we don't *know* about?

Are they *monsters*?

7

THE GETAWAY

Sometimes I live in the country
Sometimes I live in town
Sometimes I get a great notion
To jump in the river and drown.
—"Goodnight, Irene," traditional folk song,

from *Sometimes a Great Notion*, by Ken Kesey

Honeyman State Park
Florence, Oregon
July 5, 2007

When Neil Beagley was the first to fly over the ridge of the massive sand dune in his souped-up ATV, his grin was so bright that Patrick could see it from almost a quarter of a mile away. Neil's father, Jeff, watching with Patrick, bellowed praise. Neil looked like a kid who was experiencing one of the happiest moments in his life, and that automatically made it one of the happiest in his father's, too. They were tied by a bond so tight that it was a legend in the church. Their connection wasn't just an honor-thy-father thing, but a fully shared life. They had the rarest kind of father-son relationship: best friends.

Neil rocketed down the slope and looked back to see his nearest competitor fall farther behind as he crossed a makeshift finish line.

Second place went to one of the Hickman kids. There were so many of them, and just one Neil, but they always sucked his dust.

Rebel yells of male pride carried over the dunes, with Jeff leading the cheers, and Hickman patriarch, Phil, coming in second, as usual. Not that they competed. That would test the group's trust.

Patrick gave Jeff a heartfelt clap on the back. "How'd an old dude like you get such a great kid?" he said to his lifelong friend.

"Just lucky." Jeff never committed the sin of pride, which wasn't so easy, with a kid like Neil.

Patrick felt a joyful surge of unbridled camaraderie, as strong as the feeling he'd had as a kid hanging out behind the church with these same guys. His friends really were Godly men and good dudes, and had always been more like brothers than buddies. They worshipped and socialized only with one another, and most of them worked in a cluster of family businesses, like Hal's Construction and Excel Finishing, at rugged, good-paying jobs.

Patrick had felt doubt lately, and had done something he thought he'd never do. But here, now, with his brothers under God, he was certain all that nonsense was over. He'd heard that Liz was finally getting help, though it had been phrased as, "Bill's wife got kidnapped by that Band-James-Band cop." So his work was done.

Across the dunes, Neil waved at them, and Jeff saluted in return. Neil drove back up the dune to do some sand-surfing, and teach the little kids how to sand-sled.

"How come you never had kids?" Jeff asked Patrick.

"It'll happen, in God's time." Patrick had, in fact, recently asked Theresa to consider infertility treatment, but after the look she gave him he dropped the subject.

Patrick's ringtone played "Ode to Joy" and he put his phone to his ear. "Hello."

"Hi, my name is Jim Band. I'm with the Oregon City Police Department." Patrick jammed the phone against his cheek to muffle it. "I got a call from this phone just before the Fourth."

Patrick tried to keep from freaking. He'd told Theresa yesterday to get a new number, but she obviously hadn't yet. Strange. She was usually so obedient. Was she changing?

"I'm not sure what you're talking about," Patrick said.

"It was about a woman with mental health issues?"

"Um, that wasn't me. I think you've got the wrong number."

"Are you the only person who uses this . . . ." Patrick clicked it off.

"Wrong number?" asked Jeff.

"Yeah." But Jeff's eyes stayed on him. Patrick told himself he was just being paranoid. Fear always came with lack of faith, and now his doubt was coming back to haunt him. No more Judas games. He had *everything* to lose. Nothing to gain. He tried to keep the fear out of his eyes.

Patrick stared across the dunes and remembered the time Jeff had given him his first Holy Greeting, at his father's funeral. That reminded him of the first time he saw Jeff and Marci together, at the 1990 New Year's Eve party. He loved Jeff. But now Jeff felt like a stranger sometimes.

"So who jazzed up Neil's four-wheeler?" he asked Jeff.

"Guess." Jeff meant, of course, that he and Neil had done it together, working side-by-side, as always.

In the evening everybody circled around the campfire and inhaled briny ocean air and occasional puffs of cedar-smoke as salmon—some of it from the day's catch, some from the freezer—browned in butter in big black skillets. Women in jeans and denim jackets finished making a few of their most common campground side-dishes: garlic-bread in foil, twice-baked potatoes, fried chicken, venison kabobs, and corn on the cob from their gardens, as blackberry pies baked in a motor-home oven. Jeff's wife Marci, deep-frying heavily breaded chicken in a Dutch oven, said, "I miss Ellen's chicken already."

"It was the best," said one of the Cunningham women. Ellen had died the day before, at age 52, much sooner than anybody had anticipated, before she could even pass on her recipes.

Marci's daughter Katie, a couple of years younger than her brother Neil, whispered something into Marci's ear, and Marci put her hand on the girl's forehead. "You're fine," Marci said. Katie sat down at the picnic table, watching but not helping much.

One of the Hickman boys—or one of their look-alike cousins—was skinning a rabbit he'd shot. He cut a slit in one of its legs and tugged at the Achilles tendon, making the paw wave hello to a group of girls.

"*Issues!*" cried one of the girls, but the others just said "E-U" and giggled.

The Milky Way, a rare sight on the Oregon coast, was starting to color a wide stripe on a sky so bright it was blue even at night.

"God's country," sighed one of the Wylands, in a Portland Trail Blazers cap. He reached over and touched his wife's pregnant belly. "I can feel him."

"Her," said his wife. It was a joke, of course, since they hadn't done an ultrasound. But she still got a sideways glance from her husband for contradicting him in public, even in humor, so she added, "It's just heaven on *earth,* is what it is."

Then a little girl tried to take a fledgling step, right next to the fire. She pitched forward, went down on one knee, and headed face-first into the flames. Her mother, on the other side of an ice chest, froze.

Phil Hickman's hand came out of nowhere and stopped her fall. Phil—prominent and powerful, short but big-shouldered—picked the toddler up as her mother rushed over and gathered her girl in her arms, giving Phil a grateful look. "God's *will!*" she chirped.

"Good catch is more like it," Patrick said, regretting his sarcasm even before he saw the glares from the Hickmans, who preferred to see their patriarch as an instrument of God.

"Yeah," said Patrick's friend Rod Lincoln, grinning at the girl. "You're in good hands."

"With Allstate," Patrick said. Lord! He just couldn't keep his mouth shut.

Only Rod laughed. Was Rod starting to have doubts, too?

Patrick knew he had to get his mind right, and he thought he could, because the plain truth was that he loved these people, and he knew that where the heart goes, the head usually follows. With any luck, he thought, his act of rebellion over Liz would be his last.

A baby in a papoose-backpack coughed, and it sounded a little too phlegmy. "Want that little snot-getter suction thing?" asked one of the grandmas.

"No, Ava's fine," said her mother, Raylene Worthington. Raylene, a dark haired beauty, was married to Brent. "She's just stuffy from the smoke." Ava had a touchy system and got congested a lot. Brent and Raylene thought God might be giving her allergies. Something was always blooming in Oregon, and it made people feel sick without knowing why. But God knew why, so it didn't matter. Of course, if you were one of the worldly, you ran off to a doctor the first time you sneezed because the worldly thought the great white dopes could cure anything. Raylene knew better. She cooed to Ava and the cough calmed. But the baby looked befuddled as her chest kept rattling. Tears formed.

Raylene said, "Kissee?" She bent forward and anointed her daughter's lips with her own. Ava's face changed and she snuggled into her mother's chest. "Works every time," Raylene said. Raylene's mom Marci and Brent's mom Julie beamed at her. Raylene *deserved* to have landed Brent. She was such a sweet girl.

Jeff Beagley, who was in charge of the salmon, asked if anyone had seen Neil. Jeff was pushing fifty now and getting pudgy and slack-skinned, with fleshy bags under his eyes that drooped like tears. Patrick told Jeff that Neil was taking a shower. Jeff glanced down the asphalt campground road at the communal bathrooms, and held his gaze there as he jiggled the skillets. Jeff was protective—some said overly. Wouldn't let his boy grow up. But Neil didn't mind because he knew his dad's rules came from love.

After a while Jeff started piling cherry-red Chinook salmon onto paper plates, along with some skewers of venison with grilled cherry tomatoes and red peppers, but he set aside the biggest fish, one Neil had caught, for his son.

As the smell of caramelizing blackberries spread, the happiness of the whole group was palpable, and everything was funny to everybody. "A blonde, a brunette, and a redhead are on a desert island," said Brent Worthington, roasting a marshmallow, "and a genie comes and gives each girl one wish. The brunette says: 'I wanna go back home to my *mom and dad.*' Poof! She's gone. The redhead says, 'I wanna go back home to my *boyfriend.*' Poof, no more redhead! Genie's all, 'Okay, blondie, whatta you want?' And the blonde goes: 'I just wish my *friends* were back!'" The blondes laughed hardest. There were a lot of them, many related.

Patrick's wife Theresa—with long chestnut-brown hair, dimples, and a cute-smart look—said, "Three blondes are in an airplane. It crashes. Everybody dies. Who benefits?"

She took a beat as everybody waited for the punch-line. Then she did a Marilyn Monroe pout, and made her eyes go blank as she twirled a strand of chestnut hair and corkscrewed a finger into her dimple. "I forgettt," she said.

Everybody laughed but Brent, who stepped on her punch-line and said, "Society!" He got an even bigger laugh and everybody pretended he'd gotten her joke.

As cool evening air began to blow in, their joviality redoubled and dominated the campground's H-Loop, a coveted site with direct access to forty miles of the largest sand dunes in North America, the very ones that had inspired Frank Herbert to write *Dune*. The group's size alone set it off, and stood as a status symbol in the campground. In Oregon, any place that's more than about thirty miles from the trendy Pearl District of downtown Portlandia or the University of Oregon campus in granola-fed Eugene is all about family, and for the most part, bigger is considered better. At the state campgrounds, large family gatherings got special preferences, such as the better campsites.

Honeyman State Park was one of the Followers' favorite getaways, because of the world-class off-roading and the Pacific so close that the parents could stand on the ridges and watch their kids ride horses on the beach below. The kids liked Honeyman even better than the

Oregon Caves down in Sasquatch country, where they did their Squatch calls at night and rafted the whitewater of the Rogue River. Nearby was Crater Lake, the world's clearest, with vast fields of wildflowers, and Waldo Lake, the second clearest, where the kids could see the shadows of their canoes a hundred feet below. The fishing was best about an hour north, though, in Clear Lake, which had a forest on its floor that was preserved in ice water.

Usually, the Followers stayed close to home, in the Columbia Gorge—more beautiful than the Grand Canyon—where they sledded off sandbar cliffs, fished for thousand-pound sturgeon, and watched sea lions shoot out of the water with giant salmon in their jaws.

The best getaway of all, though, was the hot, flat stretch just over the Cascades, where they rented houseboats, water-skiied, jet-skiied, and rode their dirt bikes into the desert to hunt for rattlesnakes, pick them up and say, "In Jesus' name, Devil be gone," just like in the old days.

The Followers couldn't understand why so many people stayed in the crowded Oregon lowlands, away from the adventures that made the state magical. It was just one more weakness of the worldly.

As the campfire started shooting sparks, Marci leaned back in her lawn chair and checked out the shining summer moon. She was close to the fire, a privileged position for the church's inner circle, the people that God had chosen to bless with the most money and popularity. There wasn't even supposed to be an inner circle—everybody was supposed to be equal—but there were a lot of things going on that weren't supposed to be.

Marci, now in her mid-forties, was blond, plump, and feisty—maybe a little too feisty, some thought, for a woman. "Anybody seen The Crown Prince?" she asked. She meant Neil, who even at age fifteen held a special status in the group. She wasn't shy about using his regal nickname around the parents of the other kids, because everybody thought it fit. Neil already did the Beagleys' bookkeeping, and ran his father's successful port-a-potty company when Jeff was out of town. When Jeff was gone and called home, he'd have two conversations, one with the whole family, followed by a business conference with Neil. Neil was the only one who knew the combination to his family's safe, and when he worked at building sites with the men, he did one of the technical jobs instead of menial labor, like the other boys.

About the only thing Neil wasn't allowed to do was drive a truck, which he thought was silly, because he already operated four categories of heavy equipment, including a 17,000-pound, 21-foot trackhoe that he could legally operate on private property. Even though it would be four months until he turned sixteen and could drive by himself, he'd already decided on the first ride he'd buy: a '69 Camaro, the only muscle car that was up to his standards. Jeff had told Neil he'd have to pay for it and repair it himself, but that didn't faze Neil. He was short and slight for his age and seemed to get sick a lot, but he was tough as rawhide and had more money in the bank than some of the married men. He'd just finished clearing some stumps and brush off his family's new acreage, to prepare a spot for their dream house, so they could move out of the wagon-train of motor homes they lived in now, and for him that was just a little after-school chore.

Jeff told Marci that the Crown Prince was still in the showers. His eyes darted down the road every minute or two.

"Long shower," said Marci. Nobody replied. Neil was known for long stays in the bathroom. There was a rumor—there were *always* rumors—that he had Crohn's disease, or an ulcer. The Internet said that both conditions could cause bathroom problems. Most of the Followers used the Net a lot, because it was a good way to get medical information without going to a doctor. But they feared it, too, because it could put ideas into kids' heads.

Neil was never a worry, though. Jeff and Marci's only real concern was their daughter Katie, who ended up in people's prayers a lot. Katie had one kidney infection after another. She'd get feverish and start to have back pain, but then they'd give her gallons of cranberry juice, which the Internet said was *better* than medicine, and she'd feel fine in a couple of weeks. But it definitely slowed down her home-schooling.

A few minutes later Neil clip-clopped out of the dark in a cream-colored bathrobe and flip-flops, his lanky brown hair still wet, with his usual impish grin.

"Son," said Jeff Beagley, with more than a touch of grandiosity, as he prepared Neil's plate, "this thing is a whopper. Old as you."

Neil stood tall, practically levitating from the pleasure of his father's approval. Neil didn't gloat, though, which was typical of him. He was humble, and very much in the Word, an out-of-this-world kid, according to almost everybody. When Neil's Grandma Beagley had needed a driveway, he'd shown up with a road grader and had leveled the whole area himself. He'd done it without being asked, and had refused to take any money. When he'd been about ten, his big sister Nicole had found her dream car, an old junker, and he'd loaned her about two years of his family-business earnings to help pay for it, then he'd fixed it up. His only interest on the loan had been a deal with her to keep his room clean.

Neil's dad opened a lawn chair for him near the fire, among the inner circle: the cool people that God had chosen to make not only the most money but the most sacrifices. At the epicenter was Brent Worthington.

Brent had automatically become inner-circle when he'd married Raylene, because she was a Beagley, but he had a gravitas of his own, which had grown when he had bravely fathered Ava earlier that year, while still hurting from the loss of his son. Having kids counted. The only thing that added more luster was putting your faith to the ultimate test, and either winning, as people usually did, or losing, but keeping the faith.

Brent was holding Ava as his wife started cooling the pies. He loved to be seen with his baby. She could melt any heart with her long black hair and her mother's brown doe-eyes. Her symmetrical features were flawless, except for a little bump on her neck, and ears that she hadn't quite grown into yet. Those imperfections were virtually invisible when she smiled, though, because her unguarded smile radiated the warmth of a child who'd never known anything but love.

Brent stirred the fire. He had an air of control and shrewdness, which was good in these troubled times, with the cops apparently interested in them again. His friends said that he could get you to look at his left hand while his right was getting ready to do whatever it wanted.

Everybody knew he'd lead them wisely in the years to come, and that he'd do anything for his brothers and sisters. Need your house painted? Brent's company would do it at cost. Need to move? Brent would show up with some buddies and a truck. Money? Sure. And if you needed to summon the power of God because somebody was sick, you called Brent. Before you knew it, everyone in the church would be lasering their love until you could feel the heat of God's healing.

On the outskirts of the group, Patrick felt a thump against the ground behind him and heard a muffled pop that sounded like a knuckle cracking. Then he heard, "Mommy!" and spun around to see little Galen on his belly in the dust, holding his index finger delicately, with a yellow Nerf ball still in his palm.

Later Patrick would remember, "I was thinking, 'Here we go again. Martyrville. And it's usually some little kid who gets martyred.'"

In an instant all the men were gathered around Galen, including Neil, summoning the tender mercies of the Lord. Galen started getting real fussy but calmed down quickly when Come Back Jack materialized. Jack had been a medic in Vietnam, one of the Church's long line of conscientious objectors. In 'Nam, they'd dropped Come Back Jack in places that nobody else came back from, and that's how he'd gotten his nickname. When they started calling him that, he stayed humble in the Word and didn't tell anybody that there was a *reason* he always survived.

In less than an hour, far less time than an ER trip would have taken, Come Back Jack had iced the finger, settled the cracked bone back into place, and locked it stationery with a cast made of fiberglass bandages and polyurethane from his first aid kit. Everybody thought an ER doc would have just buddy-taped it to the next finger, because that would have been the quick and cheap way—like a thousand dollars "cheap." Plus, the Comeback Kid had done it without exposing Galen to hospital germs, dope, or a shot that could cause autism or God-knows-what.

Galen's mother rocked him in a hammock as he drifted to sleep in the quiet campground, now past its nine o'clock noise curfew. Galen's little sister started to murmur a prayer of comfort to her brother, but her mother put a hand on her shoulder. "Pray in the closet," she said. "The Followers don't cast pearls before swine."

The girl looked puzzled, so her mother offered the standard explanation: "Don't worry about it." It wasn't healthy for kids to stew. "Just give praise," she said, tapping her heart, "in here."

As the moon dipped behind a mountainous dune, a Hickman boy, one of the young troublemakers but still inner-circle, yanked a blazing marshmallow from the fire and started to wave the flame out—too close to some kids, judging by the dirty looks he got. He peeled off the charred skin with his teeth and put the white remains back over the coals. He was a reckless kid who drove his ATV like a maniac, but still couldn't beat Neil, who calculated his risks. Neil looked young but acted old. Some people even thought that *he'd* be the Prophet.

Phil noticed the other parents' disapproval and put his hand on the back of his boy's neck. That was the end of the dirty looks. The boy needed some TLC. He and his buddies had been in on the goose-shooting spree—killing them and throwing them in a creek—and had gotten in trouble when law enforcement had butted in. The Geese Police.

"Doesn't *get* any better than this, does it?" said Brent, and everybody agreed, some a little too loudly for post-curfew. Brent stroked his new goatee and mustache. It was an unorthodox look for a Follower, but framed his handsome face well. The pies were making their last rounds, along with fresh whipped cream to scoop on top, a platter of s'mores, and a pitcher of hot chocolate with melting marshmallows. There was no wine, yet—not in front of the kids.

Theresa came up behind Patrick as he was sitting in a sling-back chair and put her face against his hair, which was now more sandy than red from the summer sun. "You smell good, like a campfire," she said.

Patrick noticed a small, silent group at a next-door campsite, in the world. They had a scraggly fire, some KFC and cheap Rainier beer, and a boom-box with multiple headphones. They glanced over once in a while and looked envious. Not unusual. Who in the world *wouldn't* envy them? It made Patrick feel good. He needed reassurance. He just *knew* he was starting to have a devil.

Patrick went for firewood and Rod Lincoln tagged along. "So, Hot Rod," Patrick said, "who do you think Brent looks like, with that goatee?"

"I know who he'd look like if he had little red horns."

Patrick gave him a fist-bump. He was starting to think Rod might actually have a mind of his own.

"You hear the thing about Neil and Katie?" Rod asked. "Word is, one of the older kids told Neil that Katie's kidneys are fried and she needs a transplant. So Neil told her he was up for it, if God would okay it, and she went *off*. Like, *off* off. Everybody talks about *him*, but she's the tough one."

"Where'd the kids come up with the goofy idea of a transplant?"

"The usual." He meant the Net.

They headed back to the campfire as black-dark settled in and almost all the talking stopped, making the fire louder and its heat and light even more comforting. "Tell a ghost story," one of the Cunningham kids said to Dale Hickman, one of Patrick's best friends.

"The one that ends with the hook in the car door?" Dale said. Patrick thought it was typical of Dale to give away the ending. Dale was young in the mind.

"No, the cowboy ghost."

Dale settled his big frame into a sling-back chair and started telling the flashy version of the Followers' history, a traditional way of letting the little kids know that they were the chosen people. The little Cunningham boy hugged his knees and snuggled closer to the fire. His brother unselfconsciously put his arm around him.

"Once upon a time, way back yonder in the days of cowboys and Indians," Dale said, "there was this soldier, name of Brother McDonald, and he's sittin' in a wagon, all alone, on this real, real scary dark night, readin' Scripture, to stay brave. Then he hears somethin'! Real quiet at first. Then louder! And just then, a ghost! This big, floating, see-through dude comes outta nowhere! Like outer space!" Dale's arms flew outward, indicating infinity, and startling some of the kids, as intended. "And this big . . . scary . . . ghost creeeeeps up to the soldier and points to the Good Book and says, 'I want you to preach that Gospel!' Then, whoosh, he flat-out disappears. Thin air! Well-sir, a big old ghost tells you to do something, whatta you do?"

"You *do* it," a couple of the older kids said.

"Got that right." Dale told how the torch was then passed from Brother McDonald, in the Oklahoma Land Rush, to one of their direct ancestors, Charlie Smith. "Anybody named Smith here?" Dale asked.

The Smith kids beamed. One of them said, "Do the talk-in-tongues, like Great-Uncle Smith!"

"Naw," Dale said, "that'd be blasphemous." Plus, the last time he'd tried to do it, he'd sounded stupid.

"Then another direct ancestor, George Oakely, marries Charlie's sister, and one day George tangles with a bad guy and gets shot! Right through the heart!" Dale said, smacking his chest. "And he dies, a-course! But a bright light shone around him! And he comes straight back to life. For real! It's all written down." Dale was getting worked up. Even the adults were listening. Patrick thought it was too bad a guy like Dale couldn't preach at their services.

"Then Charlie Smith, who's obviously got the gift, he goes to another tongue-talkin' follower of Jesus, John Evans"—Dale pointed at the youngest Evans child—"and he tells John Evans, and these are his exact words, 'Go teach this unfriendly world, and wear a starry crown.' Then Uncle John Evans, he goes and hooks up with another born-holy person. Who knows who that was?"

"Brother John Cunningham," said one of the Cunningham girls.

Dale leaned over and gave the little girl a low-five. Dale was sweet with kids, Patrick thought, and someday he would be a good dad.

"And they all get in a wagon train, with that big white top, like in the movies, and head out West, with Indians and grizzly bears. They do some Indian fightin' on the way, but only cuz they get attacked. They never start nuthin', but they ain't afraid to finish it. And they end up in the cowboy town of Caldwell, Idaho, where there's gold mines, and serpents that they tame out in the desert, and gunslingers. Idaho, though, is plagued with sin, just plagued, but by this time they're being led by the great . . ." Dale paused. "The Prophet."

"Uncle Walter White!" the big kids shouted.

"Uncle Walter White. Is right. God bless. And Walter leads them out of the desert. To Oregon City. The Promised Land." Patrick had heard the story as a kid and still liked it. But he'd heard, as very few others had, terrible things about Walter. His mother had told him in the depths of her depression.

"Walter," said Dale, "knew they were meant to live in Oregon City, cuz he had the gift of prophecy. And it was right there, right at the end of the Oregon Trail, that all the miracles start happening!"

Dale started ticking off the miracles—incredible healings and fortunes that came out of nowhere—but with the cowboy and ghost parts over, he lost most of his audience.

Moms started tucking in their kids in family-size tents with cozy comforters. The kids felt safe and fell asleep fast. Then the women rejoined their husbands around the fire.

As the cold began to come, couples started to head to their tents and campers, the women giving everybody a hug and a peck on the cheek, the men hugging their friends' wives and giving each other the Holy Greeting.

The crowd around the fire thinned until it was just Patrick and the inner circle: the Beagleys, the Hickmans, and the Worthingtons. Nobody said much, but they all seemed to feel luxuriously secure, and reborn by the closeness of nature and one another.

Only Jeff Beagley, Brent Worthington, and Phil Hickman were still around the bonfire when Patrick joined Theresa in their tent. She was already asleep. Just looking at her soft face, unlined by any uncertainty, made him feel as if his destiny had already been fulfilled, and that he needed nothing more. Even with no children, Patrick felt complete with her, because he still adored her with the intensity of young love.

For a time, the crackle of the fire and Theresa's long breaths were all that Patrick could hear as he held her closely. Then he heard a tight, strained voice, too loud for post-curfew. "No! I *don't* think. I *know*. There's a traitor. Somebody who's startin' to call stuff in. And I think I know who it is."

Patrick went cold and could feel his heart beating hard against Theresa. He stared into the dark for so long that he started to see shapes, and felt dizzy and unreal. For all he knew, this could be his last night with his wife. By this time tomorrow she might already have begun to shun him for the rest of his life.

He might not even get the chance to tell her why he had done what he had. But that wouldn't make much difference. Theresa was brilliant, the group's only female college graduate, but he was starting to think that she'd been brainwashed.

At that moment he needed her love desperately, far more than he would ever need the peace of mind that came from doing the right thing. He longed for just a half-awake word from her, or a touch. Even so, he let her sleep. He was very protective.

He would do anything for her, and anything to keep his marriage. *Anything.* And in his fear, he thought he would feel that way forever.

8

THE SNITCH

And Judas cast down the pieces of silver in the temple, and departed and went and hanged himself.
— THE BOOK OF MATTHEW 27:5

OREGON CITY
AUGUST 12, 2007

After church, most of the families broke into sub-clans for a big Followers picnic on the banks of the Columbia, since it was almost the last day of the sturgeon season, but Patrick went to see an older woman who'd been too sick to attend the service. During the morning's announcements—the only time anyone ever talked—the speaker had urged the congregation to remember her in their prayers. That didn't necessarily mean she was dying, but it was definitely a hint to stop by and see her after church, when she'd be expecting people.

Theresa didn't want to go. She said she was sick to her stomach. But Patrick was afraid she was sick of him.

They'd started arguing just after the camp-out about his commitment to the Church. She'd heard rumors that he was talking to the police, and remained suspicious even after he denied it. He was afraid, for the first time in their relationship, that she might be losing her love for him. He couldn't even get her to admit that she was angry, though, but a Followers' wife never would. Too obedient. Most of the men liked that feminine reticence, but not Patrick. He was tired of secrets and lies, and was dying to resolve their differences. Having any argument at all was a big deal for a Followers couple, because if there was a disagreement, the wives almost always gave in. To Patrick, it wasn't some terrible sexist thing, like worldly people would think, but simple obedience to the Bible, which said, "Ye wives, be in subjection to your own husbands." But Patrick knew that the rest of the verse said that husbands had to bend over backward to please their wives. Of course, when push came to shove, it was always the husbands who shoved.

Patrick had always tried to honor Theresa's desire to stay true to Church doctrine, but ever since the dunes camp-out, he'd begun to wonder if he really could. The plain truth was, he was freaked out about all the sick people around him, and was thinking that there had to be a better way than all-prayer-all-the-time. But just mentioning that idea pushed her buttons.

He was almost sure she believed he'd been the Judas that called the cop who'd kidnapped Liz. That rumor had started just after they got back from the coast, when Patrick, in a moment of weakness—or strength—had told Rod Lincoln that he'd called James Band. Rod hadn't seemed surprised, and had promised not to tell anybody, but Patrick was afraid that Rod had told his wife, Lorene—in confidence, of course—but that was how rumors got started. For all Patrick knew, nobody had any evidence at all, but there was no way to know. Once rumors got started, they had a life of their own, and after a while, it hardly mattered if they were true or not. Rumors were rampant, because the church was as much about socializing as it was about religion—though no one ever admitted that—and gossip was a staple. The men thought the women started most of the rumors on the phone tree, and the women thought the men started them at work.

No matter what Patrick said, Theresa still acted suspicious. She wouldn't even have a direct, cards-on-the-table conversation about his presumed betrayal. To her, it was just "it," as in, "I don't want to talk about it." For weeks, they'd studiously ignored the subject of "it," but she made clear that if "it" had really happened, she'd leave him.

Dealing with her doubt was tough, because he not only adored her, but feared her intelligence. Her Internet-tech job at a bank downtown was the best of any woman in the church, since those few who did work either cleaned houses or helped a little at their husband's business, and she had an air of sophistication the other women didn't. So why was she so rigid? What was she so *afraid* of?

The obvious answer, he thought, was hell. Since childhood, both of them had been inundated with legends of the tortures that awaited the damned. One story Patrick always remembered was about somebody getting impaled on a sharp pole, done so carefully that their internal organs were spared, prolonging the pain. Why would someone tell a *child* about that kind of thing?

Patrick's mom had told him many times that he had a lot of common sense, and she didn't necessarily mean it as a compliment. In her opinion, he over-thought things. She'd always say, "Don't worry about it," but he'd been a worrier ever since his dad died.

His twin curse was curiosity. He loved the Net, and lately he'd started searching online for answers to questions like, "How often did Jesus mention hell?" Only nine times, it turned out, all in the Book of Matthew, with a few repetitions of the same stuff in Luke and Mark. The mentions were barely even fire-and-brimstone. They were mainly allegorical references to evil—like in Matthew 16:18, when Jesus said, "Thou art Peter, and upon this rock I will build my church, and the gates of hell shall not prevail against it." And Jesus never threatened anybody with hell for not believing in him. The Church came up with that. It obviously built membership, but it was shaky theology.

Hell's notorious reputation, he found, didn't even come until the Dark Ages, when Dante Alighieri, and later John Milton, invented the version that the Followers believed in: dens of snakes, rivers of excrement, a lake of fire, and a red devil with a pitchfork. Hardly any of that was in the Bible, and none of it was in the Gospel. But when you told it to a five-year-old and repeated it for about thirty years, even a brainiac with a great job in IT could find a way to swallow it.

In fact, Patrick had started reading a blog by a former Follower, Suzanne Shumaker—another smart girl; he remembered her from some party—who now railed against the Church. Even so, she still thought she might go to hell—but for having been a Follower. Once the idea got stuck in your head, it was hard to kick out.

The Net said most religions considered hell to be a fairly ordinary state of misery, or didn't exist at all. The Muslim hell was harsh, but not necessarily eternal, and Judaism didn't claim to know if hell even existed. The Hindus believed in a torturous hell, but one with a chance for redemption, and Buddhists and Sikhs considered hell to just be a scare tactic.

Patrick was actually relieved to see how complicated the whole thing was. It made him feel better about his doubt. But he had to be careful to delete his search history. If Theresa saw the kind of stuff he was looking at, she'd kill him.

When Patrick got to the sick woman's house, only two other Followers were there, and when he walked in, they took off. Bad sign. He offered to make her lunch, but she said her stomach hurt too much for that. He could tell, by the outline of her sweatpants, that she was probably wearing an adult diaper. He'd seen that before. So many of the old people in the church were just falling apart. One woman had such a severely prolapsed uterus that it protruded, forcing her to scoot around like a crab, and mostly stay in her recliner. Another man had recently let himself go blind.

But Patrick worried most about the kids, who were almost as brainwashed as the adults. He thought Katie Beagley, barely a teenager, was fading fast, and there were still rumors that her brother

Neil wanted to donate a kidney to her. But Katie was staying in the Word.

Patrick made some tea for the woman and tiptoed toward the subject of her getting medical attention, but she stopped him cold. In so many words, she said there was no way she was going to risk having this level of pain for *eternity* by losing faith now. So they prayed. Then his phone played the first stanza of "Jesu, Joy of Man's Desiring," the ringtone that meant Theresa was calling.

"Come home," she said. "I found out something." She wouldn't say what. That was a bad sign. Her voice was shaky.

When he got there her face was red with emotion. She had that look she got when she was all prayered-up.

"It *happened*," she said. "I can't believe it." She shook her head as tears glassed her eyes.

"What?" He knew what. But he wasn't going to admit it until he was cornered. He felt like throwing up.

"You know what." The tears in her eyes began to fall onto her face. She looked down and kept shaking her head.

She reached out, and took both of his hands. "Oh Patrick." She placed his palms on her belly. "I just found out. From a test I got at Walgreens. I *knew* there was a reason I was sick." She looked up, luminous, as her tears still fell.

His exhale felt like it lasted forever, and the air he inhaled was intoxicating. "What do we do now?" he asked.

"Well, we don't need a book of baby names." She looked beautiful to him, her dark, straight hair framing her face.

He held her, and they prayed aloud.

"To me," Patrick later said, "that just changed everything. I know it shouldn't have. But it did."

Patrick Robbins dropped his contact with Jim Band entirely. With a heart that was finally light, and a thrill of hope, he began to focus on the future far more than ever before, certain that it would be the most glorious time in his life.

OREGON CITY
FEBRUARY 13, 2008

When Brent Worthington got home, Ava ran to him through a field of Valentine's Day balloons on unsteady toddler's legs, holding on to furniture to keep from falling, her face shining with love. "Dada!" She raised both arms. That meant she wanted him to pick her up and hold her so high that she could touch the ceiling. He did it, as always, until his arms hurt, then put Ava down and hugged her big sister, Corryn, who was four. Corryn was a mama's girl, but Ava cuddled with everybody, especially Brent. He popped some Cheerios into her mouth, and gave her a little heart-shaped candy that said "WILL U B MINE?"

Ava crawled into a big cardboard box that was left over from the installation of a new bathroom sink and played "McDonald's" with Corryn, poking her head through a cut-out window while Corryn pedaled up to the drive-through on her trike and ordered her food. While Raylene made dinner, Brent put Ava into her Johnny Jump-Up, and she bounced while he jumped up and down beside her, in their daily contest to see who could jump the longest. Ava won, as always. Soon she got drowsy and lay down, her head drooping onto her chest. She snored a little. It was cute. Most babies didn't snore.

Ava had first started snoring around Christmas—her first Christmas, a joyous occasion. That was when Raylene's mom, Marci, noticed that Ava had a little lump on her neck. Looked like a cyst. Brent had noticed something like it when Ava was just three or four months old, and it had also popped up a little during the dune's camp-out. It kind of came and went, but most of the time it didn't look like much at all to Brent. The important thing was that it didn't seem to bother Ava. As Ava was learning her words—"mama" and "dada" were first—she'd learned to say "owie," but she never said her neck had an owie.

Brent's mom, Julie, had also noticed it, but wasn't concerned. When one of Julie's daughters had been little, she'd had almost exactly the same thing, and sometimes it would get big when she was sick, but it finally went away forever. Julie figured the neck thing ran in the family, because she'd had one on the right side of her neck, too, around the time she started kindergarten. Back then, Julie's mom wouldn't let her play outside when her neck was swollen, but once when Julie was five and the thing on her neck was puffed out about half an inch she went outside anyway and walked up behind her little brother, who was swinging a plastic baseball bat. He didn't see her and—wham!—he smacked her right in the neck. Fixed the bump right away. Never came back.

Ava ate her usual amount at dinner—Brent thought she was kind of a chowhound—but then she got a little fussy. Raylene thought it was from too much Valentine's candy. Or maybe she was teething. With kids, you never knew what was going to happen. Actually, Raylene thought, you never knew what was going to happen with anybody. That was up to God.

OREGON CITY
FEBRUARY 21, 2008

Julie Worthington wanted to get a picture of Ava and Corryn in their new hula-girl dresses. Julie and her husband, Guy, just back from ten days in Hawaii, had bought their granddaughters Hawaiian dresses and Hawaiian Barbies, and the girls were thrilled. They looked adorable. Julie forgot to bring her camera—unusual, since she was such a doting grandmother—so she used her phone.

The Followers were good with high-tech stuff, mostly because so many of them worked in the building trades, but they knew that the worldly thought they were rubes, like those people back East who still rode wagons.

For the photo, Corryn got in front. Guy picked up Ava, so she could be seen. He cuddled with his granddaughter while he had the chance, because she always ran off to play. Ava let them take turns cuddling her. When it was Julie's turn, she squeezed Ava's legs. They seemed chubby. Ava's tummy also looked fat to Julie, but she wasn't worried about her granddaughter getting overweight, because she could still see Ava's ribs.

Cuddling done, Ava started eating out of a big jar of babyfood, but then a feather from somewhere started floating around the room and Ava chased it. Julie got a picture of that, too. It was cute, like the feather floating around in *Forrest Gump*.

Guy and Julie only stayed about an hour because Ava started getting fussy again. It definitely looked like she was still teething, or catching a cold. Maybe it was the moon, which was full that night, and shining a bright winter-white. The night before there had been a lunar eclipse. Sometimes strange things happened under the grand influence of the heavens. But this night was pretty ordinary, and there was nothing better than that.

OREGON CITY
FEBRUARY 24, 2008

The mood at Brent and Raylene's Sunday-night pizza party was a little more restrained than usual, because the real estate industry had suddenly, out of nowhere, crashed and taken down the home-building business with it. In a matter of weeks, what they were now calling "the housing bubble" had burst, and some of the guys were starting to think it was more than just "a correction," like the people on TV said. It looked like the banks had been giving too many funny-money mortgages to worldly people who didn't care about paying their debts, and some of the Followers' companies were getting stiffed on bills. When work slowed, a few guys, including Patrick and his friend Rod Lincoln, had quit their jobs at Crone's Construction, Hal's, and some of the other Followers' companies, and were now freelancing in remodeling and repair.

Raylene was making a video of Ava playing with a little boy named Grady, who was almost exactly her age. It was important to Brent, Raylene, and their family and friends to document their lives, to preserve the history of their branch of the Church. It was the only one left where people were still born holy. They thought the other Followers branches—in Oklahoma, California, Idaho, and Grants Pass, Oregon—were no more in the Word than most of the worldly. The one in Caldwell, Idaho, was really wicked. Walter had told them that.

It looked to Raylene like Grady was having a hard time keeping up with Ava, which was great, because Ava had seemed puny, and the thing on her neck was starting to swell up again. Grandma Julie had noticed it in church that morning. Nobody else had, though, mostly because Ava looked so darling in a fancy new dress, and was so affectionate with everybody. Ava had just turned sixteen months, and Grandma knew that was the time when babies developed their own personalities, knew everybody, walked more than crawled, and talked up a storm in baby-talk. It was when kids first realized how irresistible they were, and it was pretty clear that Ava had figured out that she could charm the pants off people.

It wasn't really too surprising that Ava was under the weather, because a nasty bug that people were afraid was the bird flu had hit Oregon during the winter mold-and-mildew season. Men in the Followers' companies were calling in sick a lot, though probably not as often as the worldly, who got sick more easily from taking too many drugs. Even with her little cold, though, Ava was pushing her stroller full of dolls all around the house while Grady toddled after her.

A few days later, though, on Wednesday the 27th, the bump on her neck was even more swollen. But Raylene was relieved when she saw Ava playing with her Elmo doll, a favorite toy that she and her sister Corryn squabbled over, because as the doll sang, it rocked its head from side to side, and Ava did the same, which showed that the bump-thing wasn't hurting her neck.

On Thursday it looked like Ava was about ready to snap out of it and be her old self. Late in the afternoon, Raylene and Grandma Julie took Ava and Corryn for a walk, and Ava was sniffly but having fun. So was Corryn, who was learning to ride the bike she'd gotten for Christmas.

Brent soon showed up. That wasn't great. It meant work was slow at Excel Finishes and Wallcoverings, the business he ran with his dad. Brent didn't say anything about that, though. His dad had taught him a long time ago to never worry his wife or kids with that kind of thing. Followers men *acted* like men. They weren't like the worldly guys who made their wives go to work, and then told them all their problems, like that was a big favor.

Brent noticed Ava's bump, but it didn't concern him. It reminded him of his sister Danielle, and how one day her bump just went away and never came back.

The day after that, on Friday the 29th, Danielle and Julie were hanging around together—which was common, since their properties were adjoined—so they drove down the block and dropped in on Raylene, to let Danielle's two kids play with Ava and Corryn, who were very close to their ages. Ava was racing Danielle's son around an ottoman, and it looked to Raylene like Ava was holding her own, or even giving more than she got. Raylene wanted Ava to eat, so she offered her a spoonful of applesauce each time Ava ran around the ottoman. Danielle's son wanted some too, so Raylene asked Danielle if it was okay.

"It's okay with me if it's okay with you," said Danielle. "My kid's not sick."

"Mine's not either," said Raylene.

Julie, though, was pretty sure that Ava either had a bug, or was having a super-hard time teething. But teething was a good thing. It meant they were growing up. It was the end of them being babies, and that was always bittersweet, but more sweet than bitter, because they always turned into beautiful young children. Then one day they had their own kids, in families that were always together, in a cycle of sharing that was once common in America, but hardly happened anymore.

Later, Julie would remember, "It was like, 'Okay! Let's get those teeth through here!'"

OREGON CITY
SATURDAY, MARCH 1, 2008

To many people in Oregon, the first day of March is the unofficial first day of spring—not out of logic, but desperation. March usually comes in like a lion and stays that way, but at least it's not one of the four classic wet months between November and February, which account for half the year's rain. March brings a sense of relief.

Brent felt good when he woke up. Saturday was his day to play Mr. Mom and make breakfast for the kids, a chore he loved. He made Ava and Corryn scrambled eggs and some fruit, and was glad to see that Ava's bump, or cyst, or whatever, didn't look much bigger, though it was kind of hard to tell when you saw it every day.

The rest of the day didn't go so well. The bump seemed to swell up some, and Ava's breathing started to get raspy. By that point, it didn't look like she was just teething. It looked to Brent and Raylene like she probably had a cold, or even flu, and that was kind of scary with the little ones. They'd seen little ones with the flu take a sudden turn for the worse. So they gave Julie a call, and Julie called Raylene's mom, Marci. Both of the grandmas came over, and brought their husbands, Jeff and Guy. Julie's sister-in-law Kelli came over, too, and so did her niece, Leigh, as well as Julie's mom and Marci's mom: the great-grandmothers. People did some praying for Ava because, as Julie later said, they hated to see a child not feel well.

Guy wasn't entirely surprised to see that Ava was acting sluggish. He thought of her as kind of a lazy little girl, or at least low-key—never very rambunctious.

Ava just wasn't coming around, though, and when evening came, Julie stayed over, and sat at the end of Ava's bed all night while Guy hung out in the living room with some of the other men. Julie told everybody that there was no reason for people to stay, but a lot of them did anyway. Some of the people started fasting, hoping to hurry up God's healing.

Sunday wasn't good, either. Ava seemed pretty sick, and the day dragged. People came over after church to pray and before long, there was that familiar electric feeling of healing in the home. It built, and affected everybody that walked in. Ava sure seemed to be feeling it. She would get real antsy, like her energy was back, then she'd calm down, curl up, and rest.

They began to perform their most sacred ritual. They gathered around Ava, and Brent and Raylene touched their little girl tenderly as their family and friends touched them, in a web of love. Ava stirred. Everybody saw it. She suddenly seemed much, much better. Her eyes opened wide. It was incredible. Almost hard to believe. But they'd all stood witness.

It wasn't the first healing anybody had seen, or the most dramatic, but nothing in the world was sweeter than healing a little lamb of God.

Ava had gotten relief.

Freed from fear, and exhausted, the family and their friends filed into the kitchen to break their fasts. Big plates of creamed chicken, handmade pasta, and hot dinner rolls dipped in butter were suddenly everywhere.

It was an unforgettable first weekend of spring. It was a time of rebirth, and of love so strong that it had traveled to heaven and back, and relieved their precious baby from pain.

9

CRIME SCENE
INVESTIGATORS

Judas drew near to Jesus, to kiss him.
—The Book of Luke 22:47

Oregon City
Sunday, 7:10 p.m.
March 2, 2008

As evening settled in after a long, hard day of prayer and healing, Raylene thought Ava was getting fidgety again, probably because the group-healing had worked almost *too* well. They had laid hands on her more than once, and maybe that was overkill. But it looked to Raylene like it had helped.

After the last laying on of hands, though, it seemed to Raylene that Ava was suddenly almost too relaxed. They had to bounce her around just to get that happy spark of life back in her eyes. The bouncing did the trick, but made Ava a little too restless. That's how it was with kids: You couldn't get them going, and when you finally did, you couldn't get them stopped.

Raylene later recalled that after her daughter's energy returned, Ava got her favorite photo, a portrait of the family, and kept pointing at the people in it and reciting their names: "Mama, Dada, Corryn,

Ava." Then Ava snuggled between her parents and rolled over to Brent and said, with the nipple of her bottle still in her mouth, "Dada." Then she rolled over to Raylene, still nursing her bottle, and said, "Mama." Then back to Brent—again and again. Raylene thought Ava was gathering strength by the minute, but she wanted her baby to calm down, so she kissed Ava's cheek, still oily from the anointment, and held her closely.

A friend wandered into the room and Raylene held her finger to her lips. "Shhh," she said, "let me rest. She'll be up and running tomorrow, and I need my sleep." It looked like Ava was finally nodding off.

In the kitchen, people were warming up creamed chicken and corn. Nothing was more satisfying than breaking a fast after a healing. Fasting, though, didn't necessarily mean a protracted withdrawal from food. Grandma Marci's fast had consisted of just skipping breakfast.

People began to drift away, some falling asleep at the Worthingtons', and others returning to their homes. The previous night and all of Sunday had been long and frightening. As they left, most of the people bestowed upon the grandmothers the typical benediction that followed a miracle: "Our prayers have been answered."

Then Raylene screamed.

OREGON CITY
SUNDAY, 8:10 P.M.
MARCH 2, 2008

Clackamas County sheriff's deputy James Rhodes was doing the best he could to put his daughter to bed, but Sarah was two-and-a-half years old and had ideas of her own. She liked her bunk bed, but she didn't like bedtime.

She did like her daddy's new look, though. Now his face was smooth. For as long as Sarah could remember, he'd had a thick beard and scraggly hair. Sarah knew that her daddy was a police officer, just like mommy, but she didn't know that Rhodes had lived in almost constant peril as an undercover narcotics agent in the outback, meth-addicted netherworld of Clackatucky.

Rhodes, one of the department's best detectives, liked the new look better himself. Prior to his middle-class makeover, it had seemed as if his neighbors were starting to wonder about him. He also liked not going from one pucker-job to another, where he knocked down doors with his battering ram, sweating in his eighty-pound vest and balaclava ski mask, and screaming like a hyena to keep the perps off-balance.

Truth be told, the fear of that was exactly equal to the fun, but being in that line of work was no way to raise a daughter. So it was comforting, after all the years in Narcotics, to enjoy the near-certainty of fulfilling the primary mandate of law enforcement: At the end of your shift, go home alive.

Now he was working CATs, another job that he had to describe to his daughter delicately, because CAT was an acronym for Child Abuse Team. All Sarah knew was that he worked with little kids.

The phone rang. It was Dispatch, with a duty assignment from Rhodes' sergeant, who'd gotten a call from the medical examiner. The medical examiner had just been phoned by Carl Hansen, one of the board members of the Followers of Christ. A child had died, and Rhodes had to get to the scene. Fast.

Most people in the community were expected to immediately call 911 to report the death of a child, but the Followers had been granted an exception by the district attorney's office. "The theory behind the accommodation," Rhodes later said, "was that if we did it that way, they'd actually *call*. If they had to call 911, they might just dump the damn kid in the backyard."

Rhodes thought it was possible that over the past few years some children had been buried in unmarked graves in the Followers' cemetery, or maybe in old graves they'd dug up and recycled, like a gang had been doing in Portland. It was even conceivable that the Followers might have planted kids in far less public locations, without the protection of coffins—the purchase of which provoked curiosity—leaving the kids, in police lexicon, to suck mud.

Those possible burial stratagems would have been easier for the Followers than reporting dead infants as stillborn, as Brent and Raylene may have done in 2001. The Worthingtons had been investigated for that, but there had been no way to prove that their son, Baby Boy, had ever drawn a breath, and therefore been alive, so the case had been dropped.

This was Rhodes' first call-out on CATs, and he was scared. Not because of physical fear, which felt like an old friend, but because he might screw the pooch by making some rookie mistake. A Follower death was high-profile. People in CATs still talked about the unpunished death of eleven-year-old Bo Phillips ten years earlier, and about the efforts of Rita Swan to hold the people responsible for that type of death accountable. "The pressure was intense," Rhodes remembered.

"Who's the lead on this?" Rhodes asked the dispatcher.

"Michelle."

"Good call." Rhodes handed Sarah off to his wife, a state police detective, and put on a sport coat and tie. He'd learned as a narc that it was important to dress the part.

He tore out of his neighborhood like a stock-car driver and burned rubber around corners. That was the only fun part of his new job.

EASTERN CLACKAMAS COUNTY
SUNDAY, 8:15 P.M.
MARCH 2, 2008

Michelle Finn lived in the boonies, so to get to the scene on time she had to drive even faster than Rhodes. Plus, she had to drop off her kid. She hated leaving her child, but this was a time to worry about work, not parenting.

She shut down her feelings and went into cop-mode: What are the steps? What do we collect? Cameras? Computers? Phones? She knew the Followers liked to keep records, and she wanted to find them. As a local kid, she'd known about them all her life—but nobody really knew them. They made sure of that.

Who do I talk to? How do I cross-check their stories? What if their stories don't match what Ava looks like? Who'll still be there? Who split—and *why* did they split? What's Ava's health history? Anything chronic? What's the family structure?

Most important: Will there be any possible way to get a confession? How would that happen? Will mom break down? Who should interview her? Finn thought she should interview the mom while Rhodes interviewed the dad. Women were more likely to spill to another woman. And: Who's there to support the family? Because you never knew. Kids *did* die when no one was at fault. And if, God forbid, *she* was ever in that kind of situation as a mother, she'd need help. The job was never completely about thinking. Part of it was feeling. The hard part.

Finn felt comfortable leading the investigation, because she'd been working CATs for three years, and was already a crime scene detective. CSD was a step above just plain detective, and soon she would rise to the even more elevated position of crime scene investigator. The biggest difference between CSD and CSI was, as she later expressed it, "In CSI, I get to work more with dead people." Which made her laugh. It was hard to work CSI without a sense of humor. After several years of working on CATs, though, she needed the shield of not only humor, but rationality.

She was glad Rhodes was on this, because even though this was the first Followers case for both of them, Rhodes had at least been around long enough to handle a kid's death scene. Sometimes Finn made newbies go to a few autopsies before she let them come to a juvenile crime scene, so they wouldn't puke the first time they saw what parents could do to their kids. In certain ways, Rhodes reminded her of her buddy Jim Band, who'd worked Child Abuse for a long time, but now worked Everything Abuse. Thinking of him brought up another question: Why hadn't Band's snitch told him this kid was sick? Had the source stopped calling? But that was a question for another day.

One thing she did know: If this was a crime, it wouldn't be the

usual whodunit. It would be a whydunit. And a howdunit. This type
of crime was virgin territory, and its jurisdiction was in the mysterious
space that existed somewhere between the town she'd grown up in
and the very different one the Followers had: It's O.C.

When Finn rolled up to the death scene on Leland Road, parking
was a problem. She had to park three blocks away because the streets
were quickly filling up with the cars of mourners—or co-conspirators.
As she walked through the dark she put her long brown hair into a
ponytail. Michelle Finn was attractive—tall, with soft, even features
and an easy smile—but this was no time to look good, just like it was
no time to get emotional.

Rhodes was waiting for her in front of the house with Detective
Patrick Harris and his associate Jeff Green, who had worked the Bo
Phillips case in 1998. Clackamas County medical examiner Jeff Mayer
was also there. All the cops thought Mayer was a good man. He'd
worked about forty or fifty infant deaths, and knew the drill. About
70 percent of those infants had died in car wrecks, but at least 25 percent of the cases had been homicides. Mayer had arrived at the
Leland Road scene first, so he debriefed everybody as they eyed the
large group of men in the front yard who were also eyeing them.

A couple of officers from the little Clackamas County municipal-
ity of Gladstone were there, but they looked like they'd rather be
anyplace else. They volunteered to manage traffic, pick up litter—
whatever. The Gladstone sergeant who generally dealt with this type
of event, Lynne Benton, was, for reasons unknown, nowhere to be
seen. That was fine, though, because Gladstone's department wasn't
highly regarded. It was a small, underfunded force, with no captains
or lieutenants, that worked in a poor community.

The baby was in a back bedroom, Mayer said, with a captain there
to keep the scene secure. There were 200 to 300 people in the house
and yard, he said, but so far he and Captain Bruce Pearson had kept
the death scene sequestered and pristine.

Rhodes was surprised that a captain had come. It was one more
indication of the enormity of the situation. Captain Pearson was

smart and had risen through the ranks quickly. Once upon a time, he'd had a reputation as a heavy drinker, but nobody said that anymore, and tonight he'd turned in early, and gotten out of bed to come.

Mayer said he'd already taken photos to document Ava Worthington's condition and had secured some evidence: olive oil used for anointing, a baby bottle with some diluted wine, Ava's pillow, a humidifier, some Cheerios, some baby food, and pink pajamas that Mayer had removed from Ava to get photos of her body. Ava's parents had told Mayer that she'd died at 7:15, which was consistent with her state of rigor mortis, as well the pooling of her blood to the lower parts of her body that began when her heart stopped, known as livor mortis.

Finn told them that she would interview the mom, Rhodes should take dad, and Green should speak with Grandma and Grandpa Beagley. Finn would try to separate everybody before they had time to coordinate statements. It was the standard divide-and-conquer procedure.

The plan was to be even more respectful than usual, because the Followers were known to be courteous, and to respond to courtesy. Mayer would do the always-sensitive initial interview with the father—because the Followers didn't hate medical examiners quite as much as they hated the police—and after Mayer got Brent's tongue loosened, Rhodes would take over the questioning.

Finn asked Rhodes to lead them through the crowd of Followers, because he could still radiate the physical menace that had protected him in Narcotics. A year before, he'd been sixty pounds heavier, but he'd followed the Paleo Diet until his compact frame was nothing but muscle.

As they walked the gauntlet, the Followers' contempt for them was obvious—cold stares on contorted faces—and Finn wasn't sure that they would be able to squeeze through without somebody sticking them with a ballpoint pen or pocket knife, and melting into the crowd.

They inched their way to the death scene through three distinct groups: men outside, women inside, and immediate family closest to Ava. Finn wanted to get rid of most of the people, but couldn't think of a polite way. Everybody seemed to be related, and it was against protocol to shoo away family. But this was different. This extended family probably wanted to impede the investigation.

They saw Brent Worthington sitting in the master bedroom and staring at his daughter. Then Finn saw the child. There was a *huge* lump on Ava's neck! The size of a goddamned *softball*. It jutted out grotesquely and was varying hues of red, purple, and mottled gray.

"I think it's some kind of cyst," Jeff Mayer said quietly. "I've never seen anything like it."

There were so *many* things wrong with Ava's body. Rhodes had been expecting to see a toddler somewhere close to the size of his daughter, but Ava was tiny and withered. Her ribs protruded and her stomach was bloated. Her hair and face looked greasy, and she smelled like salad dressing. Her skin was a sick shade of yellow.

The baby bottle with watered-down wine was sitting on a TV tray next to some wadded tissues. A ceiling fan whirled above them, and the humidifier was still hissing. Rhodes approached Brent. "I'm very sorry for your loss," he said. "I have a daughter about the same age . . . ." He trailed off as Brent bowed his head slowly and then brought it back up.

Captain Bruce Pearson turned over the death scene to Finn and Rhodes and headed home. He told them he'd taken a sleeping pill before the sudden call-out, and wanted to get at least a little rest before his next shift.

While Finn and Rhodes examined the bedroom and adjoining bath, Mayer began to ask Brent gentle questions about Ava's recent health, and when Brent began to be somewhat more expansive, Rhodes turned on a tape recorder and took over. Finn delayed talking to the women momentarily to hear what Brent had to say, but he acted like she didn't exist.

"It was because Michelle was a female," Rhodes later said. "The *body* language on that guy! He would literally raise his chin and look over her head, then shake his head a little. It was one tell after another. I'd love to play poker with the guy. What an asshole!"

But Rhodes stuck to his strategy of courtesy, which he later characterized as "killing them with kindness."

"They're so painfully well-mannered," Rhodes later said, "that if you ask them for something nicely, it's hard for them to say no. And if you leave an awkward pause hanging, they'll fill it. I tried a lot of open-ended questions, like, 'Tell me about the laying on of hands.' And, 'Is there a special kind of oil you use?' There's not—they just buy gallon jugs of Wesson oil. I asked, 'Would you go to a dentist?' Yes. 'Would you let him inject Novocain?' Yes, if that's what needed to happen, sure. 'With a needle?' Sure. 'What if they had to put you to sleep?' He said if it was a dentist, okay, but a doctor, no. I said, 'Help me understand the difference.' But he couldn't."

With his dead daughter still in his field of vision, Brent remained calm, and almost affable. One way to describe his demeanor, Rhodes thought, would be stoic. Another would be pathologically cold.

Brent said that when he heard Raylene scream, he thought she'd hurt herself, but then she cried, "Ava's stopped breathing!" He ran into the bedroom, he said. Raylene was holding Ava and sobbing hysterically. His father, according to Brent, came in and said, "You should anoint Ava." So he did. Then the immediate family had gathered beside the baby and prayed. No one had tried to revive Ava, or call 911.

Near the end of the interview, Brent looked coolly at Rhodes and said, "So what do you think of us?"

"I think you're probably the most honest, endearing people I've met in a very long time. I think you . . . I believe you're absolutely truthful, and don't believe you've held anything back." Brent, accustomed to having his ass kissed, appeared to believe it.

Rhodes was basically telling the truth. The Followers *were* being honest—according to their own twisted view of reality. And they were genuinely likable. Rhodes later commented, "The Followers would be great neighbors. And I'd love to have one of them working for me. I'd work for them. They'd be perfect people, if they just didn't let their fucking kids die."

Rhodes then went to Brent's father, Guy Worthington, while Finn talked to Raylene. "Can you describe the difference in Ava's breathing on Sunday?" Rhodes asked Guy. "Was it different from what it had been on Saturday?"

"Shorter, I guess."

"Was she struggling to breathe?"

"Yes."

"I've heard the term 'labored breathing,' to describe someone who's having difficulty breathing," Rhodes said.

"Yeah, I'd say that's probably a good word. *Labored breathing*."

Rhodes was perceiving a scenario of a baby in deep distress.

So was Detective Green, who interviewed Grandpa Jeff Beagley. Beagley, who had been with Ava all day, told Green that she seemed to be getting worse throughout the evening, and was coughing up phlegm. However, Beagley said, shortly before Ava died, her cyst had been "smaller than it is now." That didn't make sense. She died, and *then* it swelled? Wouldn't it be the other way around? Not to the best of Mr. Beagley's recollection.

Michelle Finn was also hearing about how inconsequential the cyst was from some of the women she and the other detectives were interviewing. Brent's mother Julie said that she'd had a cyst herself as a child, on the same side, in the same area: "a big honkin' thing." Her own cyst had swelled occasionally, Julie said, just as Ava's did "when Ava was teething."

Grandma Marci described Ava's cyst as having been "flesh colored" before she died. But that implied it had gained color after death— despite livor mortis, which would have drained some of the color from it. Marci did admit that Ava had been "tired" and was "possibly coughing," and that the "possible" coughing "got worse" throughout the night. She also said that they had laid hands on Ava three times.

Marci was apologetic about one issue—giving the baby wine. She said she knew that it "sounds bad."

Finn struggled to show respect, but their story smelled rotten. The probable reality: A little girl who was thin as a scarecrow, with a horrible growth on her windpipe, slowly died while people watched, applied their most extreme measure—the laying on of hands—and then ate potluck. It looked like a criminal case—open and shut.

But in the real world: No confession, no smoking gun, no honest witnesses, a lot of evidence that was too ambiguous to be admissible—and the presumed perps, a grieving family, were also the victims. Finn later noted, "I've learned from years of going to trial that there's the detective's work product, and there's the work product that the *jury* sees. It's all a matter of the rules of the game, and the evidence we can bring in. It's a game of perception." She thought a jury would probably consider this a crime if they were here, right now. But they weren't.

As Finn, Rhodes and the others finished their interviews, Jeff Mayer loaded Ava Worthington onto a cot in his mobile unit and drove her to the Clackamas County Medical Examiner's Office. Ava's cot was unloaded with a forklift onto a stainless-steel tray. Then her body was transferred onto the metal gurney that she would remain on during her autopsy. With her clothing off, she was wheeled to a computer station with a large scale. Mayer weighed Ava, as an overhead camera took a photo of her oil-shiny, chalky face. Then she was wheeled into a large cooling unit. Ava would spend the night in the cooler, with her body temperature maintained at just above freezing.

By 2:00 a.m., the Worthingtons' house was almost empty, and Finn and Rhodes huddled outside and planned the next day. Rhodes wanted to reprise Brent's interview on videotape, to fully reveal his telltale body language to a grand jury, if the case went before one. Finn wanted to conduct more interviews as soon as absolutely possible, before the Followers could further conspire. The Followers, she thought, would be able to change the story among themselves almost instantly, because their phone tree could connect hundreds of people within minutes. That's how the crowd had gotten so huge. It had almost certainly grown *after* the death, probably to inhibit the investigation.

The solution: The next morning at exactly 10:00 a.m., fourteen detectives from Major Crimes would simultaneously knock on fourteen doors in Oregon City. The procedure was called a cold tap, and was effective against organized crime.

Just before they left, Rhodes said, "I guess Band's snitch didn't know about this one."

Finn shrugged. "There's never a Judas around when you need one." They made plans to meet at the autopsy.

James Rhodes went home and stood beside Sarah's bunk bed for quite some time. He listened to his daughter breathe, felt comforted by the sound, and tried not to think about the dissection of Ava Worthington in the morning.

OREGON CITY
MARCH 3, 2008, 3:00 A.M.

"Patrick," said Theresa, "something's wrong with the baby."

"What?" He was still mostly asleep.

"He can't breathe."

"What!" He was awake.

The baby, still virtually a newborn, squirmed in Theresa's arms. Little Paul inhaled a hard, raspy breath. The exhale was scary, like the bark of a seal. It sounded, to a frightened new parent, as if Paul was dying. Patrick reached for him, held the baby's soft ear to his lips, and whispered, "Paul, Paulie, baby boy." Theresa looked terrified, and Patrick reached out to her with his free hand. "Sweetheart, it's just croup," he said gently. "I'm sure it is. That's exactly what it sounds like. It's just a little swelling in his throat. Go run all the hot water in the bathroom and get it steamy."

When the baby began to breathe the warm, wet air his breath calmed almost immediately. Patrick rocked him in his arms and wicked sweat away from his own blue-green eyes to keep it from dropping onto his son.

Theresa finally smiled. "Where'd you learn that?" she asked.

"I'm a dad."

"You're a good dad." Theresa put her forehead against Pat and took Patrick's hand. He could tell she was praying.

Theresa's love for him had again blossomed after Paul's birth. She didn't even object when he named the baby Paul, after the apostle, instead of himself. He'd simply reminded her that he had been named Patrick only because he was born on St. Patrick's Day, and that names didn't matter. Only children.

Everybody seemed to have a virus that winter. The Net said that croup was rarely bacterial, so Patrick knew he probably wouldn't have to go to a doctor for antibiotics. He hated to think about the ramifications if he did, but he'd worry about that when it happened. He wasn't much of a worrier these days. His life, for the first time, was simple and happy. He wasn't trying to save the world, or crucify his best friends by threatening the custody of their kids. He was just trying to be a good father and husband.

He sent Theresa back to bed and got ready to spend the rest of the night in the family room, holding Paul in his work-hardened arms, just in case. On the way downstairs he drew his sleeping baby close and gave him a kiss.

The answering machine was beeping. There were two messages. Any message after bedtime was bad. Two was worse.

The first was an urgent request from his phone-tree contact to remember Ava Worthington in his prayers that night, and in the morning, too. That made Patrick very afraid of the second.

After he heard the next message he sat in his recliner, pulled Paul close to his heart, and tried not to cry, at least not out loud, because he knew how much terror it would cause Theresa if she woke up to the sound of him sobbing.

THE CLACKAMAS COUNTY MEDICAL EXAMINER'S OFFICE
MARCH 3, 9:00 A.M.

The innermost circle of hell portrayed by Dante in *The Divine Comedy* is cold, and the cold intensifies as hell's concentric circles lead to Satan's home in the center. There, in the heart of The Ninth Circle, the

Beast, encased in ice, tortures Judas eternally for committing the worst of all sins, treachery. The inner circle, called Judecca, is named after Judas.

As Detective Rhodes worked his way back to the autopsy room, going through anterooms that got colder and colder, it felt a lot like he was walking into the heart of The Ninth Circle of Hell. It wasn't just because of the cold, but the smell, too. No amount of air-conditioning could hide the thick metallic smell of death. Death had an odor you could identify the first time you ever smelled it.

The forensic pathologist who was working the case, Dr. Christopher Young, didn't want Rhodes in the autopsy room. He told him to watch with the other cops and doctors from the adjacent glass booth. Most of them were there because of the importance of the case, but some of the doctors just wanted to see how somebody could actually die from a cyst. In medical circles, that was a "novelty."

But Rhodes was adamant. He didn't want to be in the autopsy room at all, because it felt disrespectful of Ava. But in three hours he'd be interviewing Brent and Raylene again, and he was damned if he was going to do that without knowing everything he possibly could about how Ava had died. "How" would determine if a crime had been committed. Had the death been inevitable? Accidental? Preventable? An honest mistake? Malicious? An act of criminal neglect?

And even if it was criminal neglect—which is what it seemed like—it would still be hard to tag the act with one of the predictable elements that usually establish motive: anger, greed, lust, envy, and recklessness. Those were the simple, popular sins that occupied the outer rings of hell. Juries knew all about those sins, so those crimes were easy to prosecute. But prosecuting something as fucked-up as watching your own daughter die—with your parents, grandparents, siblings, and friends? That act of treachery would be a tough sell to a jury. It was unthinkable.

Dr. Young started by re-weighing Ava. That was critical in this case, because if her growth had been stunted, it would mean she had experienced the medical condition called "failure to thrive," probably because of medical neglect by her parents. Young stood on a large scale, noted his own weight, took Ava in his arms, and recorded the increase in weight. Just 23 pounds—the lowest five percentile! But that could be due to height.

He measured her. Twenty-six inches—*lower* than the one percentile mark!

Ava's height and weight were proportional, but why so tiny? At sixteen months, she was the size of a six-month-old.

Then he measured her head's circumference. It was in the 90th percentile! The growth of her body should have remained consistent with the size of her head.

Her recorded birth weight was normal as well—another sign that she'd probably been neglected.

Something had happened.

Rhodes had been to dozens of autopsies and steeled himself for what was next. He'd grown up shooting and gutting deer and he'd been in pre-med long enough to get his hands bloody, but there was something about an autopsy's first incisional step, degloving, that felt unnatural. Part of it was just the sound. Dr. Young cut through Ava's scalp, gripped it, and pulled her skin off her skull and face, toward her chin, leaving a ghoulish visage, as the skin made a sucking *"usssss!"* sound. That sound and the sight of a skinned face was like the smell of death: You couldn't desensitize yourself to it.

Rhodes, standing next to Young, wasn't sure what exactly would constitute a good day for a medical examiner, but this obviously wasn't it. Maybe that's why Young hadn't wanted Rhodes in the room. Some jobs were easier done alone.

There were nothing wrong with Ava's brain—another sign that her death was probably preventable.

Then Young snipped through Ava's ribs, using a scalpel, instead of his shears, because her ribs were so small. But when he cut across her chest cavity there was suddenly another ugly sound, very unexpected: a quick hiss, as soft and sinister as a snake's, as Ava's now severed windpipe—which had been stretched by the cyst—contracted violently and whipped back up into her neck.

"Her esophagus and trachea actually retracted by two inches," Dr. Young later said.

It was obvious that the cyst had been choking off her larynx, trachea, and esophagus. Her Adam's apple was misshapen, and the flap of skin that protected her airway during swallowing, the epiglottis, was crumpled.

Ava's cyst was filled with yellow fluid. Its largest chamber was four inches wide. Her jugular vein and carotid artery, the main vessels that served her brain, were stretched tight across the cyst, and other vessels were oozing blood. When Young touched the cyst with the tip of his scalpel, the fluid in it flooded out and the cyst began to flatten.

Ava's lungs were filled with a thick tan pus. The cyst had helped keep it in, just as it had interfered with her breathing and swallowing.

Rhodes watched Ava's neck normalize as the cyst quickly drained.

"That drainage could have been performed with a needle at any time, pretty easily, huh?" Rhodes murmured to Young.

The doctor gave him a sideways glance but didn't answer. Rhodes didn't need him to.

The official categories of causes of death vary slightly from state to state. Live-free Oregon has eight categories, more than almost all the other states, because it includes doctor-assisted suicide.

In Oregon, the eight ways to die are: (1) Natural Causes; (2) Suicide; (3) Homicide; (4) Physician Assisted Intervention; (5) Undetermined; (6) Accidental; (7) Drug Overdose; and (8) Other (a grab-bag of arcane causes, such as snake bites).

Police who deal with child abuse don't like this narrow system of classification, because it doesn't include death from *preventable* Natural Causes. Because of this, children who starve to death from neglect are classified as having died from Natural Causes, a fact that can sometimes be used to confuse a jury.

When the body of Ava Worthington was released to Brent and

Raylene later that day for embalming and interment, the copy of her death certificate that they received said she died from Natural Causes.

It was a busy day for them. They had to plan the funeral, meet with Michelle Finn and James Rhodes, and go check in on Ava at the Followers' favorite funeral home.

OREGON CITY
MARCH 3, 3:30 P.M.

With the video rolling, Rhodes, fresh from having seen that a needle could have drained Ava's cyst, asked Brent to elaborate on his willingness to get a shot from a dentist.

Brent reiterated his acceptance of a needle procedure from a dentist, and showed no emotion when Rhodes told him that a simple, out-patient needle-drain would have saved Ava's life. Raylene dabbed at her eyes, but gazed respectfully at Brent and let him do the talking.

Rhodes and Finn wanted to show that the Worthingtons were aware of Ava's increasing peril, in order to prove negligence, so Rhodes asked Brent about Ava's declining condition, day by day. But Brent painted a picture of absolute stability, until he slipped up and said, "It didn't change dramatic until Sunday, is when . . . ."

"It dramatically changed?" Rhodes asked.

"From Saturday evening until Sunday is when it, uh, dramatically changed."

Rhodes didn't push it and his patience paid off. Brent made an offhand comment about worrying that his daughter might not make it, and Rhodes casually asked, as if he were just curious, "When you, uh, when the thought crossed your mind that she might not survive, what did you do at *that* point?"

"We kept praying, and asked for prayers at the church. And then we laid hands on her again."

"So you took action—you called and asked for prayer?"

"Yeah."

"So you laid on hands? Was there anointing that occurred as well?"

"Sure."

Rhodes backed off again, and Finn tag-teamed in. "Did you talk about this with anybody in the church—friends, family?" she asked.

"Yeah. Yeah. We talked about it." Brent was looking over her head again.

"What was some of that discussion?" she asked.

"I wondered if it wasn't something to do with teething, or a gland that was swelling up."

"And everybody," Finn asked, "kind of agreed that nobody really knew?" She was working on the "reasonable person" angle. The law required all people to be as reasonable as most others in the general populace. A *reasonable* person who didn't know what was happening would, of course, have called a doctor.

The only problem was, not all people who were on juries were reasonable. Especially Clackalackie's large contrarian subgroup sometimes called Clackastanis, due to their fractious and feisty nature.

Finn asked, "Did she seem like she was in pain?"

"Uh, the coughing started to look like it was hurting her throat," Brent said. "She would stir. They kept her stirred up—keep her breathing. So they'd move her around, keep her going. She wasn't, she wasn't fussy. She like cried out once in a while."

Rhodes asked if Ava was lethargic at that point, and Brent said she was.

Rhodes went for the jugular. "Stop me if I get this wrong," he said, "but your beliefs are that if you're going to die, it's God's will?"

"Right," said Brent.

"And that no amount of effort on behalf of a doctor will change that?"

"I do believe this is how it was meant to be."

Point blank: "Could a doctor have saved Ava's life?"

"It would have been the same result."

Rhodes was shocked but didn't show it. Brent had just said that medical attention could not *possibly* have helped his critically ill daughter. That wasn't reasonable. The self-righteous little son of a bitch, Rhodes thought, had just convicted himself. In a reasonable world.

They stopped by DA Greg Horner's office, smiling, with the good news. Horner called in one of his closest associates, Deputy DA Steve Mygrant, and three other Top Guns in the department: Senior Deputy DAs Mike Regan, John Wentworth, and Christine Landers. Horner was pleased with the investigation thus far and told them in a kind and gentle way that they'd better not fucking blow it. Nobody was smiling on the way out. There was too much to do.

It was time to call on Rita Swan. If anybody knew the fine points of how to handle this case, it was her.

Rita had time to offer general advice, but was inundated at that time with other cases. Her busy schedule was one more indication of how widespread America's faith-healing scandal was, although it was still largely unknown to most of the public, even in the places where it was most common, including Oregon City.

At the moment, Rita was helping bring media attention to the upcoming trial of a mother in North Carolina, Lynn Paddock, who had killed her child during ritualistic religious punishment. Paddock had wrapped her four-year-old son, Sean, in blankets that were so tight he had to fight for breath. The little boy, already weakened by three beatings that day, suffocated.

Other punishments regularly inflicted upon Sean and his five siblings, according to the surviving children, included covering their faces with duct tape, and forcing them to eat feces and vomit. Paddock had denied that she'd made them eat feces, but did admit that she forced them to eat their own vomit, because she thought they were choosing to vomit to spite her.

Paddock had beaten the children so often and severely that one boy had a chronic limp. She usually whipped them with plastic tubing, on the advice of a book by evangelical minister Michael Pearl, entitled *To Train Up a Child*.

Pastor Pearl's book noted that plastic tubing, which he said was available as a plumbing product at most hardware stores, was a "good spanking instrument, because it's too light to cause damage to the muscle and the bone." It caused pain but left fewer marks than other objects. He called it "an attention-getter." Pearl's book, which had sold about 400,000 copies at that time and would eventually sell almost twice that many, had been published by Pearl's own organization, No Greater Joy Ministries, and was available for sale online. No Greater Joy also published a newsletter with 60,000 subscribers, sold CDs, and earned almost $2 million per year.

Pearl, when asked about his involvement in Sean Paddock's death, said that approximately one-sixth of American parents who home-schooled their children, often for religious reasons, used his materials, and that "the chances of one of them committing a crime is pretty good." Pearl had been investigated by ABC's *20/20*, but his religious affiliation had helped keep him from being prosecuted.

Two other children who were victims of Pearl's approach would also soon die. Lydia Schatz, a seven-year-old Liberian adoptee from Paradise, California, was whipped to death with plastic tubing for mispronouncing a word, and her sister was beaten so badly that she was hospitalized. In court, the parents' attorney argued that, "Few parents know that lengthy whippings can cause fatal injury."

Lydia's father, Kevin Schatz, was convicted of second-degree murder, and sentenced to life in prison. Her mother, Elizabeth Schatz, who had held Lydia down for several hours while Kevin Schatz whipped her back, was sentenced to a minimum of thirteen years in prison.

Pastor Pearl's teaching was also associated with the death of another little girl, thirteen-year-old Hana Grace-Rose Williams, of Sedro-Woolley, Washington. Hana, adopted from Ethiopia, was often beaten with plastic tubing, which her mother carried in her bra. Hana was also often starved, and locked in a dark closet for days at a time, while her parents played Hana recordings of spiritual music and the Bible. Her parents, Carri and Larry Williams, made Hana sleep in a barn, bathe outside with a garden hose, and sit outside during

Christmas celebrations. Hana suffered from hepatitis B, malnutrition, ringworm, cold sores, and parasites. The night she died, due to hypothermia, she was left outside all night, naked, in rainy, forty-degree weather.

Hana's ten-year-old brother, Immanuel—also adopted from Ethiopia, and treated much more harshly than the Williams' biological children—was often punished for "not being a good listener," even though he was deaf.

Carri and Larry Williams were charged with homicide by abuse, a murder charge in Washington. During the investigation, Larry Williams argued that the punishments had been reasonable because "people like Hana get spankings for lying, and go into the fires of hell." Their trial was repeatedly delayed.

Another case that was unfolding at this time involved a crude exorcism in Baltimore. About a year earlier, sixteen-month-old Javon Thompson had been starved to death for religious reasons, and Rita was trying to bring the case to the forefront of the Baltimore media. She hoped to influence authorities to file murder charges against the boy's mother, as well as three other members of a small church known as One Mind Ministries, including the leader, who called herself Queen Antoinette.

Javon had been ordered by his mother, Ria Ramkissoon, to say "Amen" after a blessing at a meal, but the toddler had been unable to. Ramkissoon and Queen Antoinette thought that Javon was being defiant, presumably because he was possessed by the devil.

Javon, who like most children his age had very limited language skills, was denied food and water at that meal—to drive the devil out of him—and was then given a chance to say "Amen" at the next meal. He also failed that time, and was again denied food. He failed repeatedly until he died of starvation.

After his death, his mother and the three church leaders quickly left town. They stuffed Javon's body into a suitcase, doused it with Lysol, and brought it with them, because Queen Antoinette believed that Javon might still be resurrected.

Acting on a tip from other abused children in the church, who had already been removed from their parents' custody, Javon's body was found, and all four perpetrators were arrested.

The charges were uncertain, though, because the church members were considering a plea bargain, but insisted upon being allowed to withdraw the plea if Javon suddenly came back to life.

For Rita, the bizarre and heartbreaking case was business as usual.

The prior year, in another exorcism case, Rita had helped pressure the prosecution of Sonya and Joseph Smith, who had beaten their eight-year-old son, Josef, to death because they thought he was, in their words, "demon-possessed, a soldier of the devil," due to episodes in which "his eyes rolled back in his head as if he were going through some transformation."

Josef's parents were members of a Brentwood, Tennessee, church called the Remnant Fellowship, which advocated extreme physical punishment for children. They had locked Josef in his room for weeks at a time, to pray to a picture of Jesus on the ceiling, with only a bucket for a toilet, and they frequently whipped him with implements, while forcing another son to hold him down. His dead body was covered with scars and bruises.

The local children's services division had gotten a report of the abuse from Josef's half-sister and recorded it in a memo, but took no action, indicative of a general pattern of relative carelessness that is found among some states' protective services divisions—a frequent source of great frustration among law enforcement agencies. The county children's services director argued, in his agency's defense, that "There's nothing in that memo that says the parents might beat a child to death."

The Smiths were found guilty of murder, and sentenced to life in prison, plus thirty years.

The Remnant Fellowship stayed intact, though, partly because it had a national following on the Internet. Its founder, Gwen Shamblin, who had pioneered the concept of Christian diet plans with her Weigh Down Workshop, advised parents in a video that, "If your children are not scared of a spanking, you haven't spanked them. If you haven't really spanked them, you don't love them. You love yourself."

Rita was optimistic about achieving murder charges in the upcoming trials of mothers Lynn Paddock and Ria Ramkissoon, because it was much easier for a jury to convict religious fanatics who actively killed their children, instead of those who let their children die from medical neglect. Kids often died just as painfully from neglect, but there was usually less blood and gore, which made it more difficult for jurors to comprehend the neglected children's suffering.

Also, in cases of neglect, the legal issues of intent and a lack of reasonable behavior were much harder to prove, because neglect generally occurred gradually, with no primary incident of abuse. There was often no obvious evidence that the parents were sacrificing their children to satisfy their own religious whims. Neglect tended to be so subtle that it was invisible, until disastrous diseases appeared.

Rita was also fighting to prevent an even more subtle form of medical neglect in Nebraska at this time: a proposed religious exemption for metabolic screening of infants. The procedure was the only way to protect kids from several catastrophic disorders, including an allergy-like condition called phenylketonuria that could cause brain damage. But most babies didn't have the disorders, so a religious coalition, led by Christian Scientists, was sponsoring a faith-based exemption.

If it passed, it would be a giant step backward for Nebraska—the only state with no religious shields at all, due to the efforts thirty-five years earlier of legendary state senator Ernie Chambers, the legislator who had "sued God."

In hearings, one mother who had moved to Nebraska from a state that hadn't required the screening told legislators about the emotional pain and backbreaking expense of rearing a needlessly brain-damaged child who was unable to speak. Even so, the state's Health and Human Services Committee voted in favor of the bill. It looked as if it would become law.

As the bill went to the floor, Rita faxed Senator Chambers, at this time in his record-breaking 38th year in the Nebraska State Senate. A few hours later his secretary called Rita and relayed a message from the senator: "It's all taken care of."

The bill was dead. Rita's decades of political alliances were paying off. A new day seemed to be dawning.

OREGON CITY POLICE DEPARTMENT
MARCH 4, 2008

The phone in OCPD headquarters rang. "This is Band."

"Jim, it's Patrick."

"Saint Pat! Long time no see."

"I know. I'm . . . We had a baby."

"Oh my God! I know how much you wanted one. Congratulations. Boy or girl? How's it going?"

Patrick didn't say anything. Band thought he'd lost the connection.

"Jim, I'm sorry."

"For what?"

"Ava."

"Patrick. Hey, c'mon. You can't blame yourself for that. Really."

"There's somebody I need to tell you about. A kid. It may be too late already. But I can't just . . . You know, let it go."

"Who is it?"

"One of the Beagley kids. Katie."

10

GUILT AND INNOCENCE

Guardian angels, God will send thee, all through the night.
—"AR HYD Y NOS," TRADITIONAL WELSH LULLABY

THE FOLLOWERS OF CHRIST CEMETERY
CLACKAMAS COUNTY, OREGON
MARCH 6, 2008

Patrick jiggled Paul in the back row, trying to keep him still during the graveside service for Ava. What a terrible time! No matter how you felt about what had happened, your heart had to break for the grieving parents on a day like this, or you weren't human.

Paul pushed his nose against Patrick's cheek. The baby was hungry. He was learning to tell Patrick things without words, and the quiet but clear communication felt like God's sweetest gift. Patrick reached into his shoulder bag and pulled out a bottle.

Theresa had refused to come. She hated funerals. She'd been traumatized by her brother's burial as a child and still had dreams about it. She wouldn't even tend his grave, and when her parents died, both from diabetes, Patrick had started taking care of all their graves. Many of the Followers' graves were overgrown—particularly the cheap little flat ones—so he often scuffed moss and grass off a few of them with his heel.

The truth was, he thought that some people probably neglected the graves because they felt guilty about letting their loved ones die. That was a traitorous thought, of course, the kind that used to make Patrick think he had a devil. But all that obsession with devils had ended the night he'd quietly cried himself to sleep in his recliner, holding Paul, thinking about what a sweet little girl Ava had been. It was shocking to feel how fast the world could change in just one night.

Every day since Ava had died Patrick had prayed to be forgiven for standing idly by during her suffering, but it felt to him as if God wanted more than remorse: He wanted action—true penance—and Patrick wasn't sure he was man enough to provide it. He'd been gutted of the empowering certainty that had once filled his life, and felt empty now, with an almost constant hollowness in his stomach.

For the first time in his life, he felt mortal. He finally knew he was nothing special, just another sinner, and that there wasn't going to be a Followers-only Rapture, or anything remotely like it. Heaven—if he could redeem himself enough to deserve it—would be full of the worldly, and their wild ways. Death would be as strange as life.

Brent had his arm around Raylene. They stood over the grave in lush spring sunshine that to Patrick felt wrong for the occasion. Brent seemed to be holding her up. Patrick knew that Brent came off as cold, but that Ava's death had to be killing him.

Jeff and Marci, on the other side of the grave, both looked much older than they had even a month ago—saggy jowled, slow moving, and beaten down by the death of their granddaughter. Their kids didn't look much better. Neil looked ghostly—pale and vacant—and Katie seemed to be in shock.

Patrick could see that Neil, the Crown Prince, was trying from time to time to put his hand on his sister Raylene's back, but the poor kid just didn't have the wherewithal to leave it there. Neil had always played the role of big brother to his older sisters, but today seemed to be more than he could bear.

Ava's grave, in Kids' Row, near her brother Baby Boy, was no bigger than one scoop of the backhoe-shovel that had dug it. It sat in
front of two large memorial ribbons hanging on a fence that separated
the graves from the forest.

When Ava's tiny coffin was lowered into her grave Neil seemed to
shrink even further. Neil had never been a big kid, but he'd always
projected power—the power, some Followers still thought, of the new
Prophet, or at least the prince of their intertwined businesses, which
some people now considered an even more important position than
that of their pastor. But for once, Neil looked smaller and younger
than Katie.

Patrick's friend Hot Rod Lincoln had told him that ever since Ava
had died, Neil felt guilty about being alive. It made Patrick sad that a
kid as innocent as Neil would feel so responsible. If all these *parents*
would start feeling some guilt, this craziness would stop. But just by
looking at Jeff and Marci, Patrick could tell that guilt played no part
in their grief. That was dangerous.

Patrick was worried sick about Katie. It was well-known that Katie would rather die than have a kidney transplant. She'd told people
herself. She looked too run-down to be here, but had insisted on saying good-bye to her niece, who was actually more like a little sister.

The service ended with Brent saying something about Ava being
his precious angel, the same phrase that was inscribed on her headstone. Brent and Raylene had settled for a flat one, instead of the more
expensive raised ones that the funeral home called Pillow Tops. But
nobody could blame them, because of what people were starting to
call "this economy."

Patrick tuned out Brent's speech. It was heartfelt, but hypocritical—
just one more contradiction in Patrick's conflicted new life, which was
scarier than ever. Now he might lose not only Theresa but Pat, too, in
a divorce, and if that happened, he would have been happy to kill
himself, if it hadn't been a mortal sin.

When it was over, Patrick cut through the crowd to comfort Katie
and Neil, as Vernon Thaine had comforted him at his father's funeral,

in this same place, in another lifetime. It was the right thing to do. Besides, Jim Band had asked him to get a sense of Katie's health. But as soon as he started talking to the kids, it was hard to tell who was in worse shape, Neil or Katie. Katie told him she'd been having all kinds of fevers, infections, swelling and stuff, and Neil was basically saying: Yeah, doesn't everybody? Just looking at them, Neil seemed sicker than his sister.

Patrick remembered how Vernon had lightened his heart on that awful half-remembered day with a joke, but the only one that came to mind was a wry Followers standard: You can't spell "funeral" without "real fun." That didn't cut it on a day like this.

Patrick would have to tell Jim Band about both Katie and Neil. Another alternative, Jim had said, was to call the state's children's services division, because they could legally intervene *before* a crime was committed. But Patrick was worried that it might arouse suspicion.

But so what? Having everything to lose felt surprisingly like having nothing to lose.

Patrick held Paul over his heart like a shield and walked back to his car, alone and afraid.

MARCH 7, 2008

Rita Swan, still preoccupied with the fatal exorcism of sixteen-month-old Javon Thompson, was suddenly taking on more work than ever before. She'd been brought into three more cases, all grisly.

One was a case before the Tennessee Supreme Court that involved one of the country's most notorious faith healers, Ariel Ben Sherman, a pockmarked old preacher who linked himself to various minor churches when it fit his needs, including one called the New Life Tabernacle. Sherman had convinced one of his communal girlfriends, Jacqueline Crank, to refuse medical treatment for her fifteen-year-old daughter, Jessica, who had bone cancer and a tumor as big as a basketball. Instead, they prayed for Jessica's health, not only before her death, but even over her corpse at the funeral, because Sherman had everybody hyped-up about the possibility of a resurrection.

In the mid-1980s, Sherman and Crank had run a church just outside Oregon City that had tortured children, a sickening but relatively common crime among some of the same isolated, outlaw churches that also often engaged in pedophilia. The torture was always done in the guise of corrective corporal punishment, and generally culminated in confessions, repentance, and rape. In Oregon, their parishioners had reportedly hung children from the church ceiling, whipped them, starved them, and forced them into a frigid swimming pool, hosing them down when the kids soiled themselves. Sherman and Crank had disappeared during the investigation of those crimes, which had resulted in minor sentences for some of the children's parents, and had somehow eluded prosecutors until the investigation of this new Crank case.

The case should have been a slam-dunk for prosecutors from the beginning, because before Jessica's death Sherman and Crank had been ordered by a judge to have her treated. Jessica herself had told the judge that she didn't want treatment, but the judge had said, "That's not a decision a child makes. That's a decision parents make."

Not all judges agreed. A few months earlier, in the state of Washington, a judge had allowed a fourteen-year-old boy, Dennis Lindberg, a Jehovah's Witness, to refuse, with the approval of some family members, a blood transfusion that would have kept him from dying of leukemia. The judge said that Lindberg was "giving himself a death sentence," but still invoked freedom of religion. On the day of the ruling the boy died.

Sherman and Crank had been arrested in Tennessee for manslaughter, but Tennessee had one of the toughest shield laws in the country, protecting perpetrators of faith-healing crimes from prosecution for any felony, including manslaughter, child abuse, or neglect—just like Ohio, Texas, and West Virginia. So charges were dropped for both Sherman and Crank.

Tennessee prosecutor Frank Harvey, at Rita's urging, pursued the case, though, on misdemeanor charges. "He should get a gold medal for persistence," Rita later said. Both Sherman and Crank were convicted of very minor charges, but appealed even those to the Supreme Court.

Rita's work remained complex and often frustrating. Around this time, thirty-eight states still had religious shields that could protect people from being charged with child abuse and neglect. Seventeen states had religious shields against various child-abuse felonies, and fifteen more had shields against certain child-abuse misdemeanors. Four states—Idaho, Iowa, Oregon, and Ohio—had shields against both first-degree and second-degree manslaughter, the two toughest non-murder homicide charges. In West Virginia and Oregon, religious motivation could prevent prosecution for murdering a child, and in Arkansas, there was a religious shield against prosecution for murdering anyone—a child or an adult.

Only four states, by this time, had repealed their shield laws entirely: Maryland, Hawaii, Massachusetts, and North Carolina. In those states, the dismantling of the shields had been gradual, occurring over periods of years—as far back as 1994 in Maryland—with various shields eliminated piece by piece, until, generally with little fanfare, few significant exemptions existed at all. The only important exemption left in those states was one that allowed avoiding immunizations—a religious shield that's still present in every state except Mississippi and West Virginia.

Rita still contributed material to journals and books, including a chapter on religion and corporal punishment for the *Encyclopedia of Domestic Violence,* and an article for *The Humanist.* She'd also given recent presentations in Iowa, Florida, and Maine.

Rita did have time to offer some advice on the prosecution of Brent and Raylene Worthington. Don't expect jurors to be rational about religion, she warned, and don't treat the Worthingtons like victims—treat them like perpetrators. Don't let Raylene skate on the grounds that Brent was the boss. Don't get too technical about the medical issues. Hammer away at their failure to call 911—if they didn't make that call, they're guilty, no matter what else happened. And don't make the case about religion. It's about child abuse.

Rita had endured so many disappointments lately, including the light sentences in the Jessica Crank case, that it seemed to her as if, in some areas, particularly in rural regions, the zealots were getting bolder than before. Over the last year, she was virtually certain that at least seven children had died from medical neglect, but only three of the crimes had been prosecuted, and she feared many more crimes had been committed secretly. "So often," she later said, "the deaths just get swept under the rug."

The crimes even seemed to be getting more grotesque. One woman had recently died when church members had jammed an eight-inch-long crucifix up her nose, and another died when a crucifix was shoved down her throat.

Prosecutors and cops around the country were desperate for an aggressive, multi-case attack that would set a precedent, make the news, and change the culture.

So was Rita.

OREGON CITY
MARCH 9, 2008

Marci handed Neil her cell phone. "It's for you." They were at their unfinished ranch, twenty-three acres of creek-side forest and farmland that was out in the less supervised reaches of Clackatucky. The area still had a Wild West feel to it, and was where most of the old churches were, including the 134-year-old Lower Highland Bible Church, a pioneer Pentecostal church, and the Bryn Seion Church, where a clan of Welsh people still sang, very beautifully, in their native tongue.

Neil told Marci that some of the boys from the church had called, wanting him to go for a ride. But he told them he had too much to do.

He wanted to finish moving some boulders with his trackhoe

before the rains returned and soaked the ground to mush. It had been unseasonably sunny lately, and in Oregon the weather always found a way to get even.

Neil wouldn't have gone anyway, though. He didn't feel great, and he wasn't really part of that crowd. Their idea of a good time was to go over to the house of somebody whose parents weren't home and play ridiculous games, like Vase Football, where they'd find something expensive, like a nice vase or a laptop, and use it as the ball, just for the sick thrill. Often as not, they'd break it—that was kind of the idea—and would get reamed out, but nobody ever really got punished. The same kids liked to shoplift at the Followers-owned W. B. Market, because if they got caught nobody would call the cops. Neil had recently gotten roped into helping them toilet-paper somebody's front yard, though one of his friends later said that Neil didn't seem to enjoy it.

Some of these same boys—along with guys old enough to know better—had just gotten busted for the willful slaughter of a bunch of geese over on the dry side of Mt. Hood. Dale Hickman and his brother Lee had been in on that, and so had the Crone and Pedracini boys. It was idiotic, because guys from the same families had been arrested in 2007 for exactly the same thing. This time they shot up even more Canada geese, about forty of them, in the Juniper Flats area. They breasted out seven of them, cutting away only the choice breast meat and tossing the rest, which was illegal. They dumped the other geese in a gully.

Sure enough, a rancher called a Fish and Wildlife officer, who tracked them down. Dale had offered the standard Oregon poacher's defense of It's Just Duck Meat, Not Buck Meat, but that didn't get him very far. Dale, as Patrick had once said, wasn't exactly the sharpest Christian in the Bible.

Neil got his winter jacket from his own small motor home, one of four that were gathered together on the property as their dream home, now framed and roofed, gradually rose from the muck. Someday the house, already spacious and ambitiously planned, would be a monument to the family's grit and togetherness—as would Neil's dream car, the long-sought Camaro he had finally found and was now restoring. At the moment, though, both dreams seemed distant.

Neil went out to the marshy wetlands that led down to Beaver Creek, which was still running high and noisy, and he fired up the Bobcat trackhoe, an excavator with a bucket that could lift a rock as big as a woodstove and crush it to gravel. Neil was building a parking space for his Camaro.

All afternoon he piled boulders into the mud until they stopped sinking, and then ran over them to make a nice flat roadway. Every time he climbed a boulder, the cab would buck backward like a Brahma bull and teeter on the brink of balance, and he had to extend the machine's arm to bring down the nose. It was great, like being inside a video game.

Neil also wanted to work on his mom's planter, but by the time he finished the parking space, he was almost out of daylight. He'd already built the planter's walls, out of boulders—it wasn't the easiest way, but the best—and had left about four hundred square feet in the middle to fill with river-bottom topsoil. With that kind of semi-permeable wall, the drainage would be excellent, and the planter would grow pumpkins so big he'd need his trackhoe to move them.

Fighting the night, he turned on a floodlight and pulled up stumps around the planter until he was sweaty just from the tension of not tipping over.

It got cold early, as it always did in early March, so he went into the shop, stood in front of the heater, and checked out his Camaro. His dream car was the biggest project of his life. He'd wanted the 1969 model with the 6.2-liter, 426-horsepower engine, but his dad had told him he'd never be able to afford that one unless he hit the lottery. So Neil and Jeff had watched eBay like hawks and finally found a beat-up Camaro with a smaller engine. Neil paid cash for it out of his earnings at the construction company and his dad's port-a-potty business.

Neil and Jeff pulled the guts out of the old car and rebuilt the whole thing—steering, brakes, idler arms, bearings, fenders, ball joints, gauges, and the entire front end. Neil even did the Bondo work himself, which took muscle, but would have cost a fortune at a body shop, where they charged inflated prices that the worldly ignored because their insurance covered it.

Best of all, he and his dad found a powerful engine and put that in. Then they cherried it out with a lot of chrome. Now the Camaro was fast, sick, and ready for paint. Neil refused to drive it to town until it was perfect, though.

Before he left the shop Neil cleaned some of the port-a-potties that were lined up in long rows by the back fence. It was gross, but in a couple of years he'd own the business, and Jeff had said he could sell it, grow it, or whatever. Neil had a real sense of money and a significant net worth for a kid his age. It helped that Marci let him out of home-school by noon, because that gave him the rest of the day for real work. Home-schooling also kept the local high school from butting into their business. Back when he was a kid, he'd missed a lot of days when he didn't feel good, and the school always got bent out of shape.

These days, working with the men also kept him too busy to think about things. Like Ava. Ava's death, Jeff thought, had scared Neil. Even for a Followers kid, it was hard to accept the death of someone so young.

By the time Neil was done working, Marci thought he looked like he felt a little better. Marci and the girls had dinner ready, but Neil waited for Jeff, who was working construction at one of the Followers' companies to supplement his income from the port-a-potty business.

When Jeff got home, he and Neil ate dinner and talked about the business and the Camaro. Business was off, but Jeff kept it from sounding too bad. He was like that—he tried not to worry Neil, but still treated him as an equal. Neil had written an essay about that for school.

The phone rang just after they finished a couple of slabs of black-berry pie with homemade blackberry ice cream, and Marci put it on speaker. It was the phone-tree. There'd been a horrible wreck, and they needed prayers and help.

Jeff and Neil piled into the car and burned rubber for the hospital.

Neil's friends had T-boned a pickup. It sounded like one of the teenage Hickman boys was driving, and, if that was true, he was too young to legally have other kids in the car, but the real problem was getting those kids out of the hospital before anything bad happened. Three of them had broken bones—two pelvises, and one thigh-bone, was what they heard. Somebody else had been helicoptered to another hospital by Life Flight.

About a hundred Followers were at the hospital, and more were on the way. Everybody looked grim. They gathered in small groups, and tried to talk very quietly, because they didn't want anybody to hear about their plans to get the kids out of there. They couldn't just barge into the operating room, where one of the kids was getting a steel pin put into his leg, and pull him. It wasn't that easy anymore, with the cops all over them.

The Followers decided that the parents of the injured kids should meet privately with the doctors—just like the worldly did—and tell them that they wanted to take the kids home, where they'd be comfortable. Somebody said to tell the doctors they didn't have insurance. That was a language doctors understood.

Neil was feeling drained, so he and Jeff found a couple of chairs and talked about the paint job. There was a little commotion because Patrick Robbins showed up. Some people had started to wonder about him. But Jeff went over and invited Patrick to sit with him and Neil.

The invitation was a big relief. Patrick told himself that right now he was the best friend Jeff had. He was Neil's and Katie's guardian angel. It made sense: So why was it hard for even him to believe it?

At one point some big burly kid from the world who was about Neil's age wandered by with what looked like a scratch on his arm. Dude had *tears* in his eyes. Jeff said, fairly loudly, "Neil, do you remember the time you pulled your own wisdom tooth?" Neil laughed. Patrick did, too. Jeff, Patrick thought, was probably just as brainwashed as anyone in the church, but it was impossible not to like him.

Neil said they should head out, swing by Burgerville for halibut-and-chips, a pumpkin shake, and sweet potato fries, and take some home to Katie, who didn't feel good. Then they could all watch Letterman. None of the Followers seemed too distraught about the kids in the wreck, because there were so many people praying for them. Everyone assumed they would all recover, and eventually they all did.

When Neil and Jeff took off, so did Patrick.

On the way home Neil drifted in and out of sleep. Since Ava had died, he'd had his good days and bad. This wasn't one of the best, but he'd gotten a lot done. And God had kept him out of that car.

MARCH 17, 2008
GLADSTONE, OREGON

Social worker Jeff Lewis paid an unexpected visit to the Beagleys' country home—or, more precisely, their wagon-train of trailers and campers, in lieu of the real home that Marci Beagley was beginning to doubt would ever get built. Marci had been an obedient wife to Jeff for many years, but she was starting to lose faith, she told a friend, in Jeff's drive to get things done.

Lewis' division of the state's Department of Human Services had gotten an anonymous call on March 10th stating that Katie Beagley had serious, immediate health problems that seemed to suggest kidney failure, which would cause almost immediate death. The caller said that Katie had one kidney infection after another, with symptoms of fevers, back pain, swelling in her abdominal area, and concurrent bladder infections. She even appeared to be having seizures, which indicated the possibility of a late-stage disorder. The caller was also concerned about Neil.

DHS classified the report as a Five Day Referral, which meant that Lewis, who was young and relatively new to the job, had to take action within five days. He went to the home on the fourth day, but no one was home, so he left his card. That constituted taking action.

For some reason, he hadn't gotten a response. He waited three more days, and came back.

This time Katie was there, and Neil, too. Lewis spoke with each child separately, running through his standard checklist. It focused on drug abuse, alcoholism, domestic violence, sexual molestation, and abuse due to discipline. Katie told him that her dad and mom didn't drink much, and weren't violent. She said there was no drug use in the home, that discipline consisted of being grounded, and that there was no, as Lewis had phrased it, "unsafe touching" of the children.

Lewis asked Katie if she was currently healthy, and she said she was. She told him that when she did get sick, she was treated with prayer and anointment with oil.

Neil corroborated everything. He also said that he, too, was healthy, that he had been to a dentist and an eye doctor, that no one in the home was violent or an alcoholic, and that he hadn't been molested. He told Lewis that he wasn't exactly sure what drugs were.

Upon further questioning, Lewis uncovered the fact that Katie might have a milk allergy.

Both kids looked healthy to Lewis, and the trailers they lived in looked sufficiently clean and large. Everything seemed to be in order.

Lewis spent twenty minutes there, and left.

But he wasn't finished. A couple of days later, he called a physician and got suggestions for questions that might reveal severe kidney malfunction. He telephoned Marci and asked her the questions, and Marci relayed them to Katie, who answered them. Again, there was no indication that Katie was sick.

Lewis had tried to be, as he later described it, "sensitive to their religious beliefs." By consulting the physician, he said, he had achieved "a sensitive approach to meeting everybody's needs."

He concluded, "And so we were able to avoid her going to the doctor at that point."

OREGON CITY
MARCH 26, 2008

"Oh Lord." Patrick hated it when the phone rang in the middle of the
night. The calls were hardest to handle when he was only half-awake,
but at least this time he was up, feeding Paul while Theresa caught up
on sleep.

"Neil Beagley needs you to remember him in your prayers," his
phone-tree contact said.

Patrick nervously ran his hand through his long red-brown hair,
took a breath, and reflexively held Paul tighter. "Where is Neil?"

"Norma's." Not a good sign. Taking sick kids to their grandmother's
house was not only a strategy for hiding them from authorities, but also
a ritualistic way of dealing with extreme illness. "Tell Jeff and Marci
I'm tied up with the baby," Patrick said, "but that I'll be praying."

He could have gone, of course, but that wasn't how he wanted to
help Neil. He wanted to help him in the *real* world. There was, he was
beginning to realize, such a place.

It looked, though, as if so far he hadn't been any help at all. He sat
in his recliner with the baby and idly prayed while he mulled over
more practical matters. Should he call back DHS? Call Jim? Go over
and see exactly what was happening?

At Norma Beagley's, Neil lay in his grandmother's bed, slick with
sweat, pale, his chest rattling. Marci touched his shoulder, and he
opened his eyes. "Are you sure you don't want to go to a doctor?" she
asked. He shook his head and shut his eyes.

Neil didn't even have the strength to go to the bathroom by himself, and couldn't hold down any food. Marci had already lost a cousin
to kidney failure, so she knew how fast the wildfire of kidney infection could spread.

Norma's sister-in-law Carolyn Crone, though, thought Neil's real
problem was his stomach. It was really touchy—Crohn's disease, she
thought—and it didn't help that Neil lived on junk food.

Neil's fifteen-year-old buddy Reese Eells, in an outer room with the rest of the guys, thought it looked more like the flu. Really, really bad flu. Maybe that bird flu.

Neil started to gasp. It was time to lay on hands. Again.

OREGON CITY
MARCH 28, 2008

"I should hear from Horner any time about the Worthington grand jury," James Rhodes told Michelle Finn as they met near Clackatraz for a strategy session over coffee. "It sounds like he'll let us give the Worthingtons a heads-up about the warrant, if there is one."

"That'll help," Finn said. She and Rhodes were trying to maintain a rapport with the Followers. They were convinced that sooner or later another child would die, and when they went to that death scene, they wanted to be at least slightly trusted.

To achieve that, Rhodes had asked Chief Deputy DA Greg Horner if he could notify Brent and Raylene in advance if the grand jury, which was meeting that week, handed down indictments. Horner was considering it.

Finn and Rhodes feared that the Followers had figured out that they didn't need to be as forthcoming as they'd been at Ava's death scene. Until somebody was actually arrested, they didn't have to say anything—even if that was rude. They didn't even have to give their names. In case that happened, Finn and Rhodes were planning to bring a stack of blank subpoenas to the next death scene. Then they could say, "Here's your subpoena for a grand jury, so you can tell me your name now, or spend the night in jail and tell me later."

Rhodes' phone buzzed. It was Horner. "We got a true bill," Horner said, meaning a true bill of indictment against both Carl Brent Worthington and Raylene Worthington for criminal mistreatment, and for manslaughter in the second degree of their daughter, Ava Worthington. Bail would be $250,000 each, and the Worthingtons were required to post 10 percent of that after their booking in the Clackamas County Jail.

A warrant for their arrest would be issued the following day. Until then the indictment was secret. But Horner didn't consider the Worthingtons a flight risk, because they were so involved with their community, and said it was okay to go tell them what was happening. Horner wanted to keep the rapport, too, because this smelled like the kind of trouble that wouldn't go away.

When Finn and Rhodes arrived at the Worthingtons', Raylene opened her front door. Rhodes had decided, he later recalled, to re-prise the strategy he'd used at Ava's death scene, and "kill them with kindness."

"May we come in?" Rhodes asked. "I'm afraid we have some bad news that we have to share with you."

Brent was in the living room. "There's a forthcoming warrant for your arrest," Rhodes said. "It will be out by tomorrow morning."

Raylene's eyes widened as she looked at Brent. He was impassive. "The bail will be $250,000 each." Rhodes explained the procedure for posting bail.

"If you'd like us to take you in now," Rhodes said, "we will. But the warrant isn't really out yet, so we don't have to."

Finn told them that a long process lay ahead, but that their case was now in the hands of the district attorney, and not the police.

Brent said that they wanted to meet with their attorney. They had already spoken with one, and now they had to iron out the details of hiring him.

The attorney had told them that he would need a retainer against fees that ran about $300 per hour, and would be even higher during court appearances. They would probably want two attorneys, the law-yer said, so that Raylene could have her own, to increase her chances of letting Brent take most of the responsibility. It looked as if the most expensive time in the couple's life was approaching—"in this economy."

It would be a bargain, though, if it kept them out of jail.

"Are there any questions?" Finn asked.

"No," said Brent affably, "You've been very kind." He looked happy to be avoiding even one night in Clackatraz. He was optimistic that the Lord wouldn't send them to prison, and even had a strategy for getting God to help with the bill.

That night, shortly after the local late news, Brent and Raylene went to Clackatraz, surrendered, were printed and mugged, posted bail, and left.

The next day, Mark Hass, the reporter who had first broken the Followers story—now a state senator after six years in the House—was interviewed by Dan Tilkin of KATU, where Hass had previously worked. "Ten years ago," Hass said, "I couldn't express my feelings for what was going on out there, but I can now. This is child abuse. Pure and simple. There is no other way to say it."

The story made national news, packaged with two similar incidents. In one, a member of the Seventh-day Adventist Church expressed regret for his religion-inspired decision to allow a cluster of tumors to grow to approximately the size and shape of a head of cauliflower on his face, until it blinded him. The only news photo of him was a silhouette that partly disguised his ghoulish appearance. The Adventist Church, though, commented that the surgery to correct it would have been "contrary to what is stated in Scripture."

The other was about a little girl in Weston, Wisconsin, who had died the prior week from untreated diabetes, while her parents had prayed. Kara Neumann, eleven, had been dreadfully ill and in agony as she lost control of her body. Her aunt had called the children's services division several times, but it seemed to her as if the authorities weren't very interested in a case that didn't involve drugs or blood. On the day Kara died, her aunt called the police three times, and they finally agreed to do a "child welfare check." On their way to the scene, Kara slipped into her last coma.

Kara's parents, Dale and Leilani Neumann, were members of a Followers' offshoot, the Unleavened Bread Ministries, led by David

Eells, who had relatives in the O.C. Followers. His website, Americas-LastDays.com, praised Christians "who physically fight, with flesh and blood, to take America back." Eells' defense of the Neumanns was backed by another Wisconsin preacher, known as Pastor Bob, who said that the Neumanns had been arrested for "the crime of praying."

Rita Swan was featured in an ABC News story and a *New York Times* article about Kara's death, in which she talked once again about her loss of Matthew. That was hard for her. Having told her story more than a thousand times, it was still the last thing she wanted to discuss. But reliving that nightmare publicly was her cross to bear.

Rita helped convince the University of Wisconsin Law School to defend Kara's mother, in a hardball strategy to throw out the confusing state shield law, which said some faith-healing crimes were legal, while others weren't. The internal contradiction, Rita believed, would invalidate the law. The Christian Science Church, as usual, was funding the support of the shield law.

It was a hard time to be playing hardball. For the past eight years, born-again George W. Bush had taken Nixon's Southern Strategy to new lows, pandering to fundamentalists while he simultaneously fought two wars based mostly on religious terrorism, plus a holy war against stem-cell research. To win the hearts and minds in the Mideast, he was trying to legalize torture—intended for terrorists only, of course, with a few slip-ups here and there—and was allowing it to happen semi-secretly in the meantime. Meanwhile, Shiite and Sunni Iraqis were killing and torturing each other over whether or not Muhammad's cousin had been holy, and some jihadists were still trying to figure out another way to kill the people in the Great Satan that was America.

With the age of nationalism waning, religious war was more widespread than it had been for five hundred years, and Christian/Muslim conflict seemed to be the wave of the future.

And so we beat on, boats against the current, borne back ceaselessly into the Dark Ages.

Oregon City
April 1, 2008

The Beagley case was back in play at DHS—this time involving Neil. On the last day of March, a call had come in to DHS's emergency hotline. The caller said Neil could barely breathe, that the Beagleys were hiding him from DHS, and that they should *do* something. But it was after 4:00 p.m., so the hotline worker tabled it.

The next day, the hotline worker told Jeff Lewis that the caller claimed Neil had almost died, and still might.

It didn't make sense to Lewis. Neil had looked fine a couple of weeks ago.

Lewis decided to "staff it," which meant talk to his bosses. He had two of them, one to approve his decisions, and another to review the approvals, and approve them.

Lewis and his bosses "had a staffing," he later recalled, and he told them that an "RP"—reporting party—had informed them that Neil Beagley was "showing current illness that is causing his throat to close, and making it extremely difficult for him to breathe." The bosses decided the case was an Immediate Referral, instead of a Five Day Referral, so some action had to be taken that same day. Lewis telephoned Jeff Beagley. Beagley told him that he had an attorney, and wanted to talk to him before discussing the matter further. That was enough action to fulfill the guidelines.

Lewis had another staffing with his supervisor, Pat Bowman, to decide how much time to give Jeff Beagley to consult his attorney. Lewis later recalled, "She eventually came up with the time of two o'clock" on April 2nd. The Beagleys were informed of the deadline.

At 1:50 p.m. on April 2, Jeff Beagley called Lewis and said that he still hadn't talked to his lawyer. He also said Neil was afraid that DHS would take him. But Jeff said Lewis could come over to Neil's grandmother's house, if he didn't bring any policemen.

When Lewis arrived at Norma Beagley's home, she answered the door, and Lewis introduced himself. She didn't respond. Jeff Beagley walked up behind her and invited Lewis in. Marci was there, and so was Katie, as well as Jeff Beagley's brother Steve.

The Beagleys said they had moved Neil to Norma's home because he'd caught a cold eight days ago, and his trailer wasn't warm and dry enough. Marci said that Neil was receiving adequate care, and that she'd been giving him watermelon, strawberries, and mashed potatoes with broth, along with lots of juice, water, and Pedialyte, to keep him hydrated.

Lewis went to Norma Beagley's bedroom to talk to Neil, who had a blanket over his lap. The room was sweltering, but Neil—almost elfin, with ears that looked as if he hadn't quite grown into them yet—said he liked it warm. He told Lewis that for a week and a half he'd had a sore throat and runny nose.

"Have you ever had a hard time breathing?" Lewis asked.

"I don't think so," Neil said.

Neil told Lewis that he was stiff from sitting around so much, but that he'd been getting lots of liquids. Lewis asked Neil about the color of his urine, to help determine if he was getting enough fluids, and Neil told him his urine was yellow, and not dark brown.

"Do you want to be treated by a doctor?" Lewis asked.

"No. My mom already asked me that."

Lewis asked Neil if he could take his picture, and Neil consented. The boy looked healthy enough to Lewis, and the bedroom did not appear to be, as Lewis later put it, "unsafe." The interview took ten minutes.

Lewis asked Jeff Beagley's brother Steve if he had any concerns about Neil's care. "No," Steve said, "it's just a common cold, and they're doing everything they need to be doing." Lewis asked Katie the same question and got the same basic answer.

As Lewis prepared to leave, Jeff and Marci seemed to be frightened. But it wasn't clear what they were afraid of. The authorities? The church? They didn't seem worried about Neil.

"What now?" Jeff Beagley asked Lewis.

"I'll have to go back and staff it with my bosses," Lewis said. He told them DHS might have a hearing to determine if Neil needed medical care. But Lewis, Jeff later said, told them that, "It would be an interesting hearing, because there's an ORS statute which gives Neil the ability to decide whether or not he goes to the doctor. And Neil said he doesn't want to go to a doctor."

"Oh, yeah," Jeff Beagley replied. "You know," he said, "this type of harassment is going to continue every time one of the kids gets a runny nose." His face hardened. He no longer looked scared. He looked scary.

Beagley wasn't referring to harassment by the government. He'd seen what the government could throw at him, and didn't seem impressed. He meant harassment by the Reporting Party.

BEAVERCREEK, OREGON
MEMORIAL DAY WEEKEND, MAY 24, 2008

It was supposed to be a three-day weekend for chillin' and grillin', the traditional holiday welcome to summer, but Neil was working. He was on the trackhoe, rebuilding a stone wall down by a stream that led to Beaver Creek, which was still fast and icy because of extreme snowmelt.

Neil had accidentally knocked down parts of the wall while he was logging off the area between the two barns, and he needed the wall to help protect the outbuildings from the rising creek, and to keep out the critters that were always around, even though they hardly ever saw them—the cougars, black bear, feral pigs, beavers, and wild dogs that left tracks by the creek and made the woods scary-fun. The farm was adjacent to a forested strip of power lines that ran straight to the Cascades, and the vegetation in the open area was a magnet for wildlife.

Neil rebuilt the wall as perfectly as possible, making it balanced and symmetrical, so that it would stay there forever, or until someone tore it down. Jeff Beagley later recalled that, "He tried to keep all the rocks sort of uniform, and make it look nice."

Neil liked their country place a lot more than the house in town, and always got a jolt of energy when he hopped onto the backhoe or trackhoe and felt the wind blow fresh air into his face. His energy had been building lately, and whenever that happened, he liked to pull long hours outdoors, working, and talking to God. It took him away from the world.

Marci could hear Neil's trackhoe from the kitchen. She was in the big trailer baking a cake for Katie, because it was her birthday. It was reassuring to hear the rumble of the trackhoe and the vibration of boulders landing on the ground. It meant Neil was feeling good.

She was also happy that something was actually getting done around there. Neil was so good with his hands. She remembered the time before he could walk when they baby-proofed the house with locks and he figured out how to open them. As a toddler, he was always opening the refrigerator, so they strapped it shut and put a complicated latch on it, but he figured that out, too.

Before Neil was even five, she recalled, he loved to ride behind Jeff on his motorcycle while they splashed through puddles and creeks. When Jeff would get home from work, Neil would run up to him and say, "Dada go vroom-vroom through the wawa." Then in grade school they bought him a little red Power Wheels Jeep that ran on a battery, and he figured out a way to install a car battery to make it faster, and ran it until the wheels came off.

Grade school was tough, though, because he was still in public school. When Marci dropped off Neil and his sisters, he'd hide behind a seat, refuse to get out, and miss school. She'd talked to the principal about it, but he was still critical about how often Neil was absent. The schools didn't treat the Followers with much respect, she thought, so they mostly home-schooled Neil and Katie.

That cut down on the conflict, made Neil less stubborn, and brought out a soft side of him that only she knew. Once when he acted up and got sent to his room, she heard his door open and close and thought he'd let himself out, but when she checked the hallway she found a story from his *Children's Bible* about forgiveness, and a blackboard that said, "If this person can be forgiven, hopefully my mother can forgive me."

It was hard for her to believe that Neil was almost a grown man. He was already treated like one of the men. One of the guys who owned a company had already offered Neil full-time construction work, and Neil often talked about how he had a job lined up, and was anxious to be done with the kid-stuff.

She heard his chainsaw. He was cutting up brush for one of the burn-piles.

Sweating, Neil walked down to Beaver Creek to see if it was coming up over its banks, carrying a chainsaw that was almost as big as his torso, a bantamweight version of Kesey's quintessential Oregon hero Hank Stamper. The river looked good. He was standing by the bank with his saw when Jeff stepped out from the trees, back from work.

Jeff helped Neil finish the work. It was the main way he expressed his love to Neil. Women showed their love with words, and men showed it with work.

Then it was time to head to the Claim Jumper on Sunnyside Road for Katie's birthday dinner. The Claim Jumper wasn't Burgerville, but it was good. Huge portions of comfort food.

When they were finishing dinner, Jeff asked Neil if he wanted to catch some Letterman later on.

"*Oh* yeah," said Neil.

Neil saying that with no hesitation made Jeff feel great. It was Neil's way of saying he loved him. Neil never came right out and told Jeff he loved him—it just wasn't in his vocabulary—but Neil, a hard-working man already, didn't need to. He walked the walk.

Patrick, cradling Paul while Theresa finished grilling some steaks, said a prayer in the closet for Brent, who'd looked like death itself two days ago, on Father's Day. After church, Brent and Raylene had headed off with the Beagley clan—so that Raylene could give Jeff the apple tree that she and Neil had bought for him—but Patrick could tell the absence of Ava had been a torment to them all. Patrick, trying to enjoy a Father's Day celebration of his own, still felt half-sick with guilt about not doing more for Ava, and the day had been hard on him, too, even with the sweet presence of Paul.

Theresa brought his dinner—medallions of sirloin with creamed asparagus—and put it on the coffee table in front of the TV, so that Patrick could put Paul down on the couch beside him while he ate, and touch the baby often enough to make him feel safe.

Theresa sat beside him. "This has brought out something in you I've never seen," she said.

He shrugged. "I love being a dad."

"But you look different. You really do. In the eyes. You look like, uh . . ." She dropped it.

"Like who?" Did she mean a TV star or somebody she was embarrassed to admit she liked?

"Nobody."

"Oh come on."

"Okay. Like him." She pointed to the print over the fireplace of The Light of the World, the painting of Jesus knocking on a door.

"Thanks." He was flattered, but didn't feel good about the comparison. It felt too much like an omen, or a jinx. He was starting to pay attention to silly superstitions that would once have seemed like blasphemy. He turned his attention back to Paul, who was babbling something that sounded strangely comprehensible.

Around 6:30, his cell phone played "Ode to Joy." The caller-ID said it was the phone tree.

II

THE WAGES OF SIN

Father, why have you forsaken me?

—The Book of Mark 15:34,

known as the Word of Abandonment

Gladstone, Oregon

June 17, 2008

Jim Band got the call-out at 6:30 p.m. from Dave Ruby of the DA's office. Ruby wanted Band at a death scene as fast as possible. Chief Deputy DA Greg Horner was already on his way. So was Lynne Benton from the Gladstone PD, and Jeff Mayer from the Medical Examiner's Office. James Rhodes from the Sheriff's Office was rushing there with his wife, Patti, an OSP crime scene specialist. Michelle Finn was headed in from out of town, presumably obeying the speed limits, to the best of her ability.

Ruby had an address and a body but no identity. A male from the Followers had called in a death but wouldn't name names, not even his own. The place of death was Norma Beagley's home. Band knew it wouldn't be Jeff, Marci, or Norma, because the Followers didn't have to report adult deaths. So he assumed the deceased was either Katie or Neil.

But Band had heard Katie and Neil had been okay lately. DHS

hadn't pursued the cases on them. Patrick had recently told him that DHS never did have a clue about how close to death Neil had been in March, but he said that a couple of weeks ago he'd seen the Crown Prince playing basketball with his friends.

It was probably Katie.

Either way, Band's immediate job was to start determining the cause and manner of death. That usually meant, he later said, "finding out who was swinging the hammer that hit the head." But this was nothing like that.

Lynne Benton, the Gladstone PD sergeant who worked almost exclusively within her small town's jurisdiction, was the first on the scene. Benton, a 21-year law enforcement veteran who'd been in Detectives for fifteen years, entered the Beagley property through a security gate, and encountered a large crowd of men.

Most of them glared at her. A lot of them were smoking, and even the outdoor air was cloudy as she bumped her way through them. It was against protocol to initiate any physical contact with a crowd, because push could turn to shove and end up with an officer going to ground, which was dangerous with no back-up around. But Lynne Benton was hard to scare. She was rumored to wear her bullet-proof vest to every call-out, and looked as tough as any of the male cops in town, with a no-nonsense short haircut, a muscular build, and a face that seemed tailor-made for a cop's requisite Don't-Fuck-With-Me look. Everything about Lynne Benton tended to remind perps of their manners.

Benton badged the home's occupant at the front door and was escorted to the back bedroom, where the body was. It was a young male, identified as Neil Beagley, 16, wearing plaid pajamas, with his shirt pulled up and his blankets off to the side. He was lying in his grandmother's bed, and was quite pale, with a sick-yellow tinge. His face seemed to be smeared with oil.

On the dresser next to the bed was a container of olive oil, some white flowers, and a bottle of water that appeared to be about half-empty. A blow-up bed was off to one side, and around the bedroom were numerous depictions of swans—figurines, photos, paintings, prints, you name it.

Benton kept the scene secure and waited for the other officers to arrive.

The medical examiner got there first, and was able to photograph the death scene before there was any risk of contamination of evidence— either inadvertent, or intentional—which was known as spoliation, and was often in the minds of jurors who'd seen too many movies about people getting framed.

The ME, Jeff Mayer, looked sick as a dog. His face was white and pinched, and his lips were blue. Mayer had the stomach flu, but was determined to handle this case himself. The death of Ava Worthington was fresh in his memory, and he wanted this case to be handled as competently as that one, which would soon be coming to trial.

Brent and Raylene Worthington had recently been all over the local news and on the major websites that exposed religious abuse, including Rita Swan's, Rick Ross', *Secular News Daily*, and Atheist Revolution, as well as in other national media. Turner Broadcasting's Nancy Grace had become interested in the issue of faith-healing abuse because of the Worthington case, and truTV was planning to televise the entire Worthington trial. The spotlight was on.

A block away, Michelle Finn pulled her hair into a ponytail as she strode toward the death scene past the parked cars that were beginning to glut the street. She reminded herself not to make any of the procedural errors that had occurred at the Worthington death scene, like letting people sneak off without getting their names, being too nice, or assuming that the Followers of Christ were ODCs: ordinary, decent criminals. ODCs often acted on the spur of the moment, and were sometimes almost anxious to blurt out a confession, just for stress relief. That wouldn't happen tonight. The Followers didn't fit the profile for random-acts-of-violence. They were patient, letting their kids die slowly and then waiting to report the deaths while they got their stories straight. Tonight it sounded like they'd waited an hour or two.

Rhodes, Band, and Horner were waiting for Finn in front of Norma Beagley's little purple house. Rhodes' wife, Patti, of the OSP, had already entered the home to gather evidence, with Criminalists Randy Krebs and Greg Martin.

They game-planned quietly about how to handle the scene.

Horner told the group of cops that he didn't need to go inside. "Band was there," Horner later recalled, "and he's a smart guy who knows what he's doing. And James and Michelle had been the leads on the Worthington case, so they had a good sense of the characteristics that applied to these folks." But his mere presence had made his point, which was very much along the lines of: Good luck, you have my complete confidence, this is a critically important case, and don't you dare screw something up.

Horner's biggest concern was Neil's age. In 1999, when Rita had helped pass the new shield law, she'd reluctantly agreed to an amendment that established age fifteen or older as the legal age for being able to demand medical care. But the law was much less clear about a fifteen-year-old's right to *refuse* care. Even the distinction between demanding and refusing, Rita had thought, created a gray area that would be confusing for a jury. But the compromise had seemed necessary at the time. Now it was coming back to haunt them. Neil had been 16 when he died, a year over the legal age required to demand care.

Band spotted one of the elders, Fred Smith, a white-haired, cheerful guy with thick glasses who dressed simply and commanded respect. By this time, almost thirty years since Prophet Walter White had died, none of the elders had any specific duties or powers and had to rely on their popularity and manipulative skills to keep the minor influence they had. "Fred kind of plays the country gentleman," Band later said. "He likes talking and ribbing. But he's totally passive-aggressive, and what he really likes is to incite."

Band motioned Smith over and said, "Look, the house is full, and we need people to go outside so we can take photos and talk. I want to do it as politely as possible, and I need you to help me do that. What do you think is the best way?"

Smith said it would be best if just the two of them went in together. They agreed to announce in a low-key way that all the older people could stay seated and be comfortable, and that immediate family was welcome to stay as long as they liked, but that it would be best for the others to leave now.

Smith warned Band, though, that everyone had been advised not to talk to the police. They knew their rights. "Every time we talk to you guys," Smith said, "everything gets turned around."

Band didn't care. The subpoenas they had would take care of that.

"Let's just be real respectful," Band said.

"'Course," Smith said.

Smith led Band in, and the crowd gathered around them and quieted. "Everybody listen up!" Smith yelled. "Cops say everybody out! Get outside right now! Everybody!"

"Time out," Band said in the silence. "That's not what I said at all. We know this is a very difficult time for you, and we have every respect for what you're going through. But we need to do some things here, and it will be best if those of you who aren't close family say good-night."

The warmth-factor rose by about one degree. People were still drilling stares through Band, but began to hug others and head for the door while the police filed in. With the noise in the room suddenly gone, Band and everyone else could hear somebody throwing up in the backyard. It was Jeff Mayer. Katie Beagley was watching Mayer through a window and smiling.

Lynne Benton drifted toward the door, and began to disengage. Nobody stopped her. This kind of twenty-first-century situation was better left to criminalists like Finn, Band, and James and Patti Rhodes. It was beyond the scope of the Gladstone PD, which generally dealt with less complex tasks than investigating religiously tinged deaths.

Benton was happy to wash her hands of this mess. It offered a typically fractious Clackastani, pick-your-poison choice: You could either piss off the strongest single interest group in the county—or everybody else. Benton was positioned to make a run for Chief in the next year or so, and didn't need the grief. Besides, she had personal problems. Even by the eccentric and ambiguous standards of Oregon City, she had a complex life.

Sergeant Benton was a transgender female who identified in her private life as a male. At the moment, she was strongly considering sex-reassignment surgery, which was an ordeal in and of itself, and carried career ramifications. She was constantly in the public eye as the spokesperson for the Gladstone force, and taught at the local community college, fulfilling both roles as a female. She'd been married to a man for three years, but was now in the seventh year of a registered domestic relationship with a woman.

She'd already changed her name to Lynn Edward Benton, and was registered as a male on her driver's license, which did not require proof of gender. But to be married as a male, which was her stated desire, she would need the surgery.

It was perfectly acceptable for her to function professionally as a lesbian—It's Oregon—but changing sex could turn her very public career into a carnival. Plus, her relationship was on the rocks. This was not the time to get mixed up in an extremely controversial case.

Even so, Benton stuck around, knowing she would need to make a statement the next morning, as the Public Information Officer for the death's principal jurisdiction. She stood outside the cluster of detectives as Band, Finn, and Rhodes caucused quietly on how to divide and conquer. They'd already wallpapered the crowd with subpoenas, so now they could focus their night's work on the two main players: mom and dad. Finn, as the female, got Marci, and Band got Jeff, who was almost as tall as Band, and vastly larger than Neil. Rhodes went with Finn, thinking that if anybody might crack, it would be mom.

Marci was sitting by herself near a bulletin board that had a handmade sign inscribed, TOUCH ME AND HEAL ME, SAVYOR DEVINE, next to a post-it note that said CALL LAWYER. For some reason, people were crowded around Jeff but not her.

Finn approached her. "Mrs. Beagley, I'm Detective Finn, and I'm *very* sorry for your loss. I can't imagine it. But I need to speak with you for a moment."

Suddenly some guy was in her face—too close. She could feel his breath. "You're not talking to her without Jeff," he said.

Finn couldn't tell which was distressing this man more: a death in the family, or having two lady cops in the house.

"That's not your decision," Finn said. "I will speak to Jeff. When I get to him. Right now I'm talking to Marci." Finn gave him The Look, not quite on par with Lynne Benton's, but still rich with information, and that was the end of the discussion.

Finn asked Marci, "Would you prefer to do it someplace more private?"

Marci nodded vacantly and led Finn and Rhodes down a hallway to a small guest bedroom. They passed Jeff's mother, Norma, and Rhodes was glad they weren't relying on her to open up and be honest. She looked like a classic hard case: thin, grim, and intense, with dry eyes, blood-red fingernails, and hair pulled into a severe bun. When they passed the death-site bedroom, Rhodes and Finn could see Jeff Mayer back in there, sitting by the body, which was already beginning to emit gases in the overheated home. Mayer was as bloodless as Neil, but his flesh-tone had been replaced with white and blue, instead of yellow. Rhodes saw Mayer start to stand, fail, and sit again. His stomach bug was overpowering him.

"Initially," Rhodes later said, "I just got background from Marci. At that point, we didn't know what had happened, other than the bare-bones version we'd gotten outside. So I wanted to know the history of Neil's health, and exactly how the death occurred."

Marci, who looked empty but in control, told them she was in shock, partly because Neil had looked so good lately. Last night, she said, he was walking all over and pretending his water bottles were barbells. He had been anxious for Jeff to get back from work, she said, so that they could wrestle.

Marci confirmed that Neil had been sick in March, but said he hadn't required the laying on of hands. That wasn't what Band's snitch had said, but Rhodes and Finn kept that to themselves.

"Michelle and I," Rhodes later said, "needed to pursue the issue of what a reasonable person would do, because that's what Marci's legal responsibility was." He particularly needed to know if Marci would have called a doctor, if it was up to her. A reasonable person, in a life-or-death situation, would have.

"If the choice was totally yours," Rhodes asked, "because, let's say hypothetically, your husband was deceased, and Neil hadn't told you what he wanted, would you have called a doctor?"

Marci looked like she'd never heard anything so outlandish. "There's no *way* for me to answer that question."

"Why?" Rhodes asked.

"I have no *idea*." She sounded high-pitched and supercilious, like The Church Lady on *Saturday Night Live,* a tone Rhodes had heard among the Followers before. It was a stereotype because it was real.

"No idea at all?" Rhodes asked.

"*I* don't know if it *ever* would have come to me to do that or not."

Rhodes started to grill her like she was just another perp. "I kept drilling her," Rhodes later said, "like, 'I don't give a fuck what your husband says—what would you do?' But she wouldn't say."

Rhodes switched gears. "Do you think a doctor could have helped Neil today? Made him more comfortable? Eased his pain?"

"I'm not *familiar* . . . I'm not *acquainted* with that world of medicine and doctors. So I don't *know*," Marci said.

"We got considerably more direct," Rhodes recalled, "but she kept hemming and hawing."

It looked as if Marci been practicing for this, just like the officers had. She talked in circles for almost an hour, admitting nothing. Sometimes she just sat in silence, while they listened to Jeff Mayer throwing up in the backyard.

When Marci did say things that might have incriminated her, she tied them to the actions of others, particularly Jeff, which made the testimony inadmissible. It was a smart, old-con move, since co-conspirators cannot legally incriminate one another. Finn later explained, "If you and I rob a bank, I can only talk about what I did. If I say I did this while you did that, whatever I say about you is hearsay.

And it can cause a whole statement to get thrown out in court, before it even gets to the jury. So for every fifty pages of an interview that a jury hears, there can be a hundred pages they don't hear: the co-conspiracy part. And the defense attorneys edit the interview transcripts so smoothly that the jury doesn't even realize things are left out."

Rhodes knew that Jeff and Marci would soon meet with their lawyers, and probably adopt a strategy of blaming Neil for his own death, because of his age. Neil, at sixteen, did have a legal right to demand medical care, though not necessarily to refuse it, and his lawyers were almost certain to exploit the complexity of the law, and say the whole decision was up to him.

"What if Neil was eight years old?" Rhodes asked Marci. "Would you consider medical attention then?"

"If my husband was agreeable to it?"

"Yes."

"If the law demanded it?"

"Yes."

"I probably would."

Gotcha. She had incriminated herself, to some extent, by admitting that kids, at least at *some* age, do need parental authority on matters of medical treatment.

The jury, Rhodes hoped, would think that Neil, who knew nothing about medicine and was in a mental fog, was no more able than an eight-year-old to make a wise decision: even *if* that decision was his alone to make. Jeff and Marci should have made it for him, no matter what Neil said, or the law implied. To do otherwise was unreasonable.

When they were done with Marci, Finn and Rhodes approached Katie Beagley and asked Marci's permission to interview her. Marci agreed, but said she wanted to be there. They found an empty bathroom, and Marci and Katie sat on the edge of the tub.

Katie was cheerfully robotic. "She was like a Stepford Wife," Rhodes later recalled, "talking about her brother dying, like, 'It's all good; life goes on.'"

The detectives hoped they could get Katie to be honest about the length and severity of Neil's illness. But Marci put her hand on Katie's knee, as if to be supportive, and each time Katie began to elaborate, Marci squeezed her knee.

"It pissed me off," Rhodes remembered. "Katie would be saying, 'Oh, Neil's been sick for a *long*'—then, clamp!—'well, not really a long time, more like a *short* time.'"

The house was still hot from the hundreds of bodies that had been jammed into it, and the bathroom was a sauna. "I was, frankly, sweating my ass off," Rhodes recalled, "sitting there in my suit and tie, pissed at Marci and the church for letting this happen."

A social worker from DHS suddenly appeared, and that made Katie even more tongue-tied. Rhodes, fed up, took off, and Finn completed the interview.

Katie's interview, Rhodes said later, was extremely revealing—but not in a way that could legally be communicated to a jury. There was plenty of body language in it, but not enough legal language. It meant one more problem for Horner.

GLADSTONE, OREGON
JUNE 17, 11:00 P.M.

Jeff Beagley, in another bedroom, told Jim Band that he had stayed up all of the prior night with Neil, mostly talking about cars and work. "It was kind of a Boys' Night chat," Jeff said. He said that Neil was making plans about all the things he wanted to get done that week. They watched a little TV, he said, and from time to time Neil would nap.

Every memory of Neil put so much pain in Jeff's face that it was obvious it would never go away. Band could almost see grief rising off Jeff like a vapor.

"Normally," Band later said, "I'm really happy about putting people in prison. If I work a rape case or a homicide and somebody goes to jail, it makes me feel good. But with this case, even if we won, there'd be no win. Neil would still be dead, and I like Jeff and Marci. They're really nice people. Jeff is a salt-of-the-earth guy."

Jeff told Band that Neil hadn't been sleepy the night before because he'd slept off and on all day. While he talked to Neil, Jeff said, his daughters Nicole and Katie came in, and Neil told them some blonde jokes. After they left, Neil told Jeff that he "needed to do something about" the girls. He was kidding, Jeff thought, but not entirely.

Around the middle of the night, Neil didn't feel good, and Jeff hoped the illness was peaking and would soon "go the other way."

Jeff recalled carrying Neil into the bathroom at one point, partly because Neil's knee hurt and his legs felt weak, Jeff said, but mostly as a joke. He said they were just "making fun" of the whole thing. When Neil was done in the bathroom, Jeff said he carried him back to the bed and playfully threw him down. It wasn't, Jeff said, as if he "carefully set him down."

Jeff said that it was just "a coincidence" that he stayed up all night with Neil on the last night of his son's life. The death came without warning, he said, and was a total shock. Jeff was painting a picture of a quick and easy death, and for all Band knew, it could be true.

Or not. Jeff told Band that Neil was playing basketball with his friends less than a week ago—but Patrick had said that was *two* weeks ago. Sometimes one little lie indicated deeper deceit.

Band listened very carefully to Jeff, because he almost never taped interviews, especially the first time he talked to someone. Instead, he made meticulous notes afterward. "It's something I do to get people to trust me," he later said. "And *like* me." The technique had resulted in his most successful detective work ever, when he solved a cold-case murder with a confession, something that almost never happens, except in movies. He put the killer so at ease that the perp opened up and spilled his guts one night while they were walking down a dark country road. It was all so casual that the killer somehow felt safe from retaliation. He denied the whole story later, but still faced trial.

Another reason the perp dished was because Band was sincerely nonjudgmental. "Even a child molester," he later said, "will be fairly honest if they sense that you're not judging them. A lot of cops don't get that. But you really can catch more flies with honey than vinegar."

Jeff began to breathe more deeply as the interview continued, and mentioned that they'd laid hands on Neil shortly before he died. It was Neil's idea, Jeff said: He thought it would "be nice."

In the unique context of the Followers, that act did not indicate a quick and easy death—it was incriminating. "The laying on of hands," Band later said, "is their 911 call."

Jeff told Band that Neil's decline had begun when Ava died. Neil had started complaining that his stomach hurt, and he became even quieter than usual. "Neil usually kept his feelings all bottled up," Jeff said. "I always wished he'd talked more."

During the last few hours of Neil's life, Jeff said, his breathing became a little more labored, but he was still telling jokes to Jeff's brother Steve, who was there that night. Neil was calm and quiet, Jeff said, and didn't seem to be in pain. His nose was runny, and it had been bleeding, but Jeff thought that was just because Neil had picked at it.

Jeff said that a couple of times he did consider taking Neil to the doctor, because he loved him so much. When Jeff said that, his voice was throaty and he was on the verge of tears. "But I tried to respect what he wanted," Jeff said.

If Jeff had taken his son to a doctor, Band asked, would he have been shunned? Jeff replied that he knew some people thought that Followers were thrown out of the Church for doing that, but actually, he said, "People just frown on you for a while."

"Is it a sin to see a doctor?"

"It's called lack of faith," Jeff said. He said that God could do anything, and a doctor couldn't. "It's like, when a doctor does all he can, what does he say then?"

"He says, 'It's in God's hands,'" Band said.

"Yes. It's like that." Jeff told Band proudly that no one in his family had ever been to a doctor.

Band asked Jeff if he thought now that he should have taken Neil to a doctor.

"It's hard to know," Jeff said. "It's a lot harder to walk the walk."

"Could you tell the end was coming?" Band asked softly.

"No. I didn't think he was that bad, even at the end."

About an hour before Neil died, Jeff said, he told Jeff that he wanted to take a nap, and asked Jeff to tell Marci not to wake him up to eat.

Jeff said he helped Neil rearrange his pillows, and that Neil "rolled up" into a ball and seemed to go to sleep. Jeff and Steve continued to visit, and pray, mostly in the closet.

Just before Neil died, Jeff said, they were standing above him praying. Then, with no warning, Neil stopped breathing. It was "such a shock."

Jeff's version, so far, had vindicated him and Marci. Their son's worst symptom, supposedly, was a bloody nose, which was described by Jeff as more like a runny nose—and then he died.

Band asked Jeff if Neil had requested medical attention. "I did ask Neil what he wanted to do," Jeff said, "and he didn't want a doctor."

Jeff looked squarely at Band and said, "That's what I'm most proud of. Neil held his faith to the end." He smiled slightly and his eyes stared into space for a moment, appearing no longer to be in torment, but to be seeing his son. He took a deep breath and let it out.

Jeff was quiet, but it seemed as if there was something else he wanted to mention. Band waited. Jeff took another breath. Band leaned back.

Then Jeff said he knew Neil took a turn for the worse that afternoon.

"What happened?" Band asked casually.

Jeff said that Neil started acting differently, and did something that was totally out of character.

"Differently?"

"Neil said . . ." Jeff's lower lip was trembling. "Neil said he wanted . . . He said he wanted me to know that he *loved* me."

Jeff's face contorted in warring emotions of anguish and love, unembarrassed, and fat tears fell from his eyes.

Band put his hand on Jeff's shoulder. His eyes glassed up. Even for a cop, it was hard not to get swept up in something like that.

The interview was over. Detective Band felt terrible for Jeff Beagley. And he suddenly felt hopeful that—with any luck, and some strong circumstantial evidence—Jeff had just put himself in prison.

Band headed for Norma's bedroom. On the way, Fred Smith pulled him aside. "Let me ask you one thing," Smith said portentously. "What do doctors always say when they've done everything they can?"

Band shrugged.

"They say, 'It's in God's hands now.'" Smith looked triumphant and basked in the admiring gazes of the few Followers who remained. Band kept walking.

The odor in the still-hot room where Neil was lying was now repugnant. Neil's blood had pooled in livor mortis, and he looked even more yellow.

Jeff Mayer was in a chair by the bed, about a foot from Neil's body. He was asleep: too sick to eat or stand, but unwilling to go home, and still able to catch a few quick Zs by a decomposing corpse. "Dude," Band murmured, "you've been on the job too long."

Band gently lifted a notebook out of Mayer's lap—which woke him up—and started to study it. The first page was so startling that he reflexively took a deep breath of the room's foul air, and immediately wished he hadn't.

THE LOVE OF JUDAS

For I will restore health unto thee, and I will heal thee of thy
wounds, saith the Lord, because they called thee an Outcast.

—THE BOOK OF JEREMIAH 30:17

CLACKAMAS COUNTY MEDICAL EXAMINER'S OFFICE
JUNE 18, 2008, 10:00 A.M.

Jim Band was trying to distract himself from what lay ahead. In ten minutes he would be smelling the same odor he had the previous evening, and dreaded it. He was staying as far away from the autopsy room as he could, waiting in the office of Dr. Cliff Nelson, the physician who would eviscerate Neil.

Band, restless, perused Nelson's museum-quality collection of intricately crafted model airplanes, sitting on a series of glass shelves. Each one was carefully cataloged by a small paper label in front of it. The models were obviously considered collectibles—not toys to pick up and handle—because the shelves they sat on were dusty. Band, his mind elsewhere, took a deep breath and puffed the dust away.

The labels exploded into a tornado of paper. "Shhhit!"

There was never a good time for a detective to piss off a medical examiner—but especially not now, because Band needed special access to the autopsy room for an up-close look at Neil. He grabbed handfuls of labels and starting affixing them, with no idea of what went where.

He scrambled for the autopsy room, which suddenly seemed like a good place to be, checking the hallway to see if he'd been observed.

The metallic smell of death in the autopsy room, where Dr. Nelson was beginning the autopsy, reignited Band's memories of the night before, and now the odor was mingled with a heavy antiseptic muskiness that made it even worse.

When Nelson degloved Neil's face—*usssss*—the smell went away, because Band's mind was suddenly as focused as the doctor's.

With Neil's calvarium off the top of his head, Nelson could see that his brain had no signs of pathology.

Nelson replaced Neil's skull-cap and face, and made the giant Y-incision on the boy's torso. He peeled back the flesh—and took almost a full step backward. "I saw an incredible amount of fluid," Nelson later said. "There was fluid in his tissues, fluid in every open space, fluid surrounding both lungs, fluid surrounding the heart, fluid in his abdominal cavity—fluid basically oozing out of any place I cut." Nelson estimated that there was a total of about two gallons of fluid, which had a yellow tint and the odor of an outhouse. A normal body would contain, Nelson later said, only "a trace amount" of the fluid.

Band glanced at the glass booth where Finn and Rhodes stood. Their eyes were wide. They'd seen dozens of fluid-filled corpses, including grotesquely bloated drowning victims, but never anything quite like Neil's urine-colored abdominal cavity.

It was a strong indicator of organ failure, probably of the kidneys. But why? The "why" would help determine if a crime had been committed. If the organ failure had developed suddenly and inexplicably, there might not have been any crime at all.

"My gosh!" Nelson said. He had Neil's heart in his hands. "Look at the size of that." Neil's heart should have approximately matched the size of the boy's fist, but it was almost as big as his whole shoulder.

There were no apparent signs of heart disease. It looked to Nelson as if Neil's heart had just been overworked for far too long, probably by damaged kidneys. The other vital organs looked healthy.

Band studied Nelson's face. The detective didn't know a big heart from a small heart, or the signs of kidney failure, so he read the doctor's expressions. As Nelson severed and systematically removed Neil's urinary system, his face grew agitated. Everything was just huge—both kidneys, the bladder, and the tubes that connected them, the ureters. The ureters were supposed to be about the size of a pencil, but Nelson could fit his finger into them. Maybe even his thumb.

The tissues the kidneys were made of looked sick and rotten: spongy and faded, instead of dense and pink.

"The amount of normal working kidney tissue that was left," Nelson later said, "was maybe five percent of what it should have been."

The tiny structures in the kidneys that had removed toxins from Neil's body, known as the glomeruli, were almost all dead. Nelson estimated that only about 5 percent of them, too, could still function. They had been replaced by ugly, cystic scar tissue.

That degree of damage would take years to develop, and so would the grotesque swelling of the tubes and organs.

But what had caused the slow, steady death of the organ?

Nelson focused on Neil's bladder. There was still almost a quart of urine trapped in it. It was blocked. Why?

Nelson pushed a probe through Neil's urinary tubes all the way to the outlet from his bladder. The outlet was blocked. The probe wouldn't go through.

Nelson later recalled, "Urine basically couldn't get past this blockage."

As Neil's urine had pooled behind the blockage, it had backed up, swelling the entire system, and killing cells.

Nelson kept probing and found the source of the blockage. It was a minor, common birth defect. Just a little clump of tissue. It could have easily been repaired years ago, saving Neil from chronic illness. Or it could have been done days ago, and saved his life.

. . .

When Nelson finished writing his report, Band knew *why* Neil had died. It was from heart failure triggered by the destruction of his kidneys. The medical term for it was uremic heart failure.

Now only one question remained: How suddenly had fatal symptoms surfaced? Had Neil really been a strong, healthy kid, as the Beagleys claimed? Was Neil, as Jeff had put it, "not that bad, even at the end"?

Or was Neil a chronically ill child, who suffered a gradual decline near the end of his life, marked by obvious signs and symptoms?

Neil Beagley had a *bloody nose* and then just *died*? Band didn't think so. But he'd have to prove it.

As far as Band was concerned, he already had a quasi-confession from Jeff. But that wasn't enough. He needed, somehow, to debunk the testimony from Jeff and Marci about the supposedly pleasant last night of Neil's life, as the boy descended peacefully into death.

Band thought he had a way. He headed back to his office to do some more reading from the blue notebook he'd found on Jeff Mayer's lap.

OREGON CITY
JUNE 18, 2008, 12:00 NOON

Patrick waited for the noon news alone while Theresa and the baby visited a friend. He knew the local stations would cover Neil's death, and he was afraid of how he might react to it in front of Theresa. He was closer to her than ever on one level, bonded by baby Paul, but their conflict over the Church felt like a time bomb.

Since Ava's death, he had tried to tell Theresa how he really felt, but every time he brought it up, she acted like he'd gone nuts. They mostly argued about what they would do if Paul got sick. They knew there were people who secretly took their kids to doctors, but Theresa thought that even going for a well-baby check-up could jeopardize Paul, through lack of faith.

Patrick had already ordered a few simple meds on the Net, including some Cipro and Tamiflu, so that he could at least do something if the baby caught a cold or the flu, and Patrick couldn't sneak him off to a doctor.

Patrick tried to talk to Theresa about it rationally, but she just rattled off slogans. Like all of the Followers, she'd been brainwashed since childhood, and even now it was reinforced almost every day—not in a cruel way, which he could discredit—but through limitless acts of kindness from people in the church.

The crazy thing was, the Followers were good people, all of them victims of brainwashing themselves. Sure, they were grandiose, and some of them had unusual ideas, but who didn't? Patrick remembered being grandiose himself as a young true-believer, back in his Bible-thumper days.

He'd long thought the only way he could have a happy life was to get Theresa out of the Church, but now that seemed impossible. The Church was still her whole life, for reasons Patrick could no longer fully comprehend.

Lately, though, based on what had been happening, it seemed as if he had another option: Get the Church to change its ideas about doctors. Somebody *had* to do it, because people were dying. He just wished the reformer didn't have to be him. He was an ordinary guy, not a hero, and didn't want to be a double-agent. He might lose his marriage and his son.

But this wasn't about him. It was about Ava, Neil, Katie, the other kids, and the old people. He'd been checking out Rita Swan's site a lot, and he thought that what he had to do now would be for her, too, and for kids all over the country, like that little girl in Wisconsin who had just died. The Net was full of stories about faith-healing crimes. Oregon City was just the tip of the iceberg.

If a few Followers were punished—severely, with real jail time—they'd change. He was sure of it. He knew these people. They would rationalize going to doctors the same way they rationalized going to dentists. They'd just come up with some new doctrine, like Jesus' admonition that people should follow secular law, and "render unto Caesar what is Caesar's." Most of them would probably even be happy to change, if everybody else did.

Before Jim Band and his colleagues had busted Brent and Raylene, the idea of changing the Church had felt like a fantasy to Patrick. Not anymore.

But Patrick needed Brent and Raylene to be convicted. And Jeff and Marci to be arrested. If that didn't happen, everything would fall apart.

He was optimistic that Brent and Raylene would be found guilty, because that awful blob on Ava's neck had been so obvious. And he thought Jeff and Marci weren't shrewd enough to get away with what they'd done. There was already a rift between them, because he'd heard that Marci had wanted to take Neil to the doctor on the night he died.

But Patrick had been told that the investigations of the Worthingtons and Beagleys would fall apart without an informant in the Church, uncovering more abuse, and gathering facts on what had already happened.

If that had to be him, so be it.

Patrick turned on the KATU news, which usually had the best Followers coverage. There was Lynne Benton. He'd seen her dozens of times. Usually she was talking about somebody who'd drowned in the icy waters of the Clackamas or Sandy, or frozen to death in the woods. She was always sympathetic but tough, and he was glad she was on this case.

"We processed the scene for evidence," she told the broadcaster, Thom Jensen, one of the city's best investigators, "but there was little for us to do. There were no signs of trauma or suicide. It's heart wrenching to see this happen," she said. "Of course, I'm an objective observer, so I don't know the details of their faith, but from just my own observation, it's very sad."

Patrick wished she would cut to the chase and say if they were pursuing it.

"The parents of the boy said that he declined medical attention. That's the story that the family told us during the investigation. I don't think we're going to disprove that statement.

"And unless we can disprove that," Lynne Benton said, "charges probably won't be filed in this case."

Patrick tried to take a deep breath, but sudden anger gripped his lungs.

At the Oregon City PD office, on the edge of a strip mall, Jim Band was reading the blue notebook that Jeff Mayer had found, but paused to watch the news. He turned it on just in time to see Lynne Benton inform the world that there was *no case* against the Beagleys.

Bullshit.

It was infuriating. Why was Lynne Benton suddenly such a pussy?

OCPD, WARNER-MILNE ROAD
JUNE 18, 2008

The blue notebook had turned out to be a detailed log, compiled mostly by Marci, of the last week of Neil's life. It was blowing Jeff Beagley's version of a quick and easy death all to hell.

On June 10th, the notebook showed—seven days before Neil died—he was already beginning to slip away. Marci had Neil on what was becoming his deathbed diet: "a little bit of broth, potato, and a strawberry." Underneath that was, "Threw up." A couple of hours later, Neil had some broth and part of a granola bar, and in the evening he had "3 bites of egg, one-half Glucerna," a bottled drink for diabetics, "5–6 bites banana, and finished one bottle of water." He was up at 3:30 a.m. for "one-half Glucerna."

The notebook showed that the family was researching ulcers like crazy on the 10th, trying to find out why Neil was suddenly throwing up most of what he ate. There were printouts from FamilyDoctor.org, RevolutionHealth.com, and even some information on ayurvedic medicine, from IndiaMedicine.com. Ayurveda was medicine, of course—still the leading approach in India—but it was herbal, which the Followers accepted.

On the morning of June 11th Neil had some oatmeal, "a few bites blueberry pancake," finished another bottle of water, and held it all down. He had an egg for lunch, but the 2:00 p.m. notation was only, "I tried!" Dinner was "one-quarter cup egg soup, one-half banana, and 1 cracker." Neil ate about the same amount at 10:30 p.m. but threw up.

He threw up his breakfast the next morning at 6:30, even though it was just "one Glucerna, 4 ounces of water, applesauce, and 6 more ounces of water." During the rest of the day he had some water, broth, juice, applesauce, "a bit of egg protein," with "three bites cookie, one-half jar of baby food," and some Pedialyte. In the middle of the night he threw up.

On the 13th he vomited first thing in the morning, and continued to eat sparingly. By this time he had no regular sleep schedule.

He was up at 3:30 a.m. on June 14th and ate some banana, "1 bite egg," and threw up. He was able to hold down his food for the rest of the day, but ate very little, including "dab of broth, 4–5 bites egg, water, watermelon, broth, new water, and juice with rice protein."

On June 15th he consumed mostly just small amounts of liquids, along with "one-half egg, few bites tuna sandwich, potato, and one-third banana," plus occasional bites of other foods.

On June 16th, Neil's last full day of life, the notebook said, "Give six ounce water each feeding." By that time, Marci was feeding him tenderly by hand, and holding up a cup with a straw for him to sip. The feedings consisted of "8:00 a.m., oatmeal/applesauce. Threw up. 11:00 a.m., broth, potato. 12:30 p.m., fish. Threw up. 5:30 p.m., one egg, one-third banana. 6:10, finished water."

That was the final annotation. Neil had apparently stopped eating. This was when Jeff came home for his "Boys' Night chat" with Neil, when they allegedly talked all night about the work Neil planned to do that week, and told blonde jokes. It was when Jeff supposedly tossed Neil onto the bed playfully, after carrying him to the bathroom as a way of "making fun" of the situation.

Jeff had claimed that it was just "a coincidence" that the chat was the last night of Neil's life.

Jeff, it appeared, was a relatively good liar.

The notebook was damning. But Jeff and Marci were still the only real eyewitnesses, and also the "victims." It would be a long, hard investigation, and Band couldn't even start it until other doctors reviewed the autopsy reports, which could take weeks.

Even so, before Jim Band left the office, he started making his wish list of witnesses. At the top was Marci's mother, Sandra Mitchell. Sandra, Patrick had told Band, was a genuinely honest person. She would either tell the truth, not comment at all, or at least lie very badly.

SEPTEMBER 2, 2008
AUBURN DRIVE, OREGON CITY

Sandra Mitchell's square slab of front porch wasn't big enough for all three detectives, so Band knocked on the door of the lime-green house while Rhodes and Finn waited on the walkway. No one answered, but they could hear somebody on the phone. It rang at least twice while they waited.

Sandra Mitchell came to the door with the phone in her hand. "I'm going to talk to them," she said to the caller, and hung up. She looked, as Band later put it, "like anybody's grandma—just a sweet lady."

She invited them to sit down at her kitchen table. It had been ten weeks since Neil's funeral—they'd buried him beneath a granite engraving of the Camaro he'd never really driven—and she still looked distraught. Since March she'd lost her great-granddaughter Ava, and her grandson Neil. Now her granddaughter Raylene was facing six years in prison for manslaughter, and her daughter Marci was being investigated for the same thing. Band felt for her.

Band tried to be as gentle as he could. He told Mrs. Mitchell that they were there to talk about Neil's health history and life in general. With little prompting, she volunteered that she thought he'd had Crohn's disease, because he'd felt bad "on and off" for the last couple of years. That was the first time anyone had admitted that Neil Beagley had chronic health problems.

"What was bothering him?" Band asked.

"I don't really want to answer that question. Do I have to?"

"No, not at all."

She might have been hiding something, but probably not. She was a very private person. Band backed away from specific issues, and said that he still didn't understand the Followers' faith.

"You never will," she said. "You put your faith in doctors, and we put ours in God. God has gotten me through many things."

Band didn't ask for specifics. He knew that there had never been a single extraordinary healing among the Followers—just garden-variety recoveries from common illnesses.

Rhodes, acting on the tip from Patrick, mentioned in an offhand way that he'd heard Neil was sick in March.

"Yes, I thought he was going to die in March, but we laid hands on him and he got better."

"Why did you think he might die?" Band asked.

"Well, he had symptoms, like the flu." The phone rang but Mrs. Mitchell ignored it.

"When my kids have the flu," Band said, "I don't think they're going to die."

"Fevers scare me," she said. "That's why I thought he was going to die. I still think he had Crohn's disease."

On the day Neil died, she admitted, he *had* to be carried to the bathroom. It was not a joke to "make fun" of the situation.

Rhodes edged toward the issue of Neil making his own medical decision, and said that some people thought the Followers kids were brainwashed.

"We don't brainwash our kids. The children *choose* to follow their faith. What would society say if someone claimed that the people who turn out to be gay were all brainwashed?" The phone rang again and went unanswered.

"I heard there was some kind of argument," Band said casually. "When Neil died. Between Jeff and Marci about Neil going to the doctor."

"That was in March. Not when he died. At least, I think it was then. I get my times mixed up."

She did remember that there was an argument on the night Neil died, but thought it was between Marci and Neil. "Marci lost it," she said, "and wanted to take Neil to the doctor." But Neil reprimanded her, she said, and reminded her to have faith in God. "I was there when it happened. Neil told her that it was *his* decision, not hers."

"Was there ever a time," Rhodes asked, "when Neil was too sick to make a clear decision?"

"There wasn't."

"What would have happened," Rhodes asked, "if Marci wanted to take Neil to the doctor but Jeff didn't?"

"They would have to come to a decision together, but the Bible says to obey your husband."

"Would *you* have taken Neil to a doctor," Finn asked softly, "knowing now that he could have been saved?"

Mrs. Mitchell looked down and tears floated in her eyes. "Don't ask me that," she said. She began to cry. "I can't take this anymore."

"We're not judging you," Band said softly. "I know you've lost two grandchildren." He reached out his long, strong arm and touched her gently.

The phone rang again. Sandra wiped her eyes with her sleeve and answered it. "I'm talking now," she told the caller. There was a pause. "To the detectives."

The voice on the other end became louder. "Mom," the caller said, "you're supposed to say no comment."

Sandra hung up, smiled sadly, and shrugged.

Finn waited a few moments and asked what else she remembered about Neil's last hours.

"While he was lying in bed," she said, "I asked him how he felt, and he said, 'Fine.' Then I said, 'You should make yourself eat.' I told him he wasn't a baby anymore. And he said, 'I'm trying.' He said food just didn't sound good to him."

"Did you hear anything about Neil telling Jeff that he loved him?" Finn asked.

"No." The phone rang again.

"Why would kids be allowed to die," Rhodes asked bluntly, "when they could get treatment?"

"Like Ava? It's God's will." The phone rang again, and she answered it. After she hung up it rang again, and she answered it.

Band, Finn, and Rhodes got up to leave. It was obvious Mrs. Mitchell didn't want to talk anymore, and they had gotten the information they needed:

Neil Beagley's family *did* know that he had been chronically ill.

They thought he was so sick in March that he might die. They had used their strongest weapon: laying on of hands.

When they laid hands on him on the last night of his life, it was to try to save him, not because Neil thought it would "be nice," as Jeff had described it.

Neil had been so sick on the night of his death that his mother had wanted to violate the strictest doctrine of the Church and take him to a doctor.

And a number of people were obviously trying to cover it up, including whoever had phoned and called Sandra Mitchell "Mom." Marci, just maybe?

South Canyon Ridge Drive, Oregon City
September 4, 2008

Band called Marci. He had received the review of Neil's autopsy and wanted to tell her and Jeff about it. She asked if he would be taping the interview, and he said no, that he was just trying to see things from their point of view.

"We just want to practice our faith," she said. "People should be allowed to do what's in your heart."

She mentioned—maybe because Band already knew it—that she'd told Neil before he died that maybe he should go to a doctor.

"What did he say?" Band asked.

"He got angry with me. He told me, 'My trust is in God.'"

Band asked if it would have been a sin for Neil to see a doctor.

"No, it wouldn't have been that big of a deal. My kids make decisions for themselves. We did not drill this into their heads."

Band later offered his view of the murky law on parental responsibility: "So here is a well-educated kid who had the means to go to a doctor if he wanted to, and he chose not to, and that's *okay*? What if a parent is with their sixteen-year-old kid and they get in a car wreck, and the kid is bleeding like hell and in horrible shape? And the ambulance is there, and the kid goes, 'I'm not going. I'm going to stay here.' The parent is obligated to get them to the hospital, whether the kid wants to go or not." Band hoped the jury would see it that way. So did Rita Swan, who'd recently told *The Oregonian*'s Rick Bella, "If Oregon says there's no duty to give a child medical treatment, that would be obscene. I can't believe that Oregon is that bad." Band could tell, though, that Marci was in anguish. "It must be hard," he said, "watching your kid get sicker and sicker, and all you can do is pray."

"It was a difficult time," Marci said.

Interesting. She did not deny that he was getting sicker and sicker. It was another nail in the coffin of Jeff's version of a quick and easy death. Band heard someone whispering to Marci.

"Jeff just got home," Marci said. "Why don't you come by at 6:30?"

When Band arrived at the caravan of trailers that evening with Finn and Rhodes, Marci escorted them to an outdoor patio and introduced them to a woman who identified herself only as Mary Ann. She said she wasn't an attorney, but an "advocate for the Beagleys." They presumed she was working for an attorney.

Band told Jeff and Marci that the medical specialists had confirmed that Neil's cause of death was heart failure due to collapse of his urinary tract system.

The Beagleys seemed primarily concerned about DHS interfering with their daughter Katie. The agency wanted them to have Katie's kidney function evaluated, but Marci said that if Katie required a kidney transplant or dialysis, she would rather die.

"But if she doesn't have a problem," Band said, "a test might give you peace of mind. Or if she does have a blockage like Neil's, it could possibly be fixed. Her kidneys might . . ." Mary Ann interrupted, saying something about Ava. Marci frowned. Band lifted his hand and Mary Ann, her face flushed and eyes unfocused, stopped.

"Katie's kidneys might still be fine," Band said, "even if she does have a blockage."

Band pushed the Beagleys to explain their religious justification for not treating Katie, but as Band later recalled, "Nobody said God this or God that, or look at the Bible here or there. They talked about what people in the Church would think, and who'd be gossiping. They weren't thinking as individuals. It was group-think."

Jeff and Marci began to ask medical questions about Neil's death, and seemed genuinely grateful for information. The atmosphere grew cordial, although Mary Ann kept interrupting, to Marci's annoyance.

"It was a unique dynamic," Rhodes later said. "We were potentially going to put them in prison, and we had strategized about how to kill them with kindness. But it became an intimate conversation about their faith, their family, and Neil's entire life. Now I know more about their kids than my neighbor's. We sensed their vulnerability, and wanted to answer their questions, but we're also good detectives and we had some questions of our own."

Band felt ambivalent. "I was quite certain," he later said, "that we had enough for an arrest on crim-neg-hom"—criminally negligent homicide—"because they knew a dangerous condition existed but didn't act on it. But I didn't know if it could be successfully prosecuted."

Finn asked about Neil's illness in March, but the Beagleys characterized it as a sore throat. They said they laid hands on him and his sore throat went away.

"Neil was always generally healthy," Marci said, "but like other kids . . . ." Mary Ann, smiling, conspicuously cleared her throat.

"What can you tell us about Pearson?" Mary Ann interjected. Rhodes gave her a quizzical look. "Particularly about his drinking on the night . . ."

"You mean the night Ava died?" Finn asked. She presumed Mary Ann was talking about Captain Bruce Pearson, who'd been at Ava Worthington's death scene. It looked as if the lawyers who were defending the Worthingtons—and the Beagleys, too, if they were charged—wanted to claim that Captain Pearson was drunk at the scene. Rhodes thought it was ridiculous. Pearson had once had a reputation as a drinker, but Rhodes had been at Ava's death scene, and Pearson hadn't been drunk, just tired.

Mary Ann looked confused. "Yes, his, uh . . . Where's he working now?" she asked loudly. Her words came with the smell of alcohol.

"We're talking about *Neil*," Finn said. "Not Ava."

"I want to know about Pearson," Mary Ann said.

"Are you looking for a drinking partner?" Band asked.

Marci tried not to laugh, but couldn't.

In the awkward silence, Jeff said, "Let me show you some of the things Neil built."

Mary Ann said she had to get home and called a cab. In the oddly more collegial atmosphere that followed, Jeff took them on a tour of the grounds. Their front yard nosed into a subdivision, but out back their 23 acres of skyscraper fir trees led to a vast stretch of logging wilderness that extended to the Mt. Hood National Forest, and stayed wild through the Bitterroot and Rocky Mountains all the way to Mt.

Rushmore in the Black Hills. The Beagleys, it appeared, had one foot in civilization and the other in a realm largely undiscovered. It was an epic domain, naturally grandiose, and not at all unusual in the outback of O.C.

Jeff showed them the huge rock planter Neil had built, the wall Neil had repaired, some of the equipment he ran, and the brush and stumps he'd piled, still unburned. Some of the stumps were the size of Volkswagen Bugs, with sprawling roots that looked like giant, gnarled fingers.

In the fading sunlight they sat again on the patio—Jeff visibly melancholy after visiting the sites his son had left—and drank iced tea in the shade of the trees. The smell of the season's last overripe blackberries blew in as twilight kicked up a breeze. For a few minutes they all stayed silent, united by nature, a relatively common social occurrence among strangers in Oregon. It felt surprisingly like a comfortable family gathering, not just because of the closeness of the detectives and their suspects, but also the detectives themselves.

"I don't know of three detectives who got along the way we did," Rhodes later said. "Because, honestly, with three detectives, you're always going to end up with two who think alike, but don't like the third. Law enforcement in general, and Detectives in particular, is an ego-driven profession. But ego was, like, the *last* of our concerns. I'm not saying we were a better team than others. I'm saying, well, Michelle worked about two hundred unpaid hours on this. Jim, too, probably. It's because this case was about . . ."

Finn finished his sentence: "Kids."

Jim Band agreed. "And it wasn't like we'd never worked Child Abuse. The difference was that this concerned . . ."

Finn finished: "*Lots* of kids. Here and all over the country. Kids who had been suffering this kind of thing forever. And for all we knew at that time, they always would."

As evening settled in, the five parents went to the barn to see Neil's unfinished Camaro.

SIOUX CITY, IOWA
OCTOBER 4, 2008

Rita Swan, working over the weekend on an article for the journal of the International Cultic Studies Association, as well as a chapter entitled "Religion and Child Neglect" for the book *Child Abuse and Neglect*, got a call from *The New York Times*. They wanted a statement. Jeff and Marci Beagley, they said, had just been arrested for criminally negligent homicide, pled not guilty, and released on bond.

Rita told the reporter that Neil's death was "tragic, unnecessary, and all too common."

The Beagleys' arrest was encouraging, and Rita had also recently gotten good news about two other cases she'd been worried about.

The mother of four-year-old Sean Paddock—who had been forced to eat feces and vomit, was beaten with plastic tubing, and smothered to death in blankets—had been sentenced to life in prison for first-degree murder. At her sentencing Lynn Paddock stated grandly that her punishment "was part of God's plan."

The mother of sixteen-month-old Javon Thompson, who had died when she and three other One Mind Ministries members had deprived him of food and water for failing to say "Amen," had finally been arrested. She was cooperating with authorities to save herself, turning on the three other defendants, including church leader Queen Antoinette. They had been charged with second-degree murder, and would soon receive sentences of fifty years each.

These were big victories for Rita. But they came with heartbreaking images of suffering and, unlike most people's career achievements, were hardly the type that she could savor in detail during moments of doubt or stress.

"Jeeze Louise!" Patrick regretted his profanity immediately. Swearing was bad luck. But his contact on the phone tree had said that their mutual friend Chuck had just died, and Patrick knew what had triggered it. Now he'd have to tell Jim about it.

Chuck was the fifth Follower who'd died that year from diabetes. His family had been trying to help him control his condition with diet and exercise, but they didn't know what they were doing. Because Patrick had spent hours on the Net studying medicine, mostly to protect Paul, he knew that Chuck, almost 65, needed medication. Patrick already had a stockpile of meds, and could legally order pretty much anything, without a prescription. Most of the drugs came from a pharmaceutical company in India that was as big as Bayer.

He had a drug called metformin that he had been hoping to talk Chuck into trying, but he'd been stalling, because he didn't feel competent playing doctor. He wasn't even a medic, like Come Back Jack.

The event that had caused Chuck's quick decline was supposed to be a secret, but wasn't, in the tight-knit church community. His family had put him on a treadmill, then went shopping. They forgot about Chuck, and when they got back four hours later he was still on the treadmill, disoriented and delirious. Chuck fell into a deep sleep almost immediately and then slipped into a diabetic coma. "His family was trying to do the right thing," Patrick later said—his expressive eyes still troubled by the memory—"but they killed him with kindness." It probably wasn't a crime, but that would be for Jim to decide.

Patrick had begun to give a few people medications for obvious problems—mostly just antibiotics for simple sinus or lung infections—but was afraid he was going to hurt somebody if he kept playing doctor. What would Jim do about that? Still, to stand by and do nothing would be a sin of omission, and there was no way to intervene legally with the adults in the Church.

Patrick said a prayer and left early for the Christmas party. The

first blizzard in many years had hit, and the roads were a mess because there were hardly any snowplows in the metro area. The schools
had been closed for a week. In Portland, the town sometimes closed
the schools for a single inch of snow. The year before, Portland had
closed its schools because of a forecast for snow that never came, and
justified it later as a stress-sensitivity issue.

The people at the party seemed unusually quiet to Patrick. Brent
and Raylene were sitting stone-faced among a circle of Followers who
would probably soon have to testify for them, and they didn't even look
at Patrick when he walked by. Jeff and Marci, sitting among their own
clique, still seemed to be in shock, and just murmured something when
Patrick passed them.

Patrick chained-up, an easy chore for somebody with strong, skilled
hands, but still slipped and slid most of the way to the church and was
glad, for the first time that week, that Theresa and the baby weren't
there. She'd just left for Caldwell, Idaho, to take care of her mom, who
was dying from advanced diabetes that appeared to be out of control.
It seemed strange to Patrick, though, for Theresa to leave at Christmas, for any reason.

It was possible, Patrick thought, that people were quiet only around
him. There were rumors. A lot of people feared him. They thought he
was the Judas. But there were also rumors circulating through the phone
tree and at church and social functions that he was giving people herbal
and ayurvedic remedies that worked magic, and a growing group loved
him for that. Because the Followers were all so intimately connected, it
was almost impossible to tell when and where a rumor got started, and
just as hard to determine when and where it ended—if it ever did.

He got some lobster bisque, a slice of hot buttery pumpkin bread,
a chilled goblet of Grandma Hickman's famous huckleberry-
pomegranate punch, and looked for the Thaine family. He'd promised to bring some anti-flu "herbs" for their toddler, Conrad, who had
a cold that they were afraid was turning into pneumonia.

The Thaines were in the kitchen putting pumpkin and mince pies
in the oven.

"Merry Christmas," Patrick said to Mike Thaine, Vernon Thaine's great-grandson, who was about the same age as Patrick. He gave Mike a baby bottle with a red ribbon around it. "Keep it in the fridge," he said, "and shake it up real good three times a day, and only let him drink about yay-much." He held his fingers a half-inch apart. "It's echinacea and too much will give him a tummyache." He told them to call him if they ran out before the baby was better and let him know right away if Conrad got worse.

Patrick later recalled, "I hate to lie. Can't stand it. And what I did wasn't smart legally." But he didn't know what else he could do. "If I called DHS every time a kid had the flu, they'd stop listening."

From the main room, Patrick could hear the band singing "O Holy Night." "I love that song," Patrick said to Mike. "What a message! 'Long lay the world in sin and error pining, 'til He appeared, and the soul felt its worth.' Wow."

"Christmas is so beautiful," Mike's wife Bobbie said. She was pregnant. "It's about . . . I don't know, this sounds obvious. Birth."

"Christianity is always about birth," Patrick said. "For us, even death is birth. That's why Christmas and Easter feel so much alike." The women putting pies in the oven paused and smiled, seeming to want him to say more.

Jeff came in suddenly and Patrick stiffened but tried not to show it, aware that his eyes too often gave away his feelings, and that his face reddened too easily, sometimes becoming almost the color of his hair. He'd barely spoken to Jeff since the arrest and had heard Jeff didn't really trust him anymore. But Jeff had been quiet around almost everybody since Neil died. This party had to be miserable for him.

Jeff ambled over, and Patrick said, "You hangin' in there, buddy?"

"I'm hangin'," Jeff said.

"I'm sorry, man," Patrick said.

"Me too." Patrick didn't know what that meant. It probably wasn't remorse about what he'd done, though. Jeff had held fast to the faith, and his stature in the church was immense now.

People revered Jeff, Patrick thought—but they didn't want to *be* him. It seemed to Patrick as if the church had already begun to change. More people were sneaking off to see doctors, and there was a little less talk about how bad that was.

Both men leaned forward, embraced briefly, and gave each other the Holy Greeting. Jeff had given Patrick his first Holy Greeting, at his father's funeral, and Patrick's love for his friend had endured ever since, and endured still.

But Jeff had to go to jail. So did Marci, and Brent, and Raylene. That would be the only way to make people start taking their kids to doctors, and seemed to be the only path to redemption, for them, for him, and everybody here.

Patrick felt strangely at peace. He'd had so many happy times in this building. He thought there could be new life here. Everyone was hurting, but hurt was always part of birth.

"You try this?" Patrick asked Jeff, holding up his goblet of punch.

"It wasn't out when I got here."

Patrick held it out to him. "I don't have cooties," he said.

"I'm good." The usual dark bags under Jeff's eyes now looked black. Patrick thought it was a condition called allergic shiners, in which fluid pooled because of allergies, but this was no time to get into that.

Patrick drove home very slowly on the ice, barely needing his headlights on a night made bright by a nearly-full moon shining on the snow. He found the all-Christmas station and heard "O Holy Night" again. Wow. "A thrill of hope, the weary world rejoices, for yonder breaks a new and glorious morn. Fall on your knees, oh hear the angel voices, oh night divine, oh night when Christ was born." A guy who sold alcohol for a living, Patrick recalled, had written that song. The world was complicated.

At home he got a text from Theresa. She said she needed to stay in Idaho longer.

The text was kind of cold—no merry Christmas or anything like that—but he tried to take it as a good sign. He told himself that her mother's health crisis must have passed, and that Theresa must be staying to help with her recovery.

From his backyard, in a black sky over white snow, Jupiter and Venus, in a rare conjunction, hovered together and shone on the western horizon almost as a single brilliant star, as they briefly had long ago, when proclaimed to be the Star of Bethlehem.

Patrick bowed his head to the beautiful sight, and with a sense of terrible and sweet sadness, prayed for those he loved.

PART THREE

The Book of Revelation

*And God shall wipe away all tears from their eyes, and there shall
be no more death, nor sorrow, nor crying. Neither shall there be
any more pain, for the former things are passed away. And he
that sat upon the throne said: Behold, I make all things new.*

—THE BOOK OF REVELATION 21:4–5

13

THE FIRST GREAT AWAKENING

The weakness of human nature has always appeared in times of great revivals of religion, by a disposition to run into extremes, especially in these three things: enthusiasm, superstition, and intemperate zeal.

—JONATHAN EDWARDS,

A LEADER OF THE FIRST GREAT AWAKENING

THE FOLLOWERS OF CHRIST CHURCH
FEBRUARY 24, 2009

Patrick was driving his grandmother to a special fund-raising session at the church, which would probably cost him money he couldn't afford, especially after the expense of buying medications that he gave away. The elders wanted everybody to contribute to a Defense Fund to cover the Beagleys' and Worthingtons' legal expenses.

Theresa was still in Idaho, so now Patrick was supporting not only their O.C. home but an apartment she'd rented in Caldwell. Her mom's diabetes had somehow stabilized, but Theresa wouldn't come home. She owed it to her mom. At least, that's what she said.

Patrick missed her, but it was Paul's absence that was digging a hole in his stomach. It still shocked him. You think you know everything

there is to know about love until you have a baby. Then you see that all
the love that had come before revolved around fair exchange: emotional,
physical, and even financial. And on that magical day when you begin
to love someone who gives you absolutely nothing in return—except a
smile—you find a new world.

Patrick's grandmother said something but he wasn't paying attention. He was remembering the night Paul was born. He'd been terrified
that something would go wrong—and that he would end up calling
911, or *not* calling—and after hours he'd become numb. Even after
the birth he'd felt very little, except relief, with no surge at all of the
love that he'd been certain would come. But then the midwives left
the room and Theresa fell asleep. He picked up Paul and without
thinking whispered a promise into his son's ear that was so heartfelt
he was sure God could hear: "I'm going to take care of you every day
of my life, just like my dad did me." Then the love had come like a
flood. Now, a year after the birth, he still felt like a teenager with
puppy-love.

"Patrick!" his grandmother said, breaking through. "I've been
hearing talk. You know there's folks that's *scared* of you, don't you?"

"I know."

"Know why they're scared? Too much playin' doctor. They think
you're good at it, but don't know why. Somebody even said it was devil's work."

"Don't worry, Grandma." He patted her hand, but she winced. She
had arthritis but wouldn't even take the ibuprofen he gave her, because she considered it to be medicine.

So many people were sick. One of the men who worked at Hal's
Construction had heart disease that was so advanced his feet looked
like footballs with toes. Even middle-aged people had heart disease and
diabetes from the Followers' home cooking, and dozens of people were
gimpy from untreated injuries. About half the old people had emphy-
sema, cancer, or cardiovascular disease. There was even a rumor about
somebody who was letting himself go blind, despite Walter's acceptance of eye doctors.

A big secret that only a few Followers knew was that Walter hadn't been very rigid about doctors, and once drove a man who had gangrene to the doctor himself. When Walter died, though, the last elder of that era, Glenford Eells, who died about five years after Walter, declared that nobody but Walter was fit to preach, baptize, convert, or give Communion. After that, the only thing left that made them feel special was avoiding doctors. That's how it had been ever since. They still had elders, like Fred Smith, but the elders no longer had any real power.

"I mortgaged the house for the Defense Fund," his grandmother said. Patrick forced a small smile.

When Patrick parked, four guys who were smoking under the awning rushed to his car and helped his grandmother out. One was Mike Thaine, still grateful for Patrick's help with his baby at Christmas, and another was one of the guys who Patrick knew was spreading rumors about him. As they helped his grandmother inside, Rod Lincoln ambled over and took Patrick aside.

"Some of these people think I'm Judas," Patrick said quietly. "Some think I'm Jesus, and the rest . . ."

"Don't know whether to shit or go blind," Rod said.

"Why is that supposed to be a hard choice?" Patrick asked. Rod laughed. "Who would choose to go blind?"

"My uncle," Rod said. He stopped laughing.

"Are you contributing?" Patrick asked.

"I wasn't planning to. Then I got to thinking, what if *my* son was in trouble? By the way, Marie took your advice and got that lump removed."

"Tell her God bless."

Rod was excited about the clandestine group that was beginning to gather around Patrick. It was like a church within a church, and when Patrick ran Bible Study he sounded like a preacher, with his naturally melodic voice.

Inside, Fred Smith was pumping up the crowd. In the front row were the martyrs—Jeff and Marci, along with Brent and Raylene, who were trying to have another baby.

"Using Marci is bad marketing," Rod whispered. Some people blamed Neil's death on her lack of faith.

"This is *persecution*!" Fred shouted from the rarely-used pulpit. "We're fightin' God's fight!"

The attorneys, he said, wanted a $150,000 retainer, and needed to pay doctors to testify. The church was also launching a website to attract support.

Money was tight because of the recession—Patrick's handyman business was hurting—but the atmosphere was electric. If the Followers won these two cases, they'd be free forever.

People began to stand and state their pledges: $1,500 to $2,000. One Follower who built high-end houses in the fancy western Clackalackie suburb of Lake Oswego—Lake O'Ego, the Followers called it—offered $10,000.

The martyrs in the front row—all facing up to six years in prison—gazed at people with glazed, grateful eyes.

Patrick thought about Paul, who might someday end up being brainwashed, and maybe even prosecuted.

He stood. "On behalf of Paul and Theresa Robbins," he said loudly, "I pledge three thousand dollars."

Some people looked surprised. Some of the people he'd helped clapped.

Patrick felt happy, but for conflicting reasons. He was helping people he loved. But he was also betraying them. He was sacrificing to help protect Paul. But he was trying to change a church that might destroy Paul. The days of simple thoughts were over.

At the night's end, the pledges totaled more than $800,000.

The martyrs gathered at the main exit to thank people as they left. They all hugged Patrick, the women reaching high to put their arms around him.

"Where's Theresa?" Jeff asked.

"Gone."

Jeff, off in his own world, didn't seem to hear.

As Patrick turned to leave, Jeff grabbed him. "Gone?" Patrick nodded. Jeff drew him in, and gave him the Holy Greeting, as he had at Christmas.

"My brother," Jeff said.

"My brother."

CLACKAMAS COUNTY COURTHOUSE
JUNE 25, 2009, 8:30 A.M.

Hot sun streamed in and turned the jury room into an inferno. Juror Ken Byers, still pasty from Oregon's drizzly early summer—Junuary, in local parlance—wasn't ready for it. In Chicago, where Byers had grown up, there had been four seasons, but in Oregon there was generally just the monsoon, and a hot season that veered between paradise and hell. The first days of heat always made people irritable and invariably shocked that the sun they'd longed for came with unfamiliar and ugly side-effects, such as sweating, and thirst. Byers wiped his forehead with his palm. A young blonde woman entered the room.

"Hi, I'm Ashley Santos."

"Ken Byers."

Ashley reminded Ken of his daughter. They chatted, but it was awkward because they weren't allowed to talk about the only thing they wanted to discuss: what the trial was about. They knew it was a big deal, because they'd had to fill out a fifty-page questionnaire, and the street was crammed with broadcast units, including one from truTV. They did know that it had something to do with the Followers of Christ, whatever that was.

Byers was glad to be there. Suddenly unemployed at forty-six, after a big-league career as a software project manager, he needed the distraction of jury duty—and even the money, because of the recession and his wife Jane's disability. Her doctor had botched what should have been an easy surgery, and now she could barely leave home. She'd been trying to get on Social Security disability for five years, but the bureaucrats were idiots. Byers was as alienated from Big Government as he was from Big Medicine.

The other jurors filtered in. The first was a marketing project manager for Intel, which was in the far-west exurbs of the Silicon Forest. His commute was relatively short, though, because he lived on the distant western edge of Clackamas County—as did Ken, who lived exactly nine feet within the county line—and both of them, it became obvious, skewed closer to sophisticated Lake O'Ego sensibilities than those of Clackatucky. Ashley, smart and outdoorsy, was from the ski town of Sandy. A very quiet guy with bad teeth was from the possum-ridden town of Estacada. But the other eight jurors were all from O.C., including a conservative medical-imaging technician, a logger, a farm wife, a soft-spoken man who reminded Byers of Mr. Rogers, and several others who faded into the ornate woodwork of the 125-year-old courthouse.

In the large, cooler courtroom outside the jury room, the Worthingtons' attorneys, both wearing dark suits, huddled together and ignored Brent and Raylene. Raylene's attorney, John Neidig, billed himself as "Oregon's top attorney for criminal defense, and aggressive DUI defense," and was a member of the pro-pot group NORML. Brent's lawyer, Mark Cogan, was a Portlandish liberal who had worked for the NAACP, Legal Aid, and a movement to keep nuclear-weapons factories out of Portland—not that any had asked to come. Cogan, who'd made the Oregon Super Lawyer list for the past five years, had once argued a search-and-seizure case before the US Supreme Court and had lost by only one vote to the conservatives on the bench. He was a genuine civil libertarian, and for him this trial was not just another payday but a cause, though certain to be unpopular among his many liberal friends. "Fighting for individual freedom," Cogan later said, "has always been the hallmark of my law practice. In this case, our task was not only to defend our client, but to uphold the values of freedom of religion."

Cogan had charisma and looked like Richard Dreyfuss—at least, the *Mr. Holland's Opus* version, not the *Jaws* version. He liked to deliver his message cordially and professorially, so his appearance matched his performance.

Cogan had worked with Neidig a number of times, quite success-fully, partly because both of them exuded credibility and had an un-canny ability to memorize reams of information that they could recite casually to jurors. The defense attorneys were in a bind, though, thanks to Rita Swan, who had almost single-handedly stopped Ore-gon's religious-shield law from protecting the Worthingtons from the crimes they had been charged with, second-degree manslaughter and criminal mistreatment. Brent and Raylene were the first people to be tried under the 1999 law that Rita had ramrodded through the state-house. Because the shields for those crimes had been eliminated, Cogan and Neidig could not even mention the issue of religious free-dom. Since freedom of religion was officially off-limits, references to it would have to be very subtle, or even subliminal.

Even so, Cogan liked this jury. During the early stages of selection, he'd been appalled by the extent of anti-Followers sentiment. "The questionnaires," he later said, "revealed very strong biases against our clients, based on intense, negative, and very selective media coverage of our case prior to trial." He was referring mostly to *The Oregonian*—which had a couple of smart, veteran reporters on the story, Steve Mayes and Rick Bella—and KATU, the station that had first cracked the story and still followed it closely with Portland's three best investi-gative broadcasters, Thom Jensen, Dan Tilkin, and Anna Canzano. They had won about twenty regional Emmy Awards among them, and Tilkin had kept an eye on the Followers ever since KATU's Mark Hass had exposed them more than ten years earlier. The journalists from KATU and *The Oregonian* had, almost by themselves, originated and advanced in American media the issue of faith-healing abuse, and that didn't endear them to the Followers' defenders. Cogan was worried that they would sensationalize their coverage, because "much of what the news media reports," he later said, "is packaged as entertainment."

Cogan and Neidig had winnowed the pool mostly to jurors who were anti-government, pro-religion, and pro-family. They'd also put in parents, since they believed most moms and dads wouldn't like the government sticking its nose into family matters.

Prosecutors Greg Horner and Steve Mygrant sauntered in, looking at home in a familiar courtroom. Horner was as optimistic as Cogan, partly because prosecutors usually win: If people aren't guilty, they're usually not on trial. Horner, too, had wanted parents on the jury, believing they would be even more appalled than people without kids by the photos of what he called "that God-awful thing on Ava's neck." Those pictures would remind the jury that *Ava* was the victim, not her parents. Sympathy for the perps was a real danger.

Horner had even felt that sympathy himself. "I started out," he later said, "thinking that the Followers were nice people. But I gave them too much credit. They're nice people, but they let their kids die? That's kind of a big deal, isn't it?"

Horner, as the chief deputy district attorney to head District Attorney John Foote, no longer worked many trials, but this was the county's most nationally significant case ever, so he'd assigned it to himself.

So had Chief Judge Steven Mauer, the grand old man of the Clackamas courts, who had an air of gravitas, a silver-haired senatorial appearance, and an impressive career based around deterring crime instead of just punishing it, by using diversion systems of treatment, rehabilitation, and education. This case represented one of the best chances ever for a jurisdiction to achieve complete deterrence among an organized group of longtime, repeat offenders. If Mauer could achieve successful deterrence in Clackamas County—the epicenter of faith-healing abuse in America—it could happen anywhere.

"Most of the time," Mauer later told a law school class, "deterrence doesn't have a lot to commend itself. Busting one person for shoplifting usually doesn't prevent it among all others." But the Followers could be influenced, because they were not typical criminals. They were more rational than most criminals, didn't have sociopathic mentalities or criminal intent, and were part of the community. That's why this was such a great opportunity.

And a great risk: The Followers might look like benign innocents to some jurors, or even like martyrs.

At 9:00 a.m., the bailiff unlocked the door, and Patrick, with about fifty other Followers, entered and squeezed into chairs. Brent canted his swivel chair backward and smiled at his friends.

Patrick had heard that Raylene was scared to death, but that Brent was calm. Brent thought that they'd either win, or that only he would be convicted. He'd therefore be a hero, or the ultimate martyr. Win-win.

A gracefully aging woman walked in, but there were no more seats. Dale Hickman—"young in the mind," in Patrick's opinion, but undeniably a gentleman—gave her his seat, next to his pregnant wife, Shannon, who was Walter White's great-granddaughter.

The woman thanked Dale, sat down, and texted Rita Swan: "It's starting. After all these years."

She didn't expect Rita to respond, because Rita was preoccupied with a number of new cases, including that of Kara Neumann, the eleven-year old Wisconsin girl who had died from untreated diabetes. Kara's mother was now on trial, her father having just been convicted of second-degree reckless homicide. Both parents would soon be sentenced to only six months in jail, with ten years of probation.

Rita, hoping for much harsher sentences than those that would eventually be assigned, was bringing national attention to the Wisconsin trial, and had recently spoken about it on the PBS program *Religion & Ethics Newsweekly*. She'd offered an opinion that Patrick shared: That many fundamentalists in faith-healing churches would actually welcome strict enforcement of laws against faith-healing abuse. "It takes the moral burden of decision making off the parents' shoulders," she'd said.

Wisconsin's shield law, unfortunately, offered too much leniency to perpetrators, making Rita pessimistic about the possibility of long sentences for the Neumanns. Because of that, she was working on a dual strategy in Wisconsin: publicize the trial, and gut the shield law. She was helping legislators write a new bill, and was preparing for upcoming hearings.

The necessity of changing laws one at a time, state by state, was complex and grueling for Rita. The need for individual state reform reflected poorly upon the federal government, which with one act of

Congress could have virtually eliminated the legality of faith-healing abuse nationwide. The federal lawmakers, though, just didn't have the courage to do it.

Canada, in contrast, had just announced that the government's rights to protect children in obvious cases of medical neglect superseded religious preferences. That ruling had come a couple of weeks earlier, when the Supreme Court of Canada upheld a lower court decision that a fourteen-year-old girl in the Jehovah's Witness Church was obligated to undergo a blood transfusion, even though she and her parents opposed it.

Rita was also trying at this time to publicize the death of Zachary Swezey, a seventeen-year-old boy who had recently died in the quiet rural recesses of Okanogan County, Washington. That was the same conservative, survivalist region where Rita had been involved almost twenty years earlier in the case of the ten-year-old boy who had been beaten to death for suspected masturbation.

In March, Zachary, who had been bedridden for days with extreme pain, uncontrollable diarrhea, vomiting, and a fever, died in agony from a ruptured appendix as his parents, Greg and JaLea Swezey, members of the Church of the First Born, prayed by his bedside.

The Swezeys were getting strong support from their congregation, which had significant support within the largely fundamentalist community, and Rita was not terribly optimistic about the case—rightfully so, because the Swezeys eventually received very light sentences.

A similar incident involving First Born members had also occurred in 1994 in the isolated town of Brownsville, Oregon, where Loyd and Christina Hays avoided jail time in the death of their seven-year-old son, Anthony, who died from untreated leukemia. Oregon had the worst shield law in the country at that time, enabling Anthony's mother to be acquitted of criminally negligent homicide, and his father to be sentenced only to probation. After that, when Rita asked a school principal there to report religious abuse, he told her, "I don't have anything against the First-Borner's religious practices. They're no different than the Christian Scientists or other groups who believe in readings and prayers to heal disease."

The Church of the First Born and the Followers appeared to be the two most lethal churches in America, and had been philosophically associated since the 1700s, sharing harsh doctrines of medical avoidance, literal interpretation of the Bible, lifelong shunning of presumed sinners, and extreme fear of a brutally torturous hell. Each church also believed that only its members would ascend to the celestial kingdom, while everyone else—including the congregations of the other church—would burn in hell, where fire was nine times hotter than it was on earth. Rita believed that approximately ninety children had died needlessly during recent decades in the Church of the First Born, which had about one hundred branches in twenty states.

Another case, this one in inner-city Philadelphia, also didn't look very promising, due to the Pennsylvania shield law, which Rita had been fighting for years. A two-year-old boy, Kent Schaible, had died after suffering for ten days from untreated bacterial pneumonia. His parents, Herbert and Catherine Schaible, members of the First Century Gospel Church, prayed for him as he slowly died, telling detectives, "We tried to fight the devil, but in the end the devil won."

Another new case had just broken in Oklahoma, a conservative state in which the media often resisted covering incidents of faith-healing abuse. A few weeks prior, a nine-year-old boy named Aaron Grady had died slowly from untreated diabetes. He had grown so weak that he was able to eat only pureed vegetables and drink broth or juice, and he needed to be carried to the bathroom. But his mother, Susan Grady, of the Church of the First Born, did nothing but pray, telling police, "I didn't want to be weak in my faith and disappoint God. I don't believe what I did was wrong." Mrs. Grady's prosecution was dragging, and it would be two years before she was sentenced to two and a half years in prison for second-degree manslaughter. By then, two more children from that Church had died from untreated conditions. There were 41 congregations of the Church of the First

Born in Oklahoma, more than in any other state, and Rita was planning on attending the Grady trial, hoping to gain attention in her fight against Oklahoma's strong shield law.

Also, in yet another exorcism case, this time in rural Gwinnett County, Georgia, a judge had just dismissed charges against a mother who had handcuffed her teenage son to a chair for three days, withholding food and water for twelve hours at a time, to try to drive the devil out of him. She had been charged with child cruelty, but a judge dismissed the charges, telling prosecutors, "I'm going to have a hard time believing that you're going to get anybody in Gwinnett County, Georgia, to say that Satan doesn't exist. So it's going to be really hard to claim that the basic precept behind any of her actions were false, malicious, or criminal."

Although these exorcisms tended to occur most often in ghettos and rural areas, Rita had also helped expose others that had occurred in elite environments, such as one performed by members of the University Christian Fellowship at the Ivy League school of Brown University. There, undergraduate Bobby Jindal, who by this time was governor of Louisiana, had witnessed, and to some extent participated in, an attempted exorcism of a young woman he knew.

Jindal wrote an article about it in 1994, noting that other students knelt over the woman, chanting, "Satan, I demand you to leave this woman," whom he described as smelling like sulfur, "which supposedly accompanies the devil." Governor Jindal tried to pray himself, he said, but when he did, "I felt some type of physical force distracting me. It was as if something was pushing down on my chest."

That same year, a more horrifying exorcism had occurred in Jindal's home state of Louisiana, where belief in voodoo was still relatively common among Haitian descendants, and where extremist Catholic Cajuns sometimes shunned relatives who converted to Protestantism. In Louisiana's historic Acadia Parish, two sisters gouged out the eyes of another sister, Myra Obasi, to drive the devil from her, and tossed the eyes in a garbage can. The perpetrators won a relatively light sentence on an aggravated-assault conviction, mostly because the victim testified that she was glad it happened, prompting the DA to say, "It's something you'd think you'd see on *Tales from the Crypt*."

Despite Jindal's indirect association with exorcism, and his tacit approval of creationism, he was, at this time, being mentioned as a possible presidential or vice-presidential candidate.

On top of all this, Rita had heard that in a few weeks Utah senator Orrin Hatch would introduce an ominous amendment to President Obama's historic health care reform act. The amendment would once again force the federal government to pay religious practitioners for prayer—a practice that Rita had helped abolish twelve years earlier. She feared it would allow parents to claim that prayer really was a medical treatment.

For the most part, this was a discouraging time. Things didn't look good—except, possibly, in the Worthington case.

In the Clackamas County Courthouse, the woman who had texted Rita felt her cell phone vibrate and checked it. Surprisingly, it was a text from Rita. It said: "Good, I'm glad it's starting. This case means everything."

No one recognized the woman that Rita had texted. It was Eleanor Evans, "The Widow," who'd been bitten by a black widow spider in Caldwell, Idaho, almost seventy years earlier. Eleanor recognized only a few of the oldest Followers. The last time she'd seen them all together had been at the funeral for Patrick's father in 1974, when she'd arrived with Patrick's shunned sister, Ella. Patrick still hadn't contacted Ella, though he had started to feel guilty about that.

Eleanor had enjoyed a great life as a successful businesswoman and happy wife, after several early years of grappling unsuccessfully with the ghosts of her past, a fight that she fueled, for a time, with the assistance of alcohol. Finally she realized that the only way to leave her past behind was to confront it head-on, day after day, by volunteering at a clinic for other victims of childhood abuse. These days she was serving as a source on faith-healing abuse for the producers who worked with Bill O'Reilly, Glenn Beck, and Anderson Cooper. Hardly any other former Followers would talk to them.

The door to the judge's chambers opened.

"All rise."

CLACKAMAS COUNTY COURTHOUSE
JUNE 25, 2009; 9:00 A.M.

Although trials in movies often begin with the jury filing into the courtroom, trials in real life are often virtually over—won or lost—before the jury enters the room. The most important pre-trial factors are usually the composition of the jury itself, and the acceptance or rejection of crucial pieces of evidence.

This trial, with the jury still waiting outside, was almost over.

Cogan and Neidig had already achieved a huge pretrial victory when the judge had agreed to restrict evidence about the deaths of other children in the Church. When KATU's Dan Tilkin heard that, he thought the Followers could definitely win.

But the other pivotal piece of evidence being considered at this time was the collection of photos of "that God-awful thing on Ava's neck." Horner thought that if he could get those photos entered, *he* would win.

Cogan and Neidig were afraid Horner was right, despite their own pretrial victory, but had a strategy for barring them: alleged manipulation of Ava's body by Captain Bruce Pearson, who had been at the death scene when most of the photos were taken.

Horner had seen the ploy coming, though, ever since tipsy legal assistant Mary Ann had mentioned Captain Pearson to Detectives Rhodes, Finn, and Band at the Beagleys' farm. After that happened, Horner also received eleven affidavits from Followers who said that Pearson was drunk at Ava's death scene. If that could be proved, the photos might get tossed.

John Lucy, a lawyer working with Cogan and Neidig, made a motion to Judge Mauer to restrict the jury from seeing the photos, and to let them see the affidavits. It would be a devastating one-two punch.

"There's an issue," Lucy said, "with regard to how the photographs were *taken*." He said there were two groups of photos, some shot before Pearson arrived and most after. Those taken after Pearson's entrance might have been contaminated, Lucy claimed, because "Captain Pearson was intoxicated that evening" and may have "moved and displaced evidence." Lucy began to verbally create images that were almost pornographic, asserting that, "They undressed the infant who was deceased, completely disrobed her . . . took off every garment, took disturbing and gratuitous photographs—quite shocking photos—and unclothed her." He said they "took off everything, every stitch. . . . The hair is mussed, the body stripped, the position changed. . . . The body was manhandled, touched, and contaminated." Lucy said that bacteria was introduced by Captain Pearson, "who remembers nothing of that night."

The memory loss was true, but Lucy didn't mention that it was due to a sleeping pill, not alcohol.

Cogan then got up and seemed to try to hang a drunk-driving charge on Pearson. Pearson, he said, "drove to the location under the influence of intoxicants." Cogan charged that Pearson was "unfit for duty" and was just "a trespasser with no lawful purpose in the residence."

DA Steve Mygrant quickly swatted down the unfounded charge of drunkenness, and got right to the point: "These photographs are highly relevant," he said. They were, after all, photos of the deceased.

Mauer agreed that the photos were disturbing, but said, "The death of a child is a disturbing event." He entered the photos as evidence and added, "This idea that we're going to try the driving-under-the-influence case against Captain Pearson, in the middle of this trial, just isn't going to happen."

"Well, Your Honor," Cogan said, "my only response to that is that—"

"I'm not asking for a response," Mauer said. "This is not an invitation to debate."

Cogan argued that he wasn't debating, and Mauer lost his patience. "We're not debating this any further. That is the ruling. So—"

"No," said Cogan, "I'm not—"

"So unless you're—"

"I'm not trying to debate," Cogan said.

"Well, don't interrupt me, Mr. Cogan."

"I'm not trying . . . ," Cogan said, and attempted to make his point again.

"Okay. Mr. Cogan—"

"Previously—"

"Mr. Cogan. Mr. Cogan. The time to make your record is before the court has ruled. Once the court has ruled, you don't get to go back and say, 'Well, I didn't say this and I didn't say that. The record is what it is.'"

"All right. Let—"

"And will remain. Anything else before we bring the jury in, gentlemen?"

"State's ready, Your Honor," Horner said, looking happy.

Cogan said he was ready, too, but his eyes held a look of loss.

"Members of the jury," Greg Horner said as he began his opening statement, "on March second, 2008, Ava Worthington died a needless death that could have been stopped by her parents." Horner made eye contact with every juror, then continued, "What we have to prove is that the defendants failed to be aware of a substantial risk." He didn't need to prove intent or recklessness, he said—just that Brent and Raylene weren't aware of a medical risk that a *reasonable* person would be. Ignorance was no excuse. It was just another sign of neglect.

Horner said that he had three types of evidence: the reports from the death scene, the results of the autopsy, and the testimony of doctors who could prove that Ava could have been saved.

He said Ava had been a big, healthy newborn, but wasted away because of a cyst that her parents either ignored, or just prayed would go away.

During the week she died, he said, she had a serious lung infection, which made the cyst even bigger. She couldn't fight off the infection because she was emaciated, and the cyst was choking her. But even in her final hour of life, the cyst could have easily been drained. Instead, her parents just prayed.

However, Horner said, according to Brent and Raylene: "'Oh, she was doing fine. Oh, there was no problem. Oh, she was a happy, healthy child.'"

Juror Ken Byers leaned forward. "I was blown away by the story he was telling," he later said. "It was like something out of the Old Testament."

Horner said that on the last night of Ava Worthington's life, even the Followers saw that she was "struggling to breathe." They realized "that her condition had changed dramatically." The cyst, he said, was part of her body's toxin elimination system—the lymphatic system—so as the toxins from her infection increased, the cyst swelled until it stretched from her ear to her collarbone, crushing her throat almost shut.

Horner took out the transcript of Brent's first interview with Detective James Rhodes. Reading from it, Horner said, "The question was: 'Was there a time you thought that she might not survive?' His answer: 'Yes.'"

Rhodes had asked Brent why he thought that, and Brent said: "Because her breathing got that bad."

Rhodes, Horner said, asked Brent what he did when he thought his daughter might die. "Brent said, 'Uh, we kept praying. Asked for prayers at the church.'"

As Ava lay dying, Horner said, the Followers described her as, "Oh, just a little tired—but playful." When Ava lapsed into lethargy and stopped breathing, Horner said, "They did not provide any kind of CPR or lifesaving efforts. They anointed her. They provided her with a diluted form of wine . . . and the laying on of hands. Three times." The Followers' own aggressive, if misguided, actions, Horner said, showed that, "This is not a family that's just, 'Oh, gosh, my kid's sick with a cold.'"

Even during Ava's last hour of life, Horner said, a doctor could have opened her airway, given her antibiotics, and almost certainly saved her.

There was nothing wrong with praying for Ava, Homer said, but a reasonable person would have combined prayer with medical care. Brent and Raylene didn't. "And that's why their failure to act was criminal."

Horner said that Rhodes asked Brent if he would have done things differently if he'd known that a doctor could save Ava. "'No,' Mr. Worthington says. 'No.' It wouldn't have changed his decision. Is that reasonable? No, it's not. That's why we have brought these charges," Horner said. "And it's why we will be asking you, as difficult as it may be, to convict Mr. and Mrs. Worthington. Thank you very much."

Most of the jurors were impressed by Horner. His serious unsmiling face and quick, intense movements evoked a sense of coiled energy ready to spring. The Intel manager was glad Horner stuck to the facts. He liked facts.

They took a break. The jurors, almost instinctively, began to divide into two groups: one from Oregon City, including the rural eastern wilderness of Clackatucky, and one from the more upscale environs of urban western Clackamas County, including Lake O'Ego.

"Good afternoon, ladies and gentlemen," Mark Cogan said, looking relaxed and confident. "This is Brent Worthington." Cogan put his hand on Brent's shoulder, a move that usually softened a defendant's image. Cogan said that Brent, 29, was a fourth-generation local boy, owned a local business with his dad, stayed out of trouble, loved his kids, went to a local church, lived in the church's neighborhood, and had been married for ten years to a local girl. Brent was, in other words, one of us: He's Oregon City. That wasn't supposed to matter, but of course it did.

"Brent and Raylene have never been to a doctor," Cogan said. "They did not deny medical treatment to their daughter—they never felt that it was needed."

Horner suddenly knew more about Cogan's line of defense. He wasn't going to say that Brent and Raylene knew that Ava was sick and that they'd tried to heal her spiritually, because they thought that prayer worked. They were going to pretend there was no obvious problem. It was a smart move.

But it was cynical and hypocritical. The Worthingtons wouldn't stand up for what they believed in, because that would be risky. They'd take risks with Ava's life, but not their own.

Then Cogan revealed another basic strategy. He described Brent and Raylene as part of an idyllic community: a vanished, old-fashioned Americana of close families, good neighbors, and great friends. "These people respond in times of trouble. If their house needs painting, if their car breaks down, if their child is ill, if they're in trouble of any kind, if they need a new roof, they instantly—instantly!—have dozens of people at hand."

That also helped characterize the crowd at the death scene as buddies helping out and having fun, not desperate people at a deathwatch.

"So let's talk about what happened March 2nd," Cogan said casually, referring to the day Ava died. It was the flu season, he said, and people were getting sick, then getting better—so naturally Brent and Raylene thought Ava would recover. Who knew?

Ava's failure to recover, Cogan said, had nothing to do with malnourishment. He had photos of his own, and began to flash them on a screen. In these pictures, Ava didn't look malnourished. Her arms and thighs seemed chubby. "Do you see a malnourished, starving child in that photograph?" Cogan asked. The jury was riveted.

Cogan said that Horner would try to make the jury believe that Ava was as thin as a cancer patient who was cachectic. "Cachectic," said Cogan. "Now, that's not a word that most of us use in our vocabulary. It's a word that's new to my vocabulary."

It was part of the "Who Knew?" defense: Doctors who know fancy medical words can spot danger—but not all reasonable people are doctors.

Ken Byers wasn't impressed. "He was playing the ignorance card. But ignorance wasn't a legal defense."

"Now," Cogan said, "what killed her?" It was not, he said, pneumonia—exacerbated by that God-awful thing on Ava's neck. "She was killed by a very fast-acting condition called sepsis." Sepsis, an infection of the blood, moves so quickly, Cogan said, that "treatment is often ineffective." Sepsis "just shuts people down." Cogan said he had a doctor who would prove that.

Then John Neidig began his opening statement for Raylene. He was a good fit for her—kind, patriarchal, and patrician, with an expressive face reminiscent of the Kennedy men, and eyes that teared-up easily. Neidig painted a Norman Rockwell picture of the last week of Ava's life: family, food, fun, friends, and love. Ava did have a runny nose, though, and was teething. Neidig endowed Ava with an endearing personality—spunky, cuddly, and playful—and at least two of the jurors began to feel that surely these parents must have done everything they could for such an adorable child, and must still be deep in grief.

Even when Ava began to decline, Neidig said, there was no panic, just a few casual calls by Brent asking people to, as Neidig put it, "Remember Ava in your heart. Send positive thoughts. She might not be feeling very well."

Neidig said Ava was "a chowhound," of normal weight. He produced a blow-up of a federal government chart for height and weight. Ava weighed 16 pounds and was 26 inches tall. "That's right smack-dab in the 50th percentile," he said, pointing at a highlighted line. "She was petite. But she was proportionate in height to weight."

Several of the jurors scribbled that down. The medical technician was impressed. Ken Byers was not.

Ava was fine until the very end, Neidig said, and the cyst didn't bother her. That's what *every eyewitness* saw, he said. The state's "experts" might not agree—but they hadn't *been* there.

The Worthingtons may have made incriminating statements, but Neidig asked the jury to disregard them, because Brent and Raylene had been tired and upset.

The day was done.

Patrick stayed in his seat, pretending to be sending a text, as the other Followers filed out. Patrick knew that the street outside was jammed with press, including reporters and stringers from the network news and the country's biggest papers, and for the first time in his life he was ashamed to be seen with his friends.

Horner and Mygrant conferenced quietly until the room held only themselves, Patrick, and a few others. The prosecutors noticed Patrick, but didn't know who he was. They'd had a good day. Horner and Mygrant were a tight team, and some people considered Mygrant the leading candidate for Horner's position, if Horner ever left the department, or got the top job.

Some of the jurors socialized briefly, but Ken Byers quickly headed home. He couldn't wait to tell Jane about the trial he was on. Their life had been hard lately, but now he was going to do something good. He wanted to make her proud.

CLACKAMAS COUNTY COURTHOUSE
JUNE 30, 2009

To launch the testimony, Deputy Medical Examiner Jeff Mayer—the first law enforcement official to arrive at Ava's death scene—flashed pictures that he'd taken of Ava on a large screen. Ken Byers and the guy from Intel exchanged a subtle, puzzled glance. Ava didn't look malnourished in these pictures, either.

Then came picture number seven, and they saw Horner's strategy. In the first six photos, Ava had clothes on, as she had in the photos the defense had shown, but in the seventh, Mayer had removed her clothing—as he usually did at infant deaths—and Ava looked frightful. Her ribs were sticking out, her skin was tight to her bones, and her stomach—usually chubby in a child that age—was sunken. Ava's arms and legs, the only parts of her body that were visible with her clothes on, did look relatively big, but in contrast to her midsection, they seemed more bloated than meaty. She was yellow, and the cyst was huge and discolored.

Mayer described transferring Ava to the morgue, and storing her naked body in a frigid locker as rigor mortis intensified, reducing the little girl to cold, rigid meat. It made Ava's death alarmingly real. As people tend to do, many of the jurors fancied a comforting Disney vision of death: immortal souls leaving warm, intact bodies and floating to heaven. Mayer's gritty procedural wiped that away.

Cogan tried to discredit Jeff Mayer for taking four years instead of two to finish his medical examiner's education, but Mayer said it happened because he had eight kids. Cogan backed off. He needed Mayer to be a jackbooted menace, not a family guy.

Then detectives Michelle Finn and Patrick Harris offered their own grim images of the death scene, forcing the jury to focus on Ava's suffering, instead of the Worthingtons', or on lofty ideas of philosophy, family values, and personal privacy.

During the course of the Worthington investigation, Rita Swan had talked to Finn about the importance of ignoring any spiritual abstractions, and focusing instead on the down-and-dirty reality of faith-based child abuse. Most of the Followers, Rita had said, didn't even know much about religion. Finn soon found out that was true. "At first," Finn later said, "I asked them about the Bible and their beliefs, but they didn't have much to say." They seemed more interested in the legal technicalities of guilt and innocence.

Now, Finn's testimony boiled down to plain police work—just the facts: Brent and Raylene knew Ava was dreadfully ill, didn't call a doctor, and admitted it.

Harris told the jury what it felt like to arrive at a Followers' death scene: the crowd, the food, the chaos, the cigarette smoke, and the hostility. He showed photos of olive oil on a nightstand, and oil smeared on Ava's face—a tableau simultaneously mundane and bizarre.

Cogan got Harris to admit that the Followers were cooperative with authorities, which became a staple in his defense. But the Miss Manners Defense bored the jury. What was the alternative? A shoot-out?

Cogan wanted to mention James Rhodes' comment to Brent on the night of Ava's death that the Followers were "the most honest and endearing people I've met in a long time." The attorney hoped it would bolster the image of the Followers as decent people. But Rhodes hadn't been called as a witness, so Cogan asked Finn about it.

"Do you think Detective Rhodes was stating his true feelings, or was he maybe shading things a little?" It seemed like a good question at the time, because it apparently created a double-bind: Which was it—the Followers are great, or the cop was lying?

"I don't know *what* he was thinking," Finn replied, and that was the end of that.

Horner looked happy, and he hadn't even used his two best weapons: the autopsy report, and doctors' testimony. That stuff would blow holes in the tall-tales of Brent, Raylene, and anybody else who had the guts to get on the stand and lie.

CLACKAMAS COUNTY COURTHOUSE
JULY 1, 2009

Christopher Young, MD, who'd done the autopsy, attacked the myth that Ava was "smack-dab in the 50th percentile" of normal growth. The jury had seemed to swallow that, which was bad, because Ava's failure to thrive was a huge issue. It had helped kill her, and showed that Brent and Raylene had long neglected a baby they claimed to adore. And if the Worthingtons hadn't even *noticed* it, how could they possibly be reasonable people?

Young brought out a growth chart that showed Ava's weight was even less than the lowest five percentile, at 23 pounds. That was eight or nine pounds below normal. Her height, twenty-six inches, was also in the lowest one percentile—or less.

"Less than one percentile?" Horner asked.

"Yes. A fraction of a child," said Young.

Ava, therefore, was in the 50th percentile of weight for toddlers as *short* as her, and the 50th percentile of height for toddlers as *thin* as her. She was proportional, but tiny.

Even more damning, Ava weighed ten pounds at birth: the 95th percentile. When she died, her head circumference was still in the 90th percentile. Her height and weight should have been consistent with her head circumference and her birth weight, but had lagged dramatically.

Ava was a poster child for failure to thrive, and the obvious cause was her cyst. Young said the cyst pushed against Ava's larynx and trachea so much that when he began to remove those organs, they whipped back into her neck by two inches, like rubber bands snapping. "There was a tremendous amount of pressure," Young said. Some of Ava's blood vessels were torn open and her Adam's apple was "actually misshapen, because the pressure had been there for so long."

The cyst blocking her throat had also helped to hold pus in her lungs. The sicker she got, the more her cyst swelled, until it was "the size of a grapefruit or softball," he said. "It's a vicious cycle."

Young also said the cyst could have been drained with a needle, or removed.

Mark Cogan took one last shot at establishing Ava's size as "in the 50th percentile" but the myth had been busted. Then Cogan insisted to Young that she'd died from sepsis, not pneumonia, but Young said there was no real difference, because pneumonia usually caused at least a little sepsis: It was a fake-out argument.

Neidig did, however, force Young to admit, under oath, that Ava had indeed been teething. None of the jurors wrote that down.

CLACKAMAS COUNTY COURTHOUSE
JULY 2, 2009

To once and for all bury the Legend of the Fiftieth Percentile, Horner brought in Dr. Sayonara Mato, a specialist in childhood infection, who said that Ava, at sixteen months, was the size of a six-month-old.

"Was that dramatically low?"

"Severely dramatic . . . a very big red flag."

Horner asked Mato what could have been done as Ava lay dying. "ABC," Mato said. "Airway, breathing, and circulation." A paramedic would have immediately given Ava a breathing tube, then oxygen, and then intravenous antibiotics. That almost certainly would have saved her, Mato said.

Neidig didn't really challenge the facts of Mato's testimony, but seemed to fixate on the fact that Mato was from Venezuela. He struggled with the pronunciation of her last name—all four letters—and asked why one of her credentials was "TM."

"That means 'master of public health and tropical medicine,'" she said.

"Oh, okay." He seemed befuddled.

"Tropical medicine," Cogan offered from his desk.

"Huh?" Neidig said.

"Tropical medicine," Cogan reiterated.

"Tropical medicine. Okay. I've never seen that before."

The exchange didn't meet the standards of political correctness that might behoove two Portlandia-based attorneys, but this was Oregon City.

Detective Jim Band, who was watching the trial among some Followers in the spectator area, thought that Neidig and Cogan's case was already cooked. He considered them "just not very good attorneys."

The prosecution called on Dr. James Cuyler, who'd treated about thirty similar cysts, or cystic hygromas. He said that surgical removal "has been done for decades" and was first written about "in the mid-1800s." Cuyler agreed that Ava could have been saved even during the last hours of her life.

Dan Leonhardt, MD, who specialized in child abuse, said that as Ava was dying, her struggle to breathe would have been like "breathing through a straw," until she was so exhausted that she lapsed into a generally lethargic condition called carbon dioxide narcosis. Ava simply could not have been playful, active, engaged with other people, and happy, as her parents and their friends claimed. It would be impossible.

The trial had come to a standoff: Eyewitnesses vs. Experts.

Neidig embraced the standoff. He asked Leonhardt, "Would you expect someone with carbon dioxide narcosis to be playful?"

"No."

"Or active?"

"No."

"With people?"

"No."

"Or happy?"

"No."

Neidig looked as if he'd won at least that one point. Most of the jurors didn't think so.

"State rests, Your Honor," Horner said.

As Followers began to leave the courthouse, many of them headed for a restaurant on Molalla Avenue, and even more headed for the church. Patrick, sitting in the lobby with the overflow crowd of Followers, felt his phone buzz and pulled it out of his pocket.

It was a text from Theresa, who was still in Idaho, with less of an excuse than ever to be there. He'd visited her seven times in the last five months, but things were so strained that not seeing her at all felt like the best way to keep their marriage alive. She was cold and critical, as if he'd become someone else she didn't know and didn't like.

"Baby is sick. U should come. T."

He took deep breaths and wished there were no media people outside, so he could bolt for his car and race to Caldwell.

Patrick saw Jim Band come out of the trial room. It was a shock—he didn't know Band was there, and was afraid he might somehow reveal that he'd met with Band-James-Band many times. So with his head down and his summer-lightened hair in his face, Patrick took the stairs to the lobby two at a time.

When he got outdoors, one of the TV people put a microphone in front of him and said, "Are you people going to start taking your kids to the doctor now?"

"Get that thing out of the way." He hurried off.

14

SACRIFICED ON THE ALTAR

*Though I should gaze forever
On that green light that lingers in the west,
I may not hope from outward forms to win
The passion and the life, whose fountains are within.*

—"Dejection: An Ode," Samuel Taylor Coleridge

Caldwell, Idaho
July 5, 2009

Thunderous fireworks, legal in Idaho, exploded just outside Theresa's apartment as Patrick held his son. Paul, now the same age Ava had been when she died, cupped Patrick's sunburned cheeks with his palms and babbled, showing few signs of the bronchitis he'd had. "He's getting better," Patrick said to Theresa. He didn't tell her why, but he was sure she knew.

"They always do," she said flatly.

Patrick was willing to prolong the torture of not knowing what was happening to their marriage, because if it was over, that would feel even worse than fearing it was. But he took a breath. "So," he said, in the shorthand of longtime intimacy, "what do you want to do?"

"I don't know."

"Well, what do you *need*?" His voice sounded tight, even to him, its lyricism lost.

"I need my life to mean something, Patrick. Whether I'm with you." Then she took a breath. "Or not."

There it was. The end. But he had to take one last shot. "It *does* mean something, Theresa. You're a mother. A wife. You have a great job. Great friends. We've always been happy, and now we're a family."

"I'm talking about my inner life. My spiritual life. I need to be more than somebody who takes care of kids and a husband and a job and a house. Patrick, we were *chosen*. We're different. Remember? You don't seem to."

It was time to be honest. "No, we're not. Give that up."

"And do what? Live and *die*? Be worldly? Go to hell?" Angry tears shined in her eyes. "You betrayed me, Patrick. You didn't hold fast. You gave up. You think you're so cool, with your pretty green eyes, but you have no idea what people are saying about you, and it's so humiliating. I wonder if you ever even loved me—the real me."

"I thought the real you would put your husband and family above everything, even Church stuff."

"Church *stuff*? Why don't you abandon *your* beliefs? Whatever they are."

"Because kids are dying."

She was silent, and stayed that way for a long time, to the best of Patrick's recollection.

"I've gotta leave," she said finally. She was out the door fast, her long legs, tan and thin in cut-offs, slicing like scissors.

Leave for where? To do what? Patrick thought she was playing mind games.

The pyrotechnics got louder and he could smell sulfur. He felt an urgent need to move. He put Paul in his car seat and drove off. When he passed the Simplot potato plant, he remembered the legend of a Follower's grandmother shooting at Walter White's rival for molesting some girl at a motel that used to be here. That started the whole migration to Oregon. It was the grandmother, as best he could remember, of a Followers dropout that people called The Widow. Now the

Widow was a hero to him, along with a few other ex-Followers that people gossiped about, some of whom had lost children: a remarkable woman named Myrna Cunningham, who'd had the courage to talk openly with KATU's Dan Tilkin about the Followers, and also Myrna's distant cousin Myra Cunningham, as well as Holly Divelbis, Mick Mouser, Suzanne Shumaker, Darrell Shaw, and Russ Briggs. They'd sacrificed everything by leaving the Church. But from what he'd heard, they were all okay now, and almost able to accept what they'd lost. And now Jack Simplot was the world's oldest billionaire, still selling potatoes to McDonald's with his Mormon cronies. It was funny how big things got started.

Passing streets with Mormon-derived names—Locust, Logan, and Kimball—he headed out of town on Karcher Road, toward Lake Lowell, where there was a Followers cemetery. He and Paul could check it out, watch the ducks on the lake, and wait for Round Two with Theresa.

Peaceful Valley Cemetery was identified by a sign, unlike the O.C. cemetery, which just had a no-trespassing sign. The Followers in Caldwell weren't as secretive as they were back home because there were more than a thousand of them in a town far smaller than Portland, with three congregations and three cemeteries. And they didn't need to hide from the authorities, because of Idaho's impenetrable religious-shield law. When Followers kids died from medical neglect in Idaho, their deaths were little noted, even by authorities.

The cemetery sat on a mesa under what seemed to be a perpetually azure sky, but it was tacky and thrown together. There were irregular rows of graves with gaudy, disheveled decorations, and many of the headstones were just cement poured onto the ground with names scratched into them. He recognized many of the family names: Beagley, Eells, Cunningham, Smith, Young, Morris, and Downs. So many children. In the Watson family plot, there were four graves, side by side, all with INFANT BABY scratched onto their tiny concrete headstones. Lots of lamb references dotted the cemetery: Our Little Lamb. Baby Lamb. Lamb of God. There were even more of the little sacrificial lambs here than in the Oregon cemetery. Patrick started to count the kids' graves, as Paul slept on his shoulder, with the baby's reddish-straw hair, the same color as Patrick's, keeping the sun out of his eyes.

There were 136 kids' graves out of a total of 337. One of the graves was new, but not marked, a tactic the Followers sometimes used to hide a suspicious death. There was even a rectangular, spray-painted outline of a grave soon to be dug, with a shovel in the middle, standing upright in the dirt. He took a picture of it with his phone.

At that moment, Patrick suddenly knew, with a certainty that seemed like it had been there forever, that what he was doing was far more important than losing Theresa, Paul, his only friends, his job connections, and everything else. Now he would have to follow the sacrifices of others and lead the way himself, a phoenix born of fire, with his own losses to forget.

The outer world was his inner life now.

On the spur of the moment, he took out his phone and had directory assistance put him through to the Canyon County District Attorney's Office in Caldwell. He told an assistant DA who he was and what he'd been doing for the authorities in Clackamas County and mentioned the unmarked grave. The DA told him, in the safe, non-incriminating language of a bureaucrat, that he wasn't remotely interested, couldn't do anything even if he was, and that the people of Canyon County took freedom of religion very seriously. The call lasted about two minutes.

The baby stirred. "Are you hungry, honey?" he said. "Let's go home. We've got a lot to do." He smiled at Paul and felt strangely okay, as if almost instantly comfortable with a role he'd once dreaded: the abandoned husband whose only refuge was the reformation of the Followers of Christ Church.

CLACKAMAS COUNTY COURTHOUSE
JULY 6, 2009

Mark Cogan, whose case appeared to be in big trouble to most of the jurors, called his first witness. A nicely dressed, young-looking woman took the stand. It was Julie Worthington, Ava's grandma.

Julie began to weave a tale—the Sad Story of Sudden Death—that eleven other Followers, including Brent and Raylene, would soon corroborate with the remarkable consistency of a well-coached team. Their story was the heart of the defense strategy: Eyewitnesses vs. Experts.

A cyst like Ava's, Julie said, was too common in the family to worry about, especially since Ava was so fat, active, playful, engaged with others, and happy. Julie talked about the harmlessness of the cyst she'd had herself as a child—the one that had burst from a blow by her brother's baseball bat—and blamed Ava's symptoms not on her little neck-bump, but on teething, and a cold.

Ken Byers wondered: "Do they think that none of our kids ever teethed?"

When Horner cross-examined her, Julie said that even in the last hours of Ava's life, the cyst was only "fairly swelled."

"Did you have a concern about it at that point?" Horner asked.

"I didn't."

"The cystic hygroma?"

"What is it?"

"It's called a cystic hygroma," Horner said. He sounded far more bewildered than sarcastic, seeming not to comprehend how Julie could be so lacking in curiosity about the condition that killed her granddaughter.

Julie claimed that it was quite common for a crowd to gather for a child with a cold, and for her to sleep by the baby's bed, and for them to lay on hands at 4:30 a.m.

Horner confronted Julie with her statements to Detective Jeff Green that Ava had been "raspy" and "tired," with stringy, foamy phlegm "coming from her mouth."

"That's not right," she told Horner. She said Green, who hadn't taped the interview, "made a lot of errors."

However, she said, even if Ava's condition had been very, very serious, they still wouldn't have taken her to a doctor.

Julie's testimony was hurting her son's case, but when Cogan followed up by asking her about a photo she'd taken of Ava, she began to dab her eyes and cry, and Horner felt uneasy. Julie was the first of what promised to be a long line of weeping witnesses, and if a picture of the victim was worth a thousand words, the tears of a grieving grandmother were worth two thousand.

Cogan let Julie have a leisurely cry, then jumped to an unexpected piece of evidence: a photo of Ava towering over an end table that was about the same height as her measurement at her autopsy. Julie testified that Cogan had asked her, just the day before, to look for pictures of Ava, and lo and behold, she'd found that one.

It seemed fishy to several of the jurors—"a stunt," one of them later said. "She could have been standing on a book, or whatever."

Cogan called up Julie's husband, Guy, and he backed up her story. But Guy looked equivocal when he, too, denied making statements to detectives that Ava was "wheezing" with . . . "congested-type breathing" that was "labored" and sounded like "asthma."

He said the statements were "not quite accurate."

"You were asked twice, and that was inaccurate?" Horner said.

"Yes. I am thinking that's inaccurate, yes. Somewhat, yes. Yes."

But the statements were taped, and Horner played them. Finally Guy said, "That was my words, yes," but his statement was made "after several hours of no restful sleep."

Then more friends and family members repeated the Sad Story of Sudden Death, chapter and verse.

Raylene's aunt Laina Beagley said that just before Ava died, she was "more comfortable than when I had normally seen her . . . . I was very encouraged." Then, "I heard someone from the bedroom yell, 'She's not breathing!' And I couldn't believe it." She began to cry.

Nicole Sayre—Jeff and Marci's oldest child, and Raylene's big sister—said it "crossed my mind" that Ava might die, but that, "I tend to worry about people."

DA Steve Mygrant asked Nicole, "What caused you to think she might not live? What happened?"

"I wouldn't really say something happened."

"What about her condition made you think that?"

"I wouldn't really say it was something about her condition."

"She sounded like she'd been coached," one of the jurors later recalled. "They all did."

Seth Keith, who'd grown up with Brent, said, "I actually went into the garage with Brent, and I kind of confronted him." But Brent, he said, calmed his concerns, and then he went inside and saw Ava "tossing on the bed with full orneriness," and felt even more relieved.

Keith said he was "very surprised" by the death, "because that's not something you want to see, is a little kid die." Then he began to cry.

Family friend Samantha King, a fourth-generation O.C. Follower, said she felt "really good" about Ava's condition just before she died, because she seemed to be "ready for a nap." When Ava suddenly died, King said, "I was shocked." Then she began to cry.

Jeff and Marci Beagley didn't testify, but recordings of the police interviews were played, confirming the Sad Story. Ken Byers was offended by Marci's supercilious tone in the recording. She sounded the same to him as she'd sounded to James Rhodes on the night of Neil's death: like The Church Lady on *SNL*. "She was basically telling the cops," Byers later said, "to butt out, read a Bible, and get a life." Byers didn't know that Jeff and Marci were facing a trial of their own, because that information, and that of other Followers' deaths, was considered prejudicial, and was withheld from the jury.

Family friend Steve White—the Prophet's son, who'd worked at the W. B. Market for 47 years—was brought in to show that Brent and Raylene were under no pressure from the Church to keep Ava out of a hospital. Years earlier, he said, he'd taken his own son to the hospital when the boy had gotten hit by a car and suffered a head injury.

His son had been riding his bike to the house of his girlfriend—
"which happened to be Raylene." White said that, "When you're going to meet your girlfriend, it's not *cool* to wear your bicycle helmet." It
also wasn't legally necessary, since the Followers had a religious exemption from the helmet law. Paramedics had wanted to Life Flight
his son, White said, but he wouldn't let them, though he did agree to
take the boy in himself. He was never shunned for it, he said.

White said that people had been treated without being shunned
"dozens" of times—or even "more than dozens." He told of a Follower with liver trouble who had been treated without being shunned.

"Can you give me another example?" Cogan asked.

"You make me dig deep here," White said. "I'm on the hot seat."
He recalled another case, twenty-five years earlier.

"Can you think of any more right off the bat?"

"Not right this second."

Mygrant's cross-examination of White was tricky. The DAs wanted
the case to be about child abuse, not religion, but religion was obviously the motive, and usually the rule was: no motive, no conviction.
But challenging religious beliefs was treacherous territory. A recent
Gallup poll had shown that 40 percent of all Americans thought that
people were sometimes possessed by the devil, and 70 percent believed
that angels and demons were active in everyday life. Those beliefs
were probably even more popular in Clackalackie.

But no guts, no glory: Mygrant asked White if he thought Ava's
illness was "a test of faith" for Brent and Raylene.

"Well, all of our faith is tested daily," White said.

"Do you think they passed that test?"

"It's not for me to judge how they did in the eyes of God."

Next, Jeff Beagley's brother Steve, who had reportedly swapped
blonde jokes with Neil on the night he died, said that for him, the
night of Ava's death night was mostly just a social event.

More than half the jurors thought the Sad Story was nonsense. "I
thought all of them were lying," one later said.

But every one of the jurors from Oregon City thought that such devout people would never commit perjury, even to fight an oppressive government that was trying to stifle freedom of religion.

CLACKAMAS COUNTY COURTHOUSE
JULY 9, 2009

Cogan's star witness took the stand: Janice Ophoven, MD, America's premier expert witness for the defense on child abuse, who testified in about seventy trials every year. Only eight other doctors in America were in that business. Ophoven had been a defense witness for a man convicted of murdering his wife, three children, and mother-in-law, and had helped exonerate two murder suspects who later confessed.

Cogan asked Ophoven if Ava was a victim of medical neglect.

"No," she said, speaking quickly and confidently. "This is a child who got sick and died in a little bit over 24 hours"—not from pneumonia, but infection of the blood, known as sepsis. Ophoven said that she'd seen kids with sepsis "come in walking, looking fine, holding their bottle, and they're dead by the time they hit the floor."

Ava's death wasn't her parents' fault, Ophoven said. "It's the bacteria's fault." She cited the similar death from sepsis of Muppet creator Jim Henson. In the jury box, the man who looked and often even acted like Mr. Rogers thought the link to Henson was persuasive, because Henson could afford excellent medical care. No one in the jury knew, though, that Henson had been a former Christian Scientist who'd reportedly waited too long to go to the hospital, due to his lingering religious beliefs. If Ophoven knew, she kept it to herself.

About half the jurors liked Ophoven's no-nonsense demeanor, including some of the quieter, more neutral members. Others were dubious, due partly to her appearance: pale, puffy, jowly and dour. "She didn't really look like a doctor," one juror said, "because she didn't seem very healthy, and you expect doctors to practice what they preach."

Ava, Ophoven said, couldn't possibly have died from pneumonia, because Ava had only "very early pneumonia. No apparent fever. No loss of consciousness." She said that Ava was "taking her own fluids," and had "a wet diaper and urine in her bladder."

She also said Ava wasn't emaciated. "Every child," she said, "until teenagehood, their ribs show, unless they're too fat." The doctor claimed, "This is what a normal kid this age *looks* like." She called Ava "a normal, fat little baby," and said Ava was "exactly the right weight for her height."

Dr. Ophoven criticized the way Ava was weighed by the medical examiner, claiming that Ava was weighed on "the same scale they would weigh somebody who is—"

Cogan interrupted: "300 pounds and suffering from obesity?"

"In my world," she replied, "garbage in, garbage out."

Ken Byers remembered that phrase from some trial he'd heard about in the news. A juror had said it, dismissing technical medical evidence. Byers noticed several of the O.C. jurors scribbling it down. Then he remembered where he'd heard the phrase. It was from O. J. Simpson's trial.

Ophoven also said that because Ava's trachea retracted when it was severed, the evidence from it had been compromised. The medical examiner should have tied a string around it, she said, to keep that from happening.

Ophoven intimated that Ava's recorded birth weight was irrelevant, because Ava had been born at home, and that her lungs were not sufficiently full of pus to indicate death by pneumonia. Looking at a photo of Ava's lung tissue, she said, "Air exchange is going to be perfectly fine here." Another reason she ruled out pneumonia was because of "no apparent fever," although no one had taken Ava's temperature.

Ophoven, who also worked part-time as a medical examiner, said it was unusual to undress children at the death site. "Boy," she said, "my medical examiners do not undress the babies at the scene—ever."

Ophoven concluded that blaming Ava's death on her parents was "shocking."

Ken Byers wasn't impressed. "It was clear to me that this person just rolled in for the money," he later said.

Horner went straight for the hired-gun issue. Ophoven's fee was $400 per hour, plus expenses, often including travel time. In his business, that was called "reasonable doubt for a reasonable fee."

Ophoven claimed that of the 350 to 400 trials she'd worked on over the past five years, some were either malpractice, or civil, or second opinions, or for the prosecution. Finally she admitted, "Of the criminal cases, the vast majority in the last five years have been for the defendant."

Then Horner asked what she as a doctor would recommend in a situation in which people said a child was choking on phlegm and struggling to breathe, with a father there who thought she might die.

Ophoven said she would recommend medical attention, "If that's what the people in the room actually said." But the Followers, she said, thought Ava was fine.

"Her dad thought she might die," Horner said.

"I don't know what that means."

"You don't know what it *means* for a father to say, 'I think my child might die'?"

"That was a couple of days later."

"So why would you *not* accept his statement, as it was laid out . . . and accept all the other people who were saying, 'Well, she was sitting up, and taking the bottle,' and so forth?"

Ophoven said her opinions were largely based on "the physical findings and the findings at the postmortem."

That seemed to exclude the fact that Ava did die, with pus in her lungs and a cyst crushing her trachea. Horner reminded her that Ava had "wheezy breathing," and "swelling that is persistent." If Ophoven had seen the baby at that time, he said, "You would have said, 'Bring that child in,' wouldn't you?"

Ophoven argued that even if Ava *had* been taken to the hospital, she still might have died. "Let's assume that she just got a big, honking dose of antibiotics the minute she got a little sick on Saturday, which isn't how normally medicine works, but let's assume that she got sick at the hospital—if they started antibiotic right then, it might have been a different outcome and it might not."

"Would you have said, 'Let's not waste our time'?"

"No."

"Thank you doctor. No further questions, Your Honor."

CLACKAMAS COUNTY COURTHOUSE
JULY 10, 2009

"In many trials," Mark Cogan told truTV's Jami Floyd after the trial had ended, "defense counsel doesn't commit to whether the defendant will testify until a very late stage in the trial. In this case we knew all along that Mr. and Mrs. Worthington would testify, and explain the situation from their point of view."

Cogan wanted the jury to see how much Brent and Raylene loved Ava. That would evoke pity. Once pity was in play, other emotions would follow, and if the trial was decided by emotion, the Worthingtons had a chance.

"Good morning, Mr. Worthington," Cogan said. It was Friday, so the jury would have the whole weekend to absorb images of Brent's and Raylene's grief. "I'm going to ask you a question that's somewhat blunt. Did you ever believe that your daughter would die?"

It was smart phrasing. Brent had told detectives only that he thought she *might* die.

"No, I did not."

Cogan asked if he would have made every possible sacrifice to save Ava's life.

"My family is my life to me," Brent said. "I'd do everything I could."

Then Brent gave his rendition of the Sad Story of Sudden Death, as a video on an overhead screen showed him playing with Ava, and calling to her, "Come get your daddy." Brent began to sniffle and his eyes grew glassy and distant. Most of the jurors looked distressed. Guilty or not, Brent was obviously suffering.

Brent had previously made several damaging statements to James Rhodes, and now Cogan had to undo them.

Brent admitted he'd told Detective Rhodes that the swelling had occurred when Ava was three to four months old, but now he recanted. "There wasn't swelling at that time," he said. "One side of her neck had a little more fat on it than the other side."

Brent said he was never "concerned about her life," even when they laid on hands at 4:30 in the morning. They didn't do that because she was choking, as Brent had previously told Rhodes, but because "she hadn't rested all night, and we didn't want her to get wore down."

Brent had told Rhodes that just before Ava died, they'd been trying to keep her "stirred up—keep her breathing," because she was acting "lethargic."

But now he said that just before her death, "The congestion she had sounded a lot better. I felt really good . . . to see that our prayers had been answered . . . . So we was getting ready to eat dinner." But he "heard somebody holler . . . so I ran back into the bedroom, and she had stopped breathing."

Neidig took over the questioning and asked Brent about the description of Ava as lethargic. *"Lethargic,"* Neidig said. "Did you know what that word was?"

"I still ain't sure what that word means."

The Oregonian's Rick Bella, sitting in the front row, was struck by Brent's mangling of the English language. "I thought he was putting on a hayseed act with his cowboy aphorisms," Bella later said, "to play on the jury's sympathies."

Neidig asked about the baby scale at Ava's birth that showed she weighed a robust ten pounds. "Did *you* ever work with the baby scale?" Brent said he hadn't. "Did you ever test its accuracy?" He hadn't. "Do you know if it was accurate?" He didn't.

By the end of their questions, Brent looked lost and broken, almost indifferent to his own fate.

Horner needed to puncture that image. *Ava* was the victim, not the parents who'd sacrificed her on the altar of their faith. Horner asked Brent if the tragedy had changed his view of medicine, and Brent said no—that even a doctor, Janice Ophoven, had said Ava might have died no matter what they did.

"So you acknowledge there was at least a *possibility* that modern medicine would have saved your daughter . . . but, for you, it was more important to follow your faith?"

"My point is, if medicine hadn't worked, the doctor would tell you to put your faith in God, anyway. They say, 'There's nothing more we can do for you.'"

Brent insisted that he thought Ava was improving, so Horner referred Brent to the interview with James Rhodes in which Brent had said that Ava's condition "dramatically changed" on the day she died.

"I see I said that there. I mean, it had gotten worse. I don't see it as a dramatic change, though. That would be a poor choice of words."

"That *was* your choice of words, wasn't it?"

"Yeah, it was."

Then Horner confronted Brent with his statement to Michelle Finn that Ava's cough became more painful as she began to die. Brent denied it. He claimed he had said the cough was only a little "irritating."

What about trying to stir Ava up, just before she died, to "keep her breathing"?

Brent said what he *really* meant to say was that Ava, herself, "did a lot of stirring that night, in her sleep."

"Well, that's not what you said."

"Some of my words, I picked poorly, and my explanations weren't good."

"Well, they're not good at *all* now, are they—those statements you made?"

Horner asked Brent if he would have taken her to a doctor under any circumstances.

"Like I said, she was getting better from what we was doing."

"It didn't get better at 7:20 on Sunday night."

"She did pass away. Yes, she did."

"You said, 'It was meant to be.'"

"Yeah. I don't think they could have did anything different. And, yeah, as far as God's will, they die in the hospitals, too, if I'm not mistaken."

"You think her chances were just the same laying on your bed in your home?"

"I think they were better."

"Okay, thank you. No further questions."

Then it was his wife's turn. Raylene—fiddling with a strand of beads around her neck, and pregnant with her fourth child, counting the two who'd died—looked like she would rather be anyplace else on earth. She was scared to death—not of prison, presumably, but public speaking. The first thing Neidig asked her about was her education, and why she'd dropped out of school in tenth grade. It was mostly fear of speaking in class, she said, her voice a sorrowful whisper. Besides, she was on the verge of marrying Brent.

So the jury immediately knew this: She was timid. She was vulnerable. She was grieving. She wasn't well educated. She'd been married to an alpha male her entire adult life.

In Raylene's version of the now-familiar Sad Story, Ava was a "healthy child" with "fat on her body." Raylene found it "rather insulting" that the prosecution's doctors had called Ava emaciated. The cyst on Ava's neck was "about the size of my fingertip" for most of her life, caused no discomfort, and didn't stop Ava from keeping up with other kids. The day before Ava died, Raylene said, several friends came over to pray because "you don't like it when your kids choke a little bit on phlegm." On the final day of Ava's life she was "not quite as active." As Ava's death approached, "She acted more happy, she settled down, and she was taking a nap." Then all of a sudden she died.

Neidig asked Raylene how she arrived at major decisions.

"Well, I would go to God, read the Bible. I would ask my husband how he felt," she said, because "major decisions are his to make."

"Do you disobey your husband?"

"No. . . . I am trained to live how I feel I should."

She could offer Brent her opinion, Raylene said, and decide "trivial things . . . like what I'm going to eat for breakfast." But "major decisions," including ones about health issues, were made by Brent.

Ashley, the juror from Sandy, had known couples who operated like that—but it wasn't for her. Still, she understood.

Ken Byers couldn't tell "if it was rehearsed ditziness," or not. "She did have Net access," he later said, "but Brent ran that family, and Raylene was a couple of cans short of a six-pack."

Neidig kept Raylene's testimony short, presumably to show how uninvolved she was.

Then Mygrant took over, and it was Raylene's turn to escape from her previous statements. "You were asked by Detectives Rhodes and Finn, 'Would you do things differently now?' Do you remember being asked that?" She didn't.

Mygrant asked if she'd ever before packed her house with people when one of her kids "had the flu."

"No."

Had her parents ever stayed all night before?

"No." Brent's parents? "No." Her sister-in-law Danielle? She couldn't remember. Kelli Dotson? She couldn't remember. Leigh Smith? Couldn't remember. Did Ava sleep through the night? Couldn't remember. Did she call for people to come over? She couldn't remember.

Raylene's grammar was good, but bad memory seemed to be her version of the ignorance card. She came off as weak and empty-headed. "But maybe that was the whole idea," one of the jurors later said.

The arguments were over.

"What would a reasonable person do?" Mygrant asked in his closing statement. What if that person's baby "was struggling to breathe, and choking on phlegm"—apparently because of "a cyst the size of a softball? What if their child stopped breathing?" He gave the jury a hard, long look. "They would call 911."

Brent and Raylene, Mygrant said, knew Ava was in peril, no matter what anyone said. Without using the word "lie," he made it clear that he thought they'd all been lying. And that they'd do the same thing again.

They didn't let Ava die on purpose, he said, but their intent was totally irrelevant to the manslaughter and mistreatment charges. The only thing that mattered legally was what they *did*.

Mygrant stopped short of calling Dr. Janice Ophoven a hired gun. He called her a "defense expert" doing "what she's paid to do."

Horner followed. Raylene, Horner said, "cannot hide behind the decisions of her husband." If she *wasn't* involved, that alone made her unreasonable. No one in the Church, not even Ava's parents, he said, "would stand up for Ava. Not one. This little girl, who was struggling to breathe, was lost . . . because no one had the judgment or the common sense to say, 'Enough.'"

Oregonian reporter Rick Bella thought Horner's closing argument was virtually irresistible. "It was a masterful mix of logic and emotion," he later said. Bella couldn't think of anything the defense could do to turn the case around, even if the jurors didn't find out about the Followers' prior deaths.

Horner, of course, would have liked the jurors to know that this tragedy was the last in an almost endless chain of needless death. But in the legal system, people are tried for their own crimes, not those of their family or friends.

Cogan, in his closing, stuck with the story that the cyst was "the tiniest little knot on her neck," and that "there was no evidence . . . it ever interfered with her breathing or her eating."

He said there were "really two *different* reasonable-person standards"—one for doctors and one for parents.

Ava wasn't malnourished, he said, and she died so suddenly no one could stop it.

Neidig began a PowerPoint presentation. But it included the case of another local child who'd died of a similar illness, but in different circumstances, at about the same time as Ava, and Judge Mauer had already told Neidig that it wasn't admissible. Horner objected and Mauer sent the jury away.

"This could *not* be more improper!" Mauer snapped at Neidig. "This is simply a blindingly stupid move." He accused Neidig of "subterfuge," and said, "You have tried cases for years! Where does this *come* from?" Neidig tried to justify it, but Mauer said, "Now, wait a minute. Stop right there . . . . This goes to the heart of our profession. And I must say this is absolutely improper, and I am stunned, literally stunned, that you tried to pull this stunt." The verbal whipping went on for a number of minutes.

"If I offended the court—" Neidig interjected.

"No. No, no, no. Let's not even go there! This is not a matter of any *personal* offense. This is a matter of the integrity of a process." The whipping went on for as long as half an hour. Finally Mauer said, "I'm not interested in discussing this any further. We've got a jury that's been waiting for too long."

The jury came back in, but the juice was gone from Neidig's presentation.

Mygrant and Horner felt good. It looked like they had both Brent and Raylene on second-degree manslaughter, known as man-2. That seemed to be the only reasonable possibility.

CLACKAMAS COUNTY COURTHOUSE
JULY 16, 2009

The jurors took a preliminary poll to see if they already had the necessary ten votes out of twelve to acquit or convict.

The vote was eight to four—only two votes short—to convict both Brent and Raylene of man-2, good for more than six years in state prison. On criminal mistreatment, they were 8–4 against Raylene, and 9–3 against Brent.

Three of the jurors who voted guilty—Ken, Ashley, and the Intel

project manager—were certain of the Worthingtons' guilt, and confident they could find two more votes. The other five who voted guilty
weren't as committed.

All four who voted not guilty on man-2 were from the Oregon
City contingent, and two of them were absolutely convinced that Brent
and Raylene were innocent: the conservative medical technician, and
the logger. The other two—the farm wife and the juror who resembled
Mr. Rogers—weren't so sure, and were the obvious swing votes for
a conviction.

Byers, who had steered committees to consensus throughout his
career, began sizing this one up, trying to get a feel for each person.
He didn't try to learn all their names. It wasn't necessary, and besides,
most of the jurors were intent upon retaining their anonymity, even in
the jury room, because of their close ties to Oregon City. Some even
had friends in the Church.

Byers and Ashley Santos didn't care *who* knew how they felt, and
ultimately became the only jurors who released their names to the
press, although others did speak anonymously. To sort the jurors out,
Byers assigned his own nicknames: the muscular logger was Paul Bunyan, the right-winger who worked at a hospital was Big Nurse, the
Intel manager was Bill Gates, the farm woman was Pioneer Wife, and
the Mr. Rogers–type guy was . . . guess who. The others—especially
the five Quiet Ones—were harder to caricature. For now, they were
Quiet One, Two, Three, Four, and Five.

As the jurors started talking, Ken Byers felt good about their
chances of a quick conviction—until utter chaos descended. Mr. Rogers, who was undeniably a pleaser, said he was sure that Brent and
Raylene had no intention whatsoever of harming their daughter. Bill
Gates reminded him that intent had no bearing on the case, but about
half the jurors didn't seem to understand that, and launched into a
two-hour debate about it.

To one of the quiet jurors, it seemed as if some of the people felt
like they were on a reality-TV show, and wanted to drain every drop
of overwrought Clackastani melodrama out of it.

Big Nurse—stocky and talkative, with short blond hair—began to argue that the key to the whole case was the Ninth Amendment, which said that people had rights that weren't specifically mentioned in the Bill of Rights. "She basically seemed to think," Ken Byers later said, "that the Constitution could mean whatever any citizen wanted it to. The Tea Party hadn't been created yet, but she was Tea Party to the core."

She insisted they get a copy of the Ninth Amendment from the judge. Horner and Mygrant heard about it and were bewildered. They weren't experts on the Ninth Amendment, but they knew it didn't legalize child abuse.

After looking at the amendment, Big Nurse, Pioneer Wife, and Paul Bunyan all agreed that the government had intruded on not only the religious rights of Brent and Raylene, but also the unstated right of family privacy. Tempers ignited as the sun microwaved the small jury room, now jammed with stacks of evidence and even the Worthingtons' coffee table, which was supposed to prove Ava wasn't tiny.

Day Two: July 17

Deliberations devolved further during the discussion of Ava's alleged failure to thrive. Big Nurse argued that the condition was "a subjective appraisal."

"It's a precise medical term," Byers said. "You should know. You're a medical technician."

"That's right." She gave him a hard-boiled glare.

Later in the day, as the O.C. clique glamorized the Followers' tight-knit community as an American ideal, Byers said, "You know, these guys aren't all that different than the people who drank poison Kool-Aid with Jim Jones."

"How can you possibly equate these people with Jim Jones' followers?" accused the Pioneer Wife.

"Because they blindly follow a leader."

Mr. Rodgers, Paul Bunyan, and several of the Quiet Ones—looking at Byers as if he had just burned the flag—ganged up on him and essentially said he should shut up and get some Clackalackie spirit.

Byers apologized. "You have to pick your battles carefully," he later said, "or you'll lose the big one."

Day Three: July 20

After the weekend off, Big Nurse kicked off the increasingly heated debate by parroting the testimony of Dr. Ophoven, saying that sepsis killed Ava very suddenly, and in that situation, even reasonable people could do nothing. Mr. Rogers agreed—Who knew?—and several of the Quiet Ones seemed persuaded. Byers argued that Ophoven had actually agreed that Ava should have been taken to a doctor, but people didn't seem to get that: She was a *defense* witness, wasn't she? Besides, she was being fair and honest.

Rita Swan, who'd been following the trial closely from her Iowa headquarters, had predicted the jurors' positive response to Ophoven's reasonable position on that point. It had been a mistake, she thought, for the prosecution to try to use Ophoven to make their argument.

They took another vote. Six jurors voted guilty on the manslaughter charge, and six opposed.

Ashley Santos and Ken Byers, concerned that momentum was shifting against them, began to push for declaring themselves a hung jury. Big Nurse accused them of trying to shirk their public duty. Even so, Ashley sent a note to the judge telling him that they were deadlocked, and might not be able to reach a decision.

If they were hung, Horner would have to either try the case again, or drop the charges.

Judge Mauer came in, gave them a pep talk, expressed his gratitude, and told them to take the rest of the day off.

Day Four: July 21

Ken Byers thought that emotion had almost completely overtaken logic. The O.C. clique was becoming obsessed with pity for Brent and Raylene and with anger at the government, and was gradually winning the hearts of the Quiet Ones. Byers and Santos were now the only hard-core advocates for the manslaughter convictions, and it looked as if an acquittal on all charges was inevitable if they couldn't revive rationality.

Byers got together with Bill Gates and worked out a system to simplify the case. They broke it down into separate issues and outlined them on big pieces of butcher paper that they taped to the walls.

It seemed to work. Emotions cooled and they started focusing on the main topics, such as sepsis versus pneumonia, failure to thrive, and the quality of the autopsy. Although it seemed to distress the O.C. clique, they ignored the irrelevant issues, including intent, freedom of religion, and family privacy.

But Horner was worried. As a rule, the longer a jury stayed out, the more likely it was to acquit. In movies, he later said, juries argue day after day, but in real life it was usually just one or two days at the most.

Day Five: July 22

The four people who favored the defense, all from O.C.—Big Nurse, Paul Bunyan, Mr. Rogers, and Pioneer Wife—wouldn't budge. The possibility of a man-2 conviction for either Brent or Raylene had faded away, and the jury was even two votes short of convicting both Worthingtons of criminal mistreatment.

Tempers again began to boil and people seemed desperate to be done. Byers took advantage of the poisonous atmosphere. "I can stay here until next year," he told the O.C. clique, "because I don't have a job I need to get back to. And there's no way I'm changing my vote." Two of the Quiet Ones begged him to back off and be reasonable.

Now was the time, Byers thought, to force a compromise. He'd get the jury to trade guilty on Brent for innocent on Raylene. He was determined that *somebody* had to go to jail.

Byers' usual management style was to wait patiently for someone else to head down the path he desired, then chime in, "and snap the trap."

Just before the end of the day, Byers suggested that maybe they should focus mostly on Brent, because of his power over Raylene, and the O.C. clique perked up. Then Mr. Rogers cracked. Byers had predicted that. The guy seemed to loath conflict. Mr. Rogers proposed convicting Brent of criminal mistreatment, but letting Raylene off.

"That's not a bad idea," Byers said. "That could end this thing." It looked like they needed only one more vote.

Day Six: July 23

Byers lasered his attention on Pioneer Wife. She was less rigid than Big Nurse or Paul Bunyan and seemed to identify with Raylene. "I know you think Raylene had no power to stop this," he said, "and maybe you're right and I'm wrong." But if they were a hung jury, he said, and the case was tried again, both Worthingtons might go to jail for six years.

"I'll go your way on Raylene," Byers told Pioneer Wife. "But I can't let Brent off. I just can't. And won't."

Ashley jumped on the compromise. She did think Brent and Raylene were both guilty, but also sympathized with Raylene's lack of power and loss of a baby. Bill Gates agreed, and Quiet One, Two, Three, and Four spoke up, for almost the first time, and joined the new coalition.

They took a vote. Ashley Santos asked the bailiff to tell the judge that they had a verdict.

CLACKAMAS COUNTY COURTHOUSE
JULY 23, 2009

Horner and Mygrant were already in the courtroom, working on other cases as they waited, feeling unusually tense. The jury had been out *way* too long.

"All rise."

Judge Mauer entered. The camera crew from truTV quickly reassembled, reporters ran up the stairs to the courtroom, and the crowd of Followers filed in from the lobby and stoically took their seats.

Mauer warned the spectators to behave, no matter what, then

turned to Brent and read the verdict: "We find the defendant as to Count One not guilty of the felony charge of manslaughter in the second degree." Cogan smiled and didn't try to hide it. Escaping man-2 had been their main goal. Brent sagged and released a seemingly endless breath.

Brent, noticeably less intent on the judge's words, was pronounced guilty of misdemeanor criminal mistreatment, by a 10–2 vote. Mark Cogan put his hand on Brent's shoulder and squeezed it. One of the Followers wailed in shock.

Raylene: Not guilty on both counts. She gazed impassively at the judge, and didn't look at Brent.

Several of the Followers sobbed. They didn't seem to know they'd won. With Brent's clean record, he'd be out in a couple of months. As the Followers saw Brent pumping his attorneys' hands and hugging his family with tears of relief shining in his eyes, they gradually realized the extent of their victory.

Byers was somewhat disappointed, but relieved. This seemed like a reasonable reaction to an unprecedented crime that would probably never happen again.

Then Byers saw Horner. The tough DA had his hand over his eyes and was doubled over like he'd been kicked in the gut. Byers' sense of relief vanished. What did Horner know that he didn't?

Jim Band watched Horner poll the jury to find out who voted not guilty. "Greg couldn't believe it," Band later said. "It made *no* sense."

On the steps outside, Ashley Santos told the press, "They were loving people. They didn't mean for anything to happen. We tried not to judge them on their beliefs and religion. Just because something isn't normal to you, it doesn't mean it's bad." And she did think, she said, that the Followers had an "amazing community."

When journalist Rick Bella reminded Santos that intent was irrelevant, "she seemed surprised," he later said.

Mark Cogan told the reporters that because a child was dead, "There are no winners in this case. My clients are not celebrating a victory." He did a good job of not looking victorious, and had no need to crow, because others were doing it for him, including Jami Floyd of truTV, which had televised about thirty hours of the trial. "It's a win for the defense," she said, and Cogan was "quite brilliant."

Ken Byers walked Ashley Santos to her car. "This feels wrong," he said.

"I know."

Patrick, his face still reddened by midsummer sun, sick with worry, watched television for breaking news about the verdict while he tried to put bites of a Kraft Lunchables into Paul's mouth. But the baby really wanted his bottle, or better yet, his mother. Theresa, furious at Patrick for taking Paul home from Idaho without asking her permission, refused to even talk to him. A letter from her lawyer raised the dread specter of DHS and even Family Court, saying that his religion and lack of proper child care posed a great threat to his continued access to his son. Theresa was shrewd.

Then, there it was. Video of Brent, shaking hands with Cogan as other Followers lined up to congratulate him. "A win for the defense!" the reporter announced. Brent and Raylene looked calm and victorious. Vindicated.

Oh Lord. They got off.

The broadcaster said it would have a "profound impact" on the Beagley case.

Patrick went online to check *The Oregonian*'s website with shaky hands. The headline was, "What will become of the next sick child?"

Paul, stretching for a bottle he couldn't reach, started to cry.

Patrick picked him up and cradled him.

Paul quieted. "Daddy take care of you."

"Da."

Rita Swan, working late, got an automatic update on the trial from Internet Explorer, and sagged. The Worthington verdict was a disaster. She'd been so hopeful. Horner was so good, and they had that informant. Her only remaining optimism was her hope that the Clacka-mas court had deliberately gone easy on the Worthingtons to establish its fairness, in preparation for more aggressive prosecutions. But that sunny speculation was a stretch, even for a positive person like Rita.

She paused, and quieted her anxiety, as she often did, with work. These days, she was obsessed with the fight to keep payment for prayer out of the federal health-care reform act. If the new amendment pro-posing that passed, it would grant legal legitimacy to the notion that prayer is medicine, according to federal law. Then, because federal law trumped state law, state politicians around the country would use the amendment to justify, or even amplify, their state's shield laws. If that happened, when Rita traveled the country, fighting shield laws state by state, her legal position would be almost as weak as it had been back in the 1970s.

The Christian Science Church loved the amendment, of course, and had budgeted $150,000 on lobbyists to make sure it passed. The Church had already generated 11,000 e-mails that were sent to US senators.

In the Senate, Rita was being opposed, as she had been for many years, by former presidential candidate John Kerry, who was still un-der the sway of the powerful Christian Science faction in his home state of Massachusetts, and Utah senator Orrin Hatch, who was strongly influenced by his state's Mormon community. Throughout the coun-try, dozens of newspapers supported the amendment in their op-ed pages, which tended to reflect the views of their publishers, who were often politically conservative. The editorials generally referred to praying for health as "spiritual health care," as if faith healing was part of America's new progressive, preventive medicine.

Even so, almost miraculously, Rita seemed to be winning. She'd prompted articles favorable to her position from *The Los Angeles Times*, *The Chicago Tribune*, *The Washington Post*, and *The New York Times*. *Time* magazine had run a critical article entitled "Should Universal Health Care Cover Faith Healing?" She was also being supported by the insurance companies, which were reluctant to pay for prayer.

The battle was emblematic of Rita's whole career. She was fighting, as usual, as a veritable army of one, with a modest budget, mobilizing help wherever she could find it—and slowly prevailing. "Rita Swan," religious-abuse activist Rick Ross later said, "was always a marathoner—not a sprinter. Some of the things she did took decades." That sentiment was echoed when the American Academy of Pediatrics presented Rita with an Outstanding Service Award. Her acceptance speech was entitled "Persistence in Advocacy."

Even so, although it had once seemed almost inevitable to Rick Ross that Rita would eventually succeed in her critically important Oregon campaign, things changed after the Worthington verdict. The momentum had shifted. Now people in the movement to stop faith-healing abuse were afraid that Oregon authorities might back away from the Followers' cases.

If that happened, Rita later said, "The pundits on the law channels would have said, "'These parents were doing the best they know how.' And society would have muted its outrage about the deaths. Then the whole country could become one big Idaho, where the coroner doesn't even do autopsies on these kids, because everybody agrees that the Followers have the right to let kids die."

The Beagley case, Rita prayed, would go better. If not, her entire, lifelong mission might already have peaked, and begun a downhill slide to utter disappointment.

Ken Byers went home, turned on his computer, and began to read about the shadow of death and suffering that had trailed the Followers of Christ for decades. He read about the deaths of Bo Phillips, Holland Cunningham, Alex Morris, Valerie Shaw, and Neil Beagley. He read *The Oregonian* stories by Mark Larabee and Rick Bella, watched online segments by Anna Canzano and Thom Jensen on KATU, and searched Rita Swan's site. By the time he was done he felt sick and dizzy.

"Oh my God," he said. He held his head in his hands. "What have I done?"

He told his wife about it. "How could you have *done* that?" she said. It hurt. He had wanted so badly to make her proud.

• • •

Jim Band, James Rhodes, and Michelle Finn drank coffee in The Verdict, getting psyched up to see Horner. "In *some* ways," Rhodes said, "it *was* a victory. A stepping-stone. Worthington is going to jail because it looked like he cared more about his ego than his daughter—he did it for his own pride—and now people know that."

"This is the best we've done in the last ten years," Band said.

Finn nodded, but none of them believed their own spin. Now the Followers would think they could get away with anything, because God had protected them. Things would get worse.

And the damn Beagley case was coming up.

They walked over to the courthouse and found Horner in his office, alone. "He's not a weak person," Rhodes later said, "but he looked like a broken man."

Horner looked up. "I'm sorry. I'm sorry. I wish I'd done some things differently. I don't understand."

"Hey, it's not a grand slam," Band said. "They didn't go away to jail forever, but that asshole is at least going away for a few months."

"I thought it would be about the facts," Horner said. But it had been about religion. And Big Government. And intent. And community. And family. And tears.

Horner and Mygrant, who'd picked jurors who were unable to ignore all that, and who'd failed in their efforts to enter evidence of previous deaths, had lost the case in jury selection and pre-trial. It was over before it started.

"Well," Finn said, "we've still got Beagley, and we've gotta fight that fight."

"Yeah, the Beagley case," Horner said absently. Now Beagley looked like a piece of shit. There were no honest eyewitnesses, no pictures of some God-awful thing on Neil, and the jurors might believe that Neil was old enough, based on the confusing law, to make his own medical decisions. Worst, the Followers had all the momentum. Word was already spreading around town that they were innocent, and that would poison the jury pool.

All four of them felt like losers. But it felt good to be together at this moment. Misery loves company.

Ken Byers met Dan Tilkin of KATU early that evening for an on-air interview. Tilkin—still thinking that the trial had been all but settled when the judge excluded evidence of other kids dying—asked Byers if he would have done things differently if he'd known about the other children.

"Yeah, I would have," Byers said, his voice low and slow with remorse. "If I'd known, I would *never* have changed my vote."

When it was over, Byers told Tilkin that he felt like he'd blown the case.

"Don't feel like that," Tilkin said. "This is the best the prosecutors have ever done. Because of you. Someday you'll feel like a hero."

"I don't right now."

"Nobody ever does," Tilkin said, "at the time."

"Mr. Worthington," Judge Mauer said at Brent's sentencing, "is there anything you wanted to say?"

"I'd like it to be known," Brent said magnamimously, "that I don't hold anything against the prosecution for bringing me to trial."

Mauer sentenced him to sixty days in Clackatraz.

"As a matter of symbolism," Mauer said. "Mr. Worthington will leave this court in handcuffs."

When Brent rose to be shackled, the gallery of Followers rose with him, as one. Head held regally, in sacrificial dignity, Brent Worthington gave himself over to the jailers to accept the punishment of the world, and lead the way to God's light.

15

ANGEL BABY

It's just like heaven, being here with you,
You're like an angel, too good to be true.

—"Angel Baby," Rosie Hamlin

Oregon City
August 2, 2009

Rebecca Wyland and Shannon Hickman, both pregnant and beaming wondrous smiles, were the belles of the after-church potluck, as their husbands fetched them molasses-glazed barbecue and old-fashioned strawberry phosphate sodas. It was heavenly. Everybody was glorying in the presence of pregnancy, the dream of more babies born holy, and the tantalizing end of their nightmare of persecution.

Rebecca, with a sweet, trusting face and busty figure, was prettier and more animated than Shannon, but inner-circle Shannon, descended from Walter White—who was still protecting them from heaven, with some help from God—lived her life in the Word even more than most.

One of the prospective fathers, Dale Hickman, still boyish at 24-years old, was playing Super Mario Ford Flat Track with his father-in-law, Matt White, the Prophet's grandson. Matt, a major force in the church due mostly to his lineage, was shiny-bald except for a low ring of black curly hair that matched his thick mustache, and looked alarmingly like Mario himself. Jeff Beagley, still shattered by the death of Neil, was off to one side, pretending to watch, with empty eyes. Jeff now had an aura of loss and gravitas, and stood in stark contrast to chuckleheaded Dale, who even to his friends was just a goofy car-nut, intensely invested in improving his on-screen driving, which closely approximated the way he screamed around corners in his souped-up Subaru. Dale was not as grandiose as his brother Lee, who'd been with Dale on the second geese-killing spree, but he was getting there, as his family grew from one child to two. Dale was otherwise undistinguished, as nothing more than an asphalt paver in the family business, Hal's Construction.

Patrick, restless, let Shannon coo to Paul, a toddler now, while he poured hot fudge on Grandma Worthington's homemade caramel-pecan ice cream. Next in line was Lee Hickman, who started chatting casually. But Lee was the last person Patrick wanted to see, because he'd recently reported Lee to DHS for letting his daughter's ear infection fester until she was almost deaf. Patrick had kept his involvement secret, and DHS had made sure that the girl had gotten treatment, but the incident was one more reason for him to be afraid. Lee tried to stay chatty, but he had that hot Hickman temper, and he got riled up as he told Patrick about the anonymous complaint. "I can't believe this harassment!" he said. "Next thing you know, they're gonna be at *my house* for somethin' or other!" Lee eyeballed him, but Patrick just shook his head sympathetically. "They're like the Gestapo," Lee said, "and they're starting to ask questions they know the answers to."

"Who is?"

"Those three cops—Band-James-Band, that chick, and Rhodes, the mean bastard. Plus that ugly bull-dyke, Lynne Benton."

Patrick put a finger to his lips, meaning: Watch your language.

"You think Band has a demon?" Patrick asked.

"I'd think a pious guy like you would know."

Patrick kept his face frozen and his too-expressive eyes hooded. "What are they asking about?"

"Like, how did we raise eight hundred thousand bucks for the defense fund when church dues are $40 a month? And what's the big deal in laying on hands? *You* want to tell me who the Judas is?"

Here it comes, Patrick thought. In public. He shrugged.

"Then I'll tell *you*. It's Holly."

"Holly Di?" Patrick felt so relieved he almost shuddered. "That's not a surprise," he said. But he thought: You Hickman hicks—you've got bigger problems than Holly Divelbis. She left the church years ago.

In the kitchen, Rebecca and Shannon talked with their friends about which midwives to use. There were always three at each birth, and one of Shannon's was going to be her aunt, Lavona Keith, who'd midwifed at the birth of Shannon's four-year-old, Daisy. Another easy choice was Carolyn Crone, a midwife at Shannon's own birth. If there was a problem, those experienced midwives could easily help pray it away. Not long ago, one of their friends had actually died in childbirth. Long labor. A day or two. She was cold and blue. But she'd gasped and come back. There was only one explanation, Shannon told the group: God loves the Followers.

"He so loves us!" said one of the Cunningham girls.

"Amen," said her mother. "In a way the worldly don't get."

"Modern-day miracle, is what that was," said the daughter. "It's just, wow, in modern life—us—the chosen. Too cool."

"Could a doctor have done that?" her mom said. "What do doctors always say: 'It's in God's hands now.' But they still want to be paid."

"Yeah, and if a doctor said that to somebody in the world, they'd *still* die," said Shannon.

"Lack of faith," Becca said.

"Ya think?" said Shannon, offering Paul a bite of her butterscotch pie, and scooping the whipped cream off the top for herself. At five and a half months pregnant, Shannon was already too ballooned to worry about her weight, and Dale had never cared about it. He had love handles of his own. All they cared about was having a healthy baby.

Mrs. Cunningham brought up the often-told story of a friend

who'd had terminal cancer, with gross, lumpy tumors. But the church prayed away her devil, and she died of natural causes at ninety. Happened all the time.

"But you have to hold fast," she said, giving the pregnant girls a steely stare. She started ticking off the names of babies who'd died at birth, with the insinuation that the mothers were to blame. In Shannon's and Dale's families, eight babies were already in heaven: Ross, Otis, Betsy, and Baby Girl, on Shannon's side—and Dwayne, Rita Ann, Justin James, and Baby Girl, on Dale's side. Eight babies had also died in the Smith family: Cheryl Marie, Monte, Joan Kay, Lynnee, Tommy, Monica Joyce, Maria, and Lucas. "Birth is a *test*," she said.

Patrick overheard more of their conversation than he wanted to. He looked around and saw people he had loved all his life—his family—but these days they seemed frightening. Almost freakish. Some of the older people looked bright-white from lack of circulation, a couple of people had trollish skin growths, the Follower who was letting himself go blind—Rod Lincoln's uncle—had eyes that were cream-colored, others had eyes that were too far apart, and most of the elderly people were glued to the couches and recliners, coughing and clearing their throats. Feeling lonely and repulsed, he took Paul to the backyard, lush with purple hydrangeas and yellow lilies, put him in a toddler swing, and pushed him gently as the boy's eyes grew wide.

Marie, his friend who'd had the lumpectomy, came out.

"How you doing?" he asked.

She took a breath. "*Much* better." She reached out for his work-hardened hands, squeezed them hard in both of hers, and left quickly and conspiratorially.

For a moment, Patrick was happier than he'd felt in months. Helping Marie with her cancer made the pain of being a traitor bearable. But he looked at the two pregnant women through the kitchen window and felt a troubling premonition. He'd had funny feelings about the future ever since his dad had died. Looking back, the dread had probably just been realism, considering the odds of disaster in this group. As a kid, though, the forebodings had felt supernatural, and once he made the mistake of telling his mom about them, and she beat him with a wire hanger. She called it spanking the devil out of him. Patrick said a prayer in the closet for Shannon, Rebecca, and their babies, and his anxiety lifted. Prayer was magic. There was no denying that.

A kid limped out of the house to smoke one of his Camels and walked awkwardly over to Patrick. The boy's foot had been misshapen all his life, and now he was walking on the side of his grossly distorted ankle, which was red and blue from misuse. His parents had taken him to a doctor for a leg brace a year ago, but when the doctor recommended surgery, they'd walked out. It was so hypocritical: brace good, surgery bad? Patrick knew another Follower who'd injured himself at work and gone straight to the doctor. But the same guy had let his baby die in childbirth.

Still feeling buoyed by the power of prayer, Patrick said to the boy, "Did you know you're legally old enough to make your own medical decisions?"

"Why would I do something medical?"

"It's God's will. He wants you to walk without a limp."

Patrick saw that Marci Beagley, on the back deck, was staring him, so he shut up.

He smiled at Marci, but her face looked vacant, almost paralyzed.

Marci, who would once have been the center of the gals' group, was wandering around by herself. She was on the outs, because everybody knew she'd shown lack of faith when Neil needed her most. As Neil lay dying, she'd told him she couldn't take it anymore, and wanted to call a doctor. The Crown Prince had chewed her out, but she still headed for the phone. One of the elders had intercepted her, though, and told her to forget about it. It was just one of the old men who had no formal power, but he was still intimidating.

Jeff, though, had held fast to tradition, and stayed in the Word. Now he reigned among the holiest of parents, with Brent, who had just left for jail to serve his scant sixty-day sentence. Brent's sacrifice, it was believed, had been for all of them, and now Jeff would win his battle with the world, and end the terror forever.

Patrick pushed his son high and Paul happily cried, "Daaa!"

Patrick wished Theresa was there to see it. Her lawyer's letters were becoming more pointed, accusing him of leaving Paul "with unqualified caregivers" while he was at work. Even Theresa's mere absence was a threat now, because people kept asking about her, and if they figured out she was separated from him, they might realize that he was the Judas.

Jeff came out, saw Marci, and stood next to her without talking, not even acknowledging Patrick. Jeff and Marci were often in the local news these days, and there were innumerable references to them on the Net.

Wind blew in the sweet summery smell of new-cut grass, reawakening memories of better days, and Patrick, lonely, couldn't stand to stay. He packed up Paul, drove downtown, parked behind the courthouse, and walked across the street to watch people fish off the sidewalk, over the fence, for the salmon that schooled below in the shadows of Willamette Falls.

The Falls, Oregon City's landmark, had been the beginning of the end of the greatest flood on earth, when Ice Age water twice the volume of the Great Lakes had carved out the towering Columbia Gorge at eighty miles an hour for decades, creating a huge fishing hole here used by the Indians for ten thousand years. The Clackamas Indians had built a trading center under the rainbow that often formed over the misty Falls, a place of union and reunion. It was centered around America's largest meteorite—sixteen tons of iron—that had been carried from Canada by the floods, and had sat in seeming permanence for millennia before being carted off to a New York museum.

After the trading post came the first church and first jail west of the Mississippi, followed by miners' tents, shacks, whorehouses, courthouses, and Victorian mansions, as the capital of the vast Oregon Territory rose to dominance, climaxed by the Falls' deliverance of the first electric-power transmission in America.

But Portland, closer to the Columbia, pushed Oregon City into decline and decay until it was little more than the gateway to the Willamette Valley, mildewed and hyper-pollinated, named "Willamat" by the Indians, a word widely believed to mean "Valley of Death."

Now mercury plumes from Chinese coal plants traveled here by jet stream to mix with mercury clouds that swept down the Gorge from the country's worst-polluting coal plant, which was adjacent to 95,000 acres of stored Army nerve gas.

These toxins joined the traditional poisons and new pesticides from upriver to create the perfect petri dish, one that had resulted in a dramatic belt of autoimmune disorders, cancer, allergies, asthma, and autism that confounded the local doctors, but made them unusually prosperous.

These toxic threats, though, were microscopic—invisible in this seeming Eden of crashing water and rainbows—and so it was still possible, on the right summer day, in the right circumstance, to see the glistening Falls with the same thrill of wonder and hope that the travelers of the Oregon Trail must have felt when they reached journey's end and sat on these green shores, wondering if America could possibly have a better place than this.

Patrick, calmed by the Falls, as always, went home. When he got there, a car was in front of his house.

Two people got out of the car when he pulled into his driveway. He didn't recognize either of them. They approached him. One was an older woman, and the other was a woman who was approximately his age.

"Patrick," said the older woman, "do you know who I am?"

He held Paul tightly in his long arms and looked at her. "Did I see you at the trial?"

She nodded. "I'm Eleanor Evans," she said. "I was in the Church. I've heard that people call me The Widow. We came to see you because friends of mine say that you're doing wonderful things."

He thought it was best to say nothing.

"Patrick," she said, "this is your sister."

He stared at the other woman's face, and with a shock saw her features morph into those of the big sister he'd loved and lost, long ago.

Patrick said something, but later on he couldn't recall what it was. He did remember that she asked to hold Paul.

After some time he said, "Ella. Can you forgive me?"

"There's nothing to forgive," she said.

"Will you come in?"

"Do you mind?"

"Ella, you're my family."

OREGON CITY
AUGUST 30, 2009

Dale and Shannon Hickman went on the traditional Labor Day campout and joined once more in the type of extended-family communion that most Americans no longer know. The weather was glorious, the food was legendary, the friendship everlasting, and everybody was still treating Shannon like a princess because of her pregnancy.

Shannon's mom and dad had a camper, and it made nature even more pleasant. The Followers' families tended to buy big-ticket toys en masse—Jet Skis, fishing boats, big screens, and snowmobiles—and campers were the current rage.

As Shannon was walking over to her folks' camper in the dark, she ran into a cement fire-pit and fell down—on her side and not her belly, luckily, hands-first. But it was still something to pray about, because she'd had a miscarriage less than a year earlier.

The prayers appeared to work, because she didn't suffer any obvious complications. The Followers believed in prenatal care, but not the dehumanizing medical type that exposed the babies to X-rays, hospital germs, needles in their mother's womb, and the ever-present possibility that a doctor might see something he didn't like and pressure the parents to kill their baby. Their prenatal care consisted mostly of eating a careful diet and getting enough rest. Shannon had some morning sickness, but no other apparent problems.

About three weeks later, though, when Shannon was at seven months, a rumor flew through the phone tree that her water had broken, but that she hadn't gone into labor. People remembered her in their prayers. On Friday, the 25th, Shannon woke up feeling crampy, but still wasn't concerned enough to ask Dale to see what the Net said about that. By the time her mom came over to help her with lunch, though, she was spotting, and worried. That night, Dale Hickman later said, "She was hurting."

On Saturday the 26th she developed what were almost certainly labor pains. They peaked at about 2:30 p.m. The labor, of course, could have been suppressed pharmaceutically, avoiding the possibility of a radically premature birth.

If her water actually had broken, as rumored, and amniotic fluid from the ruptured sac had leaked out, triggering labor, she could have gone to a hospital's neonatal intensive care unit. That was the only safe place to deliver a severely premature baby, since babies born that early need the constant warmth of an incubator, careful feeding, and attention to their lungs, which aren't fully developed.

Dale called for the laying on of hands. Shannon didn't get relief. At 3:30 p.m. they called her mother, Karen White, and told her they were coming over. It would either be for the traditional birth at the grandmother's house, or for emergency prayer.

The phone tree lit up. Lavona Keith, Shannon's aunt and chief midwife, rushed over to the Whites' home, just off Molalla Drive, where the church was. Then the two prospective grandfathers arrived, separately, and that was extremely reassuring for everyone, because Matt White, the Prophet's grandson, and Phil Hickman, who ran Hal's Construction, were beacons of security.

Soon dozens of people were there, far more than at most births, but this one was complicated. Shannon's dad and Dale's mom both expected a miscarriage, but kept it to themselves.

For two hours Shannon writhed and cried in the master bedroom, attended by the three midwives. None of the midwives were licensed, because that would have demanded medical training, but they were legally recognized as direct-entry midwives, which in Oregon required no training.

Dale, nervous, stepped onto the deck to smoke a cigarette and talk to his buddies. Nobody else was notably distraught. They'd all been through so much before. At 5:41 p.m. Dale heard a baby cry. His eyes widened with hope as a woman burst out of the house and said he had a son. Dale ran into the bedroom and hugged Shannon. He was the only man in the birthing room. Shannon had not yet had a chance to hold the baby, but she could hear him cry, and felt a surge of joy.

Shannon and Dale hadn't named the baby, but the presumption was that it would be named after Dale. That was a relatively common custom in America, but the Followers and some other fundamentalist sects, particularly the Church of the First Born, employed it some-what differently. They frequently didn't name their kids at birth, in case the children died shortly after they were born, as Followers and First-Born babies often did. That would mean wasting a precious family name on a dead child.

Shannon, exhausted after more than 24 hours of labor, collapsed into sleep, looking forward to the ritualistic ten days of bed rest that were given to every Followers mom, while the grandmothers did the child care.

Shannon's dad, Matt, and Dale's mom, Tanya, who'd expected the baby to be born dead, were ecstatic with relief. Another child had been born holy, and would carry their family ever closer to the hori-zon of eternity.

To memorialize the momentous religious event, midwife Carolyn Crone, confident and calming, brought out a video camera and started annotating the traditional baby's logbook, which detailed the historic significance of another child born holy. The midwives, responsible for what the Followers called night duty, took the baby into the bathroom and gave him his first bath. The baby was pink, and his lungs, based on the volume of his crying, were strong. Shannon could hear him from the other room.

Shannon's four-year-old daughter, Daisy, came in. "You have a new brother," Shannon said softly, still in pain, without any anesthetics.

They swaddled the baby in blankets and bath towels warmed by the dryer, as they always did. "Wow," Carolyn Crone said, "he keeps pulling his blankets down." She had to pull them back up to keep him cozy. Karen White turned up the thermostat, and made sure a fresh supply of warm towels was at hand.

Tanya Hickman, who had the face of an aging Snow White, framed by glossy black hair, held the baby, and he put his hands up in what she thought of as "kitten paws."

Midwife Lavona Keith was worried, though, because the baby was so premature, and so tiny. He weighed just three pounds, seven ounces, and his arms weren't much bigger than the thumbs of the hands that held him. The baby looked okay, but that seemed too good to be true. It crossed Lavona's mind that the baby might die, but she pushed the thought away, to keep from endangering the baby with a lack of faith.

At 6:00 p.m. they gave him his first sip of water, from a teaspoon, since his mouth was far too small to accept a bottle. At 6:50, as the men drifted toward Matt's camper in the driveway, the midwives gave him a teaspoon-and-a-half of water. They considered giving him an eyedropper of mother's milk, but he seemed to be doing well without it. At 8:06 they gave him small shards of ice that totaled about one-fourth of an ice cube, and did it again about forty-five minutes later.

Dale held the baby for about fifteen minutes, on and off. Most of the time, he hung out on the deck with his dad, his father-in-law, and his four brothers.

At 10:20 the midwives gave the baby almost half of an ice cube.

Sometime around 10:30 or 11:00, Dale, happily exhausted, headed out to Matt's camper and hit the sack.

Patrick's friend Marie, still energized by her newfound freedom from cancer, stayed with the midwives past midnight, but was beginning to grow concerned about the sound of the baby's breath. As the house quieted, the baby's breathing, now somewhat raspy, replaced the sound of happy chatter. The midwives and both grandmothers seemed to gradually become more alarmed.

Marie called her husband and told him that she didn't feel good about what was happening. The baby was less active and his color wasn't as good. The pink seemed to be draining away, replaced by an ominous gray.

"Get out of there, right now," her husband said. She was gone in a matter of minutes.

The baby's color continued to darken, and he grew sluggish.

"Go wake up Dale," Shannon's mother said.

Someone made a note of when they woke Dale up.

OREGON CITY
SEPTEMBER 27, 2009

"Patrick. Patrick."

Patrick's eyes opened and he saw his sister, Ella, standing over him. She'd just moved in, giving him someone to watch Paul while he was at work, and offering both of them the chance to re-create their family in the way it should have been all along.

"Is the baby okay?" He was groggy.

"Sure, he's fine. I'm sorry to wake you up, but somebody's on the phone, and he says it's important."

"What time is it?"

"I don't know."

It was Marie's husband. He said he was worried that the baby Shannon Hickman just had was in trouble.

"I thought she had that baby a week ago. Didn't her water break?"

"She just had it. Tonight. I don't know what to do."

Patrick was still half-asleep. "I don't either. But thanks."

He made a cup of coffee. He couldn't call the police. Could he? It was not a crime to have a baby. What if a baby was in trouble, though?

But Patrick didn't even know what kind of trouble. He tried Marie's cell but the call went to voice mail. This was no time to blow his cover. If the Followers started telling lies about him, he could lose custody. And Jim still needed him, because after the Worthington victory, the Followers felt like they could get away with murder. He took a long drink of coffee. It was too hot. He called 911.

All he could tell them was that a baby might be in trouble at a home birth, but that he hadn't been there himself. They said they would help as soon as they possibly could.

OREGON CITY
SEPTEMBER 27, 2009

Dale was weeping. His dead son, already in heaven but still without a name, a tiny lump barely visible in a bundle of blankets, lay at the end of Shannon's bed. Shannon's face held a look of horror that no one could look at for very long.

"Dale," Phil Hickman said to his son. "Come into the kitchen. With the men."

They were gathered around the table. They knew they had to call the medical examiner because of their long-standing agreement with head DA John Foote. But they'd learned their lessons about that the hard way. They needed a consistent story. No contradictions. Something that would clearly show they had no idea the baby was in danger. Or that if they did think there was a problem, that it was too late to do anything. The main thing was just to keep their mouths shut. They knew by now that they weren't legally obligated to say anything to anybody. And they also had to keep the cops from snooping through their records, to try to frame them.

But they couldn't appear adversarial. That alone could be twisted into an indication of guilt. Phil Hickman quoted tactical advice from the Bible. "The Book of Matthew," he said, "says something like,

Agree with your adversaries quickly. Turn the other cheek. Or your adversary will deliver you to the judge—and the judge will deliver you to an officer. And you'll get cast into prison."

"Meaning?" Dale asked. He was an asphalt paver, not a theologian.

"It means agree quickly and mind your manners, if you want to stay out of jail," his father said, with unusual patience. After this sacrifice, Dale deserved to be treated with more respect. He'd held fast.

They got their story straight, and made the call. It had been an hour and a half since the baby's death.

Church elder Robert Billings also thought it would be best to have someone take possession of the various records and tapes they'd made, for safekeeping. He gave the camera and video camera to one of the women and said, "I would get rid of this."

There was also the matter of the placenta to deal with. The cops might even want that, because supposedly you could see germs or something in it. That was just the way the worldly thought. One of them took it out back and buried it.

In the quiet that followed, as they awaited their persecutors, Robert Billings smiled slightly and looked around the table. "Bring it on!" he said.

OREGON CITY
SEPTEMBER 27, 2009

The first authority to arrive was the deputy medical examiner, Jeff McLennan, who was not a physician but would serve as the eyes and ears of the doctor that would be performing the autopsy. McLennan arrived at 5:22 in the morning, as the cloudy sky turned gray with new light. He pulled into the long driveway in front of the Whites' ranch house and was struck by the number of cars that were still there.

Fred Smith, the same elder who'd directed the Followers at the

Beagley death scene, met McLennan out front. This time Smith was
better prepared.

Fred, with snowy hair and eyes magnified by his glasses, seemed
naturally friendly as he led McLennan into the house, where about
ten men were standing around in the living room. Twenty to thirty
other people were in the hallway and the master bedroom, where the
baby still lay at the foot of the king-size bed, with the curtains drawn
and the room lit dimly by only one lamp. Dale was sitting at the head
of the bed, leaning on the headboard, next to Shannon, who was still
too weak to get up.

There was a bottle of olive oil on the dresser, some towels, framed
family photos, a camera, some baby wipes, a cup, and a glass.

"I'm very sorry for your loss," McLennan said to Shannon and
Dale. They seemed numb. He told them he needed to look at the baby.

McLennan removed the green-striped blanket and saw a tiny
baby, one that looked like a miniature replica of an actual baby, or a
doll. The baby, lying on his back with a cloth beanie on his head, was
in the early stages of rigor mortis, and his blood had begun to pool, in
livor mortis, in the parts of his body that touched the bed. The baby
seemed to be hugging himself, with his head arched back. He was
sixteen and one-half inches long, weighed slightly less than three and
a half pounds, and had an umbilical-cord stump that was about one
inch long, with a string tied around it.

"You know I'm obligated to notify law enforcement authorities,
right?" McLennan said. Dale nodded, and McLennan went to his
car, radioed the Clackamas County Sheriff's Department, and walked
back toward the house. Fred Smith intercepted him by the garage.

"I know you're only doing your job," Smith said with a tight-lipped
smile, "and that you had an obligation to call the sheriff, but I've told
people not to talk to anyone without another church member present." That was unorthodox, but within their rights.

McLennan got a short health history from Shannon: no drugs or
alcohol, no smoking, one minor fall about a month ago, and no prenatal

care from a doctor. Dale told McLennan that he smoked cigarettes, didn't drink or take drugs, and had never been to a doctor.

According to the Hickmans and the midwives, the baby had been fine until 2:15 a.m.—active, breathing well, and pink—and then suddenly turned ash-gray. His breathing became labored, and he barely responded to them. They ran out to the camper and woke Dale up. He rushed in, took the baby, saw that he was struggling, prayed, and anointed him with oil. They woke up Shannon, and she saw that the baby wasn't doing well. At 2:30, they told McLennan, the baby stopped breathing. Then the church leaders began to call other people. That's why the house was so crowded, they said.

McLennan wrapped the baby in a white sheet, carried him to his vehicle, and placed him on the cot. A few minutes later, at 7:30 in the morning, three sheriff's deputies arrived, and McLennan took the baby's body to the Medical Examiner's Office to be autopsied by Dr. Cliff Nelson.

The officers were led by Detective Brian Pearson, a young guy with a goatee and mustache who'd only been working Detectives for a couple of months. None of the Followers wanted to be interviewed. Dale did almost all of the talking, but didn't say much. He told Pearson that the birth was quick, and the baby looked strong. Dale said he went to bed somewhere around 10:30 p.m. and was awakened "sometime during the night." His son was gray and lethargic.

"Did you think he might not make it?" Pearson asked.

"Yeah, it was in the back of my mind," Dale said.

Dale said he didn't call 911, but anointed the baby and prayed to God that the baby was healthy.

It was a short interview and a brief investigation. Very little evidence was taken.

As McLennan left, he noticed that Dale had gone back to bed.

The next morning, at the Medical Examiner's Office, Michelle Finn watched the autopsy of Baby Boy Hickman. She had seen tiny children before—she'd seen just about everything—but this baby's size was shocking. It was so hard to understand. How could parents look at a tiny little creature like that and not call for help immediately? And what about the grandparents, and the other relatives, and all the friends and midwives? Most of them had cell phones, and the house had a landline. What were they thinking? They had computers, televisions, newspapers, smartphones, books, and magazines. They had all gone to school. They had jobs. Many of them owned small businesses, and some ran relatively large businesses. They had money. They lived in a modern American city. Many of them had been to doctors, even if they kept it secret. They weren't ignorant. And this had happened before—many times.

So they all looked at this terribly underdeveloped little baby and thought, *What?*

When Dr. Nelson finished the autopsy, it still wasn't clear what had gone wrong. The baby had obviously been born dangerously early, and had not been ready to live on his own. The child's teeny little lungs, which were badly infected—probably from inhalation of amniotic fluid—could have supported his system immediately after he was born, but no longer than that. He had no functional immune system. He couldn't regulate his body temperature. He couldn't really even eat.

Babies like that were born every day, though, and almost all of them survived. The procedure was pretty simple: incubate, boost oxygen with a ventilator, drip in some antibiotics, and install a feeding tube. Taking care of preemies was one of the things modern medicine did best.

But maybe the death wasn't that simple. Nelson had a strong suspicion that the baby had died from a blood infection, sepsis, that had raged through his system. If that was it, probably nothing could have saved him. Nelson sent some of the baby's blood to a lab for analysis. If it was infected, Nelson would argue against blaming the Hickmans.

Detective Pearson was also concerned about the viability of the case, and conveyed his doubts to DA Mike Regan, a dark-haired, high-pedigree legal pit-bull who was as intense as Greg Horner. Horner had just assigned this case to Regan, so that he and Mygrant could focus on the Beagley case, which had overnight become even more critical, since it was now obvious that unnecessary Followers' deaths were still occurring.

Regan didn't want to *hear* about the detective's doubt. In a series of meetings, phone conferences, and memo exchanges with McLennan and Pearson, Regan told them he thought the Followers' version of the birth was probably a lie, and to get to the truth, they needed to push the case as hard as they possibly could.

Pearson, the rookie detective, also met with Detective James Rhodes, "the mean bastard," according to some of the Followers, who told Pearson that he was sure to find evidence, if he dug hard enough.

Pearson, Rhodes later said, struggling for diplomacy, "was an inexperienced detective who did the best he could."

"There's usually a journal," Rhodes told Pearson, "and there will be a videotape of the baby being washed, shortly after birth, by Grandma."

Rhodes and Michelle Finn got a warrant, quickly went back to the Whites' home with Pearson and some other officers, and turned it upside down. Finally they found the journal.

Then McLennan remembered that he'd seen a camera in the bedroom that the detectives hadn't collected as evidence. McLennan called Dale, but Dale said he couldn't remember any pictures or video being taken. He said he was much more interested in the baby's health than in photographing the event.

The detectives couldn't find any kind of camera. Nobody would admit to having one. But Rhodes didn't think the stonewalling would last. He thought the Followers just didn't have the grit for that. But they were probably getting more desperate, and might take desperate measures, like hiding or destroying evidence.

Michelle Finn found a piece of paper that said, "Get Dale Up— 2:15." It corroborated the Followers' version of the story—that Dale got up just before the baby died. If that was true, there was a good chance he could escape blame. But it looked as if something else on the paper had been scratched out. She wanted to take it to a lab to try to determine what the scratch-out said.

Then they went to find the placenta. The Followers men inside the house had said it was somewhere out back, but weren't sure where. The detectives found it buried behind the Whites' house, just deeply enough to leave a noticeable hump.

For people with nothing to hide, the Followers were doing a lot of hiding.

It still looked like a weak case, though, no matter how hard they pushed. It was weaker than the Beagleys' case, and way worse than the Worthingtons'.

If the Beagleys' trial went as badly as the Worthingtons had, they'd probably have to drop this one. Which was a shame, because there was a baby at the morgue who shouldn't have been there.

Later that evening, when the media found out that another Followers baby was dead, and that the police had searched the parents' house, KATU's Dan Tilkin and a couple of other reporters showed up at the Hickmans' home.

Church elder Fred Smith stormed out of the house and headed toward Tilkin.

"Sir," Tilkin said, "we don't want a confrontation—we just want to tell the public what's going on."

"You don't tell the *truth*," Smith barked.

"We'd love to interview you, so we can get your perspective on—"

Smith cut him off. "Tell the *truth*! You're *liars*!"

"No we are not liars," Tilkin said. "Nobody has talked to us in ten years. We can't tell a balanced story if you don't speak to us."

Smith stuck his hand in front of the camera lens.

"You don't get the story *straight*!" Smith said.

"Okay, what is the straight story?"

"You can't *get* it straight. So why would I tell you something? Does that make sense to you?"

"It makes no sense to me, sir," Tilkin said.

Smith huffed off.

Dale and Shannon, watching from inside, were worried. They didn't know what to do. So they called 911.

OREGON CITY
SEPTEMBER 28, 2009

"James Band please."

"May I tell him who's calling?"

"His church friend." Patrick waited as the call was transferred.

"Hey Patrick, what's up?"

"I did what I could last night, Jim. I just didn't hear about it in time."

"Don't blame yourself. You can be too hard on yourself." Every time Band talked to Patrick his admiration grew. Band had worked with police informants many times, but never anyone who took such a high risk for no personal gain. They got together about once a week for coffee, and almost every time Patrick broke down, crushed by Theresa's withdrawal, and afraid that their failing marriage was just the beginning of his loss. What amazed Band most was that Patrick had alchemized his strong sense of morality in a virtual vacuum, surrounded by dishonest, self-serving people his entire life.

"Do you have a case, Jim?"

"A weak one, I think. It looks like Dale was only awake for a few minutes before his son died."

"That's not what I'm hearing. Some people think he was up for almost an hour. Somebody even saw a note somewhere about it. And I know for a fact they took some video."

"We should meet."

Patrick didn't say anything about the upcoming birth of Tim and Becca Wyland's baby. That pregnancy just felt different. Tim, one of Patrick's oldest friends, was more responsible than Dale, and Rebecca seemed smarter than Shannon. For once, Patrick wasn't worried.

Before the day was over, Dale and Shannon Hickman went to pick out a coffin. Having done business with the Followers for many years, the funeral home had a good selection of tiny coffins.

Dale and Shannon also decided on a gravesite. They had wanted to bury the baby next to his sister, Baby Girl Hickman, but that site was already taken. However, there was now a new row of children's graves, which had been started with the burial of Ava Worthington. They would bury the baby next to Ava.

The only other decision was a name. The tradition, of course, was to name the firstborn son after his father. But this baby was dead, and they wanted to have another as soon as possible. Hopefully it would be a boy. They would name him Dale. If he lived.

They named the dead baby David.

16

POLICE WORK

With a good conscience our only sure reward, with history the final judge of our deeds, let us go forth to lead the land we love, asking His blessing and His help, but knowing that here on earth God's work must truly be our own.

—Inaugural Address, John F. Kennedy

Oregon City
December 15, 2009, 1:00 p.m.

"Go see Mommy for Santa Claus?" Patrick asked Paul.

"Yeah see Mama!" Paul was scooting around the kitchen on his tricycle while Ella made hot crab-and-cheddar sandwiches for lunch.

"Are you going to Idaho for Christmas?" Ella asked Patrick.

"I wasn't invited. But the bottom line is, she gets Paul for Christmas, or she files." He shook his head. "What a be-hotch." Patrick's transition to adult profanity had been slow and awkward. "What's the worst thing I did? Help sick people?"

"Maybe you should just let go."

"I don't want to lose my family."

"I know the feeling."

Patrick had the same bewildered look that Ella had seen so often on his face as a child. She'd been trying for months to help him readjust, even though it felt like returning to a childhood she'd fought to escape. After two marriages, two bouts of heavy drinking, three Mideast deployments as a Marine Corps nurse, and one hysterectomy after a failed pregnancy, she'd been hoping for a simpler early retirement in her hometown.

"I don't know if this will help," Ella said. "But I think you're going to feel like crap until you find a way to forgive her."

"What if Band and Horner forgave every scumbag they popped?" His cop vocabulary was coming along nicely.

"It's not for Theresa, tough guy. It's for you."

That was a bit too much psychobabble for Patrick, but she was probably right. "How did you finally forgive me and Mom?" he asked.

"It was easy. Twenty years of therapy." She smiled but he didn't. "I just got it through my head that you and mom were brainwashed, too. And so was Theresa, you know."

"Did you know that the word 'forgive' is only in about twenty New Testament verses, even though it's the key concept?" Patrick, trying to make sense of his new life, had been gorging himself on religious literature, parsing it for the truth he'd been denied as a kid. He'd discovered ideas that the Followers never talked about, like the *real* source of grace: God's love, granted freely to anyone who would accept it. You didn't have to earn it, or be born into some special group. You just had to take it, and return it.

He'd also learned the pivotal role of forgiveness in Jesus' healings. Jesus' most common healing phrase was, "Your sins are released." Translated from Aramaic, it meant, "Your sins are forgiven." That's what made healing happen—not some special favor from God to the chosen few. Forgiveness wasn't penitence for the privileged. It was power, available to anybody.

Jesus, as a rabbi, offered this power humbly, with no theatrics, just a few whispered words and a touch. It was nothing like in the movies, or on a televangelist's stage. Jesus' low-key approach, Patrick thought, showed people that their forgiveness came from the power of their *own* faith. It made sense. It put the burden on the people themselves, and gave them some credit for success. They couldn't just think that they were born holy, and that God took care of the rest. And that helped them forgive themselves, which was always the hardest test.

When Jesus enabled people to dump their burden of guilt—and the fear that always went with it—it reawakened their love, and all the power it held, creating what felt like a supernatural force.

Back then, there wasn't much separation between body, mind, and spirit, and most people thought the force they called God's grace could solve just about any problem, including illness, of course.

The Disciples often described healing as casting out evil spirits—or the devil, which to them was more or less the same. But they didn't seem to think of the devil as the red guy with horns because the devil wasn't a major character in the New Testament—just 36 references. The devil was closer to being an amalgam of all fear—of death, pain, disease, and destruction—that could be swept away by the force of grace, never again to inspire such terror, if people would just accept it.

The gift of grace wasn't limited just to Christians, though, any more than it was to just the Followers. One of the things that surprised Patrick most was that faith healing had been going on long before Jesus. The ancient Romans thought Hercules could heal, the Egyptians thought Isis could, and the Hebrews credited a number of healings to the prophet Elijah. Asian shamans had been doing it long before Jesus, and so had witch doctors in Africa and the Americas. After Jesus, Muhammad performed faith healing. More than a hundred different cultures had relied on it.

Before, during, and after the life of Jesus, it was common for rabbis in Israel to do faith healings, most often in Bethesda, outside Jerusalem, where several pure springs gushed into two swirling pools. Jesus' first healing occurred there, when he approached a paralyzed man and proclaimed, "Rise, take up your pallet, and walk, and sin no more." Unfortunately, though, it was the Sabbath, and Jesus got in trouble for working, and the crippled man got in trouble for carrying his pallet. Tough town, Jerusalem.

Common sense said that the pure water itself probably cured some illnesses. And some of Jesus' healings might not have been as miraculous as they sound now, because back then psoriasis and other skin ailments were lumped together with leprosy, palsy was often called paralysis, an arthritic hand was referred to as a crippled hand, and people with emotional problems were considered to be mad.

Of the twenty-one people Jesus was generally credited with healing, twelve were lepers, four were blind, two were paralytics, and the others were a woman with chronic bleeding, an epileptic, and a man with a crippled hand. Only four of the healings were mentioned in three out of the four Gospels, and none were mentioned in all four. Only a few of the people he healed were named. The only witnesses who passed the stories on were Matthew, Luke, and John, and probably only Luke did his own writing.

It was conceivable, Patrick thought, that the healings boiled down to improved hygiene and the placebo effect—but the Bible also said Jesus resurrected three people, which required more than clean water and the power of positive thinking. Admittedly, one of them might have just been sleeping—that's what Jesus said, and it was his disciples who tried to make it more than that. Another, however, was already in his coffin when Jesus raised him, and the most famous and deadest of all, Lazarus, was so dead he stank.

Jesus' healings, even by the mystical standards of the day, captured great attention, and attracted so many desperate people that he sometimes fled. Of course, his reputation as a healer was propelled by the power of his philosophies. He became wildly popular in a short time, and this uncontrollable acclaim, coupled with his rebellious ideas, aroused such antagonism that he was quickly perceived as a political and social danger, and killed.

After that, his disciples were said to have achieved notable healings, in Jesus' name, although their healings were even harder to document than his.

Over the next two millennia, faith healing morphed from the mysticism of the early Christians into a practice that created profit and power. European noblemen—particularly in London, a hotbed of faith healing—claimed to have the unique power of The Royal Touch, and even reformer Martin Luther took credit for miraculous healings. By the 1800s, there were fifteen European holy sites that were believed to have the same healing power as Lourdes, and each had its own version of Lourdes' Souvenir Alley, gaudy markets at the holy shrines that sold mementos to the pilgrims.

It was impossible to keep the practice of praying for health from being corrupted. Praying to be healthy seemed like an innate element of human behavior—along with such irreducible essentials as striving for wealth, playing, and socializing—and was therefore vulnerable to every human urge and vice. The Followers had completely perverted it, Patrick thought, and so had the rich televangelists.

So by now, Patrick knew all this, but he still didn't know what to think about the ability of prayer to heal. At least he had Ella to talk to.

He loved to talk religion with her. He'd been starving for someone who could do more than misquote the Bible to justify their sins, even though Ella's cosmology, he'd found, consisted of about three parts liberal Christianity, one part Zen, and bits and pieces of spiritual pop culture. But it seemed to work for her. She looked far younger than her 53 years, with a glowing, unlined face surrounded by short blond hair, and a smile that always seemed to be there, even when she was serious.

As he helped her with the lunch dishes, he said, "Ella, do you think faith healing is just the placebo effect?"

"*Just* the placebo effect?" she said. "Don't blaspheme. I'm a nurse. I love the placebo effect. It works thirty percent of the time on almost everything, with no side effects. I wish I owned it."

"What about God, though?"

She got that smiley look and he knew she was about to launch into one of the stories that she called War Vet Sermonettes. "Patrick, you know that joke: 'How come God never heals amputees?' Well, we did that once, in Kuwait. It was during the second Gulf War, the bad one. We reattached an arm that had no business getting reattached. The soldier had lost it in the field ten hours earlier—which made reattachment *impossible*—and it was just a stinky piece of meat, even iced. But this kid—twenty maybe, Latino, lance corporal—he was praying his heart out while they got ready to clean up his stump. I sat down by him. Those boys, they need a lot of love. I started praying with him, and his prayer was all about: *Heal* me, I *know* there's a way. Super positive. The kid's vibe was contagious, and I thought, Let's do it. This can work. So I pulled a couple of strings and got him in the OR, and that arm pinked right up. Everybody was shaking their heads. It really was impossible—but sometimes you see impossible stuff in an OR. So you tell me: Was that God, or a big push by the placebo effect?"

"God."

"Wrong. The placebo effect. Plus good docs. Brought to you by our sponsor. God."

"Here's where you always lose me," Patrick said. "If God isn't present in everyday life, how can I have faith?"

"I think faith means hope," she said. "Optimism. Not certainty. Just a gut feeling that life is good and makes sense. And faith isn't even the most important thing to God. You know the verse: 'Faith, hope, and love—these three—'"

Patrick finished the quote: "'And the greatest of these is love.'"

"And that's what you've got goin', Patrick. You really love people. Even those dumb-ass people in the Church. That's why all this hurts you so much. And that's also why you can forgive Theresa."

"I am religious," he said, almost sadly.

"It's not about religion," Ella said.

"What then?"

Her answer came liltingly and lovingly, as soft as a song. "People," she said.

OREGON CITY
DECEMBER 15, 2009, 4:00 P.M.

Across town, Band, Rhodes, and Finn were getting ready to work overtime on the Beagley case. The trial was right after Christmas, and

Horner didn't like their position. He still needed a Church insider to take the stand and blow holes in some of the Followers' biggest myths: that they didn't shun, that they let people go to the doctor, that laying on of hands was no big deal, that nobody had known that Neil was chronically ill, and that nobody had known he might die. Horner had experts that could expose most of those myths, but Experts vs. Eyewitnesses hadn't worked in the Worthington case.

Patrick could do that, but Band didn't want Patrick to testify. He couldn't ask Patrick to further increase the risk of losing his family, and he still needed Patrick undercover. He needed information for the legal cases that only Patrick could provide, and he was also realistic about the limitations of law enforcement. Even if he and Horner got their convictions, the Church would still never change without somebody inside it pushing the others to change, creating fear about legal vulnerability, sowing doubt about the validity of the doctrines, and offering hope and support to people who needed it. The war against the Followers was ultimately a war against their self-destructive ideas, and Patrick was the only person willing to fight that war, no matter what the risk.

Fortunately, though, DA Steve Mygrant had heard about a former member who might testify, and Patrick had helped Band locate her.

It was Holly Divelbis, the woman Lee Hickman thought was the snitch. Holly didn't have much to lose. Her family was already shunning her. Band called her and arranged a meeting.

The three detectives drove out past Hillsboro, in Portland's high-tech Silicon Forest, to a house near Henry Hagg Lake, a famous bass-fishing spot. Holly was Jeff Beagley's cousin, and had dropped out six years ago, partly because her two births had been so hard that she had needed surgery to repair the damage. Her first baby had weighed almost twelve pounds, the labor had been excruciating, and Holly was terrified throughout the labor because Jacqueline Beagley, Jeff's sister-in-law, had just died in childbirth, along with her baby.

Holly, red-haired and animated, welcomed them in and made some coffee.

Band asked if she knew anything about Neil's extended health history. "Yeah, I was at a birthday party with Marci in 2000," she said, "and Marci said that Neil sometimes had a hard time urinating, and when he did, it hurt." Holly's estranged sister had also heard that remark, she said.

The Beagleys, Holly said, should have known all about urinary problems, because a cousin of Marci's mom had died from a urinary-tract disorder, a week after she'd refused to have surgery. "The fear of disappointing everyone in your life," Holly said, "keeps you from making a reasonable decision. The peer pressure is overwhelming. If she'd gotten surgery she would have been a social outcast."

"What cousin was that?" Rhodes asked. He hoped maybe the cousin had a son or daughter who could testify about it.

"Connie Nichols." It was the mother of David Nichols, the piano player who'd been convicted of sexual spying. Too bad. David was out of prison, but wouldn't be much of a witness.

"Was it hard to leave the Church?" Finn asked.

Holly, who'd been upbeat, started to answer, but suddenly broke down and began to cry. "I miss my family," she said. She hadn't seen most of them for years. Once, she had tried to attend a social event, she said, but someone started yelling at her to go home, pray and fast for forgiveness, and devote the rest of her life to her family. Band, guided by his natural empathy, touched her hand.

"Why can't family members have a difference of opinion on religion?" Finn asked.

"That's just how it is. If they do think differently, they lie about it. I saw the Worthington trial on truTV and I couldn't believe all the lying. That reminds me, ask Norma Beagley about having moles removed by a doctor. Ask her how that was okay but taking Neil in wasn't."

Band, certain that Jeff and Marci would lie about how sick they thought Neil was, asked, "On a scale of one to ten, what are the signs that somebody is really sick?"

Holly said that a cold or flu would be a three, solved by the family praying about it themselves. A high fever that lasted for a week would be a five, and people would call their extended family for prayer. A serious illness that wouldn't go away would be a seven, and people would ask for the whole church to pray. If it got worse, and they needed to lay on hands, that would be an eight or nine.

"How sick would they have to be to lay on hands?" Band asked.

"They'd have to be dying."

"What would happen then?"

"They die." That was the answer Band expected, but it was still jarring.

"I've never been there when they didn't," Holly said. "That's how it was with both of my parents. They laid on hands. Then they died."

As the detectives prepared to leave, Holly told them that she probably wouldn't be a good witness. Her grandmother had recently died, she said, and her share of the inheritance had been funneled into the Defense Fund. Her family, she thought, would probably say that she was just bitter about the money.

As darkness came, Band, Rhodes, and Finn drove back to Oregon City, talking about the advisability of calling Holly as a witness. She was articulate, well-meaning, and had inside information. Band didn't think the inheritance issue was relevant, or even admissible. However, Holly still had contacts in the Church, and she might be able to gain some information that would help them in the possible Hickman trial. But if they couldn't win Beagley, there almost certainly wouldn't be a Hickman trial. With no good eyewitnesses, it was still a shaky case, even though Medical Examiner Cliff Nelson had found out that the Hickman's baby hadn't died from a fast-acting blood infection, as Nelson had first thought.

Ultimately, though, the decision about calling Holly as a witness in the Beagley case was Horner's, not theirs.

Band dropped off Finn and Rhodes, went to his office, turned on all the lights to make it seem more like normal working hours, and called Holly's sister, Heather Silva. He asked her if she remembered Marci talking about Neil's urinary problems.

"No, I don't," she said. She sounded very defensive. Heather asked

Band if she should talk to a lawyer before saying anything else, but he assured her that she wasn't a suspect.

"What I want to know," Heather said, "is how the Beagleys can be charged after somebody from DHS told them that Neil had a right to refuse medical treatment?"

Band didn't argue the technicalities of the law with her, but just said that as a police officer, he needed to hold parents accountable for their kids' safety, whether the kids liked it or not.

Band asked if she thought the Followers were being honest with him. She wouldn't respond to that. She seemed annoyed that the officers had visited Holly, and started attacking her sister instead of offering direct answers.

Band's day was done. He'd wanted to buy some Christmas presents for his kids. But it was getting too late for that.

Oregon City
December 15, 2009, 7:30 p.m.

Bob Zegar, a semi-retired man in his 50s, was headed for his best friend's apartment, overjoyed to be back in the safe haven of Oregon City after years of exile in the class-war zones of Salem and Canby, just south of O.C., where he'd been forced to go to find affordable property. Both towns had until recently been poor-but-quaint American communities, but things had changed. The prosperity of Salem, the state capital, had always been held down by low government wages, and the economy of Canby, a farm town, had been dominated by a migrant farmworker demographic. Even so, the two towns had long been quiet, tree-shaded enclaves, safe from the Sin City ways of Portland. Canby was so wholesome that straitlaced Nobel laureate Alexander Solzhenitsyn, author of *The Gulag Archipelago*, took refuge there in a Russian Orthodox Old Believers monastery outside town, when he was being harassed by both the KGB and the FBI after his exile from the Soviet Union in the 1970s.

But around 2006, within what seemed like a matter of months, the family-friendly atmospheres of Salem and Canby had been replaced by graffiti and gunfire.

Salem had for some years been the turf of the racist Aryan Brotherhood and the Gypsy Jokers motorcycle gang, but these groups of aging troublemakers were now rivaled by two Latino gangs known as the 18th Street gang and the Norteños gang.

Canby was now home of the Brown Pride Norteños Gang and the Sureños South Side Local. These competing gangs, in their fight for control, sometimes fired stray shots at the longtime locals. It still seemed faintly ridiculous to most of the old-time townies, though, that crime gangs would want to occupy a place as bucolic as Canby, which was next-door to the little German immigrant town of Mt. Angel, where Jim Band had first been a cop, back when the biggest law enforcement problem was public intoxication during Oktoberfest.

When Zegar lived in Salem and Canby, while he was trying to finance his retirement with some apartments he owned, multicolored spray paint had begun to inundate both towns. The gang members ran out of urban targets early on, though, and were quickly reduced to tagging trees: It's Oregon.

By comparison, the only crazy thing in O.C. was the strange Kissers church, and it didn't pose much of a threat. So it was great for Zegar to kick off the holiday season there, visiting his friend, Wayne Welch, who at age 89 was really more like a father figure to him.

Welch was slow to get to the door, as he had been since the previous year's football game between the Oregon Ducks and Oregon State Beavers, known locally as the Civil War. The game had cost OSU the Rose Bowl, and given Beaver Believer Wayne Welch a stroke. Since the game, he'd had a gimpy leg.

"Bob," Welch said, settling into his favorite recliner, "I think I'm going to go on a starvation diet."

"What?"

"Yeah, I've been reading up on it and I'm gonna do it." Welch said he was tired, that his leg hurt, that his sister had died recently, and he was ready to go.

"That's a painful way to go!"

"No, I already started, and it only hurt the first couple of days."

Zegar felt sick. Wayne, a retired teacher, still had the life of the mind to live for, and Zegar hated the thought of losing their long talks about history and politics.

"But, Bob," Welch said, "you're my closest friend, and if you say don't do it, I won't."

Zegar knew right away what his answer was. "It's your body," he said. "It's your life." He hoped Wayne would change his mind. But Zegar also believed devoutly in the right of every person to make his or her own decisions, even if it meant death. And Zegar knew that he'd never change his own position on the issue. If he'd learned anything from history, it was that the only thing greater than life itself were the ideas that gave it meaning.

When Zegar got home, he hesitated to call his wife, who was out of town. She would probably try to talk him into saving Wayne's life.

He opened his mail. Damn. At a time like this, when he had so much to think about—jury duty.

CLACKAMAS COUNTY COURTHOUSE
JANUARY 5, 2010

Horner wanted more, more, more. Coming on the heels of the devastating Worthington verdict, this was now the most nationally significant case of his life, and if he lost, the whole campaign against the Church would end. He still didn't think they had enough on the Beagleys, and the trial was fourteen days away. He called Band.

Horner and Mygrant had gotten four new names of defense witnesses, and Horner wanted Band to find out everything he possibly could about them. If Band did it right, he'd find out where the defense was headed, and give Horner a jump on them.

The first person on the list, LaMont Heinbigner, a Church member, lived on a tree-shrouded acreage separated from the Beagleys only by a power line that ran all the way to Canby and then kept going. It was a quirky property, with both of the features that were emblematic of the Clackatucky outback: a beautiful two-story home, almost big enough to be a McMansion, juxtaposed with a scattered array of broken hillbilly keepsakes, including a tarp-covered pickup, piles of wood too rotten to burn, and a life-size replica of a deer, in four pieces. There was just about everything but a washing machine on the front porch. The strip of land under the power line, outside the city's no-gun zone, had a skeet-shooting launcher.

Heinbigner clearly didn't want to talk to Band. But like the other Followers, he seemed to gradually warm up to the friendly cop. He confirmed that Neil did have long-standing problems, but said they weren't urinary: "His stomach was bothering him." Heinbigner said he had been present when they'd laid hands on Neil, but claimed he didn't think Neil "was all that sick." That was one clue: The Followers were going to use the Worthington strategy of Who Knew?

One reason Heinbigner didn't think Neil would die, he said, was because "I don't think *any* of our kids are going to die." If you do think that, he said, "You are losing your faith." And if you lose faith, he said, kids can die. It was impenetrable, circular logic.

Band asked Heinbigner which time he had laid hands on Neil—in March, or in June, when he died? Heinbigner said he couldn't remember, because of his age. Too old. Bad memory.

Band asked him if he would disagree with the statement that prior to Neil's death, everybody in the Church knew he was sick. "No."

"Is there anything else you think I should know about the case."

Heinbigner chuckled softly. "No."

The next day, Band talked to another Church member on the list, Clint Duncan, who said that he thought Neil's health was fine just before his death, "although he had lost some weight." Band asked if they laid on hands for minor problems, and Duncan said no. Band asked if it was reserved just for people "who might pass away," and Duncan said yes. Clue number two: *Somebody* knew.

Band also went to Oregon City High School, to see Neil's friend Reese Eells. Reese said that when he visited Neil, "I knew he was pretty sick." Just before Neil died, he said, "I heard he was pretty bad." Band also asked Reese which time he had laid hands on Neil, March or June? Reese said he couldn't remember, because of his age. Too young. Bad memory. Clue three: The ignorance card would be in play.

The last name on the list was Gary Kishpaugh, who'd lived across the street from Norma Beagley for more than forty years, and had seen Jeff Beagley grow up. Kishpaugh wasn't a member of the Church, and all Band found out from him was how little people outside the Church knew about the Followers. Kishpaugh said that when Norma's husband died, he didn't even hear about it for a week and a half. "They're a pretty closed-mouth people," he said.

"It became very apparent," Band later said, "that not a lot of people knew Neil Beagley. Mostly just his family. And we knew what they were going to say."

As the trial's start date approached, Patrick called in a good tip. He said Marci had been to a doctor for birth-control pills. Better yet: Marci had been to a doctor to have a hangnail treated. So, Marci wouldn't take her son to a doctor to save his life, but she went for her own *hangnail*? Images like that won trials.

On the day before the trial, Band and Mygrant corraled Norma Beagley's sister-in-law, Carolyn Crone, for an interview. Horner had an audacious strategy, based partly on the tips that Band had gotten from Patrick. He was going to call three of the Followers, including Crone, as witnesses for the prosecution. He'd take the game to them, and call them on their own bullshit. They'd already made too many stupid statements to the detectives that chipped away at the Who Knew strategy. They would either have to own up or lie, and if the jury was smart enough to see through their deceit, it would be a win/win assault. The Beagleys' jury, Horner thought, would probably be more savvy than the Worthingtons' because he was going to do everything he could to pack some IQ into the jury box.

Carolyn Crone admitted that Neil had been sick for a long time, but she stuck with the story that Neil's only apparent problem was some kind of stomach ailment. She blamed Neil for that: too much junk food. That was a another clue, though: The defense was probably going to blame Neil for his own death. They'd say he had insisted on not going to the doctor, and that he was too stubborn to dissuade. Blaming the victim was venal, of course, but Horner and Mygrant knew now that the Followers wouldn't show the courage of their convictions. They would lie to stay out of jail.

As the interview wound down, Band mentioned, very casually, that he had heard there was some disagreement between Jeff and Marci over sending Neil to a doctor. Crone said that one of the times Neil was sick, Marci had hugged her and said, "I don't know if I can do this." So: *Marci* knew.

With the investigation finally over, Band went back to his office and looked at his slim folder of evidence, the product of hundreds of hours of work by him, Finn, and Rhodes, much of it unpaid. "We had this important case that was making news all over the country," Band later said, "and I had DUII reports that were longer."

Worst of all: "There was no smoking gun." He had no confession, no corroborating witnesses, and just one piece of strong circumstantial evidence: the blue notebook that showed Neil's slow decline. It would be a tough trial. Everything was up to Horner and Mygrant now.

Horner liked to have two DAs at his most important trials, and he liked to work the most critical ones of all himself, preferably with Mygrant, who was usually perceived to be his top associate.

If the Horner-Mygrant team couldn't win, no one could. And this time it was win or go home.

The receptionist called. "Lieutenant, your friend from church is on the line."

"I just wanted to say good luck," said Patrick.

"Thanks. This one's for you."

"Oh, good news for once. Tim and Becca Wyland had their baby. No problems at all. Beautiful little girl."

"Thanks. I could use some good news."

CLACKAMAS COUNTY COURTHOUSE
JANUARY 13, 2010

Defense attorney Wayne Mackeson's eyes lit up when Bob Zegar, one of the potential jurors, told Mackeson that he had recently refused to stop his best friend's death, because of his belief in personal freedom. The story, as it emerged in fragments, was that Zegar's friend wanted to starve himself to death, and Zegar had opposed the idea, but respected his friend's right of sovereignty over his own body. Hot damn. Two more people like that, and Jeff and Marci would walk.

Mackeson even liked Zegar's beard, sometimes a sign of a freethinker. A free-thinker himself, Mackeson made the Worthingtons' civil-libertarian defense attorney Mark Cogan seem conservative. Mackeson looked urbane, but boasted on his law practice's website that he was kicked out of college for publishing an underground newspaper, and on the wall of his office he had the two-thumbed, clenched-fist HUNTER S. THOMPSON FOR SHERIFF poster. He even reverently quoted "Mercedes Benz" in his blog, noting that it was the last thing Janis Joplin wrote before her o.d.

But Horner liked Zegar, too. Zegar seemed smart, and this time Horner's model juror would be Mr. Spock: all logic, no emotion. Also, he didn't want any holy rollers, Tea Partiers, conservative family-values extremists, contrarian Clackastanis, or even O.C.ers—but good luck on that last one.

Mackeson went through two more panels of jury candidates before he found another keeper: a young veterinary technician who inadvertently displayed a tattoo on the upper part of her back that said ALL YOU

NEED IS LOVE. Perfect. She was probably a softie who'd sympathize with the grieving parents. But she seemed plenty bright to Horner, and he went along.

To complete the jury, Horner and Mackeson agreed upon a TSA employee, along with a man who worked in a cardiac unit, a retired service veteran, a couple of fairly young women, a stay-at-home mom, a skinny guy who was very talkative, a part-time community-college professor, a technical writer for a software company, a feisty young woman with red hair, and a smart guy with a Boston accent who, far too prematurely, had volunteered to be foreman.

All of the jurors believed in freedom of religion, protecting children, governmental restraint, fairness, and open-mindedness—if you took their word for it. Ultimately, a lot of jury selection was just intuition, and Horner and Mackeson both had good gut feelings.

Bob Zegar, who'd actually talked one-on-one with most of the other jurors, wasn't so confident in them. Some of them—especially the Boston guy, who obviously thought he was JFK incarnate—seemed to be there just for the fun of playing God with somebody else's life, and might willingly hang the jury out of vanity, if they didn't get their way. If there was ever a time *not* to play God, Zegar thought, this was it.

Horner's case caught an excellent upward surge when Judge Steven Mauer made two critical decisions in pre-trial, before the jury was called in. He allowed Horner to bring up some elements of the Worthington case, on the grounds that it showed that Jeff and Marci had already experienced a similar tragedy and should have learned from it. Mauer also ruled definitively that Neil Beagley's right as a child older than fifteen to demand medical care didn't cancel out Jeff and Marci's responsibility as parents. That was a huge advantage for Horner, but he knew Mackeson was a smart enough lawyer to at least allude to Neil's own role in his death.

"Ladies and gentlemen," Mauer said, as the trial began, "we'll go ahead and begin with opening statements."

"Thank you, Your Honor," Horner said. "Members of the jury, on

June 17th of 2008, at his grandmother's home in Gladstone, Neil Beagley, a sixteen-year-old boy, lay in his grandmother's bed, dying." Neil, Horner said, "was so weak that he couldn't get out of bed," or even "feed himself," and had constriction in his breathing. "Had he received appropriate medical care, Neil would be here, alive today." Horner said that Neil was surrounded by friends and family as his life ebbed, but that Jeff and Marci "did absolutely nothing. No CPR. No mouth-to-mouth, or calling 911."

Then Horner told them why, hitting religion head-on: "They did nothing because that was their *belief*." All they did, he said, was pray, anoint, and lay on hands, which would have been fine if it was combined with medical treatment. Even now, he said, they would do the same thing again. Because of their callous, selfish inaction, their son lay suffering on his grandmother's bed. "And there he died."

Horner reminded the jury that the Beagleys' intent had no bearing whatsoever. By the rules of manslaughter-2, it didn't matter that they meant no harm. He knew, though, that he'd need to keep repeating that until he was blue in the face. People just didn't seem to get it.

Then Horner, with his customary intensity, making eye contact with the jurors one by one, described the details of Neil's grotesque death: a child's frail body was "absolutely sloshed with urine, filled to the max and beyond." Neil's lungs, Horner said, were "filled with fluids," and Neil's kidneys were "at a level of only about four percent of normal." Horner said that Neil's kidneys had "collapsed—with chemical markers of kidney malfunction that were twenty times higher than normal."

And even with all this damage, Horner said, "Doctors could have saved his life."

The only reason they didn't was because Jeff and Marci wouldn't take Neil in. "Why didn't they bring Neil to a doctor?" Horner asked. "Because seeking medical treatment is a lack of faith."

Horner was either going to win on the religious issue—or lose, and forget about the Hickman case, and go home.

Mackeson looked unruffled. Cogan and Neidig had beaten Horner by playing the religion card, and that was also part of Mackeson's strategy, so Horner was on his turf now. Religion had value for Horner, as a motive, but even more for Mackeson, because most people loved religion, and loved *freedom* of religion even more. Also, Mackeson, despite Horner's pretrial victories, still had a big head start, courtesy of the defense's win in the Worthington case, which was well-known throughout the county. Mackeson felt at home with the Clackamas County jury pool. Although his law firm was based in a neoclassical skyscraper in the financial heart of Portlandia, he had an office in O.C., too, and played to a blue-collar jury quite well, having been raised as an Air Force brat by a master sergeant.

When Horner finished, he smiled congenially at the jury. The jurors would soon be seeing Jeff and Marci in tears, playing martyr, and Horner wasn't going to be pushed into the role of Pontius Pilate.

Mackeson rose as casually as if he were in his own living room and sauntered toward the jury. "I would describe my client," Mackeson said affably, working up a bond with the jurors, "as an ordinary man. He's worked in construction most of his life. He started a business where they deliver and pick up portable toilets around the country." The port-a-potty reference was a nice touch—it was hard get more down-to-earth than that. Mackeson told the jurors about the Beagleys' rustic acreage, and their rural American dream of building a gargantuan garage that was big enough for all of their quintessentially Oregon outdoor toys. "And that dream, of course, came to an end when Neil died on June 17th of 2008."

"The issue," Mackeson said, "is whether the Beagleys failed in their duty as parents in a criminal way. A *criminal* way. And that requires proof that they acted in a way that was a *gross deviation* from the standard of care that a reasonable person—not an expert, not a doctor—but a reasonable person, would have observed. . . ." He'd played the ignorance card early.

Then Mackeson invoked the Who-Knew ploy. A human being's kidneys, Mackeson said, "can function down to as low as twenty percent, and you really won't know that you've lost that kidney function."

After that, though, "as the doctors would describe it, the wheels come off."

Bob Zegar made a note in his yellow tablet: 20 percent is too low. Neil was at 4 percent.

However, Mackeson said, the symptoms that begin to happen below 20 percent "are all nonspecific. Fatigue, poor appetite, nausea." Also, he said, "Some of the symptoms are sort of counterintuitive." Such as: "the *lack* of a temperature. You might say, 'Hooray, at least my kid doesn't have a temperature.'" There was, he said, "no fever, no diarrhea, no headaches. His eyes looked good, bright and clear." Even on the night Neil died, Mackeson said, "He was telling jokes with his uncle Steve," and "eating scrambled eggs, fish, and fruit." Therefore: Who Knew?

Neil was steadfastly upbeat, Mackeson said. "He kept saying, 'I'll be fine.' Neil absolutely did not want to go to the doctor."

It was the first reference to a fundamental strategy that Horner had seen coming: Blame the Victim. Neil was characterized as "headstrong, independent, and stubborn." He "saw things in black and white" because "it was his way or the wrong way." Neil would be portrayed as indulgent with junk food, secretive about his symptoms, unduly macho, noncommunicative, and condescendingly superior. At work, he wasn't afraid to tell other people, including his dad and uncle, "You guys need to pick that up. It's not my job." Of course, traits like that could have serious consequences—and whose fault was that?

When Neil did make the unexpected transition from a runny nose to dying, his parents did all they could. But it was too late.

Jeff and Marci weren't religious fanatics, because Neil had been to a dentist and an eye doctor. "Even though he didn't *want* to go," Mackeson said, "his mother made him go." That probably wasn't a great point to make, but it was out there, and Mackeson kept going.

Jeff and Marci loved Neil, and didn't want him to die, he said. "Neil was the Crown Prince of the family." And now they were grief stricken.

The Beagleys' love of Neil and their intent were irrelevant, of course, but were absolutely vital to their case.

"Did they make a mistake?" Mackeson asked. "Of course they did. Their son is dead." But was the Beagleys' approach to Neil's illness different from what a reasonable parent would do? "I submit that it was not. And they ought to be acquitted. And put all this to an end, finally."

Mackeson was good.

Band, waiting to go on as the first witness, thought Mackeson was much better than Cogan and Neidig, and would be a worthy adversary.

Patrick, sitting in the back row, felt queasy. He, too, thought Mackeson was good—maybe too good, even for his friend Jim.

The feisty red-haired juror, who came off to the other jurors as a devout, doctrinaire Christian, was ready to acquit, and thought that at least half the other jurors agreed, based on their expressions and body language.

The young woman with the tattoo thought Jeff and Marci should be put in jail for years.

Bob Zegar thought both sides were very persuasive. But he was worried about the jury. Some of them, like the JFK clone, were having too much fun. Zegar had been on a jury once that had put a seventeen-year-old boy in prison for life, and learned that when you have godlike power over somebody, it's not play, it's the world's hardest work.

Rita Swan, watching a clip of the KATU News Online in her Iowa office as she worked on other cases, didn't know what to think. Mackeson was good but Horner was better: "a superb communicator and persuader of the jury," she later said. She had high hopes. But she'd had high hopes shattered before. Too many times.

She went back to work, her source of refuge and redemption. She was editing her emotional memoir of Matthew's death, *The Last Strawberry*. It was finally going to be published.

At least, come what may, Matthew would be remembered.

17

CLACKATRAZ

Perhaps we cannot prevent this world from being a world in which children are tortured. But we can reduce the number of tortured children. And if you don't help us, who else in the world can help us do this?

—ALBERT CAMUS

CLACKAMAS COUNTY COURTHOUSE
JANUARY 19, 2010

The jurors returned from a downtown O.C. lunch scene that was devoid of interesting choices. Main Street of the West's first incorporated city was one awkward step above the main drag of a ghost town, with empty storefronts scattered among sad but surviving mom-and-pop places, along with nineteen law offices and several courthouse annexes. Main Street's primary business now revolved around convicting criminals.

Many of the jurors skipped downtown and ate sack lunches in a drab, good-enough-for-government room that didn't have enough coffee. That made it harder to concentrate. Since they couldn't mention the only matter of interest, they generally ignored each other.

After lunch, it was time for Horner to use what he'd learned from the Worthington loss: Treat the parents like perps, not victims. Hit religion hard. Keep things rational. When they cry, cut it short. When they lie, call them out. Make them look like a gang, not a church. And show they're weasels, not martyrs.

Horner called Jim Band as his first witness. He could have called Sergeant Lynne Benton, because she had been the first cop at the death scene, but she had too much baggage at the moment. She'd recently gotten the sex-reassignment surgery she'd dreamed of. She hadn't legally changed her gender yet, but planned to, so that she could get married. But it wasn't going to be to her domestic partner of the last nine years, because they'd broken up. As the Public Information Officer of the Gladstone PD, though, she was still working under her female identity, to avoid controversy. All of that was her business, and God bless—but this wasn't the time to test the jury's tolerance for the gender complexity of Mr. and Ms. Lynne Benton/ Lynn Edward Benton.

When Band took the stand, some of the jurors looked caffeine-deprived to the point of near-catatonia. Only the skinny guy looked animated, and he seemed fitful and fidgety. Tough room to work. But Band painted vivid pictures of the crime scene, bringing to life an intensely dramatic event that the legal system, as it inevitably did, was reducing to technicalities, and burying in detail.

Band and Horner, practiced at playing off one another, re-created the reality of Neil's death, and the bizarre atmosphere of Norma Beagley's home: half death-scene, half potluck. Band also told the jury about Jeff's story of a quick and easy death, but that version didn't match the grisly, overhead pictures of Neil on his deathbed: skinny, yellow, greasy with oil, limbs askew, with blood pooling in his back.

Band worked without notes, his passion evident, and jurors leaned forward. They were seeing the tough-cop side of him, one that had worked innumerable death scenes.

Neil was so weak, Band said, that Jeff had to carry him to the bathroom. Band said that Jeff characterized it as "a joke," but Bob Zegar thought that sounded ridiculous. Zegar was trying to keep an open mind, but was glad somebody like Jeff hadn't been *his* dad.

Jeff, according to Band, had admitted he knew Neil might die. "He told me that Neil started acting differently." Neil, who was normally bottled up, told Jeff he loved him.

That stuck with the jury. Pathos usually did.

Jeff was emerging as somebody with a perverse blend of adoration and indifference.

Band said that Jeff's main point of pride was that, "Neil held fast to his faith." Jeff told Band that even if he'd known Neil was dying, he would not have called a doctor—unless Neil asked him to.

It was an ugly story of a needless death, perpetrated by a man who now played the victim.

Rhodes came on next and told the jury that the Beagleys' granddaughter, Ava Worthington, had died similarly, and that Jeff and Marci had been there. Then they let the same thing happen to their son.

Several of the jurors, including Zegar, were stunned: A similar tragedy had *already* happened?

Rhodes played the tape of his interview with Marci on Neil's death night. The juror with the tattoo—Amy Slatford, the only one other than Bob Zegar who later spoke for attribution—was repulsed by what she considered Marci's condescension, and her clear obsession with her own fate, when she should have been thinking about what had happened to her son.

Then came the presentation of the logbook and its detailed record of Neil's attempts to eat. It was shocking. One of the female jurors wondered, "Who *throws up* after 'a teaspoon of egg'?"

Band and Rhodes had set the scene perfectly, and Horner was ready to roll the dice.

"State calls Norma Beagley," he said. It was extremely unusual to call a defendant's own mother to testify for the prosecution, but Horner needed to unmask the Followers. He thought Norma was just snotty, deceitful, and dumb enough to get the job done. The Followers needed to find out what hundreds of perps in this courthouse had long learned: Fuck with Horner, and you get the horn.

Horner reminded Norma that she'd told Band that Neil wanted the family to lay hands on him, a sign he was experiencing great distress.

"I don't remember saying that," she said.

"Okay."

"I'm not saying that didn't happen. I don't remember saying it."

"I see. Do you remember whether or not he was complaining about being nauseous?"

"Yes, but he had the flu."

"Okay. Do you remember whether or not he was vomiting?"

"I did not see Neil vomit."

Even if she didn't observe it, Horner asked, did she know it happened?

"I can't remember that."

"Okay. Is it your assessment, even today, that up until his death, Neil just wasn't feeling good?"

"Yes."

"There was nothing unusual about his condition, even at the time he died?"

"No."

It sounded like one lie after another to practically everyone in the room. Now it was time for the full reveal of Norma's deceit and hypocrisy.

"Have you ever been to a doctor?" Horner asked.

"I was at a doctor once. . . . I had a test to see if I was diabetic."

"So you were willing to get a treatment, or get tested . . . ?"

"Yes. That's what I did."

"Have you ever had any surgeries, or removal of anything?"

"No."

"Moles?"

No response.

"Anything like that?"

"No."

Horner raised his eyebrows and stared her down.

"Oh," Norma said. "Well. Moles." She paused. "Yes." She looked down.

Horner asked Norma if her husband had ever been treated at a hospital. She said he had been, after an accident.

"And that wasn't any kind of a big issue with you, or him?" Horner asked.

"No."

Jim Band was becoming confident. "Norma," Band later said, "came off as very stiff when she said Neil hadn't been sick at all. Right afterwards, we put up a friend of hers from the church who said she'd known for a long time that Neil was really sick. How did she know? She said: 'Norma told me.'"

Then Horner called up Sandra Mitchell, who had told Band less than a week ago that she'd thought Neil had Crohn's disease.

Sandra said she couldn't remember saying that.

Horner read her the earlier interview's transcription. "Does that help refresh your memory?" he asked.

"I—it's not accurate."

"You did not tell the detectives that?"

"I did not say that."

Horner asked her if Neil, on the night of his death, actually seemed like a kid who just had the flu.

"This is hard for me, because there was a lot going on in my family at the time. I don't remember all of his symptoms."

"What do you remember . . . ?"

"That we thought he had the flu."

Horner asked Sandra if she remembered saying that she thought Neil might die in March.

"No. I didn't say I thought Neil would die."

Horner asked if she remembered that Neil was vomiting shortly before he died.

"I don't. I don't. I don't."

"You don't remember at all?"

"I don't remember."

Several of the jurors were looking at Mitchell with undisguised contempt. Some glanced at one another, clandestinely.

Steve Mygrant took over. "Your Honor, the State calls Holly Divelbis." He and Horner, caught in a do-or-die situation, had decided to call Holly to the stand in this trial, and worry about other trials later—if they happened.

Holly told about the birthday party eight years before Neil died, when Marci was already worried about her son's urinary symptoms.

Holly's testimony was short, simple, and hard to rebut.

That job fell to Mackeson's associate Steve Lindsey, a young attorney who was still mostly working DUIIs and Druggies. Lindsey was a good-looking guy, but he had a babyface, and in what seemed like an attempt to age himself a little, he'd sprouted some stubble around his mouth and chin. But the ultimate result was that he looked like a little boy who'd eaten a chocolate ice cream cone. Lindsey was also prone to saying things like, "That's cool, Judge," instead of, "Yes, Your Honor."

Lindsey eyed Holly and said, "You sat there—at that witness stand—and took an oath to tell the *truth*." In law school, they'd taught him to always end with a question. "Didn't you?"

"I sure did," she said.

"Take that oath seriously?"

Horner objected. Mauer sustained. The first day was done.

CLACKAMAS COUNTY COURTHOUSE
JANUARY 21, 2010

Dr. Cliff Nelson told the jury that when he autopsied Neil, he found the boy's internal organs floating in a gallon of foul yellow liquid, his kidneys bloated and scarred, and his bladder stretched like a water balloon.

The blocked urinary tubes that had triggered Neil's death, Nelson said, were supposed to be about the size of shoestrings, but looked like fat, swollen fingers.

The biochemical measures of Neil's kidney destruction, he said, were "astronomical . . . just mind-boggling." The basic test for kidney function, Nelson told the jury, was a measure of a waste product called BUN, or blood urea nitrogen. In a healthy person, the BUN was between 7 and 20. Kidney failure was indicated by a BUN of 40. Neil's was 288.

Another good test for kidney function, Nelson said, was the measure of the partial-protein called creatine. "The norm for creatine is 1," Nelson said. A person with only one kidney had a level of almost 2. Anything higher than 2 required kidney dialysis. Neil's was 21.

"I've never seen a more complete destruction of a urinary tract," Nelson said. "It's remarkable to me that he lived as long as he did."

Nelson said, though, that Neil could probably have been saved just "minutes before he died."

Next up: a specialist in children's urology, Dr. Edward Guillery, who said he'd never heard of any other child dying from what Neil had.

It would have been relatively easy to save Neil, the doctor said. First, they would have put him on dialysis for three hours every day, to clear out the accumulated poisons. If Neil's urinary system could not be surgically repaired, Guillery said, they would have given him a kidney transplant—at no cost, since his parents had no insurance.

Neil's chances of having a normal life would then have been extraordinarily high. "I have a number of teenage patients who've had transplants," he said. "Some are rodeo champions, and some play baseball competitively. They go on to college, they have families, and they do very well."

Horner took a breath and stared into the faces of the jurors, one at a time.

"Prosecution rests, Your Honor."

The weekend was coming up. Horner would spend it preparing to once again meet Dr. Janice Ophoven.

CLACKAMAS COUNTY COURTHOUSE
JANUARY 25, 2010

Mackeson hoped that Ophoven and the two other docs he'd hired could shoot down the testimony of Horner's doctors. But Horner's docs were, by objective standards, more accomplished—and free. Mackeson's had cost the Defense Fund about $50,000.

Mackeson held off his big guns, and led with a Seattle doctor who just worked in an emergency room. Douglas Diekema, MD, was, however, also an author. He'd written *Christian Faith, Health, & Medical Practice.* That made him more palatable to the Followers, who weren't happy about spending fifty-grand on doctors to keep them from going to doctors.

Diekema spent what seemed like an eternity establishing his credentials. His verbal résumé came to 6,346 words. Then he used about the same number of words to address the facts of the case.

Diekema said that kidney, or renal, disease can sometimes have no symptoms.

"Is renal disease sometimes missed in the ER?" Mackeson asked.

"Probably."

"But not in your ER?"

"No, not in my ER."

It wasn't ideal testimony. He was trying to say he was a good doc but ended up saying that Neil's condition would have been relatively obvious.

Diekema said that he would definitely diagnose kidney failure in any child who had a BUN of 40, and would immediately call in a kidney specialist.

But Neil's BUN was 288, and the jury already knew that. Diekema might not have. He didn't seem well prepared to some of the jurors.

Dr. Diekema was looking like a poor value in the Reasonable Doubt for a Reasonable Fee marketplace.

Horner, looking relaxed and confident, got up for the cross-exam and asked Diekema if he thought that most reasonable parents would take a kid with symptoms like Neil's to the doctor.

"It's difficult for me to say," Diekema responded, "because I don't see the parents who never choose to bring their kids in." It seemed like impenetrable logic. For about one second.

"That's exactly right," Horner said, "isn't it? That's exactly right. Because the kids who don't get taken in, die. Don't they?"

"Eventually."

Exit ER doc. Batting second in the lineup, Dr. Janice Ophoven. She looked as unhealthy and belligerent as she had the last time she'd been in the courthouse.

Ophoven told Mackeson that Neil looked "to the outside, like a healthy adolescent male." She said that Neil was of "normal stature for his age and development," and that he had "good muscle mass and subcutaneous fat."

But those descriptions didn't match photos of Neil, and the claim fell as flat as Ophoven's assertion in the previous trial that Ava Worthington was a fat baby.

Ophoven mentioned a well-known kidney patient who was even smaller than Neil, the deceased child actor Gary Coleman, who was only 4'8" tall. Neil, at 5'5" and 121 pounds, dwarfed him. But the jury did not seem to be impressed. Horner, who did Ophoven's cross-examination, was more interested in the doctor herself than her medical opinions. He asked Ophoven when she had last treated a child. It had been 34 years ago.

Horner asked her how many other doctors made their primary living by testifying in child-abuse cases.

"There's only about ten of us in the world . . . ," she said.

Ophoven, sounding defensive, said that making her living by testifying in trials was simply "the price I pay for participating in the investigation of injuries in children. Every now and then I have to come do this."

"Well," said Horner, "it's a little bit more often than every now and then, isn't it, Doctor?"

"No . . . one year I testified maybe forty times, and other years, two or three times." She said she wasn't ashamed of what she did.

Ophoven was adamant that she didn't always testify in favor of the people who were accused of child abuse.

"In the last three years," Horner said, excluding one trial in Australia, "you've testified 65 times for the defense and none for the prosecution . . . ?"

"Yes."

Horner presented Ophoven's scorecard for the other most recent years. In 2000, it was 18–2 in favor of testifying for the defense. In 2004, it was 34–0. In 2005, it was 30–1.

Ophoven's public dismantling was movie-level drama, and even the skinny, fidgety juror settled down and enjoyed the show.

The last doctor for the defense, David Vandersteen, MD, was actually a working pediatric urologist, but didn't prove to be much of an asset. Dr. Vandersteen tried to make the case that even doctors can overlook serious problems with their own children—because he had. When his daughter was four, he said, she came down with the classic signs of childhood-onset diabetes, including lethargy, stomach aches, headaches, and pain in her eyes. "This went on for months and months," he said, "and I'm a physician, and my wife is a nurse. . . . After six months, I go, 'Let's go to the doctor'—and my daughter had terrible diabetes."

The jury stared holes through him.

Thus ended the Defense Fund's cavalcade of experts.

CLACKAMAS COUNTY COURTHOUSE
JANUARY 26, 2010

Jeff Lewis, Neil's caseworker from the Department of Human Services, took the stand. Lewis, of course, was on the prosecution's side, and Bob Zegar, who was leaning toward conviction, wanted to give Lewis the benefit of the doubt. But this wasn't a good day for that.

Over the weekend, Zegar had gotten a call from his elderly friend Wayne Welch, who had already starved himself down to eighty pounds. Wayne was freaking out. There was a cop in his apartment, threatening to handcuff him and take him to the hospital if he didn't go in voluntarily. One of Wayne's neighbors had ratted him out to DHS, and the agency had quickly flipped the case to the cops.

Wayne, unfortunately, was in a legal gray area. Technically, what he was doing was illegal, even though most Oregon agencies would not have intervened. Oregon was one of the few states with an assisted-suicide law, so Oregonians could legally kill themselves, if a doctor helped them do it. Just plain suicide, without a doctor's help, was also legal—once you were dead. But *attempting* to commit suicide in Oregon—without a note from your doctor—was a crime.

Zegar got on the phone with the cop, who assured Zegar that he would not handcuff Wayne. Just overpower him. One way or another, though, Wayne was going to the hospital.

Zegar rushed over and took Wayne to the hospital himself. A doctor amiably requested that Wayne check in, so they could make him comfortable and pursue his legal suicide.

But Wayne said he'd seen the error of his ways, and would start eating. Once he'd convinced the doctor, Zegar took Wayne home so he could finish killing himself.

But the incident left a bad taste in Zegar's mouth for Big Government, including DHS. And now he was supposed to put people in jail for failing to intervene in the death of a young man who didn't want to go to the doctor.

DHS caseworker Jeff Lewis had been called by the *defense*, though, and Zegar couldn't figure out why.

Rhodes knew why: DHS had screwed up and jeopardized the case against Jeff and Marci. "DHS," Rhodes later said, "fucked us up early on," by what seemed to be their lax attention to Neil. When Lewis went to the Beagleys' place, after Patrick's tip that Neil was very ill, he'd only spent twenty minutes, and basically dropped the case a few days later, partly because he was trying to tiptoe around the Beagleys' religion.

Dropping the case implied that either nothing needed to be done, or that Neil's problem wasn't obvious to trained professionals—so why blame Jeff and Marci for missing it?

If Lewis tried to cover his ass and shift blame onto the cops and courts, he'd still probably look guilty—but so would they—and Big Government would look like every citizen's worst nightmare: Dumb Government and Mean Government. The whole case could unravel.

But Lewis, bless him, took one for the team, and essentially said, We screwed up badly and I feel like hell about it.

It was a miracle. Good government in action.

Lewis' honesty was refreshing, and it turned the tables on Mackeson's attack. There were times, Horner felt, when you could feel a jury shift, and he thought this was one.

But Horner didn't know anything about Bob Zegar's weekend.

The defense had one more big bomb, their best: the parents. The Worthingtons had won mostly because of the jury's identification with Brent and Raylene: as fellow parents, spiritual people, Clackalackians, couples with their own issues about power within the family, and human beings who sometimes made terrible mistakes.

As Jeff Beagley waited to take the stand, Mauer asked the jury to leave while he refereed a fight between Horner and Steve Lindsey. Lindsey wanted to show the jury a veritable family album of photos and videos of Neil—flying over sand dunes in his ATV, running his Bobcat trackhoe, blowing out birthday candles, and living the latter-day pioneer life in a good family, rugged and strong.

"Your Honor," said Horner, "that would be nothing more than a memorial service for him."

Lindsey argued that it showed Neil was a bantamweight brawler up to the end—so when he suddenly died, who could have known?

Lindsey fought hard, and Mauer's evidentiary philosophy tended to tilt toward letting the jury take a peek at the big picture. The memorial service was allowed.

The jury came back in. After almost two years of attacks by the cops, the courts, and the press, it was Jeff's day in court. Looking even more haggard than usual, Jeff started telling the jury about the difficulty of carving out a country life for a wife, three daughters, and a son. It meant getting your hands dirty—really dirty, since he was a port-a-potty entrepreneur—and sometimes working far from home while Neil held down the fort. Jeff described their "little wagon train" of trailers in outback-Clackalack, and when he noticed the obvious admiration of several jurors, he warmed up to the subject and relived better days. He told them about taking on white-water rivers, sand mountains, and elk-filled forests with Neil by his side in work and play, even when Neil was "a little bitty kid." He told them about the Camaro, the dream house, the camaraderie, and the magnificent meals in Mother Nature. It had a loud ring of truth, especially with pictures flashing overhead of the Northwest American Dream.

Family life, Jeff said, was quiet and close, with "a swing in the backyard and a little dog."

Jeff said Neil was gifted with his hands, but "hardly ever wanted to go to school." He didn't mention Neil's early abandonment of the school system, resulting from his excessive absences due to illness.

Religion was the family's anchor, Jeff said, and yes—they did trust God even more than the AMA. "We try to rely on God as much as we possibly can, hold to our faith if we can, and if not, we end up at the hospital." Although, no, they'd never actually gone to the hospital. But that proved their approach *worked*.

Cue Ava's death. Bring it up before the prosecution did. "How," Steve Lindsey asked, "did that affect you emotionally?"

Jeff started to cry, as in: *That's* how it affected me. "Sorry," Jeff said. "Just a minute." Lindsey was in no rush. Jeff composed himself and said, "It affected me pretty hard. We was pretty close."

It was excellent testimony—heartfelt and endearing, with just enough bad grammar to show that Jeff was a reasonable parent but not an MD. Jeff did mention that Neil was headstrong, hard to talk to, stoic, determined to hold fast to the faith, old enough to make his own decisions, and pretty much as healthy as a horse until he got his runny nose and died.

Lindsey handed Jeff a home-school essay Neil had written about the person he most admired. Jeff read from it: "'My dad is a hardworking man. He tries to set good examples for me. He has taught me many skills that may be helpful in my future. My dad always puts his family before himself . . . .'" Jeff began to cry.

"Do you love your son?" Lindsey asked.

"Yes, I did."

"I have nothing further."

It was Horner's turn. He asked Jeff about telling Jim Band that they only laid on hands when somebody was really sick.

"I don't remember saying that."

"Was it just a coincidence," Horner asked, "that you stayed up all night with Neil the night before he died?"

"I guess it was, if you want to look at it that way."

"Did you actually carry him to the bathroom?"

"I did carry him," Jeff said. "It was kind of funny." It wasn't entirely a joke, though, Jeff added, because, "He said his knee bothered him."

Horner asked Jeff when he'd last done that, and Jeff said it was ten years ago.

Bob Zegar was struck by the image of Neil in his father's arms. Neil sounded pretty sick.

Horner asked Jeff about telling Band that Neil changed dramatically just before he died—when Neil had said, "I want you to know I love you, Dad."

"I don't remember him saying that."

"You don't remember that?"

"No," Jeff said—a denial that Jim Band, who was watching, found particularly disgusting.

Horner brought up Ava. "You had been through the same thing with your granddaughter that you loved. She also died without anybody lifting a finger, as far as getting medical care, isn't that right?"

"Judge, I object," Steve Lindsey said. "He's got no obligation to his granddaughter."

"The objection's overruled," Mauer said.

As Neil struggled for life, Horner asked, wasn't Jeff thinking: "'Gosh, what about what happened to Ava?'"

"Well," said Jeff, "*He* wasn't fighting for breath." For emphasis: "*He* wasn't fighting for breath. It's just like if you have the flu."

Horner asked Jeff if he would do the same thing again.

Jeff said he would take Neil to the hospital, if Neil asked to go. Then he suddenly recanted. He said he'd talk to Marci about it, and if they both thought Neil needed to go, they'd go.

"You've never said that to anybody before just now, have you, Mr. Beagley? Not to Detective Band? Ever?"

"Not to them." Again, the emphasis. "Not to them. Not to *them*."

"You told them you were following *Neil's* wishes."

"I was following his wishes, yes." Jeff was back where he started.

"Thank you, Your Honor, I have no further questions."

CLACKAMAS COUNTY COURTHOUSE
JANUARY 28, 2010

Marci told the jury it was thrilling to have a son. She described Neil's raw vitality, his kindness to his sisters, devotion to his father, and rebellion against school. She lyricized about family gatherings under the Christmas tree, outings at the pumpkin patch, the zoo, the lakes, and the parks, and about making Valentines.

Steve Lindsey asked generally intelligent questions—except for "Is Katie's birthday in May *every* year?" He was letting Marci keep a lid on her emotions—until just the right time.

According to Marci, Neil had risen each day like the morning star, had granted pageantry to the family's ordinary life, and glory to its sacrifices. Neil had offered all of them kindness and support—even without words—that had surpassed the limitations of conventional family relationships, and now lived beyond the boundary of death.

Horner and Mygrant, on edge, were waiting for her big scene. With good direction from her attorneys, Marci's meltdown would not reveal the negative side of her personality—superior and selfish—but would showcase the sentimentality of a classic Grieving Mother.

Presented properly, a mom's broken heart and hot tears could touch off primal waves of sympathy that would make rational thought seem cold and callous. Horner and Mygrant would just have to ride it out and cut it as short as possible.

Their chance to reveal the true acts and identity of Marci Beagley would be in cross-examination—when they could control the rhythm, timing, and content—and hopefully touch off an explosion of her condescension and self-involvement. That would inevitably include tears, though, and they weren't sure what they would do when that happened. Back off, to minimize sympathy? Or keep pushing, until she went over the edge and *showed* the jury the truth, even if she wouldn't speak it?

Mackeson, taking over from Lindsey, walked Marci through her last days with Neil, creating an image of her as a doting mother who worked day and night to keep Neil safe and happy. Marci inched toward the moment of death, her voice increasingly tight and breathy. "Neil said he was tired and wanted to rest," she said, "and said, 'Don't wake me up to feed me.'"

"So you're sort of doing the hovering-mother thing?" Mackeson asked.

"Yeah."

"And what happened?"

"I went in to lay down." She stopped. Swallowed. Tears sat in her eyes. Here it came. "And when I got up, and I went back in there, he had. Stopped. Breathing." Her head dropped and she began to weep.

Several jurors suddenly teared-up, and the woman with red hair shook her head. It seemed to be all that Mackeson needed. He stopped abruptly.

Mygrant took over.

Treading carefully, Mygrant got Marci to admit that she'd gone to the doctor for hangnails and birth control pills. Marci even flipped on her mom, and told Mygrant that her mother had gone to the doctor to fix a scar on her face.

Mygrant asked her about Neil's near-fatal illness in March, shortly before his final illness in June. She admitted that she had been more worried about him in March than ever before.

Did she think Neil might die?

"Possibly."

"Because his throat was closing up?"

"No."

"Then why was it?"

"Because he was sick." She suddenly began to cry. Mygrant instinctively backed off. He called for a recess—which made him look compassionate—and got the jury out as fast as possible.

When they resumed, he asked Marci about the last night of Neil's life. Did she think Neil was dying then?

Flat denial.

Mygrant asked Marci if she would have taken Neil to the doctor on the night he died.

"If he had felt he needed it and wanted to, yes."

"You felt he needed to, didn't you?"

"I did in March . . . . He didn't seem as sick in June."

But Neil couldn't lift his arms, or get out of bed, Mygrant said, and he'd been vomiting for a week.

"*He* was telling me he was *fine*," said Marci. She was putting her tears into battle position. It was time for the reveal.

For Horner and Mygrant, this was the moment of truth. All of the seemingly endless effort that had gone into trying to stop the Followers of Christ Church from committing child homicide and abuse suddenly seemed compacted into this time and place. They had so much to lose.

Horner and Mygrant had worked years to get to this moment, and so had Band, Finn, Rhodes, Band's snitch, and Rita Swan. It was go-time. Or give up.

Mygrant stepped up to her.

Neil said he was fine? "You're the *mother*," Mygrant snapped. It was an accusation, conveyed with utter disdain.

"He'll be okay."

"*You're* the *mother*, Mrs. Beagley." Mygrant said it plaintively, embodying the identity of his client: Neil Jeffrey Beagley.

"*I* know that." Neil's presence, more than at any other time, hovered in the courtroom.

"It's *your* call." Mygrant had become Neil. Bob Zegar and other jurors could feel the eerie transformation.

But Marci could not. To her, Mygrant was the devil. She looked enraged and confused. The jury wanted to see grief and certainty.

Wasn't she worried her son would *die*, Mygrant asked, when he couldn't *walk* and his stomach was empty even of *water*?

"No."

Did she remember Rhodes asking her if she was afraid Neil would die?

"*No.*" She looked at Mygrant with hateful condescension, and seemed somehow to feel as if this reflected her superiority in a way that others would understand.

Mygrant read her the interview that showed she did fear Neil was dying.

Marci, flustered, said that she was afraid that Neil might die every time he went fishing.

But what about the night he *did* die?

"*I* didn't believe he was going to die," Marci said, "or I wouldn't have went and laid down."

The tears came.

But this time they were cold tears, coming out of angry eyes, dripping down a face that held hate she couldn't hide.

They did not look like tears for Neil. They looked like tears for Marci.

"No more questions, Your Honor," Mygrant said.

Mygrant headed back to his desk, shedding the identity of Neil Jeffrey Beagley as he walked.

CLACKAMAS COUNTY COURTHOUSE
JANUARY 29, 2010

Steve Mygrant, standing before the jury to give his closing statement, wasn't as debonair as Mackeson or as senatorial as Judge Mauer, and he didn't exude Greg Horner's sense of bottled-up energy. Even so, Mygrant's physical presence in front of a jury was riveting. Mygrant projected the same quality that Neil Beagley had: He seemed like a guy who was tougher than he looked.

Jim Band, like all cops, often bitched about DAs who caved in too quickly on plea deals, or tossed tough cases without even trying. But several times after Band had worked cases with Mygrant, he'd gone back to the station and told his colleagues, "You guys think that nobody ever fights. *Steve* fights."

Mygrant made eye contact with every juror, something he'd learned from Horner. "This case," he said, "is about trying to be perfect. It's about trying not to have lack of faith. That's why Jeff Beagley was proud of his son—because Neil held onto his faith until the very end. And that's why Marci Beagley wouldn't have done anything differently: because this is what Neil wanted."

However, Mygrant said, Neil didn't die from some profound spiritual belief, but from a profound yearning to make his parents proud.

The decision that led to Neil's death, he said, should never have landed in Neil's own lap. His parents should have made it for him. "It's their duty. It's their obligation. It's their responsibility."

The Beagleys, he said, began to engage in criminal behavior the day before Neil died. "That's when the food journal stops. He's not taking in food . . . or liquid. It's ominous. That silence," Mygrant said, "is the loudest thing in the case. It coincided with the dramatic decline."

For over an hour, working almost entirely from memory, Mygrant reviewed the details of the medical evidence. It showed that Neil was born with a minor problem, one that was neglected until it destroyed his urinary system, and finally killed him. No other boy in the history of American medicine had died from the defect that Neil had. They had all gotten treatment.

"What would a reasonable person do under the circumstances?" Mygrant concluded. "That's the question I want you to ask yourself. You set the community standard. Nobody there said, 'Enough!'

"We're asking you. Can *you* say, 'Enough'?"

Before Mackeson's closing, during the lunch break, the usual large crowd of Followers gathered in the lobby, looking unremarkable except for their numbers. It was unheard of for anyone in the Clackamas criminal courts to have an entourage. Most people were ashamed to be there.

The Followers, as usual, were chatting animatedly among themselves, but in a virtually nonverbal way, born of decades of intimate communication, and designed for confidentiality. When someone from the world came within hearing range, the conversations became even more impenetrable. So it was unusual that the worldly woman sitting next to Marci and her mom overheard most of what they were saying.

Marci, it seemed, was not only frightened, but was devastated that every day she was portrayed in the press as a wicked woman who had let her only son die. Marci had spent her whole life trying to become indifferent to the opinions of the worldly, but it was hard. Nobody likes to be hated. Marci's mom, Sandra Mitchell, had been looking for a way to help.

"Marci," Sandra said, "I was reading the Bible this morning, and I came upon this passage. It's about *you*, and what you're going through. It said, 'If the world hates you, remember that it hated me first.' Know who said that? *Jesus*."

Marci smiled and nodded knowingly. "That's how it is," she said.

It made the worldly woman's skin crawl. How could a mother on trial for the death of her son compare herself to Jesus?

Marci noticed that they were being overheard, and turned to the woman. "Do I know you?" she asked imperiously.

Rita Swan shook her head, and Marci lost interest.

Rita had come to Oregon to dismantle what was left of the state's shield law.

After everything Rita had done, the Followers were still letting their kids die, and still feeling superior about it. One of them needed to go to jail for a long, long time. She'd known that for years, but had never before felt its urgency so deeply.

When the jury was seated again, Wayne Mackeson began his closing statement. "So. Who are the Beagleys? . . . Are they really the religious fanatics that they've been made out to be? Are they really the ignorant people they've been made out to be?"

Mackeson reminded the jurors of the Beagleys' spotless record, their All-American lifestyle, their love for their children, and their tragic losses of Neil and Ava. The Beagleys didn't spot Neil's problem in time to save him, he said, but neither did DHS, which specialized in protecting kids from harm. When DHS did ask Neil if he wanted to go to a doctor: "Neil said, 'no—my mom already asked me that question.'"

Neil's death, Mackeson said, couldn't be blamed on just what happened at the end of his life, because Neil's congenital condition, enlarged heart, and fluid build-up "didn't happen in the last week, but over sixteen-plus years."

The Beagleys didn't ignore Neil's problems, he said—they just didn't fully understand them. That could happen to any parent—including even Dr. Vandersteen, who didn't recognize his own daughter's diabetes.

And if Jeff Beagley really did say that Neil had expressed his love just before he died, "How do we draw a bad inference out of *that*? When did that become a bad thing?"

When Neil's heart gave out, it wasn't from a heart attack—which could be noticed—but from a silent disruption of heart rhythm. "He just stopped breathing," Mackeson said.

"This isn't about what a reasonable physician would do," Mackeson said. "It's about what a reasonable *parent* would do in this situation." Mackeson argued that, "You can screw up as a parent and still be reasonable."

"The real issue," Mackeson said, "was whether what happened was a gross deviation—whether it was so outrageous, so beyond the pale, that these two people should be labeled as criminals."

Mackeson said it wasn't.

"Parents make mistakes," Mackeson said. Therefore, "There's only one *just* result in this case—not guilty."

CLACKAMAS COUNTY COURTHOUSE
JANUARY 29, 2010

The juror who seemed to think he was JFK again volunteered for the position of foreman, but he wanted it so much that nobody wanted to give it to him. That might have been a mistake, Bob Zegar thought, because the guy started sulking. He might turn into a perpetual naysayer, and keep them from reaching the ten votes out of twelve that they needed for a verdict.

The technical writer got the job instead, but almost immediately lost control of the room. The jury had little cohesion, because there were only a couple of hardcore O.C.ers, and no other intrinsic cliques. The preview vote was 8–4 for conviction, but even the not-guilty bloc had disparate, Clackastani mind-sets. One of them, the redhead, was a religious zealot—a surprise, since she hadn't revealed that at selection. The college teacher tended to overthink things and wanted to err on the side of mercy. The skinny, jittery guy just didn't like cops and courts. He thought they saw everybody as guilty until proven innocent. And JFK was still sulking.

Then one of the two younger women—a blonde, who seemed like kind of a party girl to Amy Slatford—went off on a monologue about having to go to jail if somebody at her house slipped in the shower. Slatford, Zegar, and the professor got frustrated. Building to her primary point, the blonde said, "And what if that was *your* grandmother who slipped?"

The skinny guy said he got where she was headed.

Zegar stayed out of it and jotted down the primary issues: Reasonable people. Medical testimony. DHS involvement. Marci's lack of power. Possible lies. Parental pressure.

He stuck it to a corkboard, and the redhead added: Religious persecution. And: Neil made his own decision.

The professor was also interested in the religious-freedom issue, and began a lecture that was cut short by the foreman, who said they'd been ordered to disregard freedom of religion, as well as Neil's legal right to make his own medical decisions.

The day ended in the middle of a debate about teenage rights, then teens in general. They had gotten nowhere.

It was Friday, and they all looked forward to a respite—not from work, but from each other.

February 1, 2010

Most of the jurors thought that the prosecution's doctors had made stronger points. Dr. Ophoven hadn't made a good impression on several of them. Some thought she was just in it for the money.

Also, another of the defense doctors had mentioned that he hadn't read the medical evidence until he was on the plane to Portland. He should have kept that to himself.

The redhead stood up for Ophoven, and started raising her voice. She seemed to feel surrounded by a pack of heathens.

Slatford said she was troubled about the fact that Neil's condition had existed for so long. At what point, she wondered, could you suddenly say: *Now* is the time for the parents to provide treatment.

"That would be when Jeff had to carry Neil to the bathroom," Zegar said.

"Or when he threw up every bite he ate," said the TSA employee.

"But somebody said he just had the *flu*," said the skinny guy. He looked like he'd had a hard weekend.

On the other hand, Slatford said, the animals at her vet clinic got better care than Neil had.

They voted again and it was still 8–4.

The redhead kept bringing it back to religion. Why would someone think, she asked rhetorically, that Jesus could heal with the laying
on of hands, but nobody else could?

"Well, for one thing," said Zegar, "he was *Jesus*." The blonde,
who'd been voting not guilty, agreed.

As the day wound down, the skinny guy yawned widely, and that
was a mistake. Several jurors saw his black molars, and stole glances at
each other. Was that *meth mouth*? People saw that once in a while in
Clackalackie. It would explain a few things.

The redhead tried to make the case that if Neil's problem was obvious, DHS would have seen it. But the consensus was that the young
DHS social worker had been in over his head, and was honest enough
to admit it at the trial.

The not-guilty coalition was running out of steam.

There was a move to convict Jeff, but let Marci off. Amy Slatford—
who said what she believed, whether or not it supported her side—said
she thought Marci was brainwashed.

"She *was* brainwashed," said Zegar. "And so was Jeff. And probably
a whole lot of those people. So this might happen again. It's up to us to
make it stop."

The blond woman drifted off into thought, and when she came
back, she said she was ready to change her vote.

"Let's vote *again*," said the skinny guy. He seemed anxious to get
out of there, once and for all. There was just enough time to do it before the day was done.

THE CLACKAMAS COUNTY COURTHOUSE
FEBRUARY 2, 2010

Word shot around the courthouse that the jury had reached a verdict
the day before, just prior to the recess.

In the courtroom, the attorneys hammered out a few last-minute
matters, with the jury absent. Several of the Followers women—not

interested in these details, but only the climactic moment—quietly left the courtroom and caucused in the ladies' restroom, jubilant, sensing victory, planning the party.

"I say we hold it at Claim Jumper," one of the women said. "It was Neil's favorite."

"Burgerville was Neil's favorite," said a younger woman.

"I don't want to go to a fast-food place," said the older woman. She started talking about the big desserts at Claim Jumper.

A female employee of the district attorney's office, in one of the stalls, started to blurt out something angry, but stopped. The Followers' arrogance and selfishness was good. It would help bring them down.

"Before we bring the jury in, ladies and gentlemen," said Judge Mauer, "all persons must refrain from visibly or audibly reacting to the verdict in a manner which disrupts the courtroom."

Mauer took the verdict form from the bailiff. He read Jeff's first. "We hereby find the defendant guilty of the charge of criminally negligent homicide."

He read Marci's verdict. She was guilty, too.

Jeff and Marci Beagley would both be going to state prison for sixteen months, after a short stay in Clackatraz.

Several of the Followers women wept. Marci began to cry, but Jeff didn't reach out to her.

Bob Zegar didn't look at Jeff and Marci, because he didn't want to have that image of pain stuck in his mind. He looked at the jurors, three of whom were crying, and at the Followers in the gallery, who stared at him with contempt.

Zegar tried to get away from the courtroom without being noticed, but KATU's Dan Tilkin saw him, and asked him to go on camera.

Tilkin asked Zegar if he'd known that *several* other children in the Church had died.

"Not just Ava?" He wished that he had looked at Jeff and Marci.

THE HIGHLAND STILLHOUSE PUB
FEBRUARY 2, 2010, 9:30 P.M.

The Stillhouse Pub, with an ambience that fell somewhere between that of a proper Scottish pub and the basement drinking room of a frat house, was getting dangerously raucous by O.C. standards, but management had nothing to fear, because it was the cops and DAs who were raising hell. The people from the courthouse thought nobody knew who they were, but most people did. It was a big day in Clackalackie history.

The pub, nestled between Willamette Falls and a greenspace that had been named Waterboard Park long before that became ironic, had the largest selection of single-malt Scotch in the Portland metro area, and 95 bottles of beer on the wall that the law enforcers were trying to sample as thoroughly as possible.

Band and Rhodes were there, but Michelle Finn was in Quantico at the FBI Academy. She'd heard about the verdict, and was sorry she'd missed it.

Mygrant was also at the crowded table, much more relaxed than usual, and Horner, at the head of the table, looked as if a terrible burden had been lifted off him.

Band felt good for Horner. For almost two years, Horner had been trying to win what no district attorney in America ever had: three convictions in faith-healing abuse cases against a locally powerful church, in a community that was extremely ambivalent about prosecution.

"Everything about this case," Band later said, "had been very hush-hush, and we'd had to be quiet about it the whole time. It was too controversial, and too hard. I'd heard Horner and Mygrant talk, after losing the Worthington case, about driving to work every day over the I-5 bridge knowing that Beagley was an even bigger challenge.

"I've worked a lot of cases with Horner, and I know Greg very well. He's quiet, very quiet, and somber, and very measured in everything he says. But then this verdict came in, and there we were at the pub, and Greg was as loud as anybody at the table—just giddy, like a guy that I've never, ever seen."

Some toasts were made, Scotch bottles drained, and war stories told. Other officers showed up, and so did DAs who weren't involved in the case, and even the head district attorney, John Foote—Horner's boss ever since they'd moved from Multnomah County to Clacka-mas. Foote had shepherded both of the Followers cases, even though they'd threatened to cost him reelection.

At the height of the celebration, the noisy table of cops and DAs was interrupted. "There was this moment," Band later recalled, "when some Joe-Bob Citizen comes up to the table and goes, 'Hey, congratulations, you guys, that was a great case.' And there was this pause. Sudden silence. Like, oh *shit*, we've been talking loud enough for everybody in the bar to hear. We all kind of looked at each other. Everything in the pub seemed to freeze.

"But it was *okay*! We could talk about it now. It wasn't a secret anymore." The whole bar erupted. People bought them drinks.

"That was the best moment I'd had," James Rhodes later said, "since it started."

Horner was thrilled with the victory. But mostly he was relieved. The pleasure of this moment wasn't equal to the pain he'd felt after Worthington, when it looked as if they'd just made things worse.

But tomorrow when he'd drive over the bridge, he wouldn't be thinking about the goddamn Beagley case. He'd be thinking about Dale and Shannon Hickman—and about the baby they'd let die. What had they named him? Not Dale. No. David. Why bury a good family name with a dead kid?

Now that Horner had won the Beagley case, he might be able to go after the Hickmans. The case against them had gotten much stronger recently. Band's informant now thought he knew who was harboring a pivotal piece of evidence—the videotape of the baby's death night. The guy was amazing. He kept hitting home runs, time after time, al-though Band said that every time his snitch had to inform on one of his friends, it took a chunk out of his soul, no matter how right he knew it was.

The Hickman case, which would be prosecuted as a homicide—*if* Horner could get an arrest—was looming as the linchpin. The conviction of the Hickmans, with the maximum possible sentence applied, would be monumental.

How many kids would that save? Over the years? Across the country?

There was no way to know. A victory like that could roll across America from ocean to mountain and beyond. A victory like that had no boundaries.

But once again: lose, and the whole thing falls apart. Convicting bad guys was easy. Changing history was hard.

OREGON AND IOWA
FEBRUARY 2, 2010, 11:00 P.M.

Patrick stayed up for the KATU news. Paul sat on his lap, touching his father's face with his soft little-boy hands and speaking in almost full sentences. Patrick already knew about the verdict. He just wanted to see it with his son. Then they would say "The Family Prayer," and he would tuck Paul in with his teddy bear, say good-night to his sister, and try not to think about Theresa. Instead, he'd focus on the people he was trying to help, and the ideas he was trying to spread.

Rita Swan, back in her hilltop Iowa home, in another time zone— the only person in America who fully comprehended the national importance of this case—was already sleeping, peacefully. The Beagley verdict had brought her more than relief, or even joy: It had brought deeper meaning than ever to a life of too much sacrifice.

When she later heard that Marci Beagley received the same sentence Jeff did, she was gratified. Many other fundamentalist mothers had been acquitted of similar crimes, she later said, "on the presumption that the husband was the divinely ordained lord of the household."

Life had been good lately. Rita had, working virtually alone, as always, won the battle against the government paying for prayer in Obamacare. Empowered only by her passion and persistence, pouring her heart into her work, she'd prevailed once more against some of the most powerful people in America, proving yet again that work is the great equalizer: It humbles the exalted and exalts the humble.

She was also hopeful now that Horner would have the necessary momentum to prosecute Dale and Shannon Hickman, and win decisively. If he could, it would mark the greatest achievement in her life.

Even with a major victory in the Hickman case, though, she knew her mission would never end. That was a vow she'd made, to herself and her son, long ago. Even so, after today, which had ended so happily, her mission would never again feel quite so lonely.

OREGON CITY
FEBRUARY 3, 2010, 7:00 A.M.

Bob Zegar, unable to sleep, walked to his neighborhood park in the gray fog after a late dawn, and sat in the playground, alone. He went to that park a lot, because his grandchildren played there, and he knew all the kids. "I'm like the Pied Piper down there," he later said.

He went to his favorite bench, breathed in the wet winter air, and shivered as cold tears sat on his cheeks.

A woman with a dog came over. "You're that guy from the trial, aren't you?"

Zegar, his face still chilled with tears, nodded.

"Well, God bless you," she said.

He couldn't say anything.

"Are you alright?"

"I had a friend," Zegar said. "And he died this weekend."

She reached out and put her hand on his shoulder.

"God bless."

The W. B. Market
Oregon City
March 2010

Rebecca Wyland, picking up some groceries at the small store that the Prophet had once owned, was pushing her baby, soon to be her toddler, in a stroller. Rebecca didn't take little Alayna out very often, not even to church, although there was a special section in the church for moms with babies. It was at the back of the main hall, so that moms could leave the room easily if their babies started fussing.

A woman from the world, next to Rebecca in the produce section, looked down at Alayna's tiny feet, sticking out of the blanket that covered the rest of her.

"So sweet," the woman said. "Can I take a peek?"

Rebecca smiled but shook her head. "She's asleep."

"I won't wake her up," the woman whispered.

She bent and gently pulled the blanket off Alayna's face.

"Oh my Lord! What happened to her?"

18

TENDER MERCIES

The tender mercies of the wicked are cruel.

—THE BOOK OF PROVERBS 12:10

BEAVERCREEK, OREGON
MARCH 2010

Alayna Wyland's face, which would become known in the media as The True Face of Faith Healing, was rarely noticed in her hometown of Beavercreek—4.8 miles from O.C., and a mile from the Followers' Cemetery—but only because it's hard to get noticed for almost anything in the still largely unsettled Wild East of Clackatucky.

Beavercreek is so isolated, clannish, and quirky that it's considered rude there to know your neighbors. The folks next door might be older people who value privacy, or world-class eccentrics, or one of the town's many Followers families. They might even be a subset of the spooky, slow-moving country folk who seemed to study every passerby for either signs of familiarity, or threat. Beavercreek is the Christmas-tree capital of the world, but most of the money from that industry leaves town, while the locals make their livings more creatively. Many people with small acreages breed and crossbreed exotic animals, such as Tennessee Fainting Goats, emus, bison, camels, alpacas, zebras, Brahma bulls, and other outsized cattle that are beefed up with anabolic steroids. People even deeper in the woods are known to cultivate a strain of medical marijuana known as God Bud, which is intended primarily for use against autoimmune disorders with psychiatric features, such as Addison's disease, as well as chronic situational anxiety among the patient population that doctors call the worried-well. Some black-market farmers also secretly sell the much more highly controlled substance of hormone-free raw milk, considered a curative by its advocates but a source of E-coli by authorities.

The sheriff's office handles hundreds of callouts on the animals every year—usually for neglect, often quite cruel—but the pot growers and renegade dairy farmers have fewer conceits about the legality of their enterprises, and keep lower profiles.

Although the retail hub of Beavercreek consists of only a general store, a gas station, a pet-grooming business, and Buffalo Bill's Saloon, the town has ten rural churches, some as idiosyncratic as the New Martyrs of Russia Orthodox Church, the Ten O'Clock Church, and the Free Will Baptist Church, while others are more mainstream, including the two other Baptist churches and the Bible Chapel. The hamlet's fragmented population dissects its religiosity with extreme attention to doctrinal detail, and there's no such thing as a local council of churches.

There are also five recognized pioneer cemeteries, and several private family plots, including one for the dwindling Moehnke family, which is nearing the end of its genetic reign on earth. The last of the Moehnkeans is a tough and funny old man who works in the general store and tends the family cemetery, but doesn't want to be buried there, because of bad memories. He doesn't like the idea of cremation, either. When asked, he says he wants to be microwaved.

Beavercreek, like nearby Estacada, also occasionally attracts rugged individualists of a darker nature. Disgraced Olympic skater Tonya Harding lived there shortly before she took out a contract on Nancy Kerrigan's leg, and Gary Gilmore lived peacefully to the near-north before he became a famously executed murderer in Utah.

But step back from the lonely and disjointed puzzle pieces of the

Beavercreek area and a mosaic emerges of shocking seductiveness: varicolored blossoms almost too beautiful to be real, aromatic fragrances of every variety, breezes whispering down from glacial Mt. Hood, and a sense of softness born of perennial moisture and fertility, inhabited by salt-of-the-earth Americans who mind their own business, but still come through in a crisis.

Partly because people in this version of God's Country don't pry, it wasn't until early February, when Alayna Wyland was two months old, that someone outside the family first noticed the thing on her face, back when it was still fairly small. It was a woman from the world, who said, "Oh, my daughter had one of those. It's a strawberry mark. They go away." That was good to know, because Rebecca was worried. At Alayna's birth, the growth had been just a little red dot on her left eyelid, but by the time the worldly woman saw it, Alayna's eyelid was swollen.

Over the next couple of weeks the strawberry mark got even bigger. When Tim's sister Jaime saw it, she told Rebecca that she had one, too, but it was hidden by her hair. Jaime said her dad had also had one, on his leg, and it had once become swollen—but went away.

In late February, Alayna's strawberry mark started to ooze slightly, and Rebecca got in the habit of tenderly wiping the baby's eye every time she changed her diaper. She and Tim prayed about it and anointed it with olive oil. They didn't consider taking Alayna to a doctor, of course, because neither of them had ever been to a doctor, and they didn't want to threaten Alayna's eye with lack of faith. They had a computer, but didn't research strawberry marks. Even that showed a certain lack of faith. The safest thing was to hold fast to the Word.

Tim, 44, had stayed in the Word even during the death of his first wife, Monique. After that act of God, it had taken until 2008 for Tim to find someone else. He was not a great-looking guy, with a slack face and black, slicked-back hair that stuck to the top of his head, almost like a melted phonograph record. Rebecca, 22, soft-featured and busty, with full lips and shiny brown hair, was a good catch for Tim.

In March, the strawberry mark started to cover Alayna's eye, and Tim called the family together to lay on hands. It was an aggressive step. But Tim hated the idea that somehow a devil had entered his innocent daughter. The strawberry mark kept Alayna from looking as cute as she otherwise would, so they stopped taking her out much, especially after that time in the W. B. Market when the busybody in the produce section saw Alayna and freaked out.

But staying inside their rambling new ranch house with its white rail fence gave them more time with Alayna. She was the first child for both of them, and they lavished her with love. Every day Alayna seemed to find new ways to express her delight in their care and comfort.

In May, when Alayna was four months old, the strawberry mark, by then scabbed and ulcerated, covered her eye completely and blocked its vision.

It looked scary and dangerous. Tim and Rebecca desperately needed help. So on May 13th, they took Alayna to church, and asked the brethren to remember her in their prayers.

OREGON CITY
JUNE 17, 2010

The Beagley verdict in February had hit the Church like a bomb. People were changing, and becoming much more open to the ideas that Patrick was spreading. It made sense to him. The Followers, he thought, had finally realized that they couldn't get away with virtual murder—so they'd changed.

It also made *no* sense to him. At *all*. Why did the Followers let so many of their loved ones die, then suddenly reverse course? Just to avoid *county jail*?

Patrick—divorced from the Followers' group-think—was increasingly mystified by life. But Ella said that was how it was supposed to be. As you get wiser, she said, you see how mysterious life really is. Only the young and dumb, she said, indulged in certainty.

Ella, with her seemingly permanent smile, believed that mystery led naturally to hope, and she considered hope sacred—almost synonymous with faith. The only difference, she said, was that when you had hope, instead of faith, you didn't sit on your ass and expect God to be your butler.

The phone in Patrick's family room rang. It was one of his small group of friends who was starting to doubt the Church. Patrick had previously given this man some meds for his chronic lung infections, and had finally talked him into going to a doctor. Then the guy had convinced his brother, who had MS, to get it treated.

"There's something you need to know," the caller said. "I was at church today, and saw this awful thing on Tim and Becca's little girl. My daughter saw it and started to cry."

Patrick got the details and called the DHS child-abuse hotline. It was premature to call Jim, because no obvious crime had been committed, and calling the police would violate the standard process for a noncriminal situation. Government, he'd learned, loved process.

For two days Patrick phoned people in his spy network. Nobody from DHS, though, went out to Beavercreek. He called DHS again. They told him that they were processing the report, and would proceed accordingly.

Patrick called Marie and asked her to file a separate report, to get something happening. Then he asked another friend to do the same, to trigger the agency's urgent-response system. That was *his* process.

Pushing DHS was dangerous, though, because Patrick, of all people, was now the subject of a report himself. An anonymous caller had told DHS that Patrick was a member of the crazy Followers Church, and wasn't taking his son to a doctor. A caseworker came out, and opened a file on him. Patrick could have told the caseworker that he was a double agent in the Church, doing everything he could to promote medical care and change ideology, but he didn't trust DHS. Old habit. Instead, Patrick told the caseworker that he didn't object to medical care at all, that Paul had all his vaccinations, had never been sick, and was too old, at almost two-and-a-half, to need well-baby checks. He didn't mention that he'd once treated Paul with antibiotics purchased on the Net. He was afraid that constituted practicing medicine without a license, which was a Class A felony, punishable by twenty years in prison.

If the Followers were out to get him, they could probably force at least a couple of families to testify against him, because they specialized in peer pressure. And some of the people he'd tried to help had still died, even after they'd gone to a doctor. Medicine had its limits, more than he'd imagined. Doctors were great at some things, he found, including emergency medicine, and a number of issues often involving kids—birth, broken bones, and bacterial infections. But it was overrated for the things that most often destroyed lives—cancer, cardiovascular disease, diabetes, Alzheimer's, and arthritis. Most people, Patrick thought, were afraid to face their stark vulnerability to death and disease, though, so they invested doctors with godlike powers that they didn't really have, and the more money people spent, the safer they felt. That was fine with doctors, but it had made modern American medicine sometimes seem like a quasi-religion itself.

Patrick was almost certain that the snitch who'd flipped on him was somebody from church. There were so many wild rumors about him—mostly among the women who were still in touch with Theresa, he thought—that he skipped services most of the time. When he did go, he usually got into arguments with people who thought it was blasphemous to even discuss being reasonable about doctors.

It could even have been Theresa who'd turned him in. She still hadn't filed for divorce, but he was sure she would. So far, she hadn't asked him to send Paul back to Idaho, but he thought that was just because she was seeing someone, and was ashamed.

He waited two more days for something to happen with Alayna. Nothing did.

He'd never been in so much jeopardy, but he had to do as much for Alayna as he possibly could. Even more was at stake than one girl's eyesight. This case might be the final showdown in his mission to change the Church, and if it succeeded, it would validate his life. It would probably trigger change elsewhere, bringing peace to people who'd suffered from the same evils he had, invariably inflicted in the name of God.

Finally, on June 27th, he made the call.

"Lieutenant Band, your friend from church is on the line."

BEAVERCREEK
JUNE 29, 2010

After a family vacation in Yellowstone Park, Tim and Rebecca were overjoyed to return to their Beavercreek home on Leland Road, just down from Tonya Court. It was the first sunny week of the year, after an especially dismal spring, and the air itself was a drifting perfume of flowers, carrying unfamiliar summer smells.

There was a message on their machine. It was from DHS: "We have an open child-abuse assessment, and need to come out and talk to the family."

Tim called them right away. DHS said they'd had several anonymous reports about Alayna. But they'd had a separate report from the Oregon City Police Department, so instead of sending out a social worker, they would be sending out someone from the Sheriff's Office. Right now.

Tim kept a lid on his emotions, called his older sister, and she, her husband, and Tim's dad came out immediately. They waited nervously in the living room.

At 7:00 p.m. Sheriff's Deputy Emile Burley rolled up with another cop. Tim welcomed them in and offered them water. Burley, a veteran who'd seen just about everything, was jolted by Alayna's face. Something was sticking out of her eye that looked like a red golf ball. In proportion to her tiny face, it looked huge.

He asked Rebecca, holding Alayna, what she had been doing for the growth.

"Keeping it clean, anointing it, and praying," Rebecca said.

"Have you considered medical attention?" he asked.

"No."

He told Rebecca that a paramedic needed to look at Alayna, to determine if she was in immediate danger.

Firefighter and paramedic Matthew Stevens arrived in minutes from a fire station just down the road. He held Alayna and asked her mother if he could touch the eye. When he did, Alayna pulled back and began to cry. The growth was soft and spongy. The paramedic had never seen anything like it. He thought it might be cancer, a benign tumor, or a cyst. He took a photograph of it.

The paramedic asked Tim what the growth had looked like when Alayna was born, and Tim got a picture that showed it was barely visible.

The detectives and paramedic stepped outside. "Is there any chance this kid will die tonight?" Burley asked the paramedic.

"No, I can't imagine that," said Stevens, who spent about 85 percent of his time handling medical emergencies, as do many firefighters these days. "It's not an infection, and that's probably the only thing that could cause immediate danger. But she does need to be evaluated."

The detectives told Tim they'd be in touch, and left, along with Stevens. Everybody in the family felt good. The cops had been friendly. It looked like the meddling was over.

But the next day Rebecca got a call from DHS caseworker John Faber. He wanted to come out with some of his team. After having dealt with the cops, Tim and Rebecca weren't too worried about DHS. They again arranged for four other Followers to be there, to outnumber the social workers.

But Faber's group turned out to be the CAT—Child Abuse Team—consisting of four veteran cops and two social workers, headed by Detective Kristi Fryett, who had twenty years on the force, mostly in CATs.

It was obvious that Alayna, on Rebecca's lap, couldn't see out of her eye, which was covered by a huge bulge that was various shades of red and maroon, with a yellow crust on it.

Fryett took Rebecca aside, and Detective Maurice Delehant took Tim.

Delehant got close to Tim's face—intimidatingly close, in the opinion of Tim's brother-in-law, Garret Crone—and asked, "Do you think this is a serious problem?"

Tim said he thought it was—but that they had prayed about it.

"Don't you use doctors at all?" the detective asked.

"God is our physician," Tim said. Tim did say that he had once called 911, but it was for a stranger, not a Follower. Tim said he would never take Alayna to a doctor, even though he knew that sometimes children didn't recover through prayer. "Sometimes God heals," Tim said, "and sometimes God lets even children die."

In another room, Officer Fryett asked Rebecca if Alayna had been given any medical care.

"We give her the best medical care—the love of Jesus," Rebecca said.

The officer asked Rebecca if she would take Alayna to a doctor if it looked like she was going blind. "No."

Rebecca said that even if Alayna might die, she wouldn't take her to a doctor. "I believe in God," she said. "I trust him."

The detectives compared notes outside. Then they told Tim and Rebecca that they were taking Alayna into custody, and going to a hospital.

Tim began to cry. He suddenly offered to take Alayna to the hospital himself. Fryett said that wouldn't be possible, because Alayna was already in their custody.

"Please," Tim said, "I'm begging you. Let me take my daughter. She's my daughter. If you want her to go to the hospital, I'll take her." His sister had never seen him like that.

The detectives said that Tim, Rebecca, and the others were free to come to the hospital, and stay with Alayna.

They got into separate cars, drove to Legacy Emanuel Hospital, and met with Dr. Thomas Valvano, a specialist in pediatric child abuse. Valvano immediately suspected that the growth was a benign tumor known as a hemangioma. Hemangiomas occurred in the lining of blood vessels, were present in almost 10 percent of Caucasian babies, and were much more common among girls. They often appeared on the surface of the skin, and were colloquially called strawberry marks. As a rule, they grew very slowly or not at all, and usually went away by about age ten. Alayna's, however, was abnormally large and aggressive.

Treatment was usually effective and fairly easy—just a cream with a mild drug in it.

The doctor looked at Alayna's medical chart, but there was virtually nothing in it, so he asked Tim and Rebecca about Alayna's health history. They said she was born at home with midwives, had never been to a doctor, hadn't been vaccinated, and had no other significant health problems. The doctor looked for possible signs of physical abuse, but didn't find any.

He asked Tim why they hadn't given Alayna medical care. "I placed my trust in God," Tim said.

Rebecca told the doctor, as she had the detective, that even if Alayna was suffering from a life-threatening illness, she still wouldn't take her to a doctor.

The doctor thought it was a clear case of medical neglect. He told Tim and Rebecca that Alayna would need to spend the night in the hospital, and an eye specialist would see her in the morning. Dr. Valvano hated to dictate treatments to parents, under almost any circumstances. "But we can't defer to them to the point," he later said, "where the child isn't receiving the medical care he or she needs."

The police officers told Tim and Rebecca that there would be a custody hearing the following day.

Tim and Rebecca, looking stunned, began their all-night vigil in the hospital.

The next day Alayna was taken to Portland's leading eye clinic, the Casey Eye Institute, located in a university-hospital complex known as Pill Hill. The Eye Institute was the site of Portland's newest showpiece, an aerial tram that had cost $57 million, with most of the costs passed on to patients. The tram wasn't supposed to have cost so much, because the architect had planned to forgo erecting a tower and instead hang the tram cables from the top of the building—until one day late in the process when he asked, "How much can the building shake before it becomes a problem during eye surgeries?"

After examining Alayna, ophthalmologist Leah Reznick, MD, was pessimistic. The hemangioma, linked to a genetic abnormality, was enormous. It was the largest her ophthalmic technician had ever seen, and she'd seen some huge ones during a stint in Saudi Arabia, where there was a relative excess of familial intermarriage. Alayna's eye had been crushed against the socket, possibly causing permanent damage. An even bigger problem was that babies needed to train their brains to see, and Alayna wasn't getting that chance, because her eye was covered. If babies didn't learn to see out of an eye by about six months, they usually never did.

It looked as if Alayna was blind in that eye and probably always would be. Even if there was major improvement, she would probably see double her entire life, and never have much depth perception, which required the proper function of both eyes. Also, her two eyes would almost certainly not track together, but drift off in different directions. That condition generally created a strange appearance, and made people self-conscious. There was also a chance that the hemangioma had spread to areas they couldn't see, such as Alayna's optic nerve and possibly even her brain.

To recover at least some of Alayna's sight, Dr. Reznick needed to shrink the hemangioma quickly.

"Time was ticking," Reznick later said.

Reznick ordered an MRI of Alayna's brain, then reviewed the results with a neuroimmunologist and a dermatologist. It looked as if Alayna's brain and optic nerve had not been invaded. But they saw enough damage to concur with Dr. Valvano that Alayna was a victim of medical neglect.

Reznick started Alayna's treatment that same day. She applied a solution to Alayna's eye that contained a type of medication known as a beta-blocker. The drug was usually used to reduce excessive adrenaline in people who suffered panic attacks, but it also helped shrink hemangiomas.

As Reznick evaluated Alayna, Tim and Rebecca were at the courthouse, losing custody. They appeared without an attorney before a Family Court judge who told them that Alayna was being removed from their home for her own safety. She would be placed in foster care, so that she could be treated.

"Is there any chance," Tim asked, "that we can appease DHS and keep our child?"

The judge said no. And he told them to get an attorney. They would need one, because now they had even bigger problems than Family Court.

Greg Horner, in his ground-floor office, made a statement. "Any decision about criminal charges will not be made until the investigation is completed." That was all he could legally say, since no one had been indicted.

But suddenly, thanks to Band and his informant, Horner saw a possibility of the golden outcome he'd long envisioned: multiple arrests: *first* the Wylands, then—with public sentiment fully and finally on his side—*the Hickmans*. Followed by multiple convictions. And possibly, and most tantalizing of all, six-year, man-2 sentences for Dale and Shannon Hickman. He might finish the job that had engulfed him for years.

To get started, he needed evidence on the Wylands. As fast as possible. If he couldn't get any, he'd lose the bust, and never get the indictments and big-time sentences that would change the Church forever, or lead to its abandonment.

And if the Wylands were not prosecuted criminally, they would probably also prevail in the family court system, and Alayna would soon be headed back home, facing the possibility of a dark future.

. . .

James Rhodes was already on his way to the Wyland house with a warrant. The Child Abuse Team—knowing that Rhodes, Finn, and Band were the resident experts on the Followers—had called Rhodes and asked him to come search the Wylands' home with them.

Nobody was home, which was good. Evidence tended to disappear when Followers were around. A back window was open and one of the detectives crawled through it and opened the front door.

"There's going to be a diary," Rhodes told the CATs. "These people keep diaries of everything. And look for journals, notebooks, photos, and computers."

The computer was easy to find, and so were some photos, but nobody found a diary or a journal, which would have been the best possible evidence that Tim and Rebecca knew that Alayna was in danger, but didn't act.

Rhodes told the CATs Team to start over and dig deeper. He took the kitchen himself and tore it apart. He kept thinking about Ava Worthington, and Neil, and that little Hickman baby, and how close the police were to victory. Or defeat. It was a hell of a thing how so much could ride on one piece of evidence.

Then, there they were: the diary and the journal, hidden in the bottom of a drawer of recipes. Rhodes called in the lead detective and had him take over.

"The whole story," Rhodes later said, "was in that stuff: when the thing started to grow, how big it got, what they did—everything. It laid out their timeline, and made it impossible for them to deny anything."

The investigation into the blinding of Alayna Wyland was virtually over.

The detectives who reported back to Horner that day didn't have any witnesses to the possible crime, because the Wylands had kept Alayna hidden, and the defense witnesses would surely lie. But they had a diary and other records to go along with the shocking photos of Alayna

Wyland: the True Face of Faith Healing, a phrase coined by the *Secular News Daily* website, and propagated by others.

That face and the records that went with it, Rhodes and Horner thought, would be enough for an indictment, and hopefully conviction.

If they got a double-conviction in the Wyland case, and a double-man-2 in Hickman—to go with Worthington and Beagley—they would have achieved more than any other prosecutors in America.

The rest would be up to Band's inside man. If he was as good as Band said he was, he would create so much doubt, infighting, fear, and shame that the Church would finally fix itself or go under. People would desert in droves, and those who stayed would stop committing crimes of medical neglect.

If Horner could make that happen, who knew where it would end? If, if, if.

OREGON CITY
JULY 22, 2010

"This Tim and Becca thing is a crazy mess," Patrick said. We were down by Willamette Falls, fishing off the concrete esplanade high above the river for summer steelhead in an unusually productive season. After more than six months of meeting in out-of-the-way restaurants and talking on the phone, it was good to see him in his own element. He had on a green Duck's jersey that lit up his translucent aquamarine eyes, and his straight auburn hair was whipping around in the wind off the Falls.

"The judge," Patrick said, "told Tim and Rebecca that they could get Alayna back if they got insurance and applied her eye medicine in front of a webcam, but they refused to do it. Now they say they will, but she's still in foster care. At least that crap on her eye is mostly gone, but she's still blind as a bat in that eye—only 20/1,000 vision, last I heard. Jim says Horner grand-juried Tim and Rebecca and is dying to indict. He'd better. If he doesn't . . ." He trailed off and focused on his fishing.

If Horner didn't indict the Wylands, Patrick knew, the DA's office wouldn't have the impetus to go after the Hickmans, and the people in the church would regain their sense of impunity. After all his effort, Patrick was even more uncertain than before. If one of the more radical guys—like Brent, who was out of jail and wildly popular among the Followers—could get people to say that Patrick had been playing doctor, Patrick feared that he might not only lose custody of his son but go to jail. Brent had no formal authority to direct the congregants, since that would be contrary to the informal structure of the church, but as a martyr he wielded the Followers' ultimate source of power: He was loved.

Patrick was also worried about a physical attack. Some of the diehards, he said, were using bodily force to push people to hold fast. Recently they'd talked two sons of an older man with congestive heart failure who was headed out the door for the hospital into literally sitting on him until he gave up. Then they kept him home until he died. Patrick had tried to gather enough information to make a case against them, but it had been impossible.

Patrick also said that a girl had suffered a crushed pelvis in a car wreck, and that her parents had pulled her out of the hospital at the earliest legal moment, so she never fully recovered. Now she limped and cried a lot. But there was no provable crime. He was leaning hard on her parents to get her back to the doctor, but they thought Patrick had a devil.

He'd heard that two boys had gotten in a brutal fistfight over one of them talking to the police about Neil Beagley. The supposed squealer had ended up in the hospital, even though he'd resisted going. It was a mutual fight, though, so that wasn't something he could take to Jim, either.

The government wasn't as strong as people thought, Patrick said. If you really wanted to keep people in line, you had to do it yourself, with arguments, tricks, manipulation, deceit, cajoling, and all kinds of other things he was sick of doing. He was running out of steam, and needed some arrests, convictions, and lengthy sentences to get people to listen to reason. If that happened, his power to change things would be vast.

The worst things of all, he told me, were what people did to themselves. One man had a growth on his forehead that was even uglier than Alayna's, and he'd had it for twenty years. He looked like a monster, Patrick said, but was proud of it.

Patrick said he wasn't angry at anybody, though. "For some dumb reason, I still love these people, even the ones that hate me. They've been misled. They don't know about the real Bible or the real Jesus. They all think Jesus basically said, 'Take up your pallet and *limp*.' They think that when he said to love one another, he only meant other Followers. That's what happens when you go forty years without a preacher."

He was trying to change their attitudes with Bible quotes and stories, and lots of private conversations with people who were leaning his way, but he was sure his rebellion was too obvious and that he'd soon be attacked, either legally, socially, or physically. "I may have completely blown my cover last Thursday," he said. "They had this potluck, and Tim and Dale got up and made a pitch for the Defense Fund. This time they only raised about one-fourth as much as before. It was $200,000, which sounds like a lot, but lawyers go through that in a few weeks. So they hit on me, because I gave $3000 for Brent. And like an idiot I stand up and say, 'Why should I pay for your sins?'"

After church, two guys yelled at him and one even shoved him—an act that would have been unthinkable even a few months ago. He'd also gotten three threatening notes in the mail, and two nasty messages on his answering machine. Tempers were boiling among people who'd never been rational in the first place.

"I'm doomed," he said, almost happily, anxious for an end of any kind.

The KATU news van sailed by and swiveled left toward the courthouse. Less than a minute later, so did the Fox-TV truck, and the news unit of the NBC affiliate. Nothing important was scheduled at the courthouse. It had to be breaking news.

"I'll bet it's Tim and Rebecca," Patrick said. His grin lit up an already sunny day.

Patrick hurried home to his television and flipped on KATU at 5:01 p.m., just in time to catch the end of an intro to a story about Alayna Wyland, the day's lead piece. Standing in the newsroom with about twenty monitors flickering behind him was intense and square-jawed reporter Dan Tilkin—whom Eleanor Evans considered "the most handsome man on television," partly, she admitted, because of his aggressive Followers' coverage.

This has to be good news, Patrick thought, or it wouldn't be on TV at all. Even so, he reflexively held his breath. "The District Attorney's Office," Tilkin announced, "says it plans to hit the parents of this girl with an indictment for criminal mistreatment . . ." Patrick didn't hear the rest of the sentence over his exhale.

"We want to warn you," Tilkin said, "that we're going to show a picture of the kind of condition this girl has, and some may find it hard to watch."

They flashed a photo from WebMD of a girl with a growth over her eye that was about half the size of Alayna's. Patrick was glad they didn't show Alayna. There would be pictures of her on the Internet for the rest of her life, and as far as Patrick was concerned, the fewer the better.

Tilkin said that Tim and Rebecca were trying hard to get Alayna out of foster care. He quoted their Family Court judge, Douglas Van Dyk, as saying that it was important to preserve the parents' bond with their daughter.

Van Dyk was in a difficult position, because the Wylands were impossible to categorize as classic criminals. The Followers, one of Alayna's doctors later said, "love their children. When you get to know these people," said Susan Nielsen, MD, who'd previously treated other Followers kids, "they're not weird. They just have a strong faith that most of us don't understand."

But Horner wanted Alayna to stay where she was because her eyesight had already improved by 25 percent. According to Tilkin, "The District Attorney's Office had said, 'The child is still in a precarious and uncertain condition, and we cannot support returning her home.'"

Paul toddled into the room on fat strong legs and Patrick scooped him up, smiling but fighting back tears of relief and sadness, as Tilkin wrapped up with some shots of the Beagleys' compound, and a photo of a very small, fresh grave.

The next indictments came with stunning speed, about one week later—approximately the period of time required to process the paperwork.

Dale and Shannon Hickman, both 25, were charged with second-degree manslaughter in the death of their newborn son, David Hickman.

Bail was set at $500,000, and was posted almost immediately by Dale's father, Phil.

The Followers were certain that it was no mere coincidence that Dale and Shannon were indicted almost immediately after Tim and Rebecca. To them, it was a conspiracy, plain and simple. Pure politics. It was the politics of religious prejudice, paving the way for the politics of persecution.

The people in the Clackamas County Courthouse and police department saw it somewhat similarly. The indictments, they knew for a fact, were not remotely coincidental, but were pure politics: The politics of justice.

OREGON CITY
AUGUST 1, 2010

On a day of sun so brilliant that it felt almost artificial, Patrick's backyard rippled with color. The perimeter was lined by huge purple hydrangeas, with long rows of lipstick-red roses beneath, and a lush profusion of pink and yellow daylilies embracing the emerald lawn below. In the back, a pond shimmered, and played the soothing music of moving water as orange koi swirled around a fountain, and Tiger Swallowtails fluttered by a butterfly bush. Overlooking it all, with a view of snow-white Mt. Hood on the horizon, was a massive crescent-shaped redwood deck with built-in benches, an outdoor kitchen, and an intricate pattern imbedded into the glossy wood.

Even by the flamboyant standards of Oregon Yard Porn, it was a place of wonder. Five friends from the church, Patrick said, had spent half of their Sundays one summer helping him put it together, while the wives prepared the picnics.

Today Patrick was waiting for some people to come over for a fish-fry picnic of the steelhead he'd caught, but he felt jittery and detached. He'd just received the worst piece of hate-mail yet. The writer mentioned the girl with the shattered pelvis and said, "That's what your butt is going to look like after I take batting practice on it. See you when you least expect it."

Patrick hadn't mentioned any of the threats to Ella, but he was thinking about sending her and Paul away for a while. Doing that could kill his chance for custody, but he didn't know what else to do.

Ella, still glowing from the good news of the four arrests, had cedar-planked salmon on one grill, baby-back ribs with pineapple on another, and a honey-baked ham in the oven. The picnic table was heavy with ceramic pots of hush puppies, grilled asparagus, creamed Mayan onions, and pitchers of blackberry lemonade, because they were expecting up to thirty people, all members of Patrick's new church within a church. This was intended to be their first social meeting.

But only eleven people came. For Patrick, it was depressing and scary. It looked like most of the people Patrick had helped were afraid to be associated with him.

People spread blankets on the lawn and watched the kids feed the koi and chase butterflies. When everyone had filled their plates, Rod Lincoln asked Patrick, as the host, to say the blessing.

Patrick got up on the deck so people could see him, and started out with the usual bless-this-food, bless-all-of-us, blah-blah-blah, but cut it short, looked around and started to talk. Even the kids quieted down.

"This is a good week but a sad week," he said, slipping naturally into a preacher's melodic cadence. "I've known Timmy Wyland all my life and I love him like a brother. He's a good man, and so is Dale, when he thinks things through. And Rebecca and Shannon—they were under a lot of pressure to do what they did." Patrick got a couple of whose-side-are-you-on looks, but plowed ahead. "What we saw this week, real clearly, was that we've all got to find a new way to live. We saw how fragile life is and how fast we can lose everything.

"We've got to remember, deep in our hearts, that the life we have is a gift, and that when it's taken—and it will be taken—we'll all be on trial. Not for who we *are*—those days are gone—but for what we've done. So we need a new way. Me, Rod, Marie, Ella—a bunch of us—we've been talking about it, and we've started a Bible group with rules of our own.

"We think that if we want our kids to grow up right, we've gotta stop telling them what to think. Our job is to teach them *how* to think. They'll figure things out, and no matter what, it's their life, not ours.

"Guys," he said, his long arms stretching out inclusively, "if we want our wives to feel safe, we shouldn't pretend we've got everything under control. Nobody does. We've got to ask them what they want to do. And if we don't agree and it turns into an argument, we need to be the first one to make up.

"And we've all got to stop trying to one-up each other. No more inner circle, no chosen people, no Prophet. We made up all that a long time ago to feel protected, and then we kept it up because it made us feel superior.

"We need to let go of the idea that Jesus is our own personal ace in the hole. He didn't tell people how to make life easy—he told them how to be good, and that's hard.

"All these things we think we hate—like not having enough money, and not being better than other people, or getting crap from people around town—those aren't the things that ruin life. That's just life. You're not always gonna be happy, or feel like you're cool.

"But how does anybody ever learn compassion? It's not when they're happy. It's when they hurt. And do you learn kindness from being the coolest person around? Do you learn generosity by giving away something you don't need? Do you learn how to love by loving only the people who love you?

"If there's one thing I've learned, it's that we need each other. But *easy* times don't bring people together. Hard times do. There's no easy way out. And we need to be grateful for that and stop looking for one.

"If we do this stuff, we're gonna have enemies. Guaranteed. I've got some now, for the first time in my life. I have no idea what's gonna happen. Not a clue. I know heaven is waiting for me, at some point—we all do—but we don't know where it is, or what it is.

"Something I learned from Ella is that if we are going to find the kingdom of heaven, we have to start looking right now. I think it's right in front of us." He looked out at his beautiful yard, his friends, and the mountaintop beyond.

"It's here," he said, in almost a whisper.

"Hard to see, though, isn't it?"

He trailed off, and sat down, looking sad, and feeling very alone.

Patrick later said that he was trying to paraphrase the Sermon on the Mount. He called it the Sermon on the Deck. "That's what Christianity boils down to," he said. "Live and let live. Turn the other cheek. All that ugly fundamentalist stuff you see in the media these days isn't Christianity. It's people."

. . .

After everybody left and Paul was tucked in, Patrick decided to show his hate-mail to Ella. She wasn't intimidated.

"So they think they can mess with my baby brother. I don't think so. I think it's time," said Captain Ella D. Robbins, USMC, Ret., "to send in the United States Fucking Marines."

For once, Patrick didn't correct her language. He didn't know exactly what she meant, but it didn't sound like a bad idea.

19

HEALING THE BLIND

As he went along, Jesus saw a man blind from birth. His disciples asked him, "Rabbi, who sinned, this man or his parents, that he was born blind?"

"Neither this man nor his parents sinned," said Jesus. "This happened so that the works of God might be displayed in him." Jesus put his hand on the man's eyes. Then the man's eyes were opened . . . and he saw everything clearly.

—The Book of John 9:1–3;

and The Book of Mark 8:25

Oregon City
August 11, 2010

"If I'm going to a meeting like this," Ella said, sliding her Marine-issue Beretta 92F into a pocket holster, "I'm gonna go dressed."

"You're enjoying this too much," Patrick said.

"Just trying to find heaven on earth." He gave her a look. "Okay, I won't load it." Another look. "Okay. I'll put it back in the vault."

They paid a surprise visit to one of the youngest and most reasonable of the elders. Like the other elders, he didn't have any special power to stop the threats against Patrick, but he could at least spread the word to lay off. He invited them in but didn't ask them to sit. Patrick told him about the threats, and asked him to let people know that intimidation was a felony that could put somebody in prison.

The elder glared at them. "You come in here and talk about intimidation," he said, "but you don't mention those cops—the James Bond guy, the ugly one from Gladstone, the mean one that tore up Becca's kitchen, and that girl—they're all cruisin' for a bruisin'. But I can see you only care about yourself, so I'll do what I can. Just don't expect miracles. Everybody knows about your crazy ideas, and that you think you're the new Prophet."

Ella took a step toward him. "My brother is a gentleman," she said. "I wish I had his manners." She leaned forward and whispered something into his ear. Patrick never did find out what it was. Ella told him it was better not to know.

The elder's eyes flared. "You baby-killing harl—"

Ella's open hand swept forward and caught him flush on the cheek. Taller and tougher than the elder, her smile was gone, and she looked every bit like a Marine.

Patrick, shocked, saw the elder swing his own palm toward Ella's face but Patrick caught it in his powerful fist. Ella took a step backward, pulled back her jacket, and slapped her hand hard onto her hip, as if she was going for a weapon. She held it there until Patrick let the man's hand go, and they backed toward the door.

She later told Patrick her move was just a reflex from the war-zone years, and he believed her—more or less.

The elder was so shaken that he didn't seem to hear Patrick's apology as they hurried away.

Back in the car, they both started laughing, mostly out of nerves.

On the way home, Patrick said, "We ought to go down to the Coffee Creek prison and visit Marci. Nobody will come see her. Not even her family. They still blame Neil's death on her lack of faith. She comes out to the visiting room, but nobody ever shows up. And I hear she's having a terrible time with the lesbians. She told somebody there's all kinds of sexual abuse of the women out there. There's even what they call the Rape Shack. Marci was thinking prison would mean a cell—

not a dorm, with people making love in the bunk above her, and guards forcing women to have sex."

"There's no reason for me to go," Ella said. "I'm sure she's still shunning me."

"You're right. That's funny."

"It is." Neither of them laughed.

After their visit to the elder, the level of violence in the threats subsided somewhat, and Patrick didn't fear for his life . . . for another nine months.

SIOUX CITY, IOWA
SEPTEMBER 2010

At 67, Rita Swan's dream of four decades was coming close to reality. It was happening in Oregon. Rita remembered telling Terry Gustafson about the dream in 1998, after she'd already spent more than twenty years chasing it.

To end faith-healing abuse in America, she'd said, the first thing she had to do was demolish a state's religious-shield law. Then she had to find a district attorney, a police department, and a Church insider with real guts. After that, she would need multiple arrests and local publicity, to create a jury pool with no illusions. Finally: major-felony sentencing.

It was beginning to look as if the only place this could happen was in Oregon. She'd been hopeful about Wisconsin, another hotbed of faith-healing abuse, but it had become a grave disappointment. Rita had helped introduce two different bills to gut its shield, but both had just been voted down, and the meager six-month sentences in the homicide of eleven-year-old Kara Neumann had been disheartening.

Efforts to supersede state shield laws on the federal level had also failed. In April, Rita had gone to Washington to meet with sympathetic Senators Mike Enzi, from Wyoming, Tom Harkin, from Iowa, and Chris Dodd, from Connecticut, hoping to create protection from faith-healing abuse nationally, with revisions to the Child Abuse Prevention and Treatment Act.

The Democrats, sympathetic to Rita's changes, controlled both chambers of Congress, so Rita was initially optimistic. But the most important Democrats refused to fight hard enough to overcome Republican opposition. There were just too many variations and congregations of Peculiar People in America, almost all voters. The changes were discarded.

That left everything up to Oregon. Horner needed to win convictions in the two upcoming cases—especially the Hickman homicide, with the maximum sentence for manslaughter. That would gain national attention, trigger new laws, and be a model for cops and DAs around the country.

It would, she hoped, also scare the living hell out of the Followers in Oregon City, and give Jim Band's Church insider the firepower he needed to reform the Church. All of that, put together, could create a permanent shift in America's policies on crimes perpetrated in the guise of piety.

But for the next steps to happen, she needed to go back to Oregon, and finish her own part of the job: Killing the shield law entirely, so Horner could apply the charges that carried the longest sentences— murder by abuse, murder by neglect, first-degree manslaughter, and failure to provide adequate medical care.

Oregon, ironically, was the nation's leader in faith-healing prosecutions, but was still one of only three states that allowed a religious exemption to murder, and one of three that still had a religious exemption to first-degree manslaughter.

Oregon's religious shield against vaccinations was also still in place, and so was the one against giving newborns blood tests for disease, and vitamin K to prevent blindness and hemorrhaging. Even the bike-helmet shield was still there.

In addition, there was a statute in Oregon's civil code that referred to prayer as a form of "physical care," which could, in a crunch, be cited by defense attorneys desperate for a loophole in a criminal case.

On top of all that, Oregon's law about letting kids fifteen or older make their own medical decisions was still much too confusing. The existing law allowed fifteen-year-olds to demand medical care, but not necessarily refuse it, and the Beagleys had tried to exploit that law's seeming contradiction. It hadn't worked for Jeff and Marci, because their judge had denied their attempt to cite the law. But sooner or later it would probably let other parents escape blame.

"Oregon's current laws," Rita noted at the time, "still reward fanaticism and absolutism."

From her headquarters in Sioux City, Rita worked all fall and early winter on a new Oregon strategy, but she was also preoccupied with ongoing cases in California, Washington, Wisconsin, Alabama, and Oklahoma. It was becoming easier to get convictions, but many of the sentences were too light. In Philadelphia, although Herbert and Catherine Schaible had just been convicted for letting their two-year-old son Kent die from untreated pneumonia, their sentences had included no jail time, just ten years' probation.

Rita was also peripherally involved with the Catholic sex-abuse scandal, and had discovered that some of the same demented things were happening among certain sects of Orthodox Jews. Even a group of Amish people had been accused of a hate crime involving spiritual disagreements.

A sick enough person, she'd found, could twist any religion into evil.

In January, as Rita finished guidelines for a bill to present to Oregon legislators, she and Doug crammed as much of their goods as they could into their car, leaving just enough room for their dog Boomer, and headed west. It was hard to leave their beautiful country home, high on a hill, near the Missouri River, where Rita and her daughters loved to ride their horses. "Home and family were always the greatest sources of peace to me," Rita later said, and every time she left brought new pain.

As soon as they crossed into the badlands of Eastern Oregon, they hit a blizzard. "My heart sank in the desolate landscape," she later recalled. With Doug now retired from forty years of teaching, and now suffering from Parkinson's disease, daily life was harder, and religion-driven politics seemed more treacherous than ever. America's current crop of fundamentalists seemed to celebrate their irrationality and disconnection from mainstream culture, and that group was playing a major factor in the approaching Republican primaries.

Mitt Romney seemed to be the most rational of the candidates who had strong religious affiliations. But even he belonged to a Church that some people still associated with isolated sects that secretly practiced faith healing, polygamy, and child rape, including three such sects in the small town of Colorado City, Arizona, which borders Utah. The town's so-called Babyland Cemetery contained only children's graves, and the village had the highest incidence in the world of a rare form of severe mental retardation caused by familial intermarriage. The tiny town also had an even higher incidence than many entire states of a category called "accidental child death, not due to traffic accidents." Colorado City, which also had two Christian Science churches and several other faith-healing churches, including the First Assembly of God, had 416 children removed from their families in recent years, against strong local opposition.

Even in liberal Oregon, though, Rita had always faced powerful opponents. Politics had been tough enough there in 1999—when she'd had to create the Kitty Coalition—but now she needed to blunt the possible opposition of maverick groups like God's Get Well Hotel, and the Ring of Fire Ministry, as well as her old nemesis, the Christian Science Church. She'd just finished fighting Mother Church in Arkansas, where she'd unsuccessfully challenged the religious defense for murder.

Rita and Doug settled into the state capital of Salem, with the help of local physician Jim Lace, who arranged for their housing. Lace knew Rita from a heartbreaking experience he'd had with a Followers girl who suffered from life-threatening asthma, so severe she could barely finish a sentence. After weeks of talking and even praying with the fifteen-year old girl's parents, he'd had to turn the case over to DHS caseworkers, who threatened the couple's custody if they wouldn't treat their daughter. The girl did get treatment, but when she turned eighteen, she sent Lace a letter saying, "I'm free now. I don't have to see you anymore. God wants me to suffer."

The girl survived, but continued, of course, to suffer. That case was one more reason why Rita had added an amendment to the proposed new Oregon law stating unequivocally that minor children, even older than fifteen, could not refuse necessary medical care. She called it "The Neil Beagley Amendment."

Almost immediately after her arrival in Salem, though, things turned sour. One of the leading law professors in the state refused to endorse her bill, because, the professor said, "I respect others' religious beliefs."

"That was the low point of our morale in Oregon," she later recalled.

Another distraction in Salem was the controversial trial of two Russian evangelicals—part of an estimated 150,000 who'd settled in Oregon—who tortured their kids and called it Christian guidance. The punishments they inflicted upon their children were unspeakably cruel and violent, but a lot of Oregonians didn't want them punished, because they were afraid that they'd be labeled as criminals themselves just for spanking their own kids.

Rita went to the capitol every day and slowly built support. The core of her campaign was simple: Show people the True Face of Faith Healing. When opposing legislators looked at photos of the ravaged eye of Alayna Wyland, they stopped spouting slogans about family autonomy and religious freedom.

Rita once again bridged the left/right chasm, with help from Republican Bruce Starr, a friend from 1999. "Senator Starr," Rita later said, "was a conservative, evangelical Christian who was always with us, from the get-go to the finish." Starr agreed to team with Clackamas County Democrat Carolyn Tomei. Initially they had competing bills— Starr wanted to protect dependent adults, but Tomei preferred the easier and more compelling goal of keeping children safe. They compromised, though, by focusing primarily on kids, building a coalition based to a large extent around the amendment named after Neil Beagley, whose fate was now well-known by all Oregon legislators.

Then, miracle of miracles, Mother Church announced support for the bill. The Church sent a letter to the legislators saying that the deaths in Oregon were "tragic" and that they had reached "critical mass."

Rita later noted, with sad irony, that, "When we lobbied for repeal of these religious exemptions in 1999, when there were 78 children buried in the Followers of Christ cemetery, the Christian Science church fought us tooth and nail. But in 2011, when there were, to my knowledge, 83 children buried there, the deaths had reached 'critical mass.'"

Rita ended up with a dream bill: total destruction of the shield. It called for the repeal of all four of the remaining religious exemptions. If it passed, Oregon—once the state with the worst law—would join a group of six that had no shield law at all.

As summer approached, the final hearings were held, and a number of Followers sat sullenly in the gallery, inspiring opposition to the bill from legislators with fundamentalist constituents. The contentious mood began to shift, though, when a woman from West Linn, O.C.'s rich sister-city, told legislators that she would soon be attending her 50th high school reunion. When she was in school, she said, she'd had classmates who were Followers. Sometimes, though, the kids would not show up for school, and she'd later find out that they'd died. "That was fifty years ago," she said. "That's a long time." The legislators sat quietly, absorbing the magnitude of all that suffering over all those years.

"You could hear a pin drop," Rita later recalled.

Shortly before the vote, with the outcome still uncertain, *The Oregonian* ran a series of articles about the 1984 invasion of Oregon by a religious group led by the Bhagwan Shree Rajneesh, a free-sex, End-Times, greed-is-good hustler who purchased an entire town for his commune and owned more Rolls-Royces than anyone else in the world: 365, one for each day of the year. The Bhagwan's group, originally welcomed by the state, lost popularity when it swung one local election by poisoning 751 voters who weren't members of the commune with salmonella—still the only bioterrorist attack to occur in America. The Rajneeshees also tampered with the voter roll by recruiting busloads of homeless men from the streets of Portland with an irresistible offer of free-food, free-housing, free-love, and a daily parade of Rolls-Royces.

But the day after the election, the Rajneeshees kicked out the Urban Outdoorsmen, and escalated their practices to include building an arsenal, and plotting multiple murders, including that of a US attorney. The Bhagwan and his top sycophants were too disorganized to successfully kill anybody, though, and were eventually jailed or deported. By the summer of 2011, many Oregonians had forgotten how much pain a corrupted religion could cause, but the articles reminded them.

As the series of articles was ending, Rita testified in the statehouse. "Medical neglect," she told the legislators, "may not be as sensational or bizarre as what the Rajneeshees were doing, but it has been even more deadly to Oregon's children." Rita's heartfelt testimony—the painful message she'd delivered so many times—had a transcendent emotional impact and propelled the bill to approval. Everyone on the floor and in the gallery knew what Rita Swan had lost, and how much she'd sacrificed to protect others from the same suffering. Her efforts reflected the highest hope of all people who work for the public good: If you are willing to sacrifice enough, life can hold more than just the certainty of its eventual loss. Your work, if your heart is in it, can live long after you die, and travel the world, and with it, a part of your heart.

Among the legislators, state senator Mark Hass—America's first broadcaster to cover the issue, during his days at KATU—had "a kaleidoscope of images," he later said, "popping into my mind": Kids' Row at the cemetery, the name "Bo Phillips" etched on a headstone, and the look on Dr. Larry Lewman's face when he described Bo's autopsy. Hass, the only person who'd fought this war in two different roles, was proud to be associated with Rita: "an American champion," whom he considered the rare public person whose sole agenda was an ideal.

As Rita stood after her testimony, several of her friends in the gallery silently rose, and then others did, too, then the legislators, and soon everyone present was standing, except for the Followers. After a few moments, out of embarrassment, or good manners, or possibly even understanding, they rose, too, for Rita Swan.

The bill passed both houses unanimously. It was immediately signed by the governor, John Kitzhaber, who'd been so reluctant to tackle the issue in his first two terms. It was the most stunning legislative victory in Rita's lifelong crusade to end the darkest practice of American fundamentalism.

She and Doug went home.

OREGON CITY
NOVEMBER 2010

Elevated by their unprecedented success against the Followers, Jim Band, James Rhodes, and Michelle Finn all got major promotions. Band was named spokesman, or Public Information Officer, for the Oregon City PD and was put in charge of all uniformed officers. Rhodes was appointed to the same PIO position for the Clackamas County Sheriff's Office. The job was highly valued, and often led to the office of chief of police, or county sheriff. PIOs were in almost daily contact with the press, and got abundant media exposure. The position was also a personal honor, an indication that the recipient embodied the qualities that their agency wanted to project to the public.

In Gladstone, Lynne Benton, the other officer who'd been involved with the Followers' arrests—particularly in the Beagley case— was already a PIO. Benton, possibly because of her complex sexual identification, had been passed over for the police chief's job when the former chief retired, even though she was still presenting herself as a female professionally.

But Benton, in the aftermath of the sex-change operation, was legally a male now, and he had recently fulfilled his longtime hope of getting married. In October, as Mr. Lynn Edward Benton, he had married his new girlfriend, Deborah Higbee, after a brief courtship. Higbee, who was comfortable with Benton's sex change, owned a beauty parlor in Gladstone. It was a modest business, and Debbie Higbee lived frugally in an unimpressive trailer court a few blocks from her shop, but she was a popular member of the local community, and she and Benton were often seen gardening and relaxing outside the mobile home. Benton, who'd had a hard time reconciling a professional life as a female with a personal life as a male, seemed finally to be content.

Michelle Finn, after her stint at the FBI Headquarters in Quantico, Virginia, was promoted to criminalist, more commonly known as crime scene investigator, or CSI. It was the highest rank for a police investigator—very prestigious—and a valuable stepping-stone to further advancement in state or federal criminal investigation.

Band and Rhodes both missed working Detectives and being on the street, but Band stayed close to Patrick. He was still the only law enforcement official who knew Patrick's identity. Patrick valued the relationship tremendously. Band and Patrick occasionally talked about religion, and Patrick was impressed at the depth of Band's knowledge of Christianity.

"It was funny," Patrick later said, "I knew all of these people in the church who were supposed to be so strong in the faith, but if I've ever had a true brother in the Word, it's Jim." It was a great comfort for him, because by then he was certain he was marked for excommunication, a legal assault, and maybe worse.

CLACKAMAS COUNTY COURTHOUSE
MAY 24, 2011

"Does anyone presume that these people are guilty?" defense attorney Mark Cogan asked the panel of prospective jurors for the Wyland trial.

One of them, a Mr. Watson, raised his hand. Not a good start.

"Mr. and Mrs. Wyland," Cogan explained, "are innocent until proven guilty. Does anyone think that I have to prove he's innocent?"

Virtually the whole panel shook their heads—indicating they understood—but Cogan launched on a long discourse about presumed innocence, until Judge Jeffrey Jones cut him off.

"He's trying to say he doesn't need to prove his client is innocent," said Jones, "just not guilty."

Cogan's day got worse. Within ten minutes, four jurors said they'd heard about the case or had seen Alayna's photo, and didn't think they could be unbiased.

Two panels later, it seemed as if Judge Jones, a get-'er-done former DA, was bending over backward to put together a jury. Cogan asked one of the possible jurors, who seemed antagonistic to the Wylands, if he could handle working on an important case, and the guy said, "I have the attention span . . ." He drifted off and then looked confused.

Cogan jogged his memory: "The attention span?"

"Of a gnat," he said.

"Is there anything novel, or new, for you in this kind of situation?" Cogan asked.

"No, not novel. But new, yes. I'm a black-and-white person—very little gray."

"That doesn't matter," said the judge. "A lot of people are like that." He was accepted as a candidate.

It got even worse. One of the jurors had known two Followers in his youth. One of them was in the Boy Scouts with the prospective juror, and had died on a hike, from an undiagnosed heart condition. The other died of pneumonia in high school. But the juror said he wasn't biased. Cogan, taken aback, tried to coax him into admitting that the deaths would color his opinion.

"I, uh, I, uh—can you *assure* us," Cogan finally asked, "that it won't prejudice you?" Cogan's geniality was being stretched to its limits.

"He's already answered that three times," said the judge. The juror was accepted.

Then a white-haired man with glasses said it was "immoral to withhold medical care from a child."

The judge asked him if he could focus on the facts.

"I think I could." Accepted.

A juror named Jennifer Barnes told the judge that she'd seen

Alayna's picture in *The Oregonian*. It had been very small, and in black and white—a rendition the editors had chosen to help keep the trial fair, and to keep from shocking their readers—but it had still jolted her. She was accepted, to her surprise.

"This seems like a hangin' jury to me," I said to Jim Wyland, Tim's dad, who was sitting beside me in the back row. I'd known him for about a year, since the first custody hearings. The first time we met, I didn't know who he was, other than somebody kind enough to give me his bottle of water when I had a tickle in my throat and couldn't stop coughing. After I calmed my cough I offered the water back, but he declined. At first, I assumed he was just averse to possible germs, but later thought he was probably averse to any kind of close contact with someone outside the Followers. I told him I was writing a book that day, and when I assured him that I wasn't going to demonize the Followers, he just smiled.

He grew to tolerate me, chatting between sessions and introducing me to his friends, after he learned we shared a skepticism about Big Medicine. I'd written a number of books that were critical of medicine, and supportive of the healing power of prayer and other integrative approaches. I had, for the most part, dropped out of conventional medical care myself, having become much more a believer in the powers of prevention and the body's immune and recuperative responses than in the heroic, late-stage medical measures that make most people feel safe. Even by the Followers radical standards, I had at least a little health cred. But I didn't kid myself—to Jim and the others, I was just one of the better-informed people who was still going to burn in hell.

Over the year, he'd opened up more and more, but whenever I tried to pry the Followers' perspective out of him, he'd only say, "Just watch. You'll learn." He never seemed worried about Tim's fate, or Alayna's eye, and over time I took that at face value. He genuinely trusted God and never seemed to wonder why God's favored few were always so sick.

Jim even liked this jury, because God had made it. Like many of the Followers, he was preternaturally upbeat—the kind of guy who would see a mushroom cloud and start celebrating The Rapture. Brent Worthington was like that, too. He always seemed to have a smile on his face, especially after he'd gotten out of jail. Brent, still the closest thing the Followers had to a Prophet-in-waiting, had a lot to feel good about, but other Followers who still had serious problems, such as Dale Hickman, were just as perennially buoyant. They actually did seem not of this world, but of a planet of their own.

Some Followers, though, were surly and hot-tempered—but just as disconnected from the world—and their style of disconnection could be just plain scary. Once, for example, one of the younger guys tried to shove my camera practically down my throat, and seemed, by the look on his face, to derive considerable gratification from it.

It was increasingly hard to comprehend how Patrick could have re-created himself as a member of the real world, after having lived so long in a different one. And it was easier than ever to see why he was so afraid of the one he'd left behind.

CLACKAMAS COUNTY COURTHOUSE
MAY 27, 2011

Jim Wyland scooted over on the spectators' bench so I could sit down, and showed me the front page of *The Oregonian,* which had a big photo of a local boy who'd gotten an eye operation—on the wrong eye. Jim knew I had a soft spot for stories about the mythology of medical perfection, and particularly those about Death by Medicine. Unlike most people, he knew that American medicine killed about 250,000 to 800,000 people every year, mostly due to drug reactions, making it the third leading cause of death. That's why drug-commercial announcers talk so fast.

"You should hold that up," I whispered to Jim, "so the jury can enjoy it, too."

A legal veteran by now, aware of the penalties of jury tampering, he just smiled.

"This case," Senior Deputy DA Christine Landers said in her opening statement, "involves three people—Timothy Wyland, Rebecca Wyland, and the main victim in the case, Alayna Wyland." With her first sentence, she'd appropriated Cogan's primary weapon: the portrayal of Tim and Rebecca as victims—just not the victim who had been blinded.

Then, less than one minute into her statement, she unveiled her big gun: the photo of the True Face of Faith Healing, which had worked so effectively for Rita. In the first picture of Alayna, taken shortly after her birth, the hemangioma was barely visible. Then Landers, speaking in a matter-of-fact tone, showed a progression of photos that ended with the grotesque image of Alayna's eye buried under a big red ball of tangled blood veins. Landers, hand-picked by Horner to head this prosecution, was rational and restrained, and let the pictures deliver the drama.

Landers told the jury about the brave double-agent within the church who had pushed DHS into action, and triggered the visit to the Wyland's home. That had been the Wyland's final night of legal custody.

Alayna had been under state control ever since, but she did live at home now, because Tim and Rebecca had gotten a Skype account, and treated Alayna in front of a webcam every day.

Alayna's vision had improved from 20/1,000 early in her treatment to 20/360 in March, but the eye was still well past the threshold for legal blindness, which is 20/200. Alayna had no depth perception and probably never would, and the damaged eye was still pushed down and out, and looked off to one side.

Alayna, Landers said, would undoubtedly have been blinded in the eye if the anonymous caller had not reported her mistreatment. Tim and Rebecca, Landers said, had told the police that they wouldn't have taken Alayna to a doctor even if they knew she was going blind—or dying.

However, Landers said, doctors had come in, restored at least some of Alayna's sight, eliminated most of her disfigurement, and were hopeful about further improvement.

Landers said that Tim and Rebecca would argue that they didn't know anything about ocular neurology. But whose fault was that? Reasonable parents, Landers said, would have learned that term the first time they took their child to the doctor for the red, swelling mass.

Also, just depriving Alayna of sight for many months, she said, was cruel. And it had to hurt. End of story.

Landers' quick, hard-boiled recitation had the desired effect of invoking rationalism, but the downside was that the jury drifted. The only juror who took nonstop notes was Jennifer Barnes, who had big expressive eyes and an aura of intelligence.

Cogan launched his opening statement more dramatically, trying to evoke empathy for Tim and Rebecca, paint the cops and social workers as Big Gov brutes, and characterize the prosecution's doctors as Poindexters who would just use big words to confuse everybody. Jennifer Barnes took fewer notes, but gazed at Cogan raptly.

Tim and Rebecca, Cogan said, were here "at the end of a long ordeal" that began when the state, pretending to be sending out social workers, sent out a platoon of angry cops who were intent on creating a child-abuse case, telling the Wylands, "This is our child. You're not the parents anymore. The government is taking your child." Then the cops, instead of taking Alayna for the treatment she supposedly needed, took her, Cogan said, to a "*child abuse* evaluator" whose "job is to work the case up as a *child abuse* investigation."

Cogan agreed that, yes, Alayna's hemangioma had receded—but hemangiomas almost always recede. There was no proof that Alayna had been saved by "a miracle cure, as the state claims." And he would show, he said, that the eye doctors had used "an experimental medicine that is not authorized for pediatric care."

As the day progressed, it looked like this would be a shorter, simpler trial than the Worthingtons' and Beagleys'.

Cogan and Neidig were going to go for sympathy, and attack Big Government and Big Pharma. They'd do what they could with the ignorance card, but it would be hard to play the Who Knew defense against the pictures of the True Face of Faith Healing.

At the end of the day, I called Patrick and told him I was optimistic that Christine Landers would have as much success with photos of the True Face as Rita Swan had. Pleased, and tantalized by the upcoming escape of Memorial Day weekend, he said he felt more at peace than he had for some time.

He would stay that way for almost twenty-four hours.

GLADSTONE, OREGON
MAY 29, 2011

"I thought you should know something." It was Patrick on the phone, almost hyperventilating. "Something really bad happened. I don't mean to alarm you. I'm sure you're completely safe." He was trying to breathe evenly but not pulling it off. "I may not be around for a little while. I'm leaving town. But I'll stay in touch."

"What is it?" I asked.

"It's one of the police in the investigation. His wife got killed. Murdered. Not Jim—thank God—or Rhodes. It was the Gladstone cop that we don't know very well. Lynn Benton. You remember her. Used to be a woman."

"What happened?"

"It looks like somebody came into the beauty shop that Lynn Benton's wife ran, and shot her."

"Was it a robbery?"

"No, it doesn't look like it." He sounded disappointed. That would have made it less threatening. "It seems like it was some kind of revenge thing. I don't know if they were going after her or Lynn Benton, or both. I don't know who it was. I do know that some people in the Church hate Benton."

"Patrick, it wasn't the Followers. They're not like that. Even the hotheads."

"I know. I'm sure you're right. I'm just paranoid. But nobody knows what this is like for me. Not even Jim. Anyway, there's no way I can take a chance that Paul or Ella might get hurt. So I'm going to get them settled somewhere out of town. Then I'll probably need to come back and keep snooping around on the Hickman case."

"You should stay with them. Go get some sun somewhere."

The unstated advice, obviously, was that he shouldn't risk becoming a martyr. Surely there were other ways for him to save the Church from itself.

Clackamas County Courthouse
May 31, 2011

Brent, Raylene, and an exceptionally large number of Followers came out for the opening day of witness testimony, which was now as much a Followers' tradition as holiday potlucks.

It quickly turned into old-home week when Mark Cogan spotted Raylene Worthington. "Hi stranger," Cogan said. "I know you've been havin' girl talk with my wife." Raylene was very sweet to Cogan and everyone else, and Brent was as friendly as usual. Cogan genuinely liked most of the Followers. "They're hardworking people with real integrity," he later said. "They have strong religious beliefs, but no interest in converting others."

The prosecution had only a few witnesses: the police and social workers who'd removed Alayna from her home, and the doctors who treated her. Landers wanted to open fast, keep moving, avoid emotionalism, and finish up before the jury had time to push the image of Alayna's eye out of their thoughts, and start focusing on the sad parents.

Dr. Leah Reznick led off with testimony that was impossible to refute: Alayna couldn't see out of her left eye when she came in, but now had some vision in it. Reznick told the jurors how important it was for babies' eyes to teach their brains how to see. That was a crucial fact, because the Wylands' fundamental crime had been denying Alayna that opportunity. They weren't just delaying her ability to see, but destroying it.

Reznick and another doctor said that the drug Alayna was now taking, a beta-blocker—which Cogan had called "experimental" and "not authorized for pediatric care"—was a well-established medication. It was used primarily to reduce adrenaline, but had been used for years against hemangiomas. Lots of drugs, the docs said, were used for multiple purposes, but getting approval for all the uses was pointless, because they were already legal.

But the jurors didn't seem very interested in Landers' short presentation of medical information. Probably too technical. Jennifer Barnes, though, stayed engaged, following every gesture and nuance. She looked like she'd be a leader in deliberations.

Cogan made a brilliant move by calling Tim's brother-in-law as his first witness, a pivotal, first-impression position. It was Garret Crone, who'd been there the night the cops had taken Alayna away. Garret was balding, with his black hair slicked into an arrowhead that pointed down at his face, as if Eddie Munster had reached midlife with his reverse-mullet intact. Garret was the perfect choice to introduce Who Knew? He couldn't even pronounce the condition Alayna had.

"Can you take a stab at it?" Cogan asked.

"Herman-jammy-oma?"

Whatever that thing was, Garret had seen a bunch of them come and go in the family, and he didn't think it was anything to get riled up about. What did frost him, he said, was how the cops had bullied and made fun of Tim, and made him beg to take Alayna to the hospital, then wouldn't let him. The cops seemed to enjoy it when Tim broke down and cried. The government people, Garret said, seemed to have their minds made up from the get-go to railroad Tim and Rebecca, no matter what. And there was no reason for it! Alayna's eye was already better. The doctors said it was because of all those drugs that people weren't supposed to give to babies anyway—but nobody else in the family needed drugs to make their strawberry marks go away.

It was strong testimony, straight from the heart, and touched on every parent's worst nightmare of losing their kids for no good reason.

Almost all the jurors scribbled notes on Garret's testimony, some nodding, seeming sympathetic to his perspective. It looked to KATU's Thom Jensen, a veteran of the Followers trials and a savvy interpreter of legal proceedings, as if Tim and Rebecca had just won. Jensen's cameraman thought the same thing. Emotion seemed to have suddenly swept past rationality.

"I think they're finally gettin' it," Jim Wyland whispered to me, nodding at the jury.

But the afterglow was ruined when Cogan called up a psychologist from Reed College, the crown jewel of Portlandia academe. The professor fulfilled the primary cliché of academia: Using big words to state the obvious. In this case, it was that the Followers couldn't be expected to do the intelligent thing, because people often favor information that supports what they already believe, a simple phenomenon with the fancy name of "confirmation bias." He tried to elaborate, but admitted that most of the ideas he wrote about in academic journals were "unreadable" by anyone not in the field. "That's why we have textbooks," he said, "to put things in English."

As he talked, somebody in the gallery began to snore. Even the Followers were laughing.

Judge Jones cut him off and ruled his testimony irrelevant. The professor looked crestfallen.

Then Cogan called a friendly doctor who didn't say much, and a couple more family members who recited the standard defense: Tim and Rebecca were pleasant with their persecutors, cooperative, confused by Big Medicine, didn't hit their kids, and kept their house clean. Two of the female jurors nodded and smiled.

Cogan and Neidig had no further witnesses. They weren't going to call Tim or Rebecca. When Thom Jensen heard that, he was almost sure that the Wylands had won. At least, that was apparently what Cogan thought.

CLACKAMAS COUNTY COURTHOUSE
JUNE 6, 2011

DA Christine Landers gave a quick closing summary in her clipped and calm way. "Children have rights," she said, and Tim and Rebecca had violated Alayna's. The case "is not about DHS," or about Tim and Rebecca "being polite and cooperative," or about Alayna "being well fed and clean, with parents who loved her."

It was about Alayna coming to the hospital blind in one eye, and achieving partial recovery only because the state had forced treatment.

"What did Tim and Rebecca Wyland *know*?" Landers asked. "Even if they *thought* that it would go away, they still *knew* she was blind. They thought it might go away by school age. They were willing to subject their daughter to this for five more years—two thousand days—and in that time she would take her first step, learn the alphabet, go to preschool, and make her first friend.

"Alayna was blind in that eye. They hoped in five years she wouldn't be blind. They *knew* that from January to June of last year. If that's not knowledge, it doesn't exist.

"There is one victim in this case. Her name is Alayna. Tim and Rebecca Wyland are not the victims. They are the perpetrators. I'm asking you to find them guilty."

Cogan went first for the defense. "It has been my very, very profound honor to defend Tim Wyland," he said, clapping Tim on the back. "The trial may not have taken as long as predicted, but you've got a lot of good evidence." He broke it into three bite-size pieces.

First, Tim and Rebecca loved Alayna. Second, they weren't allowed to take her to the hospital when they asked to. Third, once they were caught, they complied.

Neidig, his sad eyes seeming to weep without tears, finished the closing by saying that DHS had descended "in a frenzy" and created "a mushroom cloud of misinformation, poisoned by religious intolerance."

His conclusion: "I implore you—scratch the surface, and look at what's behind these charges." It was clearly persecution, he said: "by the government, trying to punish them. Don't let that happen. Vote not guilty."

Then he unveiled a huge, happy-family photo of Tim and Rebecca holding Alayna, entitled "Alayna as She Appears Today."

Alayna looked good. All's Well That Ends Well.

Most of the journalists thought Tim and Rebecca had won, because of the jury members' body language and expressions. They thought the prosecution's intentional lack of drama, to blunt emotionalism, had backfired. Others thought it was 50/50.

The courtroom broke for lunch. Then: deliberations.

At lunch in The Verdict, Emmy-winning news photographer Rod Stevens was talking about the horror he'd seen all around the world, including walking through a mass of 30,000 dead bodies on a beach after a flood in Sri Lanka. "I've been in most of the crap-holes in the world," he said, "and as long as I look at it through this viewfinder, I'm good. But *this*? Kids? It's different."

He got a text: "Verdict in." His face fell. "That is not, not, not a good sign," he said.

On the street, Followers began to burst out of restaurants and cars, heading back to the courthouse.

The first juror out of the jury room was Jennifer Barnes, smiling. Jurors that convict usually don't smile.

The judge gave the Followers the speech about no outbursts and took the envelope with the verdict.

Tim: guilty of the most serious charge, criminal mistreatment in the first degree.

Rebecca: the same.

A sob erupted and someone said, "No! Nooo." Many of the women dropped their heads into their hands, prayed, and cried. Jim Wyland, with his son on the way to jail, looked stoic and tired. It was impossible not to feel some of his pain.

There had been little deliberation in the jury room, because the first straw vote had been 12–0 to convict. The picture of Alayna, juror Jennifer Barnes later said, had sealed the deal from the beginning. "There was really nothing to sort out after that," she said. "That's why it got boring, except for those funny relatives who thought it was nothing. The prosecution did the right thing. If they'd gone over the top, people might have started to wonder why."

But what about all the nodding and smiling at the defense presentation?

"That was just good manners," she said. "We felt bad for the lawyers. They seemed like nice guys, and they had such a loser case."

OREGON CITY
JUNE 6, 2011

I called Patrick and left a message about the verdict. There was other news, too, but it was too touchy to convey on a recording.

The body of Lynn Benton's wife, Debbie Higbee, had been autopsied, and it indicated a savage attack. It appeared as if the woman had first been shot in the back, but did not die. Then she'd been beaten so badly that she suffered at least twelve broken ribs. Her liver was lacerated, possibly by one of the shattered ribs. Her breastbone was also fractured, and she had been strangled. The medical examiner said that the murder was a case of "kill, kill, and overkill."

Patrick's initial suspicion that it was a hate crime seemed inescapable.

There was a rumor in the courthouse that there was a suspect in the case, and that the suspect had been hired by someone. Nobody knew, or would say, who had done the hiring.

It seemed as if Patrick's vacation had been a wise choice.

20

THE FATHER, THE SON

The only thing necessary for the triumph of evil is for good men to do nothing.

—Generally attributed to Edmund Burke

Clackamas County Courthouse
June 24, 2011

Brent Worthington was watching over Alayna Wyland in the lobby outside the courtroom while her parents were being sentenced. Alayna, in a red polka-dot dress and cute toddler shoes, was scooting around the floor, in and out of crowds of defendants and lawyers. She was a little clumsy sometimes, because the vision in her damaged eye was only 20/170, slightly better than the level of legal blindness. Even now, the hemangioma looked like a major birth defect—a large red slash across her upper eyelid—though it had been a year since Patrick had turned in the Wylands and triggered Alayna's treatment.

In the courtroom, Christine Landers pleaded for the maximum sentence, which for Tim and Rebecca was only ninety days. One of the idiosyncrasies of the justice system is that even though people are tried for the crimes they commit, they're often sentenced for crimes they previously committed. Tim and Rebecca had no past crimes, so they were not liable for the maximum five-year sentence.

Landers also wanted three years' probation, continual monitoring of Alayna's health, and full restitution of $26,000 in medical bills.

Patrick didn't think that even the full ninety days would be enough to scare the Followers. He was hoping for harsher sentences in the Hickman homicide case. After all this time, and five convictions, the Clackamas County war against faith-healing abuse was still in doubt.

Mark Cogan countered Landers by arguing that the Wylands had been punished enough, because the "heart-wrenching events" on the day that Alayna was taken in for treatment "will be remembered by Mr. and Mrs. Wyland for as long as they live."

Cogan offered a statement from an Oregon agency called the Court Appointed Special Advocate Association, with the acronym CASA, which said that putting Tim and Rebecca in jail would impose "harsh conditions on Alayna Wyland, who is the victim the state is alleging to protect." Ironically, CASA's stated mission was to prevent child abuse.

John Neidig said that if there had to be a prison sentence, it should be held off for about ten or fifteen years, to determine exactly how much damage Tim and Rebecca actually did to their daughter. Alayna's "tremendous improvement" to 20/170 vision, he said, was "due to Tim and Rebecca's remarkable level of care."

The judge gave the Wylands the full ninety days, the full three years' probation, and full restitution costs. Tim would head to Clackatraz first, and after his release Rebecca would go in.

Tim was handcuffed. He protested that he didn't want his daughter to see him like that. The judge shook his head. "I find it absolutely stunning," he said, "that the child would be brought to this courthouse."

Raylene Worthington, watching through a glass panel in the door, said, "Brent, they gave them both ninety days."

Brent, still in charge of minding Alayna, didn't seem to hear. He was talking to a buddy about buying a refrigerator.

Honolulu, Hawaii
June 26, 2011

Patrick sent me an e-mail from Hawaii, where he'd gone after the murder of Lynn Benton's wife. It had shocking news.

He said people in the church were saying Dale didn't wake up until 2:15 a.m., just before the baby died—too late to do anything.

But somebody at the scene, Patrick said, had called *him* before 2:15 and said the baby was in distress. He was afraid the Followers would fake a logbook to back up their version of the story.

He was on his way home, he said, to try to discover anything else he could, and to get his hands on the videotape that had disappeared. Paul and Ella were staying, to guarantee their safety.

He also said that Theresa had filed for divorce, and was marrying a Mormon. She'd finally become disillusioned with the Church.

He thought it was probably because two more kids in the Caldwell church, according to his friends back home, had just died.

Oregon City
July 6, 2011

Tim Wyland had a miserable Fourth of July, because he was in a form of solitary confinement known as protective custody, to keep the ordinary criminals from assaulting him.

The last local Crime Celeb to land in protective custody had also been a religious extremist: Mohamed Mohamud, born the same year as Neil Beagley, who'd tried to bomb a crowd of 15,000 people at last year's Christmas-tree lighting in Portland. Mohamud thought the van that he parked by the crowd had an eighteen-hundred-pound bomb in it, but the bomb was a fake, supplied by the FBI. When he tried to detonate it with a cell phone from a couple of blocks away, the feds pounced on him. A cry of "Allahu Akbar" was his last public statement.

Mohamud was inspired in part by the Portland Seven, the largest domestic terrorist group in the country to be arrested after 9/11. Tied to Al Qaeda and the Taliban, their plan to murder students at a local Jewish school had fallen apart because they couldn't agree on whether to bomb it, or shoot the students as they emerged after school. Bombing, it was argued, would kill more kids, but shooting them one by one would be more spiritually satisfying. Some of the Seven were converts to Islam, including Jeff Battle, who was later arrested with his cohorts while practicing with explosives in a gravel pit. "We was out there blowin' it up, lightin' it up," Battle later said. "We looked at it as worship, because of what our intentions were."

The Portland Seven, along with yet another Muslim jihadist group from Southern Oregon, ended up in the feds' notorious "Little Guantánamo," officially known as the Communicative Management Unit, created by former Bush attorney general Alberto Gonzalez. Other occupants of Little Gitmo, in rural Indiana, came from Oregon's Animal Liberation Front, which had firebombed a mink ranch.

Tim, to get out of protective custody, needed a job assignment, which would also shave some days off his sentence. For that, though, he would have to go to a doctor, get a physical, and be treated for any problems that arose. But that seemed like a small sacrifice, so he applied. The family prayed the job assignment would happen—and it did!

Tim got a janitor job on the graveyard shift, which gave him better access to the telephone during the day. The family thought that the scheduling, too, had been arranged by God. Rebecca went to see him as often as she could, and once she had Tim's sister sneak out of her visiting time with Tim, so that Rebecca could get twice as much. It was a dumb idea for a future inmate, but Rebecca had been reassured by God's continuing favoritism.

Tim didn't like the food, and gave away things he hated, like coleslaw, stewed tomatoes, and boiled eggs, but after a while the prisoners from the world seemed to feel entitled to it, and barely bothered to say thanks.

Near the approach of Tim's release date—the same day as Rebecca's incarceration—the family began to organize a homecoming party at the church. But the church ladies were planning a big wedding that day and didn't want it spoiled with a lot of jailhouse talk about cellmates and shower privileges.

So they kept Tim's celebration short and sweet, and at 10:00 p.m. on August 19, Rebecca went in. She, too, had been praying to pass her doctor's exam and get a job, but there were only six jobs in the women's unit, which obviously made the logistics much harder for God.

Patrick, who'd been back for a couple of weeks, had found out who had the video. He had strongly recommended that they turn it over to their attorneys, or face criminal charges. They said they would.

There was still no news on who, if anyone, had arranged for the murder of Debbie Higbee. Patrick was nervous, and not living at home.

I thought he was taking too many chances, but he said this was no time to wimp out.

CLACKAMAS COUNTY COURTHOUSE
SEPTEMBER 8, 2011

The courtroom crackled with tension. The key trial against the Followers of Christ was finally starting. Horner had been waiting years for this.

"When I woke up this morning, I was feeling troubled," Mark Cogan told a potential juror, Miss Jacobs. "There were 3,552 words in the Juror Questionnaire, but there's not one word about faith healing.

"Mr. Hickman," Cogan went on, "has beliefs you may not agree with. Do you have any strong feelings about that?"

Miss Jacobs prefaced her answer with a polite smile, grateful for the opportunity as a citizen to take a bite out of Mark Cogan's ass. She had seen him on the front page of *The Oregonian* many times, and hated what the Followers were doing, a sentiment that was spreading throughout O.C., and even into the far reaches of Clackatucky.

Jacobs also was married to a former cop, and had other policemen in her family. A common dinner conversation, she said, was how defense lawyers got clients off with technicalities and theatricalism—which she *hated*, she clarified—just to make sure Cogan understood.

"Let me point out something you just did," Jacobs said to Cogan. "You put your hand on Mr. Hickman's shoulder."

"Did you think I was trying to manipulate you?" he asked. "Make you warm up to Mr. Hickman?"

"Yes."

"Do you have some distrust about me, Mr. Neidig, Mr. Hickman, or Mrs. Hickman?"

"Well, you, so far." The DAs in the case tried not to laugh but couldn't help it.

For the final, make-or-break Followers trial, Greg Horner had chosen two of his toughest, Senior Deputy DAs Mike Regan and John Wentworth. Regan was, in many ways, a black-clad, younger version of Horner, and scared the hell out of defendants with his intensity and somber appearance. Wentworth, who looked like silver-haired, patrician commentator Anderson Cooper, was known as one of the most gifted and intellectually controlled DAs on the staff, and kept his cool partly by engaging in a set of tension-reducing habits: rocking in his swivel chair, playing with his pencil, and fiddling with papers.

Cogan continued to look for sympathetic jurors, but it was almost impossible. Many of them had seen articles about the Followers for years, and had heard about Rita Swan's latest victory in Salem. It was galling to Cogan: He thought the cases had gradually devolved into trial-by-media, and now that the most important case of all was here, he couldn't seem to find any unbiased jurors.

Prospective juror Herbert Gody told Cogan, "My mother died . . . excuse me if I get emotional . . . with a prayer cloth in her hand. I have seven grandchildren, and very mixed feelings about this case. If you bring a child into this world, you have to protect them, and I don't know that Mr. and Mrs. Hickman did everything they could."

"Do you think you could give them a fair trial?" Cogan asked.

"No, I don't. I really don't."

"If the Hickmans don't testify, will you hold that against them?"

"Yes."

Judge Herndon intervened. "You haven't made up your mind already, have you?" he asked.

"No."

Mr. Gody made the cut. Herndon didn't seem unduly concerned that the Followers' new notoriety would limit the jurors' objectivity, partly, it seemed, because he didn't think the prosecution had much of a case. Same old story: the DAs didn't have any eyewitnesses, a smoking gun, or even solid circumstantial evidence, and this time the victim's entire life had lasted only nine hours. In this case, the Who Knew defense might work fine.

In the next jury panel, a techie sneered, "As an engineer, this is ludicrous to me." He said the Followers broke the law and "used religious freedom as their lame excuse." He also told Cogan that "a lot of your questioning was a speech."

When the panel left, Cogan said the engineer "was mocking, scornful, and dismissive of the Church. My concern is that he'll come in here and spout off."

"Judge," said Mike Regan, furrowing his black eyebrows, "there will always be people who have views about faith healing."

Herndon agreed. "You're not sizing these people up," he told Cogan, "to see if you want to have lunch with them."

Regan felt good. After almost fifteen years of assailing the Followers in the media and the courts, the jury pool had soured on The Kissers. The timing of that sentiment, peaking at the outset of the linchpin trial, was perfect.

In the next panel, a woman named Evelyn Jensen told a dramatic story about prayer helping heal her cancer, but she was upstaged by a guy who looked like a starving Jesus, and ranted that "the whole system is bullshit," and that "TV reporters, judges, prosecutors, and defense lawyers are all scum."

"Well," said Regan, who was interviewing him, "at least you're consistent."

Starving Jesus didn't make it, but Miss Jacobs and Evelyn Jensen did. So did Colin Fleming, a man who was "not religious" but had a Buddhist wife, along with Sophie Marks, who had taken half of her graduate courses in medical subjects. Others were a fisherman who had two cop friends, a young woman who was a caregiver, a woman whose daughter had been killed by a drunk driver with a good lawyer, and the former assistant manager of Clackatraz.

"Two. Full. Months," said DA Mike Regan in his opening statement, staring down the jury down with his dark eyes. "That's how premature David Hickman was." The moment the baby was born, Regan said, his parents should have called 911. "The entirety of this case is: 'Did you care enough to push one button?'"

Dozens of people, Regan said, had been at the birth and death, and "These folks have cell phones, landlines, computers, and TVs. We're not talking about Appalachia here."

Then he dropped a bomb. Everybody who'd been there was complicit in the death. "They could *all* have been charged," Regan said.

No one had ever said that before. It was a grave threat to the Church. There was no statute of limitations on manslaughter in Oregon. Texts went out and the phone tree lit up.

This new threat was especially disturbing for Robert "Bring It On" Billings, who had apparently orchestrated an alibi, helped dispose of the videotaped evidence that Patrick had recovered, and waited an hour and a half to call in the death.

It was also frightening for his wife, Carol, and three other family members, because they were all being called as witnesses—by the prosecution—which raised the specter of possible perjury charges if they didn't play straight. That threat alone was scary, and emblematic of Regan's style.

"Regan," Jim Band later said, "shows even more emotion than Horner and Mygrant. I had one case with him where the defendant stabbed a guy almost to death, and the defendant's girlfriend was in the lobby on the day of the trial being a total, absolute pain in the ass, and Regan got into a real pissing match with her, right outside the courtroom. I'm like, 'Mike, let's go outside.' Normally, *they're* the ones reining *us* in."

Baby David, Regan told the jury, "came out strong, arms pumping, crying, vital and vigorous, looking pretty cute." But in ninety minutes, Regan said, the baby was struggling to breathe, "gasping harder and harder, needing assistance, with lungs not ready to support life." Regan trained his intense eyes on Dale and Shannon. "These two people watched that happen. Then they went to sleep. At 2:30 Baby David passed. 911 was not called. The defense will say there were only fifteen minutes of distress, and that it was too late by then." But Regan said he would show that was a lie.

"So many wrongs in our society," Regan said, "have been committed in the name of God. You should find Dale and Shannon Hickman guilty, so you can leave here, lay your head on a pillow, and go to sleep with a good conscience."

"I have no ax to grind with law enforcement," Mark Cogan said in his opening statement. "But there are times when law enforcement goes too far. You, ladies and gentlemen, are our protection against tyranny."

Cogan painted Dale and Shannon as grieving parents who were being persecuted because of religious bigotry.

He offered the usual anti-government, pro-religion, and pro-pity litany that had worked so well before. But the jury looked repulsed.

Cogan and Neidig, though, had three aces, and Cogan started laying them out for the jury.

The first was the dependable Sad Story of Sudden Death, which was particularly plausible in this case. Cogan had a doctor who thought the baby had died from a sudden blood infection. Better still, the doctor was the Medical Examiner, Cliff Nelson, who usually testified for the prosecution, as he had in the Beagley case.

What Cogan couldn't tell the jury, unfortunately for him, was that Cliff Nelson had told the press that because he thought the death was sudden, he considered the Hickman case to be a "witch hunt." Cogan and Neidig had been excited by that, and had prepared a whole analogy between this trial and the Salem Witch Trials of the Pilgrims. Judge Herndon, however, had said that they couldn't use Nelson's specific remark, because it was too prejudicial. But maybe it would slip out anyway.

Cogan did tell the jury, though, as his opening statement continued, that there had been a big fight between Cliff Nelson and people in the DA's office, who were pushing Nelson to attack Dale and Shannon. Therefore, this wasn't just a trial of the mild-mannered Hickmans, but also the arrest-happy, publicity-hungry office of Greg Horner and his band of bullies.

Cogan's second ace was a notation in a journal. It said: "Wake Dale Up—2:15." He said the notation showed that it was already too late for Dale to save the baby, who died fifteen minutes later.

Third, they had a video. It had gotten misplaced for a while, but when it turned up, it showed the baby looking healthy. The video did, however, only show the baby shortly after birth, then ended rather abruptly, but the video that was there depicted a baby that looked fine. Of course, the baby would soon die, but Who Knew?

Cogan finished back where he started: "This is a case of the prosecution of innocent people who did not commit a crime . . . . Jurors, you are our only protection against tyranny." Cogan returned to the defendants' table, putting his hand on Dale's shoulder as he sat down.

Dale looked bewildered, as if he still didn't understand why he was here. Patrick had once said that Dale often looked puzzled when he was out in the world, because he was, as were so many of the Followers, innocent. He was not a worldly man. Many of his pursuits, such as drawing cartoons and talking about his favorite foods, were childish, and he was loved by the children in the church because he played with them on their own level. Even mild profanity was outside his sphere. The idea of spending the next six years and three months in jail on a man-2 bid was almost certainly incomprehensible to him.

After Cogan's opening, his daughter, who worked with him, couldn't find a seat, and sat in the press section, next to *The Oregonian*'s Steve Mayes. "I see you're sittin' with the enemy," Mayes said to her, and they both laughed.

Almost everybody in the courtroom—except Dale and Shannon—looked completely at home: even the jurors, who were caught up in the drama. The single most horrifying element of a criminal courtroom is that most of the people in it are having fun, making money, feeling important, and thinking about their plans, while to the defendants—terrified, bleeding money, humiliated, and uncertain—that happy existence seems as unattainable as the kingdom of heaven, and being in its midst is the cruelest torment of all.

Jim Band, across town, was reliving the good old days of drivin' fast and kickin' ass in a patrol car alongside a sergeant—all part of his new job as a supervisor—when he saw somebody scream through a red light so flagrantly that he had to pull them over, something he didn't normally do. "I don't like writing tickets," he later said, "because I don't like getting them."

"I'm sorry," the driver said, handing him her license. "I've got a lot on my mind."

"I don't need your license, because I know who you are," Band said.

"I know who you are, too." It was Sandra Mitchell, Marci's mom, Neil's grandmother, and Ava's great-grandmother.

The last time they'd seen each other was at the Beagleys' trial, when Band had challenged Sandra's lies about Neil's failing health, and exposed her to a perjury charge.

"You know," said Sandra, "the last time I saw you, I was very upset with you. And I want to apologize. I know you were doing your job." She was sweet. Band remembered sitting in her kitchen with Finn and Rhodes, when she wept about the deaths of her grandchildren and the frightening fate of her daughter.

"I'm sorry about having to send Marci and Jeff to jail," Band said. "They're good people. The whole thing was so sad. How are they doing?"

"Still tryin' to get that house built," Sandra said. It was harder without Neil's help.

Sandra Mitchell and Jim Band, by the side of the road, began a long and pleasant conversation about the family.

CLACKAMAS COUNTY COURTHOUSE
SEPTEMBER 15, 2011

DA Mike Regan, ready to launch his attack, knew that Medical Examiner Cliff Nelson would soon testify for the defense, against him. That was strange, and wouldn't look good to the jury. So Regan had to head off Nelson's testimony, and show the jury that Nelson's opinions were, in part, apparently related to hurt feelings, instead of legitimate professional differences.

Nelson's feelings were hurt, Regan thought, because the DA's office had hired another doctor to help Nelson with the important task of determining David Hickman's age, which would indicate the baby's degree of risk. Nelson seemed to have felt slighted by that, which seemed petty to many of the people who had worked so hard on this case.

The fight had started right after the autopsy. Nelson had gotten the impression, during the autopsy, that the baby had died from a sudden blood infection. But later testing showed that a sudden infection almost certainly did not kill Baby David. Even now, though, Nelson was clinging to the possibility of the Sad Story of Sudden Death, and that's the main reason Cogan and Neidig were going to call him to the stand. If Nelson could get the jury to believe in sudden death, Dale and Shannon would win. And if the "witch hunt" comment happened to emerge, so much the better. The judge would have it stricken from the record—but so what?

To blunt Nelson's upcoming testimony, Regan called, his first witness: Nelson's close associate, investigator Jeff McLennan, who'd been the first to arrive at the death scene.

Regan asked the investigator what the death scene had looked like—to make the tragedy real to the jurors—and McLennan described the tiny baby lying at the end of the bed, hugging himself, his neck arched back.

Regan asked McLennan if it was important to determine exactly how old the baby was at his birth. McLennan said yes—Baby David's age would determine if he could have lived without life support. Even more important, if the baby had not reached a certain age, his death would have come gradually, over hours, instead of minutes, as the Followers claimed.

Then defense attorney John Neidig cross-examined McLennan and went in for the kill. He tried to prompt McLennan to say that he thought no crime had been committed. But McLennan said making that determination wasn't his job. Neidig brought up the fight between Nelson and the district attorneys.

"Dr. Nelson believed no crime had been committed, didn't he?" Neidig asked.

DA John Wentworth, rocking in his swivel chair, only slightly short of the point of propulsion, snapped, "Object!"

"Sustained!" said Judge Herndon, with less body language, but even more emphasis.

But Neidig had done a good job of letting the jury know about Nelson's disaffection, and putting the DAs on the defensive. DA John Wentworth got up to put out the fire. Wentworth said that all of a sudden, it seemed as if the district attorneys were on trial.

But the DAs, he said, had a good reason to get in a tiff with Cliff Nelson. They had brought in another doctor because they needed someone who specialized in determining the age of babies, and that wasn't Nelson's specialty. Bringing in a specialist hadn't been intended as an insult to Nelson, it was just the safest course of action.

By the time Wentworth was done, the DAs were back on offense.

Then the detective who'd been at the death scene played a recording of his interview with Dale. Dale admitted, in the recording, that he thought the baby "might not make it" because he was so tiny, was unable to nurse, and kept getting cold. Dale said he thought it was God's will that his son had died.

The Sad Story of Sudden Death scenario was evaporating into thin air.

But Regan had more.

Regan introduced the logbook that said, "Wake Dale up—2:15." It was supposed to be the Hickmans' strongest piece of evidence. But Michelle Finn had directed the laboratory examination of the evidence and completely flipped its significance. It did say, "Wake Dale up—2:15." But just before "2:15" was a scratch-out, in blue ink. It had been unreadable when Finn had found it. But she had taken it to a crime lab to remove the blue ink, and see what was under it. It looked a great deal as if the notation had originally said, "Wake Dale up—1:45."

The Hickmans' prime piece of evidence suddenly looked like a fake.

Then Regan began to play the videotape of the baby's birth, when he looked strong—the tape the Hickmans thought would prove the Sad Story of Sudden Death. The tape—even though it did end abruptly, as if the last part of it might have been erased—showed what seemed to be a healthy baby. Regan's next witness cut that possibility to shreds.

What the tape really showed, said child-abuse expert Dr. Dan Leonhardt, were the classic signs of a baby boy looking good immediately after birth—but actually headed for certain death, without medical treatment. Very early preemies, the doctor said, often seem fine right after they're born because they're still strong from being in the womb. Despite that, they are not developed enough to breathe adequately, eat enough to live, or stay warm enough to survive. Any one of the three would kill them, and the combination was absolutely lethal.

It was ridiculous, Leonhardt said, to try to substitute hot towels for an incubator, and tiny sips of water and milk for a feeding tube. Those absurd efforts, he said, doomed the baby, who would almost certainly have survived in a hospital.

Very shortly after Baby David's birth, the doctor said, he would have begun struggling to breathe, and would not have looked "anything *close* to a normal, healthy baby." David would have suffered a slow, obvious decline into death, Leonhardt said, that couldn't possibly have happened in fifteen minutes. There would have been hours of extreme distress in which Dale and Shannon should have called 911.

"You don't call 911," the doctor said, "when he's going gray . . . ."

Cogan took a shot at establishing that only a doctor would know what to do. Leonhardt's response: You wouldn't need to be a doctor—you'd just need to be a decent mom or dad.

Juror Evelyn Jensen glanced around the jury box. She couldn't be sure, but she had a strong feeling that the Hickmans were in a hole as inescapable as the grave.

OREGON CITY
SEPTEMBER 19, 2011

I met Patrick for lunch at The Verdict. He made no effort to hide who he was, as he had when we'd met first met there, during the Beagley trial. He was living back at home, with Ella and Pat. Two weeks ago he had learned that the investigation of the murder-for-hire of Lynn Benton's wife had narrowed to one person, who was definitely not a Follower. He didn't know who that person was. He didn't care. His full focus was now on the trial.

He looked bronzed and strong and his hair was lighter than ever, but his eyes still looked haunted. "We're so close now," he said. "The atmosphere of the church is like End Times. People are freaking.

Half of them love me and half of them hate my guts. Nobody knows if this trial is going to put the Church in heaven or hell, but either way, it feels like the end is near."

"Dale seems to be in a daze."

"That's just Dale. We used to have so much fun together. He was a terror on his ATV. And he was always funny. I'm going to miss him, either way."

"Either way?"

"If we lose, I'm outta here. As far away as I can get. I've pushed my luck too far, and I'm still too vulnerable to people trying to destroy my life. If we win, I'll stay, and finish reforming the Church. But Dale will be gone."

The fleet of TV news units in front of the courthouse grew larger as the appearance of Medical Examiner Cliff Nelson loomed.

"You should go back in," Patrick said. "I'm not coming. It would cause a scene, and I'm so sick of drama."

Nelson's testimony, though, turned out to be anticlimactic. He had been under a lot of pressure to get over his hurt feelings.

"Cliff Nelson," James Rhodes later said, "had been ill-advised to make that 'witch-hunt' remark. It made him look like a grandstander. But he came around."

Michelle Finn agreed. "He seems like an angry guy sometimes, and he isn't a great team player, but he is a professional."

When Nelson took the stand, Cogan couldn't get him to talk about the fight with Horner's office, and he even backed away from the Sudden Death scenario.

Cogan and Neidig didn't have much left—just the usual parade of Followers. But even those usually dependable witnesses were hinky now, because the Hickmans had already been caught in two Big Lies: the Fifteen Minute Lie, and the Sad Lie of Sudden Death. With all of this talk about putting even more people in jail, it was a bad time to commit perjury.

KATU's Dan Tilkin, who had single-handedly uncovered the

deaths of the two Followers kids in Idaho—a feat Rita Swan considered "groundbreaking"—had learned from his sources that there was another issue with the timeline of the birth: That Shannon's water hadn't broken hours before her delivery, but days. Even if that was true, it might not have harmed the baby, but the talk about it seemed to show that the Follower's solidarity was crumbling.

For the next three days of the trial, the friends and family of Dale and Shannon dug the hole even deeper with contradictions, claims of memory loss, and the Followers' single most self-destructive trait: delusions of grandeur, crowned with the narcissistic assumption that God prioritized their needs over those of everyone else on earth. When Regan asked Shannon's mother if she thought preemies were at high risk, she said, "Well, *I* believe in God. So I don't know." When she thought the baby was failing, why didn't she call 911? "I put my faith and my trust in *God*." Did she think the baby might die? "I could get hit by a truck *tomorrow* and die."

Shannon's father looked like a liar when he said that the reason someone hid the videotape was because "in the event this ever came to trial," The Followers, "I didn't want it destroyed, either accidentally or on purpose."

Wentworth asked one of Dale's relatives if she had any concerns about the baby's health. "No, no, no, no. Because God had taken a hand in that day, and we were just there to take part in it."

When Dale finally took the stand, he seemed wan and beaten. He spoke humbly and cried believably.

But Shannon was not at her best. Her thin lips were too tightly pursed, and her nose was canted too high to capture sympathy.

"Should you have called 911?" Wentworth asked.

"I can't take it back. So it's irrelevant. . . ." She smiled at him contemptuously. "Have you ever given birth?" she sneered. "What happened, happened. . . . Anyway"—she shrugged—"it's not my decision."

Wentworth asked if she had read a popular book on pregnancy, and she said she'd read only the parts on nutrition. "But then it got wet, so I threw it in the garbage."

"Did you read about infections in premature labor?"

"Like I said," she huffed, "I only read the diet part." Anger stretched the skin of her face white.

Wentworth asked her how Dale looked when he brought in their dying son.

"I don't remember. I think he was crying. I seen the baby, and he was pale. I watched him take a breath, and I had to lay back down."

"You heard your son take a breath?"

"I didn't hear him."

"You said you did."

"I seen him."

"You saw him?"

"I seen him open his mouth and take a breath." She said she saw the baby take two breaths in five minutes. "There was a long time between breaths." She looked at Wentworth as if he had a devil.

"And you did nothing to get him medical care?"

"I did not," she said sullenly.

"I have no further questions, Your Honor."

Neidig, looking even sadder than the mother who'd lost her son, tried to clean up the mess by injecting the proper level of pathos, but the show was over, and the jury was restless.

The bare arrogance of Shannon Hickman, the Prophet's great-granddaughter, had ended whatever chance the Followers of Christ had to preserve the moral authority of a Church that had arrived in America almost three hundred years ago, had thrived throughout four Great Awakenings, and had nurtured the spirits of fifty generations.

America, over many centuries, has tolerated and even celebrated wild differences, and has forgiven untold sins. America, at this moment personified by twelve jurors, could accept the Peculiar People, and even defend their rights—because we are all, in one way or another, peculiar people.

But nobody likes a narcissist. Especially one on trial for the death of her child.

Deliberation took a matter of minutes.

Dale: Guilty, man-2.

Shannon: Guilty, man-2.

Outside the courthouse, Brent had his arm around the shoulder of one of the Hickman boys.

I called Patrick and told him the outcome. "Good," he said. His voice was flat. "I'll celebrate when I hear the sentences. Hopefully."

21

IT IS FINISHED

We'll forgive all our enemies, and pray for their souls,
And ask for God's mercy, for their hearts to be whole.
—Dale Hickman

Oregon City
October 31, 2011

"Your Honor," Mike Regan said at the Hickmans' sentencing, "I'd like to make an analogy, exaggerated on purpose. Imagine a group of people wearing black robes and black masks, in a forest, around a bonfire, holding hands—and sacrificing a sick child to the fire. We would punish that to the fullest extent, because it would personify evil."

The Followers, he said, had been "sacrificing lives, year after year, decade after decade." Regan explained that the Followers usually would name a firstborn son after his father. "But to Dale and Shannon Hickman," Regan said, "David Hickman wasn't even worth wasting a name on."

Looking hard into Judge Herndon's eyes, Regan said, "Someone has to speak up about this false, man-made belief that evil equals faith."

Regan said that a source within the Church—someone they had come to trust—had told the DA's office that the Followers were changing—rapidly, historically—but that the evil in the Church would never end without the imposition of maximum, life-changing prison terms.

"This has to stop, Your Honor. The only way we can do that is to sentence them to the fullest extent of the law."

Dale, looking broad-shouldered and sharp in a nice suit and new haircut, seemed to grow smaller with each word. Shannon, her hair stringy, gelled, and matted, looked as if she'd given up.

Mark Cogan looked defeated, too—almost sentimental. For almost three years, he'd been fighting for a principle, even more than for his clients, enduring snubs and insults from his liberal Portlandia coterie, and even death threats from other "progressives." He longed for a respite—"not just for me and the staff," he later said, "but for our families, too"—and there was overlap in that, since his daughter had worked with him for years.

He began with a remarkably bland comment: "This case is rather perplexing." The main reason to show Dale and Shannon mercy, he said without irony, was so that they could take care of their children: Daisy, and their new baby, Dale—named after his father—who was still an infant, born just before the trial. Putting the Hickmans in jail, Cogan said, would be "unspeakably cruel" and "barbarous" to "their innocent children." Cogan pled for probation. Dale wiped away a tear. Wentworth rocked, and Regan did paperwork.

Judge Herndon, looking at the Hickmans with lingering incomprehension, said, "There has never been a single night during this trial that I didn't awaken." When the trial started, he said, he thought a guilty verdict would be "a stretch." But the jury ruled unanimously: "in a stunningly quick time."

Herndon looked at the Followers in the gallery. "You folks could be a beacon of faith in this community. But your tortured views about doctors make you otherwise."

He announced the sentence. It was the max: six years and three months for both of them, with no time off for any reason, followed by three years of supervised probation.

A jolt shot through the courtroom. Women looked at their laps and wept. This was a blow to the gut of every Follower. Horner's office had declared open season on anybody at a child's death, not just the parents. And there was still a Judas in the church—maybe even a dozen, it sometimes now seemed.

Eleanor Evans, sitting with Ella, texted Rita Swan. Some of the Followers glanced nervously at them, but the two happy women, joyfully preoccupied, shunned them.

For Rita, the length of the sentences was a satisfying shock. But she felt it was tragic that the Hickmans, who had neglected their child for hours, would now have to suffer more than the Worthingtons, Beagleys, and Wylands, who'd neglected theirs for months or years.

She prayed that Dale and Shannon would not be demonized in prison.

After all the horror that Rita Swan had seen and suffered, and all that she had learned from it, there was one lesson she held most closely to her heart: Human beings are not demons—they can do evil things, but they do not have devils in them, and they all have the right to redeem themselves.

And yet in the realm of politics and justice—in the service of the greater good—the finest thing that some who have sinned can do, as redemption beckons from afar, is to suffer.

Suffering, sadly enough, is often an indispensable impetus for change, and after decades in pursuit of a single goal, Rita Swan was seeing—quite suddenly, it seemed—the sprouting seed of transformation in America.

"The difference in jury attitudes, and the state's degree of success over the four trials, was striking," she later wrote in her CHILD Newsletter, which by this time had Internet archives that were encyclopedic in depth. "The amazing saga of Oregon was a strong message for the country."

Her assessment was proven true within a matter of months, when a rural Oregon boy who was Neil's age, Austin Sprout, died from a treatable condition, and his parents, members of The Church of the

First Born, didn't even try to fight charges of negligent homicide. They confessed, pled guilty, and agreed to provide their other kids with medical care. For their cooperation, they were sentenced to five years' probation, with close monitoring of the surviving children. Other Church members, the local DA later said, were "very receptive" to understanding the current law, and obeying it. And in Philadelphia, Herbert and Catherine Schaible—punished only with probation in their child's 2009 death—were charged with third-degree murder in the death of their two-year old son, Brandon, and faced 40 year sentences. It showed a huge shift.

The court adjourned for ten minutes while the bailiff got handcuffs.

In the hallway, Jeff and Marci Beagley sat together, not talking. Brent and Raylene Worthington stood on the outside of a quiet group. Brent nodded politely to me. Tim Wyland had his arm around Rebecca, who was still jail-pale after her recent release. Tim's father, Jim, was typically unruffled, but white-haired elder Fred Smith scowled as he led away the man who'd let himself go blind. Rebecca stared me down, I stared back, and she looked away.

In the courtroom, *The Oregonian*'s Steve Mayes scribbled into his yellow tablet while the other reporters tapped on laptops. Somebody just behind me couldn't stop crying.

For reasons I didn't understand at all, tears formed in my eyes. To hide them, I looked down, and focused on things that made me mad. I thought about the two grown sons sitting on their dying father while he begged to go to the hospital, and the woman with a prolapsed uterus scooting around the floor like a crab. I pictured Alayna's eye, and Ava's cyst, and little Baby David hugging himself in death. And there were always mental images of Neil in that courthouse—revving his Camaro, operating his Bobcat, flying over dunes in his ATV. Sometimes his spirit seemed to hover here like a specter, lost, looking for a way home. I felt I knew Neil well by this point.

I thought about the personal abuse that Rita Swan, a genuine American hero, had endured from fundamentalists, lobbyists, and legislators, decade after decade, with barely a penny of help from a vast American religious community that should have revered her.

And I thought about Patrick, abandoned by his wife for reasons that would never make sense.

As the bailiff approached with handcuffs, Dale held Shannon one last time and didn't cry until his cuffs clicked shut. They would not be able to see each other for the next six years.

Outside, as the Followers drifted off—many to the church—DA John Wentworth, his silvery hair shining in the sun, stood beaming outside The Verdict.

"You guys did a hell of a job," I said. "Twelve eye-witnesses versus two doctors who weren't even there."

No comment on that. Just an even bigger smile.

I called Patrick.

"Meet me at the cemetery," he said.

In the parking lot behind the courthouse, a line of prisoners in jumpsuits, wrist restraints, and leg manacles shuffled from the basement to a white van. They looked jailhouse. Dale emerged looking dazed and bug-eyed. Then a line of women came out, and Shannon, on her bad-hair day, fit right in as she did the perp-walk with eyes locked straight.

"Crowded in that van," I said to the bailiff. "Dale's not accustomed to that."

"He'll get used to crowds."

OREGON CITY
OCTOBER 31, 2011

At the church, midway between the prison and the cemetery, about forty men gathered out back. The teenage boys were off to one side, smoking their Camels, with home-school, it would appear, done for the day. The women were in the kitchen, preparing a feast for the canonization of the church's two greatest martyrs, the dutiful Shannon and the legendary Dale, who would still be in his early thirties when he got out of prison, just the right age to be the new Prophet.

But prison would change him. How could it not? Year after year, he would be among people who would consider his beliefs to be ridiculous at best, but mostly just inconsequential, as he blended into a prison population of men struggling to find new lives. For the first time in his life, Dale would be, in a strange way, free.

Patrick was standing by his father's grave when I arrived.

'Where's Gabriel?" he asked.

"Back at college." My son had been helping me all summer with the interviews, the trials, the transcripts, and the manuscript. For months before that, he'd been in charge of the Beagley case and all of the tech-support. "It's not much fun since he left," I said. "There's nothing like working with your son."

"Did he charge you?"

"The stuff I usually do myself was free, because he said a monkey could do it. The tech work cost me tuition."

"Did he learn a lot?"

"He did. But not from me—from Neil. Partly because they're the same age, you know. Just a few weeks apart. I think he learned how to be a man."

"You don't mean like a tough-guy macho-man, right? That doesn't sound like Gabriel."

"No Pat, not at all. To me a man is somebody who doesn't just give his love to people, but his work, too. And Gabriel really came through for me. I think he got that from Neil."

It was dry and sunny but a rainbow was forming in the west, horizon to horizon. It must have been raining in the coastal mountains.

"A weird thing happened at sentencing," I said. "I got all glassy-eyed, and I don't know why."

"You don't?" he said, with infinite patience, looking at me with blue-green eyes that were finally at peace. "It was because you felt bad for them."

His own war now over, finally won, Patrick looked to the sky—still bright-shining blue—as sparkling drops of rain began to fall, one by one, creating colors as dazzling as diamonds, like a shower of flowers sent down from the sun. It was common and magical weather for that time of year.

"What's the latest in the Church?" I asked.

"More and more changes. Faster than ever."

"I think history changed today," I said. "Mostly because of you."

"The history of the Followers?"

"That's the story I'm going to tell. But that's just the start of it."

"How does it end?"

"I don't think it does."

COFFEE CREEK CORRECTIONAL FACILITY
THANKSGIVING, NOVEMBER 24, 2011

Dale loved state prison. It was so much better than Clackatraz.

He told his family that his only complaint—an unusual one in state prison—was that, "There just aren't enough hours in the day."

Of course, it wasn't always easy to hold fast and forgive. He had a new cellmate named Michael who wouldn't shower or flush their combined toilet-sink—which Dale called the Flushinator 2000—but even Michael was better than no cellie at all.

Michael would converse along the lines of, "Wow, this book I'm reading is so good—guess what page I'm on? I can't believe I'm reading so much. My tooth hurts. I'm used to sleeping on concrete. Guess what page I'm on?" All that while he was still reading. Then he'd put down the book, pace, and ask Dale, "Are you saying 'pow'?" Dale would say no, and Michael would keep asking. One of the saddest aspects of American prison is that now millions of the mentally ill end up in jail, as in antiquity.

A week ago, Dale had gotten into trouble for trying to mail home a drawing of the Flushinator 2000, on the grounds that any depiction of the facility was part of an escape plan. Dale, raised with good manners, didn't react sarcastically to that accusation, so they just cursed at him and dropped it.

Dale was drawing more and more, and had just finished an entire comic book about a caveman who created modern inventions, such as a Swiss Army Rock. Dale's brother Lee had sent him the book *How to Draw Cars,* and his first attempt, a 1956 Chevy Bel Air—their dad's favorite car—was extremely promising. He was also practicing for a talent show in an a cappella group that was learning Billy Joel's "The Longest Time."

Dale especially loved the mess hall, where he was considered the cellblock clown. Once he made an inmate with a life sentence spew tea out his nose just by saying, "What goes in prison, *stays* in prison."

The food tasted good, and after Dale had been there long enough, it tasted great. One favorite meal was pork chops, cornbread, rice, and salad. Mexican night was tacos, red beans and rice, and tortillas. Lunch was dependable but not spectacular. Breakfast, he recently wrote his family, "was eggs, toast, Facon (fake bacon), and hash browns—nothing to write home about. Oh wait—never mind."

He'd seen two fights, and once it had sounded like a riot had broken out, but it was just the Ducks losing a big game. He got more letters than anyone in the cell block, and had to trade his fruit for more envelopes, because he only got two every month.

He couldn't believe it was already Thanksgiving. Time was flying.

As Dale sat down in the mess hall to say grace, his mother, back home, read aloud his most recent letter to his daughter, Daisy, as the blessing for their Thanksgiving potluck. Daisy was doing well, partly because now she had to go to a doctor when she got sick. Little Dale was also under court order to get medical care, like the kids in the Beagley, Wyland, and Worthington families. But that was actually a relief, after so much tension about it. Because the inner-circle families were going to the doctor, a lot of other families had started, and some were quite open about it. Sometimes, for many of them, it was hard to imagine what all the uproar had been about.

"We have so much to be thankful for," Dale's letter said. In language that was equally familial and ethereal, he bestowed upon his daughter the blessing of having her in his heart, if not his arms, conjuring comforting images that even a child could see of her beauty, innocence, and charm. At the end he wrote, "Keep being the sweet loving girl that you are. I love you more than a lion's roar. I love you with all my heart, and more." Underneath it was a fine pencil sketch of Little Dale, his large eyes filling his small face, with ringlets of curls above, radiating the joyous purity found only in a child's love.

After saying grace for his mess-hall table, Dale began to pass around a salad that was much nicer than usual. "Wow!" he said loudly. "This salad is awesome! Who brought it?"

Everybody at the table roared. The joke shot around the room, all the inmates started riffing on it, and hilarity reigned. Dale pushed it to a new level with his traditional Thanksgiving turkey call.

The prison felt, at least for a few moments, like a family gathering. A guard told Dale that had never happened before.

OREGON CITY
DECEMBER 15, 2011

"Did you hear the news?" Rod asked Patrick. "There was a story in the paper today by those guys that cover the Followers, Bella and Mayes. It looks like the person who hired the murder of Lynn Benton's wife was Lynn Benton, himself. Or herself. That's what the shooter said. She told the DA—John Wentworth, that guy in Dale's case—that Benton gave her two thousand bucks to go shoot his wife. The gun the shooter used was the same make as Lynn Benton's gun.

"But the bullets didn't kill her. So somebody—guess who—came over and beat the wife to death."

"Oh, Lord."

"Some of the people in the Church think it's the greatest thing ever. Not because they hold a grudge against Lynn Benton, God forbid. They think, here's this woman who's playing God with her own body by getting doctors to change her sex. And people are thinking that her doctors were probably giving her huge amounts of male steroids. So she goes into a roid-rage, they think, and does something way worse than any Follower ever did. I even heard a rumor that she had something to do with the death of her first husband. All of that's just speculation—but the Followers feel pretty good about themselves."

"That's a heck of a way to feel superior."

"It's mostly just the hotheads that are gloating. Things are so different. It's almost the way we dreamed about, all those years ago."

"That's what I hear. I'm on my way to visit Dale. You want to come?"

"Sure. I miss Dale."

"Me, too. I miss a lot of things."

DECEMBER 16, 2011
SIOUX CITY, IOWA

Rita Swan was preparing for a cold and bittersweet Christmas. It would be the last she and Doug would share in their Sioux City home, where for the last 28 years they had been able to see pastures and pine trees stretch for miles in the green valley below. Over the years, Rita had left this cherished home many times, often for trials and hearings that were heartbreaking, always longing to return to Doug, Catherine, and Marsha, and ride horses with them in dappled autumns, summer sun, and icy-clear winters.

But Marsha had moved to Dublin, Ireland, where she worked in publishing, and had written a novel—something Rita might have done herself if her life had been different. Catherine was in Lexington, Kentucky, where Rita and Doug were now headed to live.

They had found a house there that was laid out well for Doug, whose mobility was limited by Parkinson's disease. But it was small, and the lot was tiny, in a flat subdivision.

Doug and Rita planned to work for social-justice groups in Lexington, and Rita was still fulfilling a vow of almost forty years: to spend all of her life on a mission that had already kept countless other mothers from suffering what she had, and had, in one sense, made her the godmother, or at least protector, of thousands of children she would never meet.

But packing memories into boxes, for a house that could not hold enough of them, was very difficult.

Even so, she and Doug had each other, and were blessed by a bond that had not been broken by sorrow, but deepened. Soon Catherine would be close. And when Marsha came home, as she did several times a year, they would all be together again.

Life would be good.

For Rita Swan, family, as always, was everything.

Her love was still young-hearted, her dreams still alive, and even now she was at the peak of her powers, facing her future with the resilient everblooming courage of youth, when a heart can be broken and still remain open, and days can unfold like flowers.

WEST LINN, OREGON
DECEMBER 17, 2011

As the winter days darkened, Jim Band, Michelle Finn, and James Rhodes got together for the first time in a long time, and for all they knew, the last time, to tell war stories about the glorious days of pain in the Clackamas County Children's Crusade.

Rhodes, now a lieutenant and desk jockey like Band, poised for big things, sipped a beer—a relatively rare pleasure for somebody on the Paleo Diet—and reminisced longingly about the days he'd once prayed would end. Finn had recently gone on the same diet, going from toned to more toned. Band, though, hadn't changed much—he still did the Navy SEAL level of CrossFit, and still looked ripped.

"It was a fun time," Rhodes said. "I know that's a horrible thing to say. Kids died."

"But that's the reality of our lives," said Finn, who still went to crime scenes, working CSI, rather than Detectives.

"You get immune to it," Rhodes said. "As a PIO, I talk to people now outside law enforcement, and shit that I think is funny, they don't."

"What I don't miss," Band said, "is that every night in Detectives you go home thinking, 'What did I forget?'"

"I know," said Finn. "What didn't I do? Who should I have called? Who was lying? Why? Know how I finally shut that off?" Finn asked.

"How?"

"Got out of Detectives," she said.

"I've got friends now," Band said, "who aren't on the job. We talk about kids and stuff. I don't talk Cop all the time,"

"I know an easier way to do that," Rhodes said. "Don't have any friends. I've got a gate at my place now. A barbed-wire fence. Dogs. Cameras."

"He does," Band said. "I've been there. It looks like the Beagleys' place. Five trailers."

"Headstones," said Rhodes. "Our own cemetery."

"I'll say this about the Followers," Band said. "I've had cases that haunted me way more. The ones that break your heart have victims who want to be victims. The Followers just want to be martyrs."

"Or talk their kids into it," Rhodes said.

"But we had something special with the Followers," Finn said, "that we'll probably never have again. The system worked like it's supposed to. Even when we lost, with Ava, it made stuff happen all across the country. You could see it on the Net. When we got better at it—with Neil, and Alayna, and the Hickman baby—I pulled up stuff about it from all around the world. People were saying, 'Look what Oregon's doing.'"

"We did protect some kids," said Rhodes, pouring himself another half-glass from a pitcher.

"My friend from the Church," Band said, "still doesn't realize how much he changed things. He's not worried like he used to be, because he doesn't have much left to lose, so he's pushing those people harder than ever. What a great guy."

"A great man," said Finn.

"I'll drink to that," Band said. "And to Rita Swan and Greg Horner. She got us the law and he enforced it."

They touched their glasses.

"I always saw this whole thing as being about Katie Beagley," said Rhodes. "I'll never forget her sitting on that bathtub, lying her ass off every time Marci squeezed her leg, with her brother dead in the other room. If your snitch hadn't stepped in, Katie would be with Neil now, suckin' mud. But she's fine and Horner's making sure she stays that way. But know what? There's not one of us in this room that wouldn't give our life for her or her parents, and they still wouldn't piss on us if we were on fire."

"Good for them," Band said. "It's a free country. I remember when we flat-out told the Beagleys and Hickmans, 'You may not know it, but the police are there for you, too. If you need help, call.'"

"Remember when the media was at Dale's house, and he called 911?" Finn asked.

"I know why he did that," Rhodes said. "Lack of faith."

They had another round, toasted the wondrous days of doubt— gone for good now, God willing—and went home to their families.

EPILOGUE: EXODUS

The showdown had been coming for a long time, and now that it was here, Patrick felt almost relaxed as he pulled into the church parking lot, crowded with the cars of people preparing for the Christmas party. He had brought a cedar-planked whole salmon, with a Bing-cherry-and-cashew crust. It was his mom's recipe—Salmon Lorraine. She'd passed it on to him, and he'd given it to Ella.

Coming to the Christmas party felt surreal. So many memories. The oldest one was from 1974, when the Christmas party was just after his dad's funeral. Back then the church had seemed huge, and the kids had run in circles at parties just to burn off the thrill. That was when Tim Wyland and Vernon Thaine had been so kind to him, and Jeff Beagley, who'd just met Marci, gave him his first Holy Greeting. He'd been so cruel to Ella that day, but thank God she had Eleanor Evans with her.

His best memory was the New Year's Eve Party of 1990, when he'd first kissed Theresa. Vernon Thaine had just died, but Jacqueline

Beagley and Monique Wyland were still alive. He remembered saying "The Family Prayer" that day, because two or three kids had just
died. That was when it had felt as if they'd all be together forever.

He remembered the Christmas party three years ago, driving
through a blizzard with medicine for Mike Thaine's little kid, Conrad. That was the year he met Jim, and turned in the Beagleys and
Worthingtons. It was when the people he loved most stopped loving
him. Even Theresa.

As Patrick walked through the halls of the church, he got the re-
ception he'd expected. Half the people treated him like family, and
others looked at him like he had a devil.

Patrick found Brent and gave him the salmon.

"I remember this dish," Brent said. "It's Salmon Lorraine." He
looked wistful.

"It's Salmon Ella now," Patrick said. "I know it doesn't sound as
good, but what can I do?" Brent laughed.

"I'm not coming to the party," Patrick said. "Too many people
blame me for what's happened. That's why I haven't been coming to
services. I still know everybody, though, and I know things have
changed. I know you're doing the right thing with your kids. God
bless. I hope you're letting others do it, too."

"It's not up to me," Brent said.

Patrick waved away the excuse. "What you did with Ava"—Brent
looked away—"look at me, Brent. What you did with Ava is between
you and God. But what you do now is between you and me. That's
how it has to be. And if somebody dies here for no good reason, or some
little kid suffers, I'm going to come to the service and rebuke whoever's responsible, and ask people to leave with me. And that'll just be
the beginning."

Patrick looked around. Every inch of the church felt like home.
"So that's my gift to you: motivation to use the love I know you have
in the right way."

"I understand," Brent said. He looked as if he did.

"Merry Christmas."

"Merry Christmas."

That was the last time Patrick Robbins was ever in the Church of the Followers of Christ.

Patrick had hoped he would feel better after the confrontation. But he felt as empty as he had when he'd lost his dad. He sent a Christmas text to Theresa and her new husband, put a Christmas CD in the player, and advanced it to "O Holy Night." When the song got to "a thrill of hope, the weary world rejoices," he pushed EJECT.

He wished he was welcome at the party. Paul, at almost four, would be old enough to feel the shock of joy that Patrick remembered so well.

OREGON CITY
EASTER SUNDAY, APRIL 8, 2012

The early Oregon spring had been a gray plague of rain, rain, and record rain, in a region famous for record rain. With the rain came a new illness that swept through Oregon City, Portland, and most of the Valley. It was labeled, in the fashion of old-school medicine, as whooping cough, but was probably closer to being a nonspecific cluster of maladies that were triggered by an endless invasion of multiple, mutating viruses, bacteria, fungi, allergens, and probably mercury rain from China. Who knew? All anybody knew was that everybody was sick.

And so it came as a shock when Easter morning dawned fair and bright, glistening in the crystalline clarity that always followed heavy spring rains.

It was a minor miracle, not to last, but meant to savor.

The backyard was even dry enough for Patrick to hide Easter eggs and brightly wrapped candy for the first time in Paul's life, instead of hiding coins, which couldn't be ruined by rain. Because the eggs and candy were bigger than coins, they were harder to hide, but Patrick matched their colors with his flowers for camouflage, and they looked beautiful and strange among the red and blue primroses, purple crocuses, sunlit daffodils, and pure white lilies.

Patrick and Ella had stayed up half the night painting the eggs, and trying to find a past when happy days had been common. Savoring an excellent Syrah-Cab from the Oregon Pinot Club, Ella told Patrick that she remembered cradling him in her arms once for so long that their mother had to pull him away, and she said that she had been afraid they'd pulled him away forever when they began to shun her. That feeling of losing him, she said, lasted long after their parents had died, until the day she finally forgave him for hurting her, and for never trying to find her. The forgiveness had come during the war, she said. "I figured, what the hell, if I could give those wounded boys in Iraq so much love, why couldn't I give some to my only brother? Love's not like money—the more you give, the more you have. That's when I came back."

Patrick couldn't remember the rest of it. He'd had some wine himself, and wasn't accustomed to it.

So they had their egg hunt, and Paul—at age four looking much more like a little boy than a toddler, except for cheeks that were still baby-pink—was overjoyed, delighting when his eyes distinguished colored eggs from flowers as he ran around the yard with bunny ears on. The sun, so rare, was like gold, and they sat on the back deck and drank it in, pure vitamin D, the elixir against illness and depression, feeling as warm on their faces as the hand of God. The sun shot right through Patrick's white shirt and melted knots of muscle that felt like they'd been there all winter. Maybe all his life.

Then Ella gave Patrick a long list of things to get at the grocery store, because she was making an Easter brunch, she said, that he'd never forget. Patrick didn't want to go to the Fred Meyer store on Molalla, because he didn't want to see any Church people, so he went to Gladstone, driving past the beauty shop where Lynn Benton's wife had been murdered. Now it was the Free Spirit Tattoo parlor. It now looked as if the shooter in the case might have been helped by her son. He would soon be arrested. So would Lynn Benton, for aggravated murder, and conspiracy to commit murder. Benton's nightmare was just beginning, as Patrick's ended. It was just one more tragedy in a year too full of tragedies—one more innocent person sacrificed for something that probably seemed important at the time, with other lives shattered for the commission of the crime.

When Patrick got back, Ella opened the door for him.

Inside was everybody—at least, everybody that he wanted to see. There were dozens of people, and those closest to the door said, "Surprise!" when he walked in. Out back were dozens more, maybe even a hundred, and the picnic table was piled with cakes, hams, a turkey, a glistening icy punchbowl, cherry-crusted salmon, pies, deviled eggs, and divinity. All the women hugged him and the guys shook his hand. They were mostly people who were still in the Church, or who'd left it. Rod and his wife, Lorene, were there, of course, and so were Bill and Liz, Marie and her husband, some of the longtime dropouts, Eleanor Evans, Mike Thaine and his brothers, and the widow of an old friend who'd recently died peacefully in a hospital. There were even people from the world, including a doctor that Patrick often referred people to, and some folks from the Baptist church that a lot of the ex-Followers were attending. Kids were everywhere, mostly by the koi pond. There was the kid who'd almost died from asthma before Patrick had convinced his parents to get him treated, and others that he'd helped with sinus infections, lung infections, and the kinds of little problems that kids had once actually died from, for reasons that now seemed not even bizarre, but quaint, like musty relics from an attic.

Overwhelmed, uncertain, Patrick asked Marie, "What's up? Why'd everybody come over here today?"

"For you, silly." She threw her arms around his neck. "Because of you, Patrick." He took a deep breath. Held it. Touched her arms.

"Patrick," Rod yelled from the yard, "say grace. I'm starving!"

"Where's my son?" asked Patrick.

Ella brought him over, and Patrick picked up Paul, still wearing his bunny ears, chocolate on his face.

"Can you say 'The Family Prayer' with me?" he asked Paul. The little boy nodded and his bunny ears bobbed.

"May the love of our family," Patrick and Paul Robbins said together, "made eternal by each new generation, rise above discord, difficulty, and even death, as it heads toward the horizon of time."

Paul, who usually said the prayer at night, kept going. "And God bless and watch over Mommy, and God bless Daddy, and Aunt Ella, and all of the people who love us, and all of the people who don't. And forgive us for doing bad things, cuz nobody's perfect. World without end. All family. All friends. Amen."

"Amen," they said.

INDEX

Adventist Hospital, 123
Ahearn, June, 33–35, 36–38, 60
allergic shiners, 235
American Academy of Pediatrics, 292
AmericasLastDays.com, 194
Animal Liberation Front, 416
The Apostle, 90
Arizona, 104, 394
Arkansas, 182
Aryan Brotherhood, 326
Asser, Seth, 83
autopsies. *See specific children autopsied*

Babyland Cemetery, 394
Baker, Mark, 8–9, 11–12
Baker, Mary, 8–10
Baldwin, Vic, 16, 17
Band, James ("Jim"), 119–20, 398, 442
    in Beagley case, 201–2, 204–5, 210–18, 226–30, 323–25, 327–31, 338, 341, 350, 362–63
on Followers of Christ, 443
Horner and, 123–25, 204
Mitchell and, 223–24, 423–24
on Mygrant, 355
Nichols, D., and, 112, 113
on Regan, 421
Robbins, Patrick, and, 121–22, 127–28, 142, 145, 176, 180, 314, 363–64, 373, 380, 399, 444
Smith, F., and, 204–5
Worthington case and, 263, 264, 289, 293
baptism, 111
Barnes, Jennifer, 400–401, 404, 407, 410, 411
Battle, Jeff, 416
Beagley, Jacqueline, 74, 76, 322
Beagley, Jeff, 296
    in Beagley case, 2–3, 188–89, 195, 196–97, 210–13, 231, 338–39, 348–51
    as father, 74, 126, 127, 130, 132–34, 186–88, 198–99

Beagley, Jeff, (*continued*)
  Robbins, Patrick, and, 21, 128, 187–88, 234–35, 242–43
  Worthington case and, 162, 178, 350
Beagley, Katie, 178
  in Beagley case, 209–10, 444
  sickness of, 133, 137, 144–45, 176, 179, 180, 188–89, 228
Beagley, Laina, 271
Beagley, Marci
  in Beagley case, 206–10, 221–23, 226–29, 231, 329, 351–54, 360
  doubts of, 220, 225, 227, 242, 299, 330
  medical treatments of, 91, 329, 352
  as mother, 74, 129, 198–99
  in prison, 390–91
  Worthington case and, 178, 272
Beagley, Neil, 183–85, 230. *See also* Beagley case
  autopsy of, 215–17, 228, 342–43
  as brother, 137, 144–45, 178, 179
  death of, 201–28, 332–33, 338–39, 352
  DHS and, 188–89, 195–97, 325, 346–48, 360
  father of, 74, 126, 127, 130, 132–34, 186–88, 198–99
  mother of, 74, 129, 198–99
  notebook about, 221–23
  refusal of care by, 197, 204, 209, 293, 325, 332, 339, 351, 355, 357, 359
  sickness of, 133, 180, 190–91, 195–97, 224, 323, 328, 329, 330, 335, 340, 341–42, 344, 350, 351, 353, 355–56, 357
Beagley, Norma, 207
  in Beagley case, 195–96, 338, 339–40
  medical treatment for, 323, 340–41
Beagley, Steve, 273
Beagley case, 293
  Band in, 201–2, 204–5, 210–18, 226–30, 323–25, 327–31, 338, 341, 350, 362–63

Beagley, Jeff, in, 2–3, 188–89, 195, 196–97, 210–13, 231, 338–39, 348–51
Beagley, K., in, 209–10, 444
Beagley, M., in, 206–10, 221–23, 226–29, 231, 329, 351–54, 360
Beagley, Norma, in, 195–96, 338, 339–40
Benton in, 201, 202, 205–6, 338
Crone, C., in, 190, 329, 330
Defense Fund, 241–42, 324, 344–46
DHS in, 188–89, 195–97, 325, 346–48, 360
Divelbis in, 322–23, 342
Finn in, 203, 206–7, 225–26, 229, 323
Followers of Christ in, 356, 360–61
Horner and, 201, 204, 311–12, 321–22, 327, 329–30, 331, 332–33, 336, 337–41, 343, 344–45, 348, 352, 362–63
jury in, 331–32, 334, 336, 337, 339, 354, 358–60, 361
laying on, of hands in, 212, 226, 229, 329, 340
Lincoln, R., and, 137, 179
Mackeson in, 331–32, 333–36, 344, 352, 357–58
Mauer in, 332, 350, 361
Mayer in, 201, 203, 205, 207, 214
Mitchell in, 223–26, 341–42, 356, 423–24
Mygrant in, 311–12, 322, 327, 329, 352–53, 354–56, 362
Nelson in, 215, 216–17, 342–43
Ophoven in, 343–44, 345, 359
Rhodes, J., in, 201–2, 207–10, 224–25, 228, 339, 363, 444
Robbins, Patrick, and, 190, 218
Swan, R., and, 336, 356, 364
verdicts in, 361
Zegar in, 331, 332, 335, 336, 339, 346, 354, 358, 359, 360, 361
Beavercreek, Oregon, 367–69
Bella, Rick, 227, 245, 278, 282, 289

Benton, Lynne
    in Beagley case, 201, 202, 205–6, 338
    wife of, 398–99, 405, 411–12, 417,
        427, 440–41, 448–49
    in Worthington case, 158, 220–21
Bernard, Gwen, 100
beta-blocker, 407
Bible, King James Version, 119
Bible Believers Fellowship, 81
Billings, Robert, 308, 420
bioterrorism, 396
blacksnakes, 14
blood transfusion, 181, 248
blood urea nitrogen (BUN), 343, 344
Book of Matthew, 143
The Book of Mormon (Smith, Joseph), 10
The Boston Globe, 69
Bow, New Hampshire, 8–12
Bowman, Pat, 195
brainwashing, 224–25
Briggs, Lorraine, 99
Briggs, Russ, 98–99, 268
Broussard, Eldridge, 92
Brown, Kate, 98
Brown Pride Norteños Gang, 326
Brown University, 250
Brownsville, Oregon, 248–49
Bryn Seion Church, 183
Buddhism, 144
BUN. *See* blood urea nitrogen
burial, 155–56, 179
Burley, Emile, 373
Bush, George W., 194
Byers, Ken
    Tilkin and, 294
    after the Worthington case, 292, 294
    in the Worthington case, 243–44,
        255, 259, 272, 275, 281, 284, 285,
        286–88, 289, 290
Byrne, Rhonda, 64

Caldwell, Idaho, 14–18, 45, 149,
    268–69
Canada, 82, 248
Canby, Oregon, 325, 326

Canhoto, Kira, 82
Canyon County, Idaho, 269
Canzano, Anna, 245
carbon dioxide narcosis, 263–64
CASA. *See* Court Appointed Special
    Advocate Position
CAT. *See* Child Abuse Team
Chambers, Ernie ("the Maverick of
    Omaha"), 36, 175–76
Charfoos & Christensen, 66
CHILD. *See* Children's Healthcare Is a
    Legal Duty
child abuse
    deaths from, 172–74
    medical neglect as, 102, 175, 180–81,
        183, 397
    Ninth Amendment and, 285
    religious-shield laws and, 49
Child Abuse and Neglect, 231
Child Abuse Prevention and Treatment
    Act, 392
Child Abuse Team (CAT), 155, 374,
    379
childbirth, 43, 44, 78–79
Children's Healthcare Is a Legal Duty
    (CHILD), 66–67, 80, 434
The Chosen People, 11
Christian Science. *See* First Church
    of Christ, Scientist
The Christian Science Monitor, 67
Christopher, Warren, 68
Chuck (Followers of Christ member),
    232
Church of England, 7
Church of Scientology, 100
Church of the Firstborn, 91, 117,
    248–49, 304, 434–35
Clackalackie, 55
Clackamas County, Oregon, 41–45, 54,
    96, 120
Clackastanis, 170
Clackatucky, 90
Clark, Joni, 79
Clark, Libby, 79
Cochrane, Jacob, 12–13

Cogan, Mark, 277, 331, 406
  in Hickman case, 417–18, 419, 421,
    427, 433
  in Worthington case, 244–45, 252,
    253–54, 256–58, 260–61, 262,
    271, 277, 282, 333–34
  in Wyland case, 399–400, 404, 405,
    409–10, 414
cold tap, 163
Coleman, George, 44
Colorado, 104
Colorado City, Arizona, 394
Columbia Gorge, 132
Columbus, Christopher, 10
Come Back Jack, 135–36
Communicative Management Unit
    ("Little Guantánamo"), 416
confirmation bias, 408
Congress, 247–48
Conley, Michael, 106
Conscientious Objectors, 21
Cottrell, Terrance, 81
Court Appointed Special Advocate
    Position (CASA), 414
Crank, Jacqueline, 180–81, 182
Crank, Jessica, 180–81
crime scene investigator (CSI), 157, 399
Crone, Carolyn
  in Beagley case, 190, 329, 330
  in Hickman case, 297, 304, 305
Crone, Garret, 375, 407–8
CSI. See crime scene investigator
Cult Awareness Network, 85
Cunningham, Baby Girl, 103
Cunningham, Carter, 41
Cunningham, Dale, 16–17
Cunningham, Holland, 41–42, 87
Cunningham, Myra, 268
Cunningham, Myrna, 267–68
Cutler, Joni Clark, 79
Cuyler, James, 263

Dante Alighieri, 143–44, 165–66
Davis, Skeeter, 18
deal-making, 31–32

deaths. See also specific people
  categories of, 168–69
  child abuse, 172–74
  in Church of the Firstborn, 248,
    249
  classification of, 44–45
  during exorcisms, 81–82, 173–74,
    180
  among Followers of Christ, 41–44,
    50, 53, 91, 106–7, 155, 203, 232,
    249, 268–69, 298, 396
  graves, 155–56, 177–78, 268–69
  hidden, 155–56, 173–74, 183
  from medical treatment, 402
  reporting, 155–56
  smell of, 166
Defense Fund, 241–42, 324, 344–46,
    382
Defoe, Daniel, 8
The Deist's Manual (Gildon), 7
Delaware, 104
Delehant, Maurice, 375
Democrats, 392
dentistry, 90–91, 116, 161, 169, 219
Department of Human Services
    (DHS), Oregon, 296
  in Beagley case, 188–89, 195–97,
    325, 346–48, 360
  in Wyland case, 371, 373–74
depression, 115, 116, 118
Detroit Free Press, 65–66
Deuteronomy, 11
DHS. See Department of Human
    Services, Oregon
Diekema, Douglas, 344
distant healing, 29
District Attorneys Association,
    Oregon, 94
Divelbis, Holly, 268, 297, 322–24,
    342
The Divine Comedy, 165–66
divorce, 46–47
Dodd, Chris, 391
domestic violence, 120
Donahue, 65

Duncan, Clint, 328–29
The Dunkers, 11
Duvall, Robert, 90
Dyer, Wayne, 63–64

Ecclesia, 92
Eddy, Gilbert, 12
Eddy, Mary Baker, 8–9, 11–12, 27–28
    on evil, 64
    in Massachusetts, 36
    "Mother's Evening Prayer" by, 34
    silent prayer, 30–31
Eells, Reese, 191, 329
Eels, Darryl, 23
Eels, David, 193–94
Eels, Glenford, 241
Egypt, 81–82
Ehrlichman, John, 35
Emerson, Ralph Waldo, 63
Encyclopedia of Domestic Violence, 182
"The End of the World," 18
End Times, 10, 18
End Times Ministries, 79
England, 7, 82
Enzi, Mike, 391
evangelicals, 11
Evans, Donny, 18–19
Evans, Eleanor ("The Widow"),
        251–52, 383
    doubts of, 20
    faith healing of, 14–16, 18–20
    Robbins, E., and, 21–22
    Robbins, Patrick, and, 301–2
Evans, John, 13, 138
evil, 64
exorcism, 77, 118
    belief in, 250–51
    deaths during, 81–82, 173–74, 180
    legalities of, 250
Eye Institute, 376–77

Faber, John, 374
failure to thrive, 166–67, 261–62
faith, 27, 28
Faith Assembly Church, 78

faith healing. See also religious-shield
        laws
    belief in, 63–64
    deal-making and, 31–32
    distant healing in, 29
    of Evans, E., 14–16, 18–20
    history of, 318–20
    medical treatment and, 11, 31, 33,
        37, 38, 39, 392
    placebo effect as, 320–21
    subsidization of, 35, 80
    terminology for, 71
    The True Face of Faith Healing, 367,
        380, 403, 405
Faith Tabernacle Church, 81, 82–83
Falls, 300
fasting, 154
Finn, Michelle, 230, 442
    in Beagley case, 203, 206–7, 225–26,
        229, 323
    on hearsay, 208–9
    in Hickman case, 310–11, 312, 426
    job of, 298, 399, 443
    on Nelson, 428
    Swan, R., and, 260
    in Worthington case, 156–60,
        162–63, 169–70, 191, 260, 261,
        279, 293
First Amendment, 66
First Century Gospel Church, 249
First Church of Christ, Scientist,
        12, 25
    criticism of, 40
    Cult Awareness Network and, 85
    famous members of, 67
    Jesus in, 25
    lawsuits against, 66, 70
    lobbyists for, 291
    medical treatment in, 71
    Nixon, R., and, 35, 39, 51
    pain medication in, 27
    politics and, 35–36
    Principia College, 28, 68
Fitzwater, Bruce, 100, 101
Five Day Referral, 188

Fleming, Colin, 420
Florida, 69, 94
Floyd, Jami, 277, 290
Followers of Christ. *See also* Beagley
    case; Hickman case; shunning;
    Worthington case; Wyland case;
    specific church locations; *specific
    church members*
    Band on, 443
    in Beagley case, 356, 360–61
    beliefs of, 249, 260
    branches of, 148–49
    deaths among, 41–44, 44–45, 50, 53,
        55, 87, 91, 106–7, 155, 203, 232,
        249, 268–69, 298, 396
    devil for, 318
    Hass and, 50–54, 89, 98, 397
    hell for, 143–44
    history of, 7–8, 11, 12–13, 137–39
    informant in, 2, 121–22, 127–28, 142,
        176, 195, 197, 202, 219, 220, 269,
        296–97, 306–7, 314, 322, 363–64,
        371, 372–73, 380–81, 444
    medical treatment for, 90–91, 187,
        232, 273, 352, 439
    names of, 117, 304, 315, 363,
        432
    Rhodes, J., on, 261, 443
    sickness in, 240–41, 323–24
    Tilkin and, 53–54, 107, 193, 245,
        252, 294, 361, 383, 384
The Foot Washers, 11
Foote, John, 124, 246, 307, 363
force-feeding, 118
forgiveness, 317–18
Foster, Anne Marie, 82
Foster, Daniel, 82
Foster, Patrick, 82
Fourteenth Amendment, 66
Fourth Great Awakening, 63–64
Franklin, Benjamin, 9
Fraser, Caroline, 70
free love, 12
Fryett, Kristi, 374

gender, 206
Ghana, 81
Gildon, Charles, 7–8
Gilmore, Gary, 368
giving back, 32
Gladstone, Oregon, 46, 158, 338
Glory Barn, 78
God Bud, 367–68
God's Perfect Child (Fraser), 70
Gody, Herbert, 418–19
Gonzalez, Alberto, 416
Good Morning America, 66
Gospel of Jesus, 119
Gottschalk, Stephen, 68, 69
Grace, Nancy, 203
Grady, Aaron, 249
Grady, Susan, 249
Graham, Sylvester, 9
graves, 155–56, 177–79, 268–69
Great Awakening, 8
Great War, 14
Green, Jeff, 55
    Phillips and, 86–89, 98, 100–101
    in Worthington case, 158, 162
Guillery, Edward, 343
guilt, 318
The Gulag Archipelago (Solzhenitsyn),
    325
Gustafson, Terry, 48–50, 55–56, 94
    indictment of, 96
    Phillips and, 90–91, 95, 96
    Swan, R., and, 57–60, 85, 91, 92, 93,
        95–96, 391
Gwinnett County, Georgia, 250
Gypsy Jokers, 326

Haiti, 81
Haldeman, Robert, 35, 51
Hansen, Baby Girl, 107
Hansen, Carl, 155
Harding, Tonya, 368
Harkin, Tom, 391
Harris, Patrick, 158, 260
Harvey, Frank, 181–82

Hass, Mark
  Lewman and, 50–51, 52
  as politician, 107, 193
  as reporter, 50–54, 89, 98, 397
Hatch, Orrin, 251, 291
Hawaii, 104, 182
Hays, Anthony, 248
Hays, Christina, 248
Hays, Loyd, 248
health care reform act, 251, 291
hearsay, 208–9
heaven, 10
Heinbigner, LaMont, 328
hell, 143–44, 165–66
helmet law, 273
hemangioma, 369, 375–78, 404. *See also*
  Wyland case
Hemphill, Ray, 81
Henson, Jim, 274
Hermanson, Amy, 68–69
Herndon (judge), 419, 422, 433
Hickman, Baby Boy. *See* Hickman,
  David
Hickman, Baby Girl, 314–15
Hickman, Daisy, 439
Hickman, Dale, 137–38, 184, 295,
  296, 302
  health history of, 310
  in Hickman case, 303–6, 307–8,
    309, 313, 314, 384, 415, 421, 426,
    433, 436–37
  personality of, 422–23, 428
  in prison, 437, 438–40
Hickman, David, 314–15. *See also*
  Hickman case
  age of, 424, 425–26
  autopsy of, 311
  birth of, 297, 303–5, 426–27,
    429
  death of, 305–7, 324, 421, 424, 427,
    430
  investigation of, 307–11
  name of, 315, 363, 432
  placenta of, 308, 313

recordings of, 304, 308, 312, 363,
    415, 417, 420, 422, 426–27, 429
  size of, 310–11
Hickman, Julia Lynn, 107
Hickman, Lee, 184, 296–97, 439
Hickman, Phil, 105, 129, 307–8, 384
Hickman, Shannon, 295, 302
  childbirth of, 297, 303–5, 426–27,
    429
  health history of, 309–10
  in Hickman case, 384, 421, 429–30,
    433, 436
Hickman, Tanya, 305
Hickman case
  Cogan in, 417–18, 419, 421, 427, 433
  Crone, C., in, 297, 304, 305
  Finn in, 310–11, 312, 426
  Hickman, Dale, in, 303–6, 307–8,
    309, 313, 314, 384, 415, 421, 426,
    433, 436–37
  Hickman, S., in, 384, 421, 429–30,
    433, 436
  Horner in, 418, 422
  jury in, 417–20, 421, 427
  Neidig in, 425, 430
  Nelson in, 310, 324, 421–22, 424–26,
    428
  Pearson in, 310
  recordings in, 304, 308, 312, 363,
    415, 417, 420, 422, 426–27, 429
  Regan in, 311–12, 418, 419, 420,
    421, 424, 432–33
  Rhodes, J., and, 312
  Robbins, Patrick, and, 427–28
  sentencing in, 432–33
  significance of, 364
  Smith, F., and, 308–9
  Swan, R., and, 434
  Tilkin and, 313, 429
  verdict in, 431
Higbee, Deborah
  death of, 405, 411–12, 417, 427,
    440–41, 448–49
  marriage of, 398–99

Hinduism, 144

The Holy Greeting, 13, 21

home schooling, 172, 186, 198–99

homosexuality, 113

Horner, Greg
Band and, 123–25, 204
Beagley case and, 201, 204, 311–12,
    321–22, 327, 329–30, 331, 332–33,
    336, 337–41, 343, 344–45, 348,
    352, 362–63
in Hickman case, 418, 422
in Worthington case, 171, 191, 192,
    246, 252, 254–56, 259, 261,
    270–71, 276, 278–80, 282, 287, 293
in Wyland case, 378

house arrest, 118, 119

The Humanist, 182

hypothermia, 173

Idaho, 45, 182, 268, 292
Caldwell, 14–18, 45, 149, 268–69
Canyon County, 269
religious-shield laws, 45, 182,
    268, 292

Immediate Referral, 195

Indiana, 77, 78

infants, 44, 78–79, 175. See also specific
    infants

International Cultic Studies
    Association, 231

International Year of the Child, 62

Iowa, 182

Islam, 144, 416

James, Williams, 63

Jamestown, North Dakota, 61

Japan, 82

Jensen, Evelyn, 419–20, 427

Jensen, Thom, 220, 245, 408, 409

Jesus
faith healing by, 318, 319
in First Church of Christ,
    Scientist, 25
forgiveness by, 317–18

jihadists, 194

Jindal, Bobby, 250, 251

John, 319

Johnson, Harrison, 81

Johnson, Kelly, 81

Johnson, Wylie, 81

Joki, Dean, 39

Jones, Jeffrey, 399–400

Judaism, 144

Judas, 119, 165–66

Judecca, 166

KATU, 50, 53–54, 99, 220, 245

Keith, Lavona, 297, 303

Keith, Seth, 272

Kellogg, John, H., 9

Kennedy, Ted, 36

Kerry, John, 36, 291

kidney functioning, 190, 334–35, 343

King, Ashley, 69–70

King, Samantha, 272

Kishpaugh, Gary, 329

Kissers. See Followers of Christ

kissing, 12–13

Kitzhaber, John, 49, 56, 95, 103, 398

Kleber, Doug, 80–81

Knefler, Sharon, 37, 64

Krebs, Randy, 204

Krogh, Egil, 35

Lace, Jim, 394

LaCroix, Sharon, 103

Laitner, Jeanne, 24, 28, 29, 30, 31, 40
Ahearn and, 33–34
former healings by, 27, 39, 60

Landers, Christine
in Worthington case, 171
in Wyland case, 403–4, 406, 409, 413

Larabee, Mark, 98

Larry King, 66

"The Last Strawberry" (Swan, R.), 40,
    65, 336

Law of Attraction, 63–64

laying on, of hands
in Beagley case, 212, 226, 229,
    329, 340

history of, 9–10
significance of, 324, 328–29
in Worthington case, 153, 161, 170
Wyland case, 370
Lazarus, 319
Leonhardt, Dan, 263, 264, 426–27
leukemia, 248
Lewis, Jeff, 188–89, 195–97, 346–48
Lewman, Larry, 44, 55
Cunningham, H., and, 41–42
Hass and, 50–51, 52
Morris, A., and, 42–43
Phillips and, 89–90, 98
Shaw, V., and, 45–46, 48
testimony of, 100
Lincoln, Lorene, 142
Lincoln, Rod, 129, 142, 148, 241
Beagley case and, 137, 179
on Benton, 440–41
Lindberg, Dennis, 181
Lindsey, Steve, 342, 348, 349–50, 351
Liz (Followers of Christ member)
depression of, 115, 116, 118
in house arrest, 117–19, 121–22, 123
Lloyd, Jerry, 74, 75
Louisiana, 250
Lourdes, France, 320
Lower Highland Bible Church, 183
Lucy, John, 252–53
Luke, 319
Lundman, Doug, 70
Lundman, Ian, 70
Luther, Martin, 320

Mackeson, Wayne
background of, 334
in Beagley case, 331–32, 333–36,
344, 352, 357–58
magnets, 9
malicious animal magnetism, 11–12, 29
Mannix, Kevin, 101
manslaughter, 49, 94, 181, 420
marijuana, 367–68
Marks, Sophie, 420
Martin, Greg, 204

Maryland, 104, 182
Massachusetts, 36, 69, 104, 182
materia medica. *See* medical treatment
Mato, Sayonara, 262–63
Matthew, 319
The Matthew Project, 61, 65
Mauer, Steven
in Beagley case, 332, 350, 361
in Worthington case, 246, 253–54,
282–83, 286, 288–89, 294
Mayer, Jeff
in Beagley case, 201, 203, 205,
207, 214
in Worthington case, 158, 160, 163,
259–60
Mayes, Steve, 245, 423
McCullough, Dan, 99
McDonald, Jacob, 12–13
McDonald, James, 11, 12
McKown, Kathleen, 70
McKown, William, 70
McLaughlin, Sue, 71
McLennan, Jeff, 308–10, 312, 425
Meade, Charles, 79
medical neglect, 102, 175, 180–81,
183, 397
medical treatment, 232. *See also specific*
people
deaths from, 402
dentistry and, 90–91, 116, 161,
169, 219
for depression, 115
faith healing and, 11, 31, 33, 37, 38,
39, 392
in First Church of Christ, Scientist, 71
for Followers of Christ, 90–91, 187,
232, 233, 273, 352, 439
for pain, 27
right to, 45
right to refuse, 197, 204, 209,
392–93, 395
Medicare, 35, 80
Melody Maker's Music, 112
meningitis, 37, 39, 40, 60, 68
Mesmer, Franz, 9

Mesmerism, 9–10
metabolic screening, 175
Michigan, 39, 66
midwifery, 43, 106, 303–4
Milton, John, 143–44
Minnesota, 70–71, 80, 94, 104
Mitchell, Sandra, 223–26, 341–42,
    356, 423–24
Moehnke family, 368
Mohamud, Mohamed, 415
Mormon Church, 10
Morris, Alex, 42–43
Morris, Dale, 99
Morris, Les, 23
Mother Church. *See* First Church of
    Christ, Scientist
"Mother's Evening Prayer"
    (Eddy, M.), 34
Mouser, Mick, 268
Mt. Angel, Oregon, 326
Mudd, Leah, 78
Mudd, Natali Joy, 77, 78
Muhammad, 318
Multnomah County, Oregon, 124
Myers, Hardy, 95, 96
Mygrant, Steve
    Band on, 355
    in Beagley case, 311–12, 322, 327,
        329, 352–53, 354–56, 362
    in Worthington case, 171, 246, 253,
        259, 272, 273, 281–82, 283, 293

nationalism, 194
Nebraska, 36, 175–76
Neidig, John, 244
    in Hickman case, 425, 430
    in Worthington case, 244, 245, 252,
        258, 262, 263, 264, 278, 280, 281,
        282–83, 333–34
    in Wyland case, 410, 414
"The Neil Beagley Amendment," 395
Nelson, Cliff
    in Beagley case, 215, 216–17, 342–43
    in Hickman case, 310, 324, 421–22,
        424–26, 428

Neumann, Dale, 193
Neumann, Kara, 193, 247
Neumann, Leilani, 193
New Life Tabernacle, 180–81
Nichols, Connie, 323
Nichols, David, 111–13, 323
Nichols, Ernest, 47
Nielsen, Susan, 384
911, 155, 182–83
Ninth Amendment, 285
The Ninth Circle, of hell, 165–66
Nixon, Dennis, 82–83
Nixon, Lorie, 82–83
Nixon, Richard, 35, 39, 51
Nixon, Shannon, 83
No Greater Joy Ministries, 172
The No Name Fellowship, 80
Norman, Aaron, 80–81
Norman, Bob, 80–81
Norman, Judith, 80
NORML, 244
North Carolina, 55, 104, 182

Oakley, George, 138
Obasi, Myra, 250–51
ODCs. *See* ordinary, decent criminals
Ohio, 181, 182
Oklahoma, 13, 249
Oklahoma Land Rush, 13
O'Leary, James, 44
One Mind Ministries, 173, 231
Oneida, New York, 12–13
Ophoven, Janice
    in Beagley case, 343–44, 345, 359
    history of, 345–46
    in Worthington case, 274–77, 286
ordinary, decent criminals (ODCs), 203
Oregon. *See also specific Oregon locations*
    assisted-suicide law in, 347
    DHS, 188–89, 195–97, 296, 325,
        346–48, 360, 371, 373–74
    District Attorneys Association, 94
    manslaughter in, 420
    midwifery in, 43, 303–4
    provincialism of, 54

religious-shield laws in, 45, 49–50, 55, 59, 93–94, 95, 97–104, 182, 245, 248, 357, 392–93, 396–98
Oregon Caves, 131–32
Oregon City, Oregon, 18–20, 54, 300–301. *See also* Clackamas County, Oregon
Oregon Super Lawyer, 244
Oregon Trail, 18
The Oregonian, 95, 98, 227, 245, 396, 402
Orieso, Anne, 82
Orieso, Sylvester, 82

Paddock, Lynn, 171, 175, 231
Paddock, Sean, 171, 172, 231
pain medication, 27
Pastor Bob, 194
Peaceful Valley Cemetery, 14–15, 45, 268
Pearl, Michael, 171–72
Pearson, Bruce
   in Hickman case, 310
   in Worthington case, 158–59, 160, 229, 252
Peculiar People, 11
pedophilia, 181
Pennsylvania, 249
Pentecostalism, 10–11, 76–77
The People's Republic of Eugene, 101
Perfectionism, 12–13
perjury, 93, 95, 274
phenylketonuria, 175
Phillips, Bo, 90, 91, 103
   death of, 86–89, 100–101
   sickness of, 88–89
   trial for, 95–96, 156
Pilgrims, 7–8
PIO. *See* Public Information Officer
placebo effect, 320–21
placenta, 308, 313
The Plain People, 11
platonic ideal, 63
Police Officer Hold, 123

Portland, Oregon, 54, 90, 96, 123–24, 300–301
Portland Seven, 416
prayer, 29–31, 291. *See also* faith healing
Principia College, 28, 68
Prohibition, 16
Prozanski, Floyd, 101
Public Information Officer (PIO), 398

Queen Antoinette, 173, 231

Radical Reformation, 11
Rajneesh, Bhagwan Shree, 396–97
Ramkissoon, Ria, 173, 175
Rather, Dan, 90
Red Israelites, 10
refusal of care, right to, 197, 204, 209, 359
Regan, Mike, 171
   Band on, 421
   in Hickman case, 311–12, 418, 419, 420, 421, 424, 432–33
religion, freedom of, 48, 57, 332, 334
Religion & Ethics Newsweekly, 247
"Religion-Based Medical Neglect," 56–57
religious-shield laws, 35, 92, 291
   age in, 204, 293
   Arizona, 104
   Arkansas, 182
   changes in, 84, 97–104, 182, 391
   child abuse and, 49
   CHILD and, 66–67, 80
   Colorado, 104
   Congress and, 247–48
   Delaware, 104
   Florida, 69, 94
   Hawaii, 104, 182
   Idaho, 45, 182, 268, 292
   Indiana, 78
   Iowa, 182
   Maryland, 104, 182
   Massachusetts, 36, 69, 104, 182
   Michigan, 39
   Minnesota, 70–71, 80, 94, 104

religious-shield laws, (*continued*)
    Nebraska and, 36, 175–76
    North Carolina, 104, 182
    Ohio, 181, 182
    Oklahoma, 249
    Oregon, 45, 49–50, 55, 59, 93–94,
        95, 97–104, 182, 245, 248, 357,
        392–93, 396–98
    Pennsylvania, 249
    Rhode Island, 104
    South Dakota, 79
    Tennessee, 181
    Texas, 181
    Washington, 81
    West Virginia, 181, 182
    Wisconsin, 81, 194, 247, 391
Remnant Fellowship, 174
repentance, 39
Republican Party, 36
Reznick, Leah, 377–78, 406–7
Rhode Island, 104
Rhodes, James, 154–56, 230, 442
    in Beagley case, 201–2, 207–10,
        224–25, 228, 339, 363, 444
    on Followers of Christ, 261, 443
    Hickman case and, 312
    promotion of, 398
    in Worthington case, 155, 156,
        159–64, 166–68, 169–71, 191,
        255, 278, 279, 293
    in Wyland case, 379
Rhodes, Patti, 201, 204
Rhodes, Sarah, 154–55
Robbins, Ella, 317, 320
    brother of, 21, 22, 105, 251, 301–2,
        306, 316–17, 320–21, 370–71, 388,
        390, 447–48
    Evans, E., and, 21–22
    shunning of, 21, 22, 74, 105, 391,
        448
Robbins, Patrick, 131–40, 236, 241,
    437–38
    Band and, 121–22, 127–28, 142, 145,
        176, 180, 314, 363–64, 373, 380,
        399, 444

Beagley, Jeff, and, 21, 128, 187–88,
    234–35, 242–43
Beagley case and, 190, 218
childhood of, 20–23, 75
childlessness of, 104–7, 127, 145
doubts of, 106, 107, 116, 118–19, 127,
    128, 129–30, 141–42, 178, 218–20,
    298–99, 370, 372–73, 381–82
Evans, E., and, 301–2
as father, 164–65, 177, 200, 218–19,
    239–40, 242, 264, 316, 371–72,
    447–48, 449–50
at funeral, 177–80
Hickman case and, 427–28
as informer, 2, 121–22, 127–28, 142,
    176, 195, 197, 202, 219, 220, 269,
    296–97, 306–7, 314, 322, 363–64,
    371, 372–73, 380–81, 444
job of, 148
Liz and, 114–19, 121–22
marriage of, 105–6, 115, 116,
    140–43, 164–65, 200, 218, 219,
    235, 239, 264, 266–67, 290, 300,
    314, 316, 317, 372, 415, 436
medical treatment and, 232, 233
at New Year's Eve Party, 72–76,
    445–46
Nichols, D., and, 111–13
at Peaceful Valley Cemetery,
    268–69
Sermon on the Deck by, 385–88
sister of, 21–22, 105, 251, 301–2,
    316–17, 320–21, 370–71, 388,
    390, 447–48
threats against, 389–90
vacation of, 405–6, 412, 415
Worthington, C., and, 116, 117, 200,
    446–47
Worthington case and, 259, 264–65,
    290
Wyland, T., and, 21, 72, 75
Wyland case and, 372–73, 383
Robbins, Paul. *See also* Robbins, Patrick
Christmas for, 316
health of, 371–72

name of, 165
sickness of, 164, 264, 266
Robbins, Theresa, 127
    child of, 164–65, 218–19, 239–40,
        264
    childlessness of, 104–7, 115, 131, 145
    marriage of, 105–6, 115, 116,
        140–43, 164–65, 200, 218, 219,
        235, 239, 264, 266–67, 290, 300,
        314, 316, 317, 372, 415, 436
Romney, Mitt, 394
Ross, Rick, 85, 292
The Royal Touch, 319–20
Ruby, Dave, 201

Salem, Oregon, 325, 326
Salem Witch Trial, 11–12
Sandy, Oregon, 47
Santos, Ashley, 243, 284, 286,
        288, 289
Satan, 77, 273, 318
Sayre, Nicole, 271–72
Schaible, Catherine, 249, 393
Schaible, Herbert, 249, 393
Schaible, Kent, 249, 393
Schatz, Elizabeth, 172
Schatz, Kevin, 172
Schatz, Lydia, 172
Schilke, John, 44
"The Scientific Statement of Being,"
        64–65
Second Great Awakening, 10, 63
The Secret (Byrne), 64
Secular News Daily, 380
Senate, U.S., 80
sepsis, 258, 262, 274, 286
Sermon on the Deck, 385–88
Sermon on the Mount, 30
Seventh-Day Adventists, 10, 99–100,
        193
sex, 72–74
sex-reassignment, 206, 338
Shamblin, Gwen, 174–75
Shaw, Darrell, 46, 268
Shaw, Tyler Duane, 107

Shaw, Valerie, 45–46, 48, 53, 87, 103
Shelley, Percy Bysshe, 26
Sherman, Ariel Ben, 180–82
"Should Universal Health Care Cover
        Faith Healing?," 291
Shumaker, Suzanne, 144, 268
shunning, 212, 273, 322. See also
        specific people
    consequences of, 46, 47, 75
    history of, 249, 250
Siegel, Jeffrey, 80–81
Silva, Heather, 324–25
Simplot, Jack, 268
Slatford, Amy, 339, 359
Smith, Charlie, 138
Smith, Fred, 214, 241–42
    Band and, 204–5
    Hickman case and, 308–9
Smith, Josef, 174
Smith, Joseph, 10, 11, 12, 174
Smith, Sonya, 174
snake handling, 14
Solzhenitsyn, Alexander, 325
South Dakota, 79
Southern Strategy, 36, 194
Souvenir Alley, 320
Soviet Union, 325
spanking, 174–75
spiders, 15–16, 21–22
spoilation, 203
Sprout, Austin, 434–35
Starr, Bruce, 98, 395
Starr, Ken, 68
Stevens, Matthew, 374
Stevens, Rod, 410
stillbirths, 44, 91, 156, 298
strawberry mark, 369, 375–76
suicide, 75
Supreme Court, U.S., 80
Sureños South Side Local, 326
Swan, Doug, 24, 26, 393, 442
    health of, 441
    in Jamestown, 61
    son of, 25, 27, 28–35, 36–40, 60
Swan, Marsha, 61, 65, 441

Swan, Matthew, 27, 194
  birth of, 25
  death of, 39–40, 60
  "*The Last Strawberry*," 40, 65, 336
  sickness of, 28–35, 36–39
Swan, Rita, 23–24, 441
  activism of, 40, 57–71, 76–85, 91–92,
      93–94, 97–104, 156, 171–76,
      180–83, 194, 227, 231, 247,
      249–50, 291–92, 357, 364, 392,
      393, 394, 395–96, 397–98, 434,
      435–36, 442
  Beagley case and, 336, 356, 364
  father of, 29, 33, 34
  Finn and, 260
  Gustafson and, 57–60, 85, 91, 92,
      93, 95–96, 391
  Hickman case and, 434
  "*The Last Strawberry*," 40, 65, 336
  son of, 25, 27, 28–35, 36–40, 60, 65,
      194, 336
  Worthington case and, 251, 260,
      286, 290–91
Swezey, Greg, 248
Swezey, JaLea, 248
Swezey, Zachary, 248

Tennessee, 180–81
Texas, 181
Thaine, Mike, 234, 241
Thaine, Vernon, 16, 19–21, 22, 75, 234
Third Great Awakening, 16
Thompson, Javon, 173–74, 180, 231
Tilkin, Dan, 53–54, 107, 193, 245, 252
  Beagley case and, 361
  Byers and, 294
  Hickman case and, 313, 429
  Wyland case and, 383, 384
Time, 98, 291
Tippecanoe Township, Indiana, 77
To Train Up a Child (Pearl), 171–72
Tomei, Carolyn, 395
Town Hall, 50
The True Face of Faith Healing, 367,
      380, 403, 405

truTV, 203, 277, 289, 290
20/20, 97, 172
Twitchell, Robyn, 69

United Church of Christ, 40
United Nations, 61–62
University Christian Fellowship, 250

vaccinations, 392
Valvano, Thomas, 375–76
Van Dyk, Douglas, 383–84
Vandersteen, David, 346
voodoo, 250

Waldheim, Kurt, 62
Walker, Laurie, 68
Walker, Shauntay, 68
Wantland, Andrew, 70
War Vet Sermonettes, 320
Washington, 81
Washington County, Oregon, 91
Weigh Down Workshop, 174
Welch, Wayne, 326–27, 346–47, 365
Wentworth, John, 171, 418, 425, 429–30
West Virginia, 181, 182
White, Karen, 303, 305
White, Matt, 295–96
White, Steve, 272–73
White, Walter, 74, 75, 204
  medical treatment and, 90–91, 241
  as prophet, 17–20, 47, 114, 116–17,
      139
White Israelites, 10
whooping cough, 447
Wiccans, 47–48
Willamette Valley, Oregon, 300–301
Williams, Carri, 172–73
Williams, Hana Grace-Rose, 172–73
Williams, Immanuel, 173
Williams, Larry, 172–73
Winterborne, Dawn, 82
Winterborne, Roger, 82
Wisconsin, 81, 194, 247, 391
witchcraft, 12
World War II, 21

Worthington, Ava, 314–15. *See also* Worthington case
  death of, 156, 157–64, 166–71, 177–80, 191–92, 229, 246, 255–56, 260, 274–75, 280, 339
  sickness of, 146–48, 149, 150, 151–54, 162–63, 165, 254–56, 258, 263–64, 270, 271, 272, 276, 278, 282
  size of, 166–67, 258, 259–60, 261–63, 275, 278, 280
Worthington, Baby Boy, 106–7, 117, 156
Worthington, Carl ("Brent"), 402, 414. *See also* Worthington case
  family of, 106–7, 134, 146–62
  at funeral, 178, 179
  popularity of, 131, 135, 381
  Robbins, Patrick, and, 116, 117, 200, 446–47
  in Worthington case, 163, 166, 169–71, 182–83, 191–93, 203, 255, 272, 278–80, 287–89, 294, 299
Worthington, Corryn, 146, 147, 149, 150
Worthington, Julie, 150, 151, 270–71
Worthington, Raylene, 406, 414
  as mother, 130, 148–54
  stillbirth of, 106–7, 117, 156
  in Worthington case, 161, 182–83, 191–92, 193, 203, 245, 280–81, 287–88, 289
Worthington case
  Band and, 263, 264, 289, 293
  Beagley, Jeff, and, 162, 178, 350
  Beagley, M., and, 178, 272
  Benton in, 158, 220–21
  Byers and, 243–44, 255, 259, 272, 275, 281, 284, 285, 286–88, 289, 290, 292, 294
  Cogan in, 244–45, 252, 253–54, 256–58, 260–61, 262, 271, 277, 282, 333–34
  Finn in, 156–60, 162–63, 169–70, 191, 260, 261, 279, 293

Green in, 158, 162
Harris in, 158, 260
Horner in, 171, 191, 192, 246, 252, 254–56, 259, 261, 270–71, 276, 278–80, 282, 287, 293
jury of, 243–44, 245, 283–88, 289, 293
Landers in, 171
laying on, of hands, in, 153, 161, 170
Mauer in, 246, 253–54, 282–83, 286, 288–89, 294
Mayer in, 158, 160, 163, 259–60
Mygrant in, 171, 246, 253, 259, 272, 273, 281–82, 283, 293
Neidig in, 244, 245, 252, 258, 262, 263, 264, 278, 280, 281, 282–83, 333–34
Ninth Amendment in, 285
Ophoven in, 274–77, 286
Pearson in, 158–59, 160, 229, 252
photos in, 252–53
Rhodes, J., in, 155, 156, 159–64, 166–68, 169–71, 191, 255, 278, 279, 293
Robbins, Patrick, and, 259, 264–65, 290
Swan, R., and, 251, 260, 286, 290–91
verdict in, 288–90, 294
Worthington, C., in, 163, 166, 169–71, 182–83, 191–93, 203, 255, 272, 278–80, 287–89, 294, 299
wrongful-death suit, 66
Wyland, Alayna, 366, 369, 400–401. *See also* Wyland case
  custody of, 373–76, 378, 380, 383, 403
  medical treatment for, 375–78, 403, 406–8
  sight of, 377, 379–80, 403, 404, 406–7, 409, 413
  as The True Face of Faith Healing, 367, 380, 403, 405
Wyland, Jim, 401–2, 408, 411

Wyland, Monique, 72, 76, 369
Wyland, Rebecca, 295, 297, 314, 331
  marriage of, 369
  in Wyland case, 366, 375, 376, 378,
    383, 403, 404, 409, 410, 417
Wyland, Timmy, 314, 331
  marriage of, 369
  Robbins, Patrick, and, 21, 72, 75
  in Wyland case, 373–75, 376, 378,
    383, 403, 404, 409, 410, 415–17
Wyland case
  Cogan in, 399–400, 404, 405,
    409–10, 414
  Crone, G., in, 375, 407–8
  DHS in, 371, 373–74
  Horner in, 378
  jury in, 399–400, 404, 407
  Landers in, 403–4, 406, 409, 413
  laying on, of hands, for, 370

Neidig in, 410, 414
recordings in, 379–80
Rhodes, J., in, 379
Robbins, Patrick, and, 372–73, 383
sentencing in, 413–14
Tilkin and, 383, 384
verdict in, 410–11
Wyland, R., in, 366, 375, 376, 378,
    383, 403, 404, 409, 410, 417
Wyland, T., in, 373–75, 376,
    378, 383, 403, 404, 409, 410,
    415–17

Young, Christopher, 166–67, 261–62

Zegar, Bob, 325
  in Beagley case, 331, 332, 335, 336,
    339, 346, 354, 358, 359, 360, 361
  Welch and, 326, 346–47, 365